Milano (Milan)

GENOA AREA BY AREA

THE OLD CENTRE
Pages 48–65

THE STRADE NUOVE
Pages 66–79

FURTHER AFIELD
Pages 80–89

Cremona

Orba

LOMBARDY

Scrivia *Coppa* *Trebbia* *Nure*

Arda

Ceno

EMILIA
ROMAGNA

Taro

Lago di
Brugneto

Trebbia

LIGURIA

Genoa

Lavagna

Vara

La Spezia

Isola Palmaria
Isola del Tino
Isola del Tinetto

**THE RIVIERA
DI LEVANTE**
Pages 104–129

D0289694

THE
ITALIAN
RIVIERA

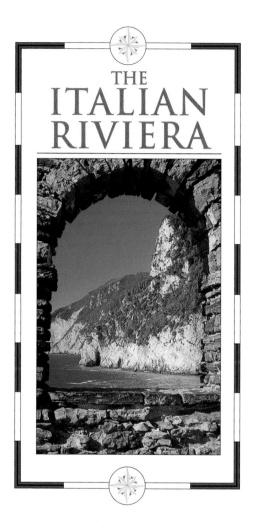

EYEWITNESS TRAVEL GUIDES

THE
ITALIAN
RIVIERA

DK

LONDON, NEW YORK,
MELBOURNE, MUNICH AND DELHI
www.dk.com

PRODUCED BY Fabio Ratti Editoria Srl, Milan, Italy

PROJECT EDITOR Emanuela Damiani
EDITORS Emanuela Damiani, Giovanna Morselli
DESIGNERS Silvana Ghioni, Alberto Ipsilanti, Modi Artistici

CONTRIBUTORS
Fabrizio Ardito, Sonia Cavicchioli,
Maurizia De Martin,Gianluigi Lanza

PHOTOGRAPHER
Lucio Rossi

ILLUSTRATORS
Andrea Barison, Gianluca Fiorani

CARTOGRAPHY
Roberto Capra, Luca Signorelli

Dorling Kindersley Limited
PUBLISHING MANAGERS Fay Franklin, Kate Poole
SENIOR ART EDITOR Marisa Renzullo
TRANSLATOR Fiona Wild
EDITOR Emily Hatchwell
CONSULTANT Leonie Loudon
PRODUCTION Linda Dare

Reproduced by Colourscan (Singapore)
Printed and bound by
South China Printing Co. Ltd., China

First American Edition, 2005

02 03 04 05 10 9 8 7 6 5 4 3 2 1

Published in the United States by DK Publishing, Inc.,
375 Hudson Street, New York, New York 10014.

Copyright © Mondadori Electra SpA 2003.
Published under exclusive licence by Dorling Kindersley Limited.
English text copyright © Dorling Kindersley Limited 2004.
A Penguin Company.

ISSN 1542-1554

ISBN 0-7566-0911-9

FLOORS ARE REFERRED TO THROUGHOUT IN ACCORDANCE WITH EUROPEAN USAGE;
IE THE "FIRST FLOOR" IS THE FLOOR ABOVE GROUND LEVEL

**The information in this
Eyewitness Travel Guide is checked regularly.**
Every effort has been made to ensure that this book is as up-to-date
as possible at the time of going to press. Some details, however,
such as telephone numbers, opening hours, prices, gallery hanging
arrangements and travel information are liable to change. The
publishers cannot accept responsibility for any consequences arising
from the use of this book, nor for any material on third party
websites, and cannot guarantee that any website address in this
book will be a suitable source of travel information. We value the
views and suggestions of our readers very highly. Please write to:
Publisher, DK Eyewitness Travel Guides,
Dorling Kindersley, 80 Strand, London WC2R 0RL, Great Britain.

◁ **The spectacular stretch of coast between Fiascherino and Tellaro**

CONTENTS

HOW TO USE
THIS GUIDE 6

Ecce Homo by Antonello da
Messina, Palazzo Spinola, Genoa

INTRODUCING
THE ITALIAN
RIVIERA

PUTTING THE ITALIAN
RIVIERA ON THE MAP 10

A PORTRAIT OF THE
ITALIAN RIVIERA 12

THE ITALIAN RIVIERA
THROUGH THE YEAR 28

THE HISTORY OF THE
ITALIAN RIVIERA 32

GENOA
AREA BY AREA

GENOA AT A GLANCE 46

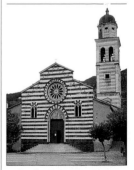

Sant'Andrea in Levanto

IL CENTRO STORICO 48

LE STRADE NUOVE 66

FARTHER AFIELD 80

GENOA
STREETFINDER 90

THE ITALIAN
RIVIERA
AREA BY AREA

The delightful scene at Paraggi, near Portofino

THE ITALIAN RIVIERA
AT A GLANCE 102

THE RIVIERA
DI LEVANTE 104

THE RIVIERA
DI PONENTE 130

TRAVELERS'
NEEDS

WHERE TO STAY 174

WHERE TO EAT 184

SHOPPING
198

OUTDOOR
ACTIVITIES 200

ENTERTAINMENT 202

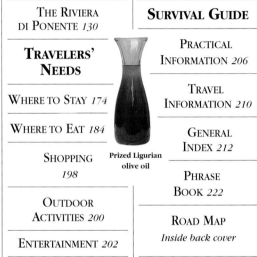

Prized Ligurian
olive oil

SURVIVAL GUIDE

PRACTICAL
INFORMATION 206

TRAVEL
INFORMATION 210

GENERAL
INDEX 212

PHRASE
BOOK 222

ROAD MAP
Inside back cover

The port of San Remo

Genoa's revamped
Porto Antico

HOW TO USE THIS GUIDE

THE DETAILED INFORMATION and tips given in this guide will help you to get the most out of your visit to the Italian Riviera. *Introducing the Italian Riviera* maps the region of Liguria and sets it in its historical and cultural context. The section *Genoa Area by Area* describes the main sights in the regional capital. *The Italian Riviera Area by Area* describes the sights and resorts east and west of Genoa along the Riviera di Levante and the Riviera di Ponente respectively, using maps, photographs and illustrations. Restaurant and hotel recommendations can be found in the section *Travellers' Needs*, together with information about shopping, outdoor activities and entertainment. The *Survival Guide* has tips on everything from transport to making a phone call.

GENOA AREA BY AREA
The centre of Genoa has been divided into two sightseeing areas, each with its own chapter. *Further Afield* describes areas outside the city centre. All the sights are numbered and plotted on an *Area Map*. Detailed information for each sight is presented in numerical order, making it easy to locate.

Sights at a Glance lists the chapter's sights by category: Churches, Museums and Galleries, Historic Buildings, Streets and Piazzas.

All pages relating to Genoa have red thumb tabs.

A locator map shows where you are in relation to other areas of the city centre.

1 Area Map
All the sights are numbered and located on a map.

2 Street-by-Street Map
This gives a bird's eye view of the heart of each sightseeing area.

Stars indicate the sights that no visitor should miss.

A suggested route for a walk covers the more interesting streets in the area.

3 Detailed information
All the sights in Genoa are described individually. Addresses, telephone numbers, opening hours and admission charges are also provided.

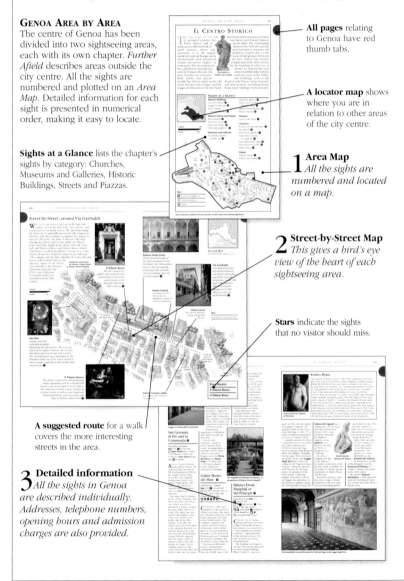

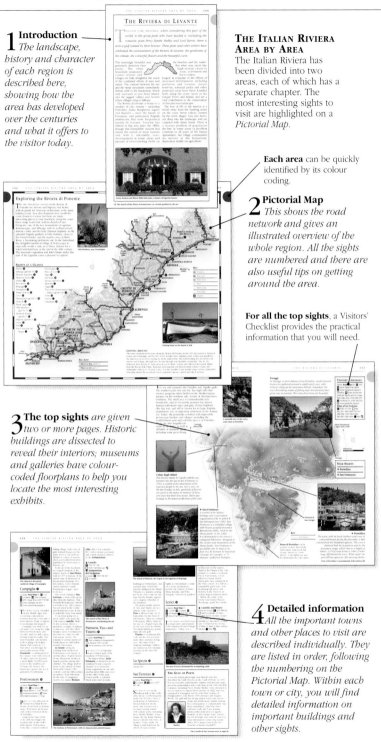

1 Introduction
The landscape, history and character of each region is described here, showing how the area has developed over the centuries and what it offers to the visitor today.

THE ITALIAN RIVIERA AREA BY AREA
The Italian Riviera has been divided into two areas, each of which has a separate chapter. The most interesting sights to visit are highlighted on a *Pictorial Map.*

Each area can be quickly identified by its colour coding.

2 Pictorial Map
This shows the road network and gives an illustrated overview of the whole region. All the sights are numbered and there are also useful tips on getting around the area.

For all the top sights, a Visitors' Checklist provides the practical information that you will need.

3 The top sights *are given two or more pages. Historic buildings are dissected to reveal their interiors; museums and galleries have colour-coded floorplans to help you locate the most interesting exhibits.*

4 Detailed information
All the important towns and other places to visit are described individually. They are listed in order, following the numbering on the Pictorial Map. Within each town or city, you will find detailed information on important buildings and other sights.

Introducing the Italian Riviera

Putting the Italian Riviera
on the Map 10-11

A Portrait of the Italian Riviera 12-27

The Italian Riviera Through
the Year 28-31

The History of the Italian Riviera 32-43

Putting the Italian Riviera on the Map

Liguria covers 5,418 sq km (2,090 sq miles) and is the second smallest region in Italy. Administratively, it is divided into four provinces: from west to east, these are Imperia, Savona, Genoa and La Spezia. Squeezed between the Mediterranean and the peaks of the Maritime Alps and the Apennines, Liguria's population is concentrated largely along the stunning coastal strip of the Riviera di Levante and the Riviera di Ponente, known collectively as the Italian Riviera – a term commonly used to describe the region of Liguria as a whole.

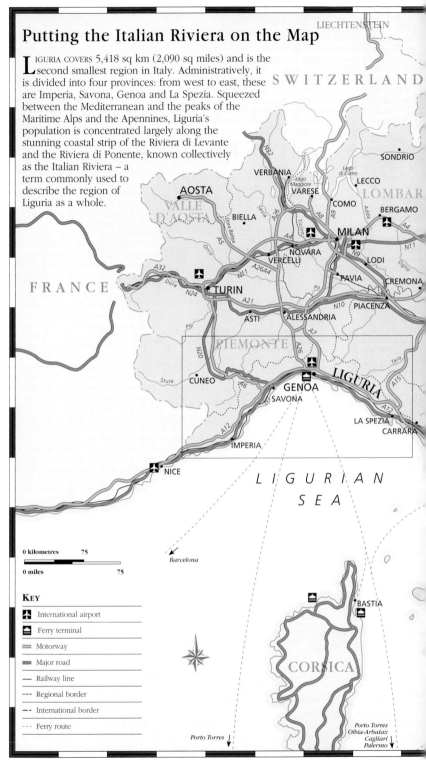

KEY

✈	International airport
⛴	Ferry terminal
▬	Motorway
▬	Major road
—	Railway line
---	Regional border
––	International border
---	Ferry route

0 kilometres   75

0 miles   75

◁ **Detail of the beautiful Byzantine mosaic in the Baptistry in Albenga**

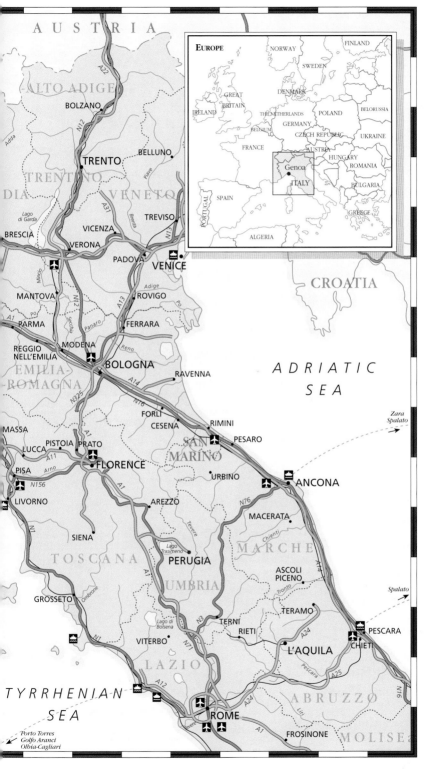

A PORTRAIT OF THE ITALIAN RIVIERA

*T*HE BLUE WATER *of one of the loveliest stretches of sea in Italy laps the coast, with its rocks, maquis and pastel-coloured villages proud of their maritime tradition. Just behind, hills that are often silver with olive trees rise steeply to the Apennines, which separate Liguria from the other regions of northern Italy.*

Bound to the north by alpine Piedmont, to the south by rolling Tuscany and to the east by the plains of the Po Valley, Liguria is a world apart: no other Italian region has such a generous climate or mountainous landscape, nor one where the sea and the mountains are in such close proximity (in Liguria you are never more than 35 km/22 miles from the Mediterranean). This is a region that was always more easily reached by sea than by land.

Monument to sailors

The characteristics of Liguria derive from the geology that has shaped it. The margins of the region are clear: the mass of the Alps, partly handed over to France after World War II, lead as far as the threshold of the Colle di Cadibona, which marks the point where the long chain of the Apennines begins, running first east- and then southwards. To the south of these mountains is the narrow strip of land where, over the course of millennia, the Ligurian civilization developed: the people were naturally more inclined to turn to the sea and the large islands of the Mediterranean than towards the peaks behind.

It would be wrong, however, to assume, when pausing to admire the waters of Portofino, Genoa or Camogli, that a Liguria of the hinterland does not exist. Reached

The spectacular rocky coast of the Cinque Terre, plunging into the sea

◁ **A staircase decorated with plants in one of Liguria's typical *carrugi* (narrow alleys)**

The seaside resort of Camogli

along steep roads, en route to the mountain passes that were once crucial staging posts on any journey northwards, are fascinating towns such as Dolceacqua, beloved of Monet; Triora, known as the village of witches; or the villages of the Val di Vara. These places are just as Ligurian as the gentrified ports of the jet set.

THE PEOPLE

The temperament of the Ligurian people can be said to vary according to the character of the coast, being generally more open and sunny on the beach-rich Riviera di Ponente and more terse and taciturn along the rockier Riviera di Levante. The writer Guido Piovene noted in his *Viaggio in Italia, published in the 1960s, that* "The greatest diversity can be observed going from Genoa to the west. Here, the air of Provence breathes on a Liguria that is closed, laconic ... and lacking imagination, creating a loquacious, colourful Liguria of storytellers, a halfway link between the Genoese and the Marseillais".

There is also a third Liguria, that of the mountainous region behind the coast. Traditionally, the people of the mountains mistrusted not just the coastal folk but the people living in the valleys. And the inhabitants of one valley would almost certainly be suspicious of the inhabitants of a neighbouring one. Such complex relationships are still part of everyday life in Liguria. To further complicate matters, there has been a steady exodus of people from the mountains towards the coast. While agriculture in the interior is in decline, tourism on the coast is booming.

Demographically, Liguria is in deep water. It has the lowest birth rate in Italy, making it the lowest in Europe, and an unusually aged population: 25 per cent of Ligurians are over 65 years old; one reason for this is the influx of retirees, attracted by Liguria's warm climate.

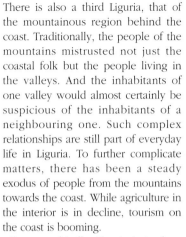

Retirees playing *bocce*, the local version of *boules*

TOURISM

The tourism industry started in the Italian Riviera in the 19th century, and it is now the dominant industry. The main attraction is, of course, the coast, with its 300 km (186 miles) of sandy or pebbly beaches, cliffs and small islands. Many of the towns and even the old fishing villages, from San Remo to Portovenere, are now devoted to tourism. While in the most

A typical *gozzo*, fishing dinghy

Fishermen, here on the beach at Spotorno, pulling nets in at dawn

famous seaside resorts you will find grand hotels built for the visiting aristocrats of the 19th century, many of the old fishing villages have a harbour rather than a beach and are riddled with the characteristic *carruggi* (the narrow alleys found in every medieval *centro storico* in Liguria), which rise and fall between tall, pastel-coloured houses.

Genoa, the Ligurian capital regally positioned at the centre of the region, is not easy to get to know. There is an abrupt change between the open spaces of the port and the narrow alleys of the town. The former has been the subject of a major but gradual regeneration, which has seen the creation of, among other things, the futuristic Aquarium, considered one of the finest in Europe. However, a Mediterranean soul can still be found in the streets of Genoa's historic centre, still redolent of those

distant centuries when the galleys of "Genoa The Proud" were familiar in all the ports of the Levante.

When you have had your fill of the wealth, ostentation or over-development of the coast, then you should head into Liguria's interior, which is attracting growing numbers of visitors. They come looking for an unspoilt land of woods, rivers, lakes and peaks, where towns show another aspect of the history and people of Liguria.

Ligurian olives, used for some of Italy's finest oils

THE CUISINE

Getting to know the Italian Riviera also involves trying the local food and wine, which is offered in most local restaurants. Liguria's olive oil can compete with Italy's best, the fish and seafood are superb, and there are all sorts of other traditional foods, including delicious snacks, known as *stuzzichini*.

The food is just one facet of a region which, even to the most ardent fans of the sea, should not be regarded as merely a seaside resort.

Apricale, in the hinterland behind Imperia

The Landscape of Liguria

FOR MOST VISITORS to Liguria, the region means only one thing – the beaches, luxuriant vegetation and rocky slopes of the Riviera. Behind the coast, on the fertile plains and in the valleys, agriculture takes over – in particular, the age-old cultivation of olives and a burgeoning modern horticultural industry. Step further back and you're in the mountains, with their isolated villages and silent forests (Liguria is the most forested region in Italy). In winter, snow whitens the peaks just a short distance from the Mediterranean.

The rocky coast of Portovenere

THE COAST

Liguria's coastline would measure 440 km (274 miles) if a line were traced following the shore into every inlet and cove. To the west, the beaches are wider and the coastline gentler, while to the east, the landscape is characterized by cliffs and mountains reaching down to the shore, making beaches a rarity. The Ligurian Sea is the richest area for cetaceans (whales and dolphins) in the Mediterranean.

__Dolphins__ can be seen in the Ligurian Sea, especially in the sea off the coast of the Cinque Terre, as well as sperm whales and the occasional marine turtle. It is not unusual to see groups of these friendly creatures following the wash behind ferry boats, emerging from the water and performing somersaults.

__The palm tree__ ("la palma" in Italian) was imported from North Africa and is now so common on the Riviera that it has given its name to a stretch of the Riviera di Ponente.

THE COASTAL PLAINS

Although the plains occupy just one per cent of the region, they have always performed an important function. The climate is temperate and favourable for agriculture, and the soil very fertile. As a result, the plains are crammed with cultivated fields, as well as industries that cannot be located in rockier areas. This is the most densely populated part of Liguria: despite large areas of natural landscape, the plains have an average population of more than 300 inhabitants per square kilometre.

__Mimosa__, originally from southwestern Australia, brightens up many parks and gardens with its bright yellow flowers in spring.

__Glasshouses__ are a common feature of the plains. The cultivation of vegetables, fruit and flowers is one of Liguria's prime economic resources.

WILDLIFE IN LIGURIA

The natural habitats of Liguria are very varied and the animal species that live there are equally diverse. In addition to the rich marine life, including whales in the waters extending southwards towards Corsica, there are many species of seabird (cormorants, shearwaters, gannets and terns). The hills are home to small mammals such as the fox, marten, badger and wild boar. In some areas roe deer and fallow deer have been reintroduced. At higher altitudes, in a gradual recolonization of the Apennine mountains, wolves have returned.

Roe deer, found in the hills

Seagulls, never far away

THE HILLS

Thirty per cent of Liguria consists of hill slopes, where the economy is based on the cultivation of olives (producing high-quality olive oil), ornamental plants, flowers and vines. In places where nothing is grown, the natural shrubby vegetation of the Mediterranean (known as maquis or *macchia)* dominates, followed, at higher altitudes, by pine woods and woods of chestnut and oak.

THE MOUNTAINS

The Maritime Alps, to the west, and the Apennines, to the east, account for the largest chunk of Ligurian territory: as much as 69 per cent of the region is over 1,000m (3,281 ft) high. The proximity of the mountains to the Mediterranean has resulted in some botanically fascinating close juxtapositions of alpine and coastal plant and flower species. At the highest altitudes, conifers such as Scotch pine, silver fir, Norway spruce and larch predominate.

Olives are cultivated on hill terraces, often overlooking the sea, as in the area of the Cinque Terre. The best-quality olive variety is the taggiasca, *which yields a fine extra virgin olive oil.*

Edelweiss, a lovely alpine flower, is found at higher altitudes. Look out for it during the flowering period, from July to August.

The wolf has been gradually moving up through the Apennines and has recently appeared in the Parco Naturale Regionale dell'Aveto, close to the border with Emilia-Romagna.

The fox, like other small mammals, is a constant presence in hillside woods. They can also be seen in inhabited areas, searching for food.

Parks and Nature Reserves

THE WILDEST and most unspoilt natural areas of Liguria are found, not surprisingly, in the hinterland. Here, a crisis in upland agriculture has seen the abandonment of mountain villages, with many vineyards and olive groves left to lie fallow; plants and wildlife are the main beneficiaries of such depopulation. Liguria's protected areas make up around 12 per cent of the region's land area and include six national parks, as well as nature reserves, mostly in the mountains. Each has a different character, from the Alpine valleys on the border with Piedmont, to the hills close to Tuscany. On the coast, after decades of tourist development, a series of marine and coastal reserves aims to conserve the last remaining unspoilt fragments of the Ligurian coast.

The Parco del Finalese (p144), *above Finale Ligure, has fascinating karst formations.*

THE ALTA VIA DEI MONTI LIGURI

Created around a series of mule tracks which criss-cross the region and traverse more than one regional park, the Alta Via dei Monti Liguri is a protected trail which extends the length of Liguria *(see p201)*. It can be explored either on foot or, for the more energetic, by bike.

The Alta Via dei Monti Liguri, offering stunning walks and views

Isola Gallinara *(see p151)* and Isola Bergeggi *(see pp140–41)*, already regional nature reserves, are set to become marine reserves.

Parco Naturale Regionale del Beigua

The Parco del Monte Beigua (see pp134–5) *is a park of high mountains. Its territory includes Monte Beigua and a series of other peaks which are only 6 km (4 miles) from the coast and yet exceed 1,000 m (3,280 ft) in height. Towards the border with Piedmont, the vegetation is typically alpine, while lower down, pines and larches give way to chestnut forest and then to Mediterranean maquis.*

PIANA CRIXIA

Fiume Bormida

BEIGUA

Varazze

Savona

FINALESE

Finale Ligure

ALPI LIGURI

Albenga

ISOLA GALLINARA

Imperia

Ventimiglia

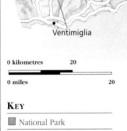

0 kilometres   20

0 miles   20

KEY

⬜ National Park

⬜ Regional Nature Reserve

⬜ Other protected area

⬜ Marine reserve

— Alta Via dei Monti Liguri

The Val d'Aveto is protected by the park of the same name (see pp114–5). It includes the highest peaks in the Ligurian Apennines and valleys where upland agriculture was introduced by monks during the Middle Ages. The park encompasses the forest reserve of Le Lame, which has numerous (originally glacial) lakes and teems with wildlife.

Along the rocky ridge *separating the Alta Valle Scrivia from the Val Trebbia is the Parco dell'Antola (see p108); all kinds of excursions are possible, including a complete circuit around the artificial lake of Brugneto.*

ANTOLA

Lago del Brugneto

Torriglia

Santo Stefano d'Aveto

AVETO

Fiume Trebbia

Genoa

AREA MARINA DI PORTOFINO

Portofino

PROMONTORI E ISOLE DEL LEVANTE

Ceparana

Fiume Magra

CINQUE TERRE

La Spezia

AREA MARINA CINQUE TERRE

MONTEMARCELLO MAGRA

The Parco di Portofino *(see pp110–11),* a coastal conservation area since 1935, is exceptionally pretty. The natural beauty of the promontory (Monte di Portofino), a meeting point between the Mediterranean and the Apennines, is not confined to dry land; in 1999, a marine reserve was created to protect the sea beds.

The Parco di Montemarcello-Magra *(see p126) includes the estuary of the River Magra, on the border with Tuscany, and the eastern side of the Gulf of La Spezia. From the summit of the promontory the view stretches from the Alps to Portovenere. The rich flora of the park includes Mediterranean maquis and flowering plants such as the cistus (shown here).*

The most famous protected *area in the region is the Parco Nazionale delle Cinque Terre (see pp118–9), now also a World Heritage site. Crammed into narrow inlets between cliffs that plunge into the sea, the five villages of the Cinque Terre are an eloquent expression of the ancient relationship between humans and their environment. The villages look up to sculpted terraces carved into the steep slopes between the sea and the mountains.*

The Italian Riviera Coastline

T HE DENSITY OF THE POPULATION along the Italian
Riviera's coast is due largely to the fact that, unlike
the marshy shores of Tuscany, Liguria's often rocky
shores are eminently habitable and, historically, easy to
defend. The beaches are more often pebbly than sandy,
with pebbles at San Remo and Rapallo, for example,
but sugar-fine sand at Alassio. Many beaches show a
Blue Flag and have gorgeous, limpid waters.

**The shores around
Savona** are generally
low-lying. From Albissola,
Celle Ligure and Varazze,
pebbly and sandy beaches
alternate as far as Arenzano,
at the western edge of the
sprawling city of Genoa.

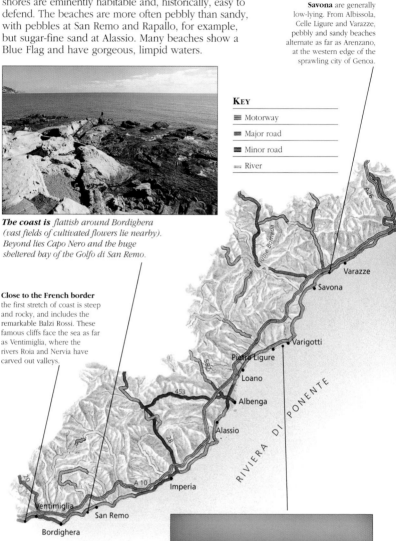

The coast is *flattish around Bordighera
(vast fields of cultivated flowers lie nearby).
Beyond lies Capo Nero and the huge
sheltered bay of the Golfo di San Remo.*

KEY

- ▨ Motorway
- ▬ Major road
- ▬ Minor road
- ⚬ River

Close to the French border
the first stretch of coast is steep
and rocky, and includes the
remarkable Balzi Rossi. These
famous cliffs face the sea as far
as Ventimiglia, where the
rivers Roia and Nervia have
carved out valleys.

Varazze

Savona

Varigotti

Pietra Ligure

Loano

Albenga

Alassio

Imperia

Ventimiglia

San Remo

Bordighera

RIVIERA DI PONENTE

Before reaching the *sandy beaches of
Alassio, the coastal landscape alternates
between rocky stretches and shallow bays,
while inland lies the plain washed by the
River Centa. Coastal resorts follow in
succession – Albenga, Loano, Pietra Ligure
and Borgio Verezzi – as far as the cliffs of
Finale and Capo Noli.*

Within the province of La Spezia, the coastline is rocky and dramatic, with the road forced through numerous tunnels. The drama culminates in a vertiginous 20-km (12-mile) stretch of coast in the famous Cinque Terre.

East of Greater Genoa, where steep cliffs predominate, every scrap of level ground has been terraced and cultivated for centuries. Along here, you will find the lovely fishing village of Bogliasco and stunning Camogli, with a rich seafaring tradition.

0 kilometres   20

0 miles   20

At Rapallo the cliffs dip, only to rise again near Zoagli, overlooking the Golfo del Tigullio. The mouth of the Entella torrent has created a narrow plain around Chiavari.

LAGO DEL BRUGNETO

Genoa
Nervi
Camogli
Portofino
Rapallo
Santa Margherita Ligure
Chiavari
Sestri Levante
Moneglia
RIVIERA DI LEVANTE
Levanto
Monterosso
Vernazza
Manarola
Corniglia
Riomaggiore
Portovenere
Isola Palmaria
La Spezia
San Terenzo
Lerici

The Monte di Portofino is best explored by foot or by boat from Portofino or Santa Margherita Ligure, the two most exclusive and romantic towns on this stunning promontory.

Portovenere is the gateway to the Golfo della Spezia, with its indented and rocky shores on the west side and gentler coastline, with the beaches of Lerici and Tellaro, to the east. The long headland of Punta Bianca faces the plain formed by the River Magra, beyond which lies the border with Tuscany.

Art in Liguria

SINCE THE TIME OF THE ROMANS, Liguria has always been an important region, even a rich one from time to time, but it has never really been at the centre of events, whether political, cultural or artistic. Of crucial significance artistically, however, was Liguria's role as a major crossroads between the European mainland and the Mediterranean (and, beyond, the rest of the world). This meant not only that works of art from foreign parts passed through Liguria, but that foreign artists (including from other Italian states) visited and even stayed on to work.

ANTIQUITY

THE EARLIEST evidence of artistic expression in Liguria include Paleolithic carvings linked to famous sites such as Balzi Rossi *(see p169)*.

Surprisingly few traces of the Romans survive in Liguria. Much of their energy was spent gaining control of the area (only Genoa gave in willingly). The city of Luni *(see p127)*, founded in 177 BC, has some examples of Roman sculpture, but these are best described as well-made crafts rather than works of great artistic merit.

Crucifixion (1138), in Sarzana cathedral

probably the only work of significance from the 12th century in Liguria. In fact, in the 13th and 15th centuries, it was generally easier to find Tuscan artists rather than local ones working in Liguria.

In terms of sculpture, one of the period's most significant works was the funerary monument (1313–14) of Margaret of Brabant, now in Genoa's Museo di Sant'Agostino *(see p57)*. It was commissioned by emperor Henry VII from the Tuscan Giovanni Pisano. The same museum has the remains of a 14th-century statue of Simone Boccanegra, the first doge of Genoa.

Political and territorial upheavals increasingly opened up Ligurian cities to the influence (and presence) of artists from Lombardy and Flanders: the

MIDDLE AGES

LIGURIA IN THE Middle Ages, which consisted of walled towns linked to one another by sea rather than by land, was of greater interest architecturally than artistically.

The first important examples of figurative art from this era emerged from the Lunigiana (the area around Luni, an important port until the 12th century), which was culturally close to Tuscany. One such example is the *Crucifixion (1138)* now in the cathedral of Sarzana *(see p128)*. The work of a Tuscan called Maestro Guglielmo, this is

Funerary monument of Margaret of Brabant

Crucifixion (15th century) by the Pavia artist Donato de' Bardi, now in Savona's Pinacoteca Civica *(see p136)*, was one of the first "Nordic" works to find favour.

Trade with Flanders and Burgundy brought a series of painters (David, Provost, Van Cleve) to Genoa; their religious works are now found throughout the region.

Equestrian portrait of Gio Carlo Doria by Rubens

THE RENAISSANCE AND BAROQUE PERIODS

IN THE 16TH CENTURY, an era in which Genoa's top families became rich through their dealings in international finance, new artistic genres reached Liguria, including the art of fresco-painting.

Among Liguria's best-known fresco painters was Luca Cambiaso, born in Moneglia in 1527 and active mainly in Genoa. His works can be seen in the Cappella Lercari in Genoa's San Lorenzo cathedral *(see pp52–3)*, and also in the Santuario della Madonna delle Grazie, not far from Chiavari *(see p114)*.

In the 17th century Genoa was a rich city, in terms of both commercial banking and art, and several of the city's fine private art collections were begun in this period: the city's newly wealthy families needed a large number of paintings to fill their vast palaces. The work available in the city attracted artists from all over

Annunciation by Paolo di Giovanni Fei (14th century)

Italy, as well as from abroad. In general, most of the works commissioned or bought by Genoa's noble patrons were not by Liguria's home-grown artists.

It was around this time that works by Flemish artists started to reach Liguria, evidence of the cultural and commercial influence that the Low Countries had on Ligurian merchants. The Palazzo Spinola gallery in Genoa *(see p64)* houses several international masterpieces dating from this period, such as the *Ecce Homo* by Antonello da Messina and *Equestrian portrait of Gio Carlo Doria* (1606) by Peter Paul Rubens. The latter arrived in Genoa in the early 17th century,

and fell in love with the city. He became a major influence in the development of Genoese Baroque. Another influence at this time was Antony Van Dyck, some of whose works are on display in Genoa's Palazzo Rosso gallery *(see pp72–5)*. Among other fine Renaissance works on show in the same gallery are *Judith and Holofernes* (c. 1550–80) by Veronese, *San Sebastiano* (1615) by Guido Reni and *The Cook* (c.1620s) by Bernardo Strozzi. There are also some fine portraits by Dürer, Pisanello and Paris Bordone.

The Pinacoteca Civica in Savona *(see p136)* has interesting works of art from the same era, including works by Donato De' Bardi and Taddeo di Bartolo.

La Spezia's Museo Amedeo Lia *(see p124)*, affectionately known as the "Louvre of Liguria", houses various Renaissance works of considerable value. Among these are the *Portrait of a Gentleman* (1510) by Titian and an *Annunciation* by Paolo di Giovanni Fei (14th century), as well as works by some of the great artists of the 16th century – including Raphael and Veronese. Liguria's greatest fresco painters, both active in the 17th century, were Gregorio De Ferrari and Domenico Piola, rivals whose work can be seen side by side in Genoa's Palazzo Rosso.

Anton Maria Marigliano (1664–1739), from Genoa was a pupil of Domenico Piola, but made his name as a sculptor of wood. His fine crucifixes can be found in churches all over Liguria.

NINETEENTH CENTURY TO PRESENT DAY

THE 19TH and 20th centuries in Liguria have been more remarkable for the developments in architecture than in art. Modern art in Liguria lacks a strong regional identity.

Among the most significant collections of modern art in Liguria are the Villa Croce in Genoa *(see p57)* and two collections in Nervi *(see p.89)*.

Portrait of the *Contessa de Byland* by Boldini (1901)

These are the Raccolta Frugoni in Villa Grimaldi, and the Raccolta d'Arte Moderna. The latter's vast collection of drawings, sculptures, paintings and engravings dates from the 19th and 20th centuries. The core of the collection consists of the art owned by Prince Oddone di Savoia, which was donated to the community in 1866. The museum's collection is largely regional with some works by national and international artists.

The Museo d'Arte Sandro Pertini in Savona *(see p137)* is devoted to modern art, mostly Italian. There are paintings by Morandi, De Chirico, Rosai, Guttuso and Birolli, and sculptures by Henry Moore and Joan Miró.

Fresco by Cambiaso, Santuario della Madonna delle Grazie, Chiavari

Architecture in Liguria

THE TRULY CREATIVE EXPRESSIONS in Liguria's past lie less with art, or sculpture, than in the people's exceptional capacity to adapt their buildings to the contours of an often harsh and difficult landscape. Perched above the sea and hemmed in by the Apennines, the cities of the Italian Riviera developed in a totally individual way. In Genoa, in particular, the defining characteristic of the city was as a meeting point between the port – the hub of commercial traffic – and the city streets.

Coloured marble on the façade of San Lorenzo, Genoa

ANCIENT ARCHITECTURE

The first examples of individual buildings were Bronze Age settlements which, although they bore similarities to other megalithic structures of the same period, introduced a new element: a fortification capable of defending people and their work. In the Roman era various cities were built or expanded, among them Luni, Genua (Genoa) and Albingaunum (Albenga), which were all given typical Roman features, such as bridges, aqueducts, amphitheatres, and trading quays in the ports. The most impressive amphitheatre in Liguria can be seen among the ruins of ancient Luni, at the foot of the Apuan Alps (a source of white marble much in demand in ancient Rome). The remnants of a Roman road also survive between Albenga and Alassio.

Settlements called "castellari" were fortifications on high ground made up of concentric circles of dry-stone walls designed to protect villages and pasture.

The houses were usually cabins.

Defensive wall

THE MIDDLE AGES

Medieval architecture in Liguria shows similarities with the building styles that developed in other areas along the Tyrrhenian coast. In Genoa, the main development in architecture involved the construction of mansions for rich families of merchants, grouped together in small districts and headed by families linked by business connections. Genoese churches constructed in the Romanesque and Gothic styles were typically built with black and white stripes, and laden with materials from earlier (including Roman) eras. Elsewhere in Liguria this was a period of local rivalries and disputes characterized by the construction of numerous castles and tower houses. Liguria's pretty hilltop villages are another symbol of the Middle Ages, many of which still preserve their medieval structure. Of particular note are the region's famous *carrugi*, the narrow and usually steep lanes that penetrate into the heart of these often labyrinthine settlements.

The church of San Lorenzo in Genoa (see pp52–3), begun in 1118, is the most famous example of Ligurian Gothic.

The doors are flanked by rich decoration in marble.

RENAISSANCE PALAZZI

In Genoa, the 16th and 17th centuries were a boom period – referred to as the "Genoese Century" – during which a handful of powerful families financed the construction of numerous grand palaces. A figure of particular importance in Genoese Renaissance history was Andrea Doria (1468–1560), admiral and patron of the arts, who built the magnificent Palazzzo Doria Pamphilj (*see p78–9)*. The laying of Via Garibaldi, or "La Strada Nuova", in the mid 16th century, was a great example of civic town planning. The palazzi along this monumental street, including Palazzo Doria Tursi, symbolized the power of the great Genoese families. Other impressive schemes included the construction of the Molo Nuovo (new quay) and of the famous Lanterna (lighthouse), both in the port. Such was the reputation of Genoa's architects that they exported their palazzo designs and materials to Spain, France and northern Europe.

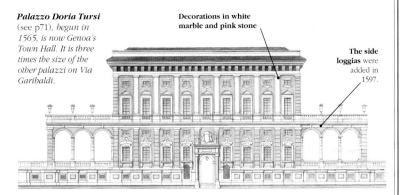

Palazzo Doria Tursi (see p71), *begun in 1565, is now Genoa's Town Hall. It is three times the size of the other palazzi on Via Garibaldi.*

Decorations in white marble and pink stone

The side loggias were added in 1597.

THE ARCHITECTURE OF TODAY

After decades of crisis, years during which Genoa's historic centre was abandoned to its own devices, the city has rediscovered pride in itself and a capacity to undertake grand projects. The 500th anniversary of the discovery of America by Columbus (1992) provided the impetus to revamp the port area, which had long been blighted by the presence of the coastal motorway; and Genoa's role as European City of Culture in 2004 has prompted renovation and building work elsewhere. One of the aims of the restoration of the port area was to link it, finally, to the narrow alleys of old Genoa.

The colossal structure of the Bigo (see p60), designed by local boy Renzo Piano, echoes the cranes of Genoa's mercantile past, while the sphere is a glasshouse containing palms and vast ferns. The Aquarium was built in 1992 for the Columbus celebrations.

The "arms" support a panoramic lift.

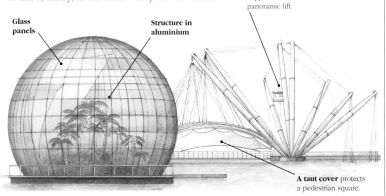

Glass panels

Structure in aluminium

A taut cover protects a pedestrian square.

Literature, Theatre and Music

LIGURIA'S TALE HAS BEEN RECOUNTED many times, by Ligurians, Italians and foreigners, and featured in songs, literature and paintings perhaps more than any other region in Italy. From the verses of Dante and Ariosto onwards, some exceptional writing has been inspired by Liguria's towns and landscapes. Meanwhile, the modern music created by Ligurian singer-songwriters, a tradition influenced by the French *chansonniers*, has provided a soundtrack to accompany the lives of new generations of Italians.

The Genoese singer-songwriter Gino Paoli in performance

MUSIC

NICCOLÒ PAGANINI, born in Genoa in 1782 (he died in 1840), is Liguria's only musician to have achieved world renown. He found early fame as a violinist, performing in public for the first time at the age of 12, and rapidly conquered the whole of Europe with his astonishing technique.

In terms of classical music, there is not much else of home-grown interest, though there were some important visitors to the region in the 19th century. Tchaikovsky (1840–93) was attracted to San Remo by the town's Russian emigré community, and composed his opera, *Eugene Onegin* here (1879).

In modern times, Liguria's best-loved artists have been singers. In the 1960s, the young singer-songwriter Gino Paoli, together with Luigi Tenco and Bruno Lauzi, composed many successful songs. The artistic career of Fabrizio De André was inspired by similar

traditions but went even further, blending social commitment with music influenced by melodies and dialects from the wider Mediterranean rather than just Genoa.

To some Italians, Liguria's most important contribution to the country's music scene is the Festival della Canzone Italiana (Festival of Italian Popular Song), staged in San Remo. This pop festival had its heyday in the 1950s and '60s (Domenico Modugno's song *Volare* was the festival's biggest international hit, but still excites passions in Italy.

A more respected contest (musically) is the Premio Tenco, staged in San Remo in October. This has featured all the best Italian songwriters (such as Guccini, Venditti, Branduardi, Paoli, Finardi, Benigni and De André) and is open to international artists, too: Tom Waits and Elvis Costello are both past prize-winners.

Beppe Grillo during a theatre performance

THEATRE

IN GENOA, there are two main venues for theatrical performances. Of these, the most important is the Teatro Carlo Felice, designed by Carlo Barabino (the most famous Genoese architect of the period) in 1826 and inaugurated two years later with a performance of Bellini's opera *Bianca e Fernando*. The theatre was renovated at various times after that, but then suffered serious bomb damage during World War II. Following decades of debate locally, the theatre was finally rebuilt in 1991 *(see p55)*.

The actor Paolo Villaggio

The reconstruction of Teatro Carlo Felice means that Teatro dell'Archinvolto is the only 19th-century Genoese theatre still in operation; all of Genoa's

Interior of the Carlo Felice theatre, Genoa

other theatre spaces have gone, the result either of urban restructuring or bombing during the war.

The theatre scene in Genoa is very much alive. Among the most famous contemporary personalities are Carlo Dapporto (born in San Remo), Lina Volonghi (born in Quarto, just outside Genoa, in 1916), Paolo Villaggio, Tullio Solenghi and Beppe Grillo, the author of caustic monologues in which dialect plays an important part. Vittorio Gassman was one of Italian theatre's greatest stage actors to have performed during the 20th century.

LITERATURE

LIGURIA'S GREATEST men of letters were Edmondo De Amicis (1846–1908) and Eugenio Montale (1896–1981), who was awarded the Nobel prize for Literature in 1975.

Generations of students in Italy have studied De Amicis' work *Cuore* (Heart), and he wrote marvellous travel pieces. Montale's poetry (available in English) captures the

The poet Eugenio Montale

quintessence of the Cinque Terre. His *Ossi di Seppia* (Cuttlefish Bones) is justly renowned.

Of much less renown was an Italian writer called Giovanni Ruffini, whose collection of short stories (called *Doctor Antonio*), printed in English in 1855 and set in Liguria, sparked the first interest in the region: the first wave of tourists and writers, from both England and northern Europe soon followed.

Among the foreign writers who wrote about Liguria were Charles Dickens, Hans Christian Andersen, DH Lawrence, Ernest Hemingway and Nietzsche. Edward Lear lived in San Remo towards the end of his life.

In 1922 Ernest Hemingway wrote of Liguria: "Outside the villages there were fields with vines. The fields were brown and the vines coarse and thick. The houses were white, and in the

Edmondo De Amicis, author of *Cuore* and numerous travel books

streets the men, in their Sunday clothes, were playing bowls".

Perhaps the deepest impression was left on the region by the turbulent group of English writers and poets who landed here in 1821 and took up residence in the Golfo di Lerici.

Casa Magni, at Lerici, became a base for a group of English non-conformists who proceeded to throw this fishing village into disorder. They included Lord Byron and his great friend Percy Bysshe Shelley and his wife Mary Wollstonecraft Shelley, their son William and Mary's half-sister, Claire Clairmont (Casa Magni was the Shelley home). The group's habits provoked scandal locally: rich, cultured and liberal, they survived on a meagre diet which consisted mainly of tea, fruit and bread, along with large doses of laudanum for the poets. To the English the local inhabitants appeared to be boorish peasants who spoke an incomprehensible dialect, despite the fact that they lived in this almost impossibly beautiful setting. The awkward encounter between the poets and the village is commemorated in a plaque on the façade of Casa Magni and the verses of *Lines Written in the Bay of Lerici* by Shelley.

THE DIALECTS OF LIGURIA

Conversations in local dialect can often be heard when strolling around villages in Liguria. It is, however, hard to understand these languages, which took root in the remote past and which have retained words, sounds and influences from the entire Mediterranean region. The dialect of the Riviera del Ponente is similar to French, while in the province of La Spezia the local tongue is closer to Tuscan in its cadences and vocabulary. Traces of the language of Genoese merchants can still be found in places far from Liguria: in Bonifacio, for example, in the far south of Corsica, and in Carloforte and Calasetta on Sardinia.

Actor Gilberto Govi, who performs in Genoese dialect

THE ITALIAN RIVIERA
THROUGHOUT THE YEAR

Advert for the
Battaglia di Fiori

HE PLEASANT and mild typically Mediterranean climate, the intense contrasts of light and colour, the romantic coastline and the equally fascinating interior have made Liguria a desirable destination for tourists since the mid-19th century. The clear blue sea, the beaches and the stunning and lush coastal scenery are

consistent attractions all year round, but there are also numerous special events which can add extra local colour to any trip. These events include many religious and gastronomic festivals and also historical re-enactments and regattas, the latter a colourful reminder of the importance of the seafaring tradition to this part of Italy.

The mid-May fish festival at Camogli

SPRING

MILD TEMPERATURES and pure air characterize spring in Liguria, which welcomes visitors with colour and unforgettable scents. The profusion of colourful flowers contrasts with the blue of the sea and the snow-capped peaks of the Ligurian Alps.

MARCH

Festival della Canzone Italiana, San Remo *(late Feb, early Mar)*. Annual pop music festival, with international guests and televised *ad nauseam*.

Sign for the theatre hosting the Festival della Canzone Italiana

Rassegna dell'Olio d'Oliva, Balestrino. This village north of Albenga is proud of its 17 different types of olive. During the festival the public can taste different types of oil and olives as well as other traditional foods.
Fiera di San Giuseppe, La Spezia *(19 Mar)*. Immensely popular festival in honour of the town's patron saint, with more than 800 street stalls and vendors and abundant entertainment for all the family.
Milano–San Remo *(1st Sat after 19 Mar)*. A classic, long-distance cycle race.
Festa di Primavera *(all month)*. Music, art and flower shows along the Riviera dei Fiori, to celebrate the advent of spring.

APRIL

Good Friday processions. Good Friday (Venerdí Santo) has a fervent following, especially on the Riviera di Ponente. It is celebrated with processions in which local confraternities file past, with *casse* (carved wooden sculptures) portraying scenes from the Passion. The processions in Savona and Genoa are particularly popular, but similar events take place in the Ligurian hinterland, too.
Settimana Santa, Ceriana. Processions of confraternities and representations of the Descent from the Cross *(Calata della Croce)*, with religious songs.

MAY

Sagra del Pesce (fish festival), Camogli *(second Sun in May)*. A gigantic frying pan is used to fry a huge quantity of fish, which both

The tasty, typical focaccia of Recco

locals and visitors are then invited to eat: a lovely gesture done in the hope that the seas will be equally generous to the fishermen.
Festa della Focaccia con il Formaggio, Recco *(fourth Sun)*. A bustling festival held to celebrate the famous cheese focaccia of Recco, a small but gastronomic town just north of Camogli. Abundant tastings on offer.

AVERAGE DAILY HOURS OF SUNSHINE

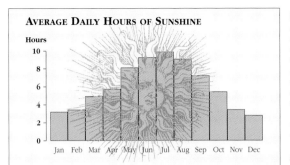

Hours
10
8
6
4
2
0
Jan Feb Mar Apr May Jun Jul Aug Sep Oct Nov Dec

Sunshine
In both spring and summer the long days of sunshine, which are never excessively hot, are perfect for swimming and sailing. The light and colours of autumn, meanwhile, are delightful, while a clear winter's day means that the white peaks of the Alps are visible in the distance.

SUMMER

THE HIGH SEASON for tourists, summer is hot and sunny along the coast and fresher and wetter in the interior.

JUNE

Infiorata *(1st week of Jun)*. To celebrate Corpus Domini (Corpus Christi), many towns strew carpets of flowers along processional routes; the best take place in Sassello, Imperia, Diano Marina and Pietra Ligure. There is also a *Battaglia di Fiori* (battle of flowers) in Ventimiglia.

Regata delle Antiche Repubbliche Marinare, Genoa *(early Jun, every four years)*. A regatta in which teams from the cities of the four ancient maritime republics (Genoa, Pisa, Amalfi and Venice) compete in old sailing ships; there are processions, too. Genoa is the host every four years (the last time in 2004).

Girl in historical costume

Festa di San Giovanni, Genoa *(24 Jun)*. Celebrations in honour of St John. Also in Laigueglia, where 5,000 lit candles are placed on the water, and Triora.

Festa e Palio di San Pietro, Genoa *(29 Jun)*. A race with traditional boats, as well as illuminations.

Palio marinaro del Tigullio *(Jun/Jul)*. Regattas in resorts along the Tigullio coast, including Chiavari, Rapallo and Lavagna.

JULY

Raduno delle Fiat 500, Garlenda *(early Jul)*. Participants come in their Fiat 500s from all over Europe.

Cristo degli Abissi, San Fruttuoso di Camogli *(end Jul)*. Nocturnal mass and torchlit procession of divers to the massive statue of Christ on the sea bed.

Sagra delle Rose and Sagra delle Pesche, Pogli d'Ortovero *(end Jul)*. A celebration of the roses and peaches grown in this area near Albenga. A chance to try local specialities.

The Muretto of Alassio, during a beauty competition

AUGUST

Stella Maris, Camogli *(first Sun)*. A festival of the sea, with a procession of boats to the Punta della Chiappa, with thousands of little wax candles bobbing on the waves.

Torta dei Fieschi, Lavagna *(14 Aug)*. The re-enactment of the lavish 13th-century wedding between Opizzo Fieschi and Bianca de' Bianchi, with a historical procession and the cutting of an enormous cake.

Castelli di Sabbia, Alassio *(mid-Aug)*. National competition for the best sandcastle on the beach.

Processione dell'Assunta, Nervi *(15 Aug)*. Evening procession, with a blessing of the sea and a firework display.

Festa della Madonna Bianca, Portovenere *(17 Aug)*. At 9pm torchlights are lit during a procession to the headland of San Pietro.

Miss Muretto, Alassio *(end Aug/early Sep)*. The prettiest girl is elected and given the title dedicated to the town's famous "Muretto" (wall) of celebrities.

An enormous carpet of flowers, part of an Infiorata

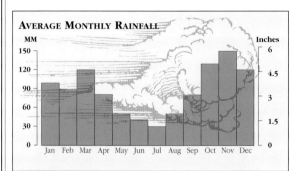

AVERAGE MONTHLY RAINFALL

MM												Inches
150												6
120												4.5
90												3
60												1.5
30												
0	Jan Feb Mar Apr May Jun Jul Aug Sep Oct Nov Dec											0

Rainfall
Liguria's weather is characterized by a fair amount of rainfall, especially during the autumn, when violent storms may occur and sometimes rivers may flood. The Riviera di Ponente is generally drier and sunnier than the Riviera di Levante.

Yachts at their moorings in Imperia

AUTUMN

A UTUMN, with its warm colours and still balmy and sunny days, is the ideal season for visiting Liguria. Towns and villages are less crowded, and it is easier to find accommodation; in short, you can get to know the area's sights, towns, culture and gastronomy in greater peace.

SEPTEMBER

Regata Storica dei Rioni, Noli *(1st or 2nd Sun)*. The four districts of the town challenge each other to a rowing race; processions in historical costume, too.
Sagra del Fuoco, Recco *(7–8 Sep)*. Festival in honour of the patron saint, Nostra Signora del Suffragio.
Raduno di Vele d'Epoca, Imperia *(second week)*. This fun event is held every two years. Hundreds of historical

Bottle of Pigato white wine

boats from all over the world take part in a regatta.
Sagra del Pigato, Salea di Albenga *(early Sep)*. A festival in honour of Pigato wine, with exhibitions, food pavilions, dancing and sporting events.
Festa della Madonna della Villa, Ceriana *(early Sep)*. Solemn candle-lit processions and a music festival of folk music in the village square, with choirs singing traditional songs.
Commemorazione della Battaglia Napoleonica, Loano. Exhibitions, ceremonies and parades in historical costume are staged in order to commemorate the Battle of Loano, in 1795, in which the French revolutionary army succeeded in routing the Austrian army.
Sagra dell'Uva, Varazze. A traditional festival with tastings and the sale of local

wines. A similar festival is held at Vezzano Ligure *(see below)*.
Sagra dell'Uva, Vezzano Ligure *(mid-Sep)*. A festival in honour of the grape *(uva)*, including a costumed procession, a challenge in dialect and a series of contests between grape harvesters.
Sagra della Lumaca, Molini di Triora *(last week)*. Enormous frying pans full of snails *(lumache)* are cooked following an ancient recipe once used by the village's noble families, who would present them as the pièce de resistance at sumptuous banquets, because of their supposed magical powers.

OCTOBER

Salone Internazionale della Nautica, Genoa *(first and second week)*. This is the largest nautical fair to be held anywhere in the Mediterranean, with yachts, motorboats, inflatables and associated nautical paraphernalia.
Sagra della Farinata, Voltri *(late Oct)*. Tastings of local, mostly Genoese, gastronomic specialities, including

A motor launch on display at Genoa's nautical fair

AVERAGE MONTHLY TEMPERATURE

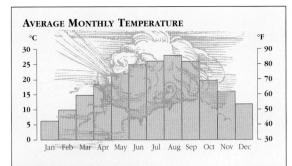

Temperature
The coastal strip, exposed to the south, experiences sea breezes which refresh the hottest and sunniest summers and temper the winter temperatures; the latter are never too severe, even in the interior. Autumn and spring offer warm and clear days.

Festa dei furgari at Taggia

Liguria's famous baked chick-pea snack *(farinata)*.

NOVEMBER

Olioliva, Imperia *(late Nov)*. Held in the area where *taggiasca* olives are grown. Visits to olive presses *(frantoi)* are arranged, and a produce market is held at Oneglia. Restaurants offer special menus.

WINTER

ALTHOUGH IT can be windy, winter in the Italian Riviera often provides days with full sun, making it a good time to explore the region's medieval towns and villages.

DECEMBER

Natale Subacqueo, Tellaro *(24 Dec)*. The village is illuminated with 1,000 torchlights, and at midnight divers emerge with the statue of Baby Jesus, which is welcomed with fireworks.
"U Confogu" (Confuoco), Pietra Ligure and Savona *(Sun before Christmas)*. Traditional ceremony with a costumed procession and the lighting of a propitiatory bundle of laurel: auspices for the coming year are divined from the resulting flames.

JANUARY

Festa di Capodanno (New Year), Genoa. The city's *carrugi* and the Porto Antico are thronged with people, to the sound of boat sirens, a memorable start to the year.

FEBRUARY

Festa dei Furgari, Taggia *(early Feb)*. Dedicated to San Benedetto. *Furgari* (bamboo canes filled with gunpowder) are set alight, while banquets and feasting go on all through the night.
Fiera di Sant'Agata, Genoa *(5 Feb)*. Stalls sell knick-knacks and sweetmeats, on the Sunday closest to 5 Feb. (Also in San Fruttuoso.)
Carnevale, Loano. Allegorical carriages with groups in costume parade through the town; the *Palio dei Borghi* is held at the end.
Sagra della Mimosa, Pieve Ligure. Floral carriages and costumed processions.

PUBLIC HOLIDAYS

New Year's Day (1 Jan)
Epiphany (6 Jan)
Easter Sunday
Easter Monday
Anniversario della Liberazione (25 Apr)
Labour Day (1 May)
Festa della Repubblica (2 Jun)
Ferragosto (15 Aug)
All Saints (1 Nov)
Immaculate Conception (8 Dec)
Christmas (25 Dec)
Boxing Day (26 Dec)

Mimosa in flower, brightening the gardens of the hinterland

THE HISTORY OF THE ITALIAN RIVIERA

HE HISTORY OF LIGURIA *is linked inextricably with the sea. The coastal climate encouraged early settlement and the Romans built the first ports. Most importantly, from the start of the second millennium, the Republic of Genoa became a major seapower whose tentacles reached all over the Mediterranean and beyond.*

The climate and geography of Liguria were highly favourable to humans in the far distant past. The coast was suitable for settlements and navigation on the open sea, while travel to what is now the Côte d'Azur and France was made easy by the low coastal hills. As a result, the population of this part of the Mediterranean was very scattered. Proof of this comes from the numerous traces of tombs and hearths found in the caves and on the hills of the region, forming an almost uninterrupted line from Liguria to Provence.

Roman amphora in Albenga

The first Ligurians appeared during the Bronze Age. In an era of migration and battles to occupy the best positions, the Ligurians fortified their settlements with walls to defend villages, pasture and access to the sea. They were mentioned for the first time (under the name of Ligyes) in the 7th century BC by Greek sources, who described how the land controlled by the ancient Ligurians extended far beyond the current boundaries of the region, as far as the limits of Catalonia and the

Cévennes. While clashes and power struggles were taking place both in the lowlands and in the mountains to the north, new arrivals turned up on the Ligurian coast: the Greeks and the Etruscans who were, at the time, in total control of the Mediterranean and its markets. The Greeks were by then firmly installed in Marseille, and sought space to settle in the Ligurian valleys. The Etruscans had founded ports and trading cities along the Tuscan coast.

A series of settlements was established during this period, including proper villages at Genoa, Chiavari and Ameglia. Traces of necropoli in which the ashes of the deceased were buried have been discovered.

The onset of the Roman era was marked by the arrival of Roman legions in around 218 BC; this represented a much more significant change for the region than the disruptions caused by previous populations of travellers and merchants. For Rome, Liguria represented a fundamental transit point for expansion into nearby Gaul.

TIMELINE

300,000 BC	100,000 BC	50,000 BC	10,000 BC	1,000 BC	100 BC
240,000 BC First burial in the cave at Balzi Rossi	**80,000–60,000 BC** Presence of Neanderthal man in Ligurian sites		**12,340 BC** Date of hand and foot prints found in the Grotta di Toirano	**218 BC** The Romans establish their first base in Liguria	
	Finds in the Balzi Rossi museum	**36,000–10,000 BC** Era of *Homo sapiens sapiens*	*Footprints in the Grotta di Toirano*	**First millennium BC** Golden age of the Ligurians and contact with the Greeks and Phoenicians	

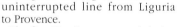

◁ **Detail from the frescoes by Perin del Vaga in the Loggia degli Eroi, Palazzo Doria Pamphilj, Genoa**

Prehistoric Liguria

Stone finds from the Balzi Rossi

THE LONG ROCKY COAST, with steep, vertical cliffs facing the sea, made Liguria a particularly attractive destination for our ancient ancestors. The rise and fall of the sea level, over the course of millennia, has brought about the emergence and disappearance of hundreds of caves which have been inhabited by man since the prehistoric era. As well as offering coastal shelter, food and fishing possibilities, Liguria also provided a series of staging posts between the coast and the hinterland and the plains of the Po valley. At the end of the prehistoric era, man regularly made use of the remote Monte Bego and the Vallée des Merveilles, just across the border into France. In the western Riviera, in the meantime, a new urban and military set-up had emerged: the settlements known as *castellari*, which protected villages and pastures from invasion by peoples approaching from the sea, intent on expanding their dominion in the hinterland.

Monte Bego
In the area around Monte Bego, a sacred mountain, and in the Vallée des Merveilles, prehistoric man has left over 100,000 rock carvings of religious significance on rocks smoothed and etched by the passing of ancient glaciers.

The Triplice Sepoltura (Triple Grave)
Found in the Barma Grande at Balzi Rossi, this provides important evidence of human presence in the area. Accompanying the skeletons of one adult, a boy and a girl was a rich collection of funerary objects.

Pieve di Teco

Triora

Imperia

Taggia

San Remo

Ventimiglia

The caves of the Balzi Rossi form part of a reddish, calcareous wall jutting out over the sea. There are 12 caves in all.

CRAFTMANSHIP IN LIGURIA

The first crafts to be discovered in the region date back 35,000 years, to the late Paleolothic period. Treasures from the Balzi Rossi caves (now in the museum) include a unique Przewalskii Horse incised on a wall of the Grotta del Caviglione 20,000 years ago, and 15 soapstone Venus figurines, symbols of fertility, found in the Barma Grande.

Venus figure

Przewalskii horse

Arene Candide
*The "white sands" cave
(a sand dune once covered it)
is closed to the public. Finds
from it are in the archeological
museum at Pegli near Genoa.*

Grotte di Toirano
*In the Grotta della Bàsura
are hand-, knee- and
footprints of Cro-magnon
men, women and children.*

THE CAVES OF LIGURIA

The women of Liguria's most ancient ancestor died in the Grotta del Principe around 240,000 years ago. The great cave complex of Balzi Rossi, however, continued to be used by Neanderthal man even after that. Groups of hunter-gatherers lived in many other Ligurian caves, too: at Arma di Taggia near San Remo, and in the Grotta delle Fate at Toirano near Finale Ligure. With the passing of millennia, our closest ancestor *(Homo sapiens sapiens)* settled in Liguria, where traces of his presence have been found at Balzi Rossi, at Toirano and in the grotto of Arene Candide in Savona province, where archaeologists found 20 graves, including the famous tomb of the Giovane Principe (Young Prince).

WHERE TO SEE PREHISTORIC LIGURIA

The interior of the Balzi Rossi museum

Some of Liguria's most significant prehistoric sites are also fascinating places to visit, in particular the site of the Balzi Rossi, with its museum *(see p169)* and the Grotte di Toirano *(see pp146–7)*. Breathtaking hikes can also be taken along the Alpine paths of the Vallée des Merveilles and Monte Bego, which lie just across the border in France.

Hikers in the Vallée des Merveilles

Ruined Roman villa at Alba Docilia, now Albisola

along the coast. The most important of these Roman settlements were: Portus Lunae (Luni), Ingaunum (Albenga), Alba Docilia (Albisola), Genua (Genoa), Portus Delphini (Portofino) and Segesta Tigulliorum (Sestri Levante). Roman Liguria, however, was never more than a backwater: the result of its distance from the main routes of communication through Italy, and the fact that the Romans' most important ports were elsewhere.

ROMAN LIGURIA

The focus of the Romans was to establish landing stages for merchants and ships, but they did not have an easy time establishing their presence in Liguria. Genoa was one of the few places that fell to the Romans without conflict; it was incorporated into the Roman empire in the 2nd century BC.

The toughness of the Ligurians attracted the Carthaginians (under the command of Hannibal and his brothers Hasdrubal and Mago), who co-opted as allies the tribes of the Intumeli and Ingauni. In 205 BC, the Carthaginians besieged and destroyed Genoa. The Romans prevailed, however and, once the Carthaginians had been driven back, they continued their expansion, attacking Gallic tribes and extending the road network, which became a vital means of communication within the empire. The Via Postumia reached Roman Genua (Genoa) from Mediolanum (Milan) in 148 BC, although the road of greatest significance was the Via Julia Augusta, which was laid along the coast; the modern Via Aurelia follows its route.

As they conquered territory, the Romans also colonized it, gradually establishing a whole series of towns,

BARBARIAN INVASIONS

The armies of the Visigoths under Alaric reached Liguria from North Africa in 409 AD, and after that the region was raided by the Goths and their allies, the Heruli. Armies came and went, while both the political and military situation in the whole Italian peninsula was in a constant state of flux. In 536 AD Italy was invaded by the forces of the Eastern Empire, under the leadership of Justinian I. They eventually overcame the Goths, and a fairly peaceful period under Byzantine rule followed. Bishoprics had

Rotarius, king of the Longobards, who reached Liguria in 641

already started to emerge in the 5th century, and continued to be created under the Byzantines, including that of Albenga. Liguria was given the name of *Provincia Maritima Italorum* by its new rulers.

The period of Byzantine rule came to a close with the arrival in 641 of the Lombards, led by King Rotarius. The towns of Liguria became part of a

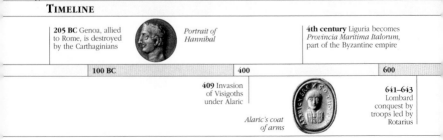
TIMELINE

205 BC Genoa, allied to Rome, is destroyed by the Carthaginians

Portrait of Hannibal

4th century Liguria becomes *Provincia Maritima Italorum*, part of the Byzantine empire

100 BC | 400 | 600

409 Invasion of Visigoths under Alaric

Alaric's coat of arms

641–643 Lombard conquest by troops led by Rotarius

Frankish territory which included tracts of land which now form part of Tuscany. The Saracens made incursions in 901, often from bases in the south of France. Later in the 10th century, during the reign of Berengarius, northeast Italy was divided into three: *Obertenga,* to the east, included Genoa, *Aleramica,* in the centre included Albenga, and *Arduinica,* to the west, included Ventimiglia. The families that had control of these territiories (such as the Del Carretto) found themselves in a powerful position that lasted for centuries.

Battle with the Saracens, a 14th-century miniature

THE RISE OF GENOA

Around the year 1000, the golden age of the free communes dawned. Their main activities revolved around maritime trade and the arming of commercial or military fleets. In this era of economic and political development, Genoese predominance became increasingly noticeable, though life was not entirely peaceful. In the mid-12th century, the city built a new wall to protect it against the ravages of Emperor Frederick I, known as Barbarossa. Nevertheless, after the independence of the Genoese commune was recognized, it began to compete with Pisa for control of the Mediterranean islands of Corsica and

Sardinia. Genoese ships from the ports of Noli and Savona also took part in the Crusades.

GENOA EXPANDS ALONG THE COAST

Besides its growing power at sea, Genoa also sought to expand its sphere of influence, both commercially and militarily, on dry land; they gained control of cities, valleys and the mountain passes linking the coast to the Po valley, and even extended their dominion along the banks of that great river – a move crucial to a republic dependent on agricultural provisions.

After a century of clashes, battles and alliances, by 1232 virtually the entire Riviera di Levante coast was effectively under Genoese control. Among the cities which clashed most violently with Genoa were Ventimiglia (which fell in 1262) and Savona, which, following a long fight for independence, capitulated in 1528.

The port of Genoa as portrayed in a 16th-century painting

890 Beginning of raids by Saracens based in France

984 Benedictines rebuild the Abbey of San Fruttuoso

1099 The "Compagna", a pact between the districts of Genoa, is set up

1133 Genoa becomes the seat of a bishopric

800

1000

935 Sacking of Genoa by the Arabs

Cross of a knight who took part in the first Crusade

1097 Genoa contributes ten galleys to the first Crusade

1162 The Holy Roman Emperor recognizes the autonomy of Genoa

Genoa's Golden Age

A genovino d'oro coin, minted in the 13th century

THE ENTERPRISING TRADING activities of Genoa's great shipowning families made the city into a Mediterranean power from the beginning of the 12th century. The exploits of aristocratic dynasties such as the Doria family took the Genoese to all corners of the known oceans. The growth in Genoa's power was consolidated with increasingly close links to other cities in Liguria, which were often in Genoese control, and to the area around Asti (in Piedmont) and Provence, indispensable suppliers of salt, grain and agricultural produce. Simone Boccanegra became Genoa's first lifetime Doge in 1339, although the most powerful institution during this period was the Banco di San Giorgio (Bank of St George). In a city riven by violent struggles between rival factions, the bank maintained a neutral position. At that time, thriving commercial houses from all over Europe were represented in Genoa, and the emissaries of the Banco di San Giorgio became familiar figures in treasuries all over Europe.

THE MEDITERRANEAN (1250)

— *Genoese trade routes*

— *Pisa trade routes*

— *Venetian trade routes*

Oberto Doria, founder of the illustrious Genoese dynasty, acquired the town of Dolceacqua in 1270.

The Pisan fleet consisted of 72 galleys. The defeat of Pisa was dramatic: 5,000 men died and 11,000 prisoners were taken in chains to Genoa.

Rivalry with Pisa and Venice
Genoa struggled against two rival powers, Pisa and Venice. Pisa was defeated at Meloria but, with the advance of the Turks, Genoa saw her possessions in the East increasingly under threat, and the republic's rivalry with Venice intensified.

Genoa expands its rule along the coast
Many cities along the Riviera di Ponente were in Genoa's orbit at the time, including Albenga, which was forced to sign increasingly restrictive pacts, until its final subjugation in 1251. Ventimiglia yielded in 1261, followed in 1276 by Porto Maurizio. Left is an engraving (1613) by Magini of ships off the western riviera.

GENOA AND THE CRUSADES

The taking of Jerusalem in the First Crusade (1096–99)

During the 250 years of the Crusades, the maritime republics vied for supremacy in the struggle over trade routes, colonies and beneficial alliances. The two Crusades that brought about the conquest of Jerusalem saw the Genoese take an active role in the naval front line, with their *condottiero* Guglielmo Embriaco. In the ports of Acre and Haifa (in modern Israel), Genoese merchants built homes and warehouses, as well as churches. At its peak, the city of Acre had 50,000 inhabitants and 38 churches; it was the last place in the Holy Land to be conquered by the Arabs, in 1291. When the Christian kingdoms present in the Holy Land found themselves in trouble, Genoa frequently allied itself to the Knights of St John, the Armenians and even the Tartars in the fight against Venice, Pisa, the Templars and the Mameluks of Egypt.

The Meloria rocks (after which the battle was named) lie off Livorno, some 7 km (4 miles) offshore.

Battles between the Guelphs and Ghibellines
During the long struggle between the Papacy and the Holy Roman Empire, the Guelphs supported the former, the Ghibellines the latter. Towns seldom had fixed loyalties but noble families did: the Doria were famously Ghibelline.

THE BATTLE OF MELORIA

One of the events that confirmed Genoese dominance in the Mediterranean was the Battle of Meloria, which saw Genoa fight and defeat her rival Pisa over possession of Corsica. In August 1284, a Genoese fleet under the command of Oberto Doria, took up position close to Porto Pisano. The battle was violent and the victor uncertain until the arrival of a second group of Genoese galleys, which took her adversary by surprise. Shown here is *Battle of Meloria* by Giovanni David, in Genoa's Palazzo Ducale.

The Genoese fleet was made up of 93 galleys.

Meloria was also the setting for another battle, in 1241, in which the Pisans, allied to Holy Roman Emperor Frederick II, defeated the Genoese.

Banco di San Giorgio
Founded in the early 1400s, the Bank of St George not only ran the domestic treasury, but was also directly involved with Genoa's colonies, such as Famagusta, in Cyprus. Shown here, an "8 Reali" coin minted by the bank.

Andrea Doria in a portrait by Sebastiano del Piombo

CLASHES WITH OTHER MARITIME REPUBLICS

The centuries that witnessed the great geographical and commercial expansion around the Mediterranean of Italy's maritime republics, also saw Genoa extend its tentacles in all directions. With the Crusades – from the first, which brought about the capture of Jerusalem, to the ill-fated expedition of King Louis IX of France to North Africa – Genoa acquired ports and also *maone* (associations involved in the financing of commercial enterprises), in all corners of the Mediterranean. She then extended her sphere of influence towards the east and the ports of the Black Sea, important trading stations on the Silk Road.

It was a time of increasingly tough alliances and clashes: although Genoa succeeded in eliminating Pisan influence from the Tyrrhenian Sea and from its major islands, taking decisive control of Corsica and defeating Pisa at the Battle of Meloria in 1284, the conflict with Venice was more protracted.

The Genoese defeated the Venetian fleet in the Battle of Curzola in the Adriatic in 1298, but were unable to reap the fruits of this victory and turn the situation in the East to their advantage. Turkish pressure led to an alliance with Venice (1343) which was of brief duration. The last war between Genoa and Venice (a result of both cities setting their sights on Cyprus) was decisive. The battles of Pola (1379) and Chioggia (1380) led to the Pace di Torino (Peace of Turin), which heralded the final decline of Genoese hegemony.

THE REPUBLIC OF GENOA

The period of the great continental struggles between the papacy and the Holy Roman Empire by no means spared Genoa and other Ligurian cities. The international nature of the struggle meant that foreign princes – such as the Visconti of Milan, summoned by the Ghibellines of the Riviera di Ponente, or Robert of Anjou, who intervened in favour of the Guelphs – got involved in Liguria's local conflicts.

During this period, Genoa was governed for almost two centuries by life-appointed doges, a position inaugurated in the 14th century. In 1522, however, their relatively peaceful rule over Genoa was shattered by the arrival of Spanish troops. Andrea Doria later put the city under the

Emperor Charles V, allied to Andrea Doria

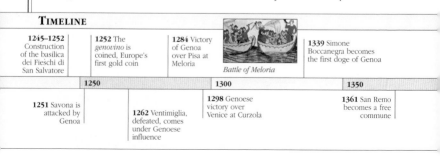

TIMELINE

1245–1252 Construction of the basilica dei Fieschi di San Salvatore	**1252** The *genovino* is coined, Europe's first gold coin	**1284** Victory of Genoa over Pisa at Meloria		**1339** Simone Boccanegra becomes the first doge of Genoa
	1250		**1300**	**1350**
1251 Savona is attacked by Genoa		**1262** Ventimiglia, defeated, comes under Genoese influence	**1298** Genoese victory over Venice at Curzola	**1361** San Remo becomes a free commune

Battle of Meloria

protection of Charles V, King of Spain and Holy Roman Emperor – a demonstration of how power in the city had shifted. Andrea Doria, a talented soldier and admiral, and a member of one of Genoa's great families *(see p79)*, chose his alliances carefully.

In 1553, for reasons connected to the wars between France and Spain, the French decided to land on Genoa-dominated Corsica, intending to establish a base in the Mediterranean Sea. Many Genoese fortresses fell, but a peace treaty eventually forced the French to withdraw.

Columbus, a native of Genoa

This was not the end of trouble in Corsica, however. The defeat of the Ottoman fleet at the Battle of Lepanto in 1571 led to instability (and also pirate raids) in the Mediterranean. The 17th century saw numerous revolts by the Corsicans, as well as renewed attempts by the colonial power to impose its authority. But the decline of Genoa, along with widespread dissatisfaction among Corsicans, provoked yet more revolts in the early 18th century, eventually resulting in the annexation of Corsica to France.

OTHER LIGURIAN CITIES DEVELOP

Albenga, which had long sought to resist the power of Genoa, finally came under Genoese control following a clash between Guelphs and Ghibellines. The town of San Remo was acquired by the Doria family but managed to liberate itself in 1361, becoming a free commune within the Genoese republic.

After years of autonomy, Savona was defeated by the Genoese in 1528 and the conquerors' first action was to rebuild the port. A great new fortress, Il Priamàr, was built, but the local population went into decline. La Spezia, subject to Genoa and, from 1371, seat of the Vicariate of the Riviera di Levante, was fortified at the end of the 14th century and remained under the control of the Genoese until the early 19th century.

Smaller towns also managed to find a role for themselves in a region dominated by the Genoese. Camogli, Portofino and Chiavari all lived off the sea, and their shipyards prospered.

A 16th-century view of the Battle of Lepanto

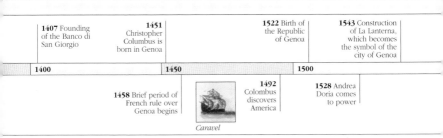

1407 Founding of the Banco di San Giorgio	**1451** Christopher Columbus is born in Genoa	**1522** Birth of the Republic of Genoa	**1543** Construction of La Lanterna, which becomes the symbol of the city of Genoa
1400	1450	1500	
	1458 Brief period of French rule over Genoa begins	**1492** Colombus discovers America	**1528** Andrea Doria comes to power

Caravel

The bombardment of Genoa by the French fleet in 1684

THE DECLINE OF GENOA

Two important constitutions were established in Genoa in the 16th century: one by Andrea Doria, in 1528, and another in 1576, which created the hierarchical structures that were to rule the city. But, as time went by, Genoa became decidedly more important for the financial power wielded by its banks than for its political or military strength. A striking sign of the diminished political role of "Genoa La Superba" (Genoa the Proud) was the 1684 bombardment of Genoa by the French fleet under Louis XIV.

With the decline in Genoese power, a series of autonomous political entities arose in the region, such as the Magnifica Comunità degli Otto Luoghi ("magnificent community of eight towns"), set up in 1686 around Bordighera. However, in a Europe in which the role of nation states was increasing in importance, there was no longer much room for such autonomous powers. The rich families of Genoa increasingly moved away from commerce in order to concentrate more on financial investments.

The 17th and 18th centuries passed with no great incident, though Corsica was finally sold to the French in 1768. Liguria also found itself in conflict with the expansionist policies of Piedmont. Occupied in 1746 by the Austrians and the Piemontese, Genoa responded with a revolt provoked by the gesture of a young boy named Balilla, who sparked off an insurrection by hurling a stone at an Austrian cannon.

PIEMONTESE LIGURIA

The arrival of Napoleon Bonaparte's French troops in Italy completely upset the political equilibrium of Liguria. In 1794 the troops of Massena and Bonaparte conquered the mountain passes which gave access to Italy. Three years later the Republic of Liguria was established, becoming part of the Napoleonic empire in 1805. Napoleon's defeat at Waterloo and the Congress of Vienna in 1815 finally put an end to the independence of Genoa and Liguria: the region was assigned to Piedmont and became part of the Kingdom of Sardinia, governed by the House of Savoy.

The only port of any size in the Kingdom of Savoy, Genoa was linked to Piedmont and to France by new

Genoese-born Giuseppe Mazzini

TIMELINE

1576 Second constitution of Genoa	**1686** The Magnifica Comunità degli Otto Luoghi is set up around Bordighera	**1768** Permanent loss of Corsica

1550	1600	1650	1700	1750

	Louis XIV, king of France	**1684** The French fleet bombards Genoa, causing considerable damage	**1746** Balilla sparks off a popular revolt against the Austro-Piemontese

communication routes. The city was also greatly altered by House of Savoy architects. In 1828 Carlo Barabino built the Teatro Carlo Felice and, in 1874, construction of the new port of Genoa began. (It was greatly enlarged again in 1919 and in 1945.)

**The architect
Renzo Piano**

Perhaps due to Liguria's traditional resentment of Piedmont, the Risorgimento movement, which sought a united Italy, was particularly strong and heartfelt in Liguria. Giuseppe Mazzini, one of the key leaders, was born in Genoa, and it was from Quarto (now a Genoese suburb) that Garibaldi's "Thousand" set sail for the south in 1860. Eventually, a united Kingdom of Italy, which Liguria joined in 1861, was formed.

TOURISM AND LIGURIA TODAY

The building of the railway line along the coast, following the line of the Via Aurelia, represented a crucial stage in the future development of the region. The smaller towns, such as Bordighera, San Remo, Alassio, Santa Margherita and Lerici, became popular destinations with a growing number of visitors, largely the wealthy and the aristocratic of Europe. In the 1930s Genoa was reshaped by Mussolini-era demolition in the heart of the historic centre. Further modifications were carried out in the 1960s and 1970s.

The ports and harbours of Liguria were badly damaged during World War II and, in the valleys and the mountains of the Apennines, the Resistance fought hard against German occupation. Postwar Liguria has seen attempts to develop the

region's industry, and to adapt its ports to the needs of tourism. Many industries have faced crisis, however, and Liguria has had more success in the field of agriculture, in particular the cut-flower industry. Tourism is also, of course, of prime importance economically.

The building of the motorway in the 1960s has increased the speed of development on both sides of the Riviera, which are crowded with visitors for most of the year. As the coast has become more prosperous and, in some cases, very rich (as in Portofino), so the neglected villages of the interior have met a rather different fate: many people have moved away, while there has also been a historic lack of investment in the interior.

Genoa, on the other hand, has been the focus of attention for more than a decade. The port was revamped (with the help of local architect Renzo Piano) in the run-up to the celebrations in honour of Columbus's "discovery" of America, and more money poured in prior to Genoa's year as Europe's City of Culture (2004).

Good motorways, important for tourism

1782 Niccolò Paganini is born in Genoa	1805 Giuseppe Mazzini is born in Genoa	1828 Carlo Barabino designs Teatro Carlo Felice in Genoa	1874 Construction of a new port at Genoa begins		1940–45 Genoa is badly damaged by bombing in World War II		2004 Genoa is European City of Culture
	1800	**1850**		**1900**		**1950**	**2000**
	1797 The Republic of Liguria is established	**1815** Liguria becomes part of the Kingdom of Sardinia	**1860** The expedition of the Thousand departs from Quarto	*Garibaldi departing from Quarto*		**1992** Columbiadi (Columbus celebrations) held in Genoa	*Logo of the Colombiadi*

GENOA
AREA BY AREA

GENOA AT A GLANCE 46-47
IL CENTRO STORICO 48-65
LE STRADE NUOVE 66-79
FURTHER AFIELD 80-89
GENOA STREET FINDER 90-99

Genoa at a Glance

THE CAPITAL OF LIGURIA, "Genova la Superba" (Genoa the Proud) has enjoyed a dominant role in the region, both commercial and political, for centuries. It is a fascinating city in a spectacular site and with many important monuments. First built by the sea, around the basin of the Porto Antico (the old port), the city could only then expand upwards. A labyrinth of medieval *carruggi*, Liguria's distinctive narrow alleys, was created up the steep hills behind the port, followed by new streets laid out in the 16th and 17th centuries, lined with grand palazzi built for Genoa's merchant families. The 19th-century and modern quarters of the city climb steeply again, adapting to the rising terrain. This scenic but inflexible landscape has created the need for various funiculars and lifts, some of which provide fantastic views. The current dynamism evident in Genoa is thanks largely to the Columbus celebrations of 1992 and the city's status, in 2004, as European City of Culture.

Palazzo Reale (see p77), *built in the 17th century, belonged to the Balbi family, to the Durazzos and finally to the Savoys, and is now the seat of the Galleria Nazionale.*

Palazzo Doria Pamphilj (see pp78–9) *was the private residence of the great 16th-century admiral and politician Andrea Doria. It still has apartments decorated for him and paintings he commissioned from artists such as Perin del Vaga and Sebastiano del Piombo.*

Fontana del Nettuno

Palazzo Reale

The Aquarium

IL CENTRO STORICO
(see pp48–65)

The Aquarium (see pp62–3), *first opened in 1992 in the attractive setting of the Porto Antico, has become one of the most popular tourist destinations in Italy. It is extremely well laid-out, and features a rich variety of animal and plant life.*

◁ **The Porto Antico, with Renzo Piano's sphere and the building nicknamed "Matitone" (Big Pencil)**

FURTHER AFIELD
(see pp80–89)

Voltri

Pegli

Boccadasse

Nervi

0 kilometres   7.5

0 miles   7.5

Via Garibaldi (see pp68–9) *was laid out in the 1550s as a residential quarter for the chief aristocratic families of Genoa. Celebrated for centuries by travellers, its impressive architecture has remained remarkably well preserved.*

San Lorenzo (see pp52–3) *is Genoa's cathedral, built from the 11th to the 13th centuries in Romanesque-Gothic style. There is fine sculpture both inside and out, and the chapels of Lercari and San Giovanni Battista are of special interest.*

Palazzo Bianco

LE STRADE NUOVE
(see pp66–79)

San Lorenzo

Palazzo Ducale

Palazzo Ducale (see p54) *was the principal seat of the Doge of Genoa, and was enlarged to majestic dimensions in the 16th century. Today, the spacious palazzo is used for major exhibitions.*

0 metres   400

0 yards   400

IL CENTRO STORICO

THE OLD HEART OF THE city is grouped around the Porto Antico and is made up of a hilly network of small piazzas, alleys and staircases. It is the largest medieval centre in Europe and is exceptionally well preserved, despite persistent neglect in some parts. The area is home to the cathedral of San Lorenzo and the Palazzo Ducale, the seat of power for centuries. Both public and private wealth has left its mark in the old town: Palazzo San Giorgio and the Loggia dei Mercanti on the one hand,

Decoration at Palazzo San Giorgio

the Doria family mansions in Piazza San Matteo and Palazzo Spinola on the other. The relationship between the old town and the port has been a centuries-old problem, largely due to the lack of integration between the two, which was further complicated in the 20th century by the building of a flyover. A chance to redeem the area and re-establish links with the seafront came in the 1990s: old buildings, such as the Teatro Carlo Felice, were restored, and new projects, including Renzo Piano's port buildings, were launched.

SIGHTS AT A GLANCE

Historic Buildings
Casa di Colombo ⑪
Loggia dei Mercanti ⑲
Porta Soprana
  or di Sant'Andrea ⑩

Historic Streets and Piazzas
Piazza Banchi ⑱
Piazza De Ferrari ④
Piazza San Matteo ㉒
Porto Antico pp60–61 ⑮

Museums and Galleries
Accademia Ligustica
  di Belle Arti ⑤

Aquarium pp62–3 ⑯
Museo Civico di Storia Naturale
  Giacomo Doria ⑧
Museo di Sant'Agostino ⑫
Palazzo Spinola ⑳

Theatres
Teatro Carlo Felice ⑥

Churches
Il Gesù (or Sant'Ambrogio) ③
San Donato ⑬
San Lorenzo pp52–3 ①
Santa Maria Assunta
  in Carignano ⑨
Santa Maria delle Vigne ㉑
Santa Maria di Castello ⑭
Santo Stefano ⑦

Palazzi
Palazzo Ducale ②
Palazzo San Giorgio ⑰

0 metres   400
0 yards   400

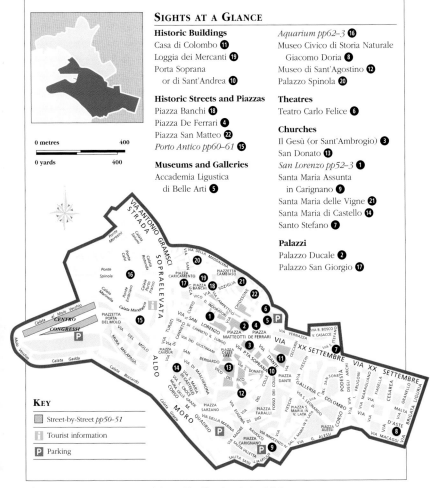

KEY

| Street-by-Street *pp50–51* |
| Tourist information |
| P Parking |

◁ **La Lanterna, symbol of Genoa and the world's oldest functioning lighthouse**

Street-by-Street: around Piazza Matteotti

WITHIN THE DENSE WARREN of the Centro Storico, the square overlooked by the cathedral, Piazza San Lorenzo, and Piazza Matteotti, in front of the Palazzo Ducale, create welcome open spaces. Nearby is Piazza De Ferrari, a 19th-century project developed to link the old city with the western, modern and industrial part of Genoa. Within this maze of streets there is almost no sense of the nearby sea, except when you get a sudden glimpse of a blue horizon. There are numerous places and monuments of interest in this area: churches of ancient origin such as Santa Maria di Castello, Santa Maria delle Vigne and Sant'Agostino; a variety of public spaces (Piazza Banchi, Piazza San Matteo, Via di Sottoripa); as well as public and private buildings, including the supposed birthplace of Christopher Columbus, the aristocratic Palazzo Spinola, and Palazzo San Giorgio, from whose frescoed façade there are beautiful views of the sea.

★ Piazza San Matteo
At the heart of the district that was home for centuries of the Doria family, this medieval piazza preserves its original appearance. The beautiful church of San Matteo is also medieval.

Palazzo Spinola   PIAZZA CAMPETTO

PIAZZA SAN MATTEO

SALITA S

VIA DI SCURRERIA

VIA ARCIVESCOVADO

★ San Lorenzo
The cathedral was surrounded by the medieval city until the building of Via San Lorenzo along the church's right-hand side and the addition of a flight of steps up to the façade, both dating from the mid-19th century ❶

The port, Piazza Banchi and Palazzo San Giorgio

VIA SAN LORENZO   PIAZZA MATTEOTTI

★ Palazzo Ducale
The seat of the Doge of Genoa, this building was begun in the Middle Ages, but was much altered in the 16th and 18th centuries. The palazzo has two large courtyards and contains valuable works of art ❷

SALITA POLLAIUOLI

VICO TRE RE MAGI

Museo di Sant'Agostino
The cloisters of the ruined church of Sant'Agostino house a collection of sculpture and architectural relics from around the city, including this moving Penitent Madonna *(1796) by Antonio Canova* ⓬

Chiesa del Gesù

Reconstructed by the Jesuits in the late 16th century on the site of the older church of Sant'Ambrogio, the Gesù has a sumptuous interior reflecting Genoa's golden age. Inlaid marble, stuccoes and frescoes create an ornate setting for two important works by Rubens, the Flemish artist who painted for various Genoese nobles **3**

LOCATOR MAP
See Street Finder, maps 2, 3, 5 & 6

0 metres   100

0 yards   100

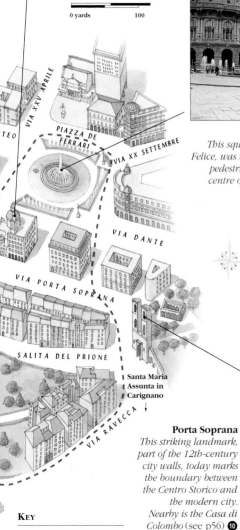

Piazza De Ferrari

This square, home of the famous Teatro Carlo Felice, was radically redesigned and made into a pedestrian area in 2001. The fountain in the centre of the piazza was designed in 1936 by Giuseppe Crosa di Vergagni **4**

STAR SIGHTS

★ **Palazzo Ducale**

★ **Piazza San Matteo**

★ **San Lorenzo**

Santa Maria
Assunta in
Carignano

Porta Soprana

This striking landmark, part of the 12th-century city walls, today marks the boundary between the Centro Storico and the modern city. Nearby is the Casa di Colombo (see p56) **10**

KEY

- - - - Recommended route

San Lorenzo ❶

The dome of the chapel of San Giovanni

THE CHURCH OF SAN LORENZO (St Lawrence) was founded in the ninth century and was chosen as the cathedral because of its secure position within the city walls. Romanesque-style reconstruction began in the 12th century but was never completed. The cathedral's present, primarily Gothic appearance, including the lower part of the cheerfully striped façade, dates from the 13th century. Important alterations followed later, however, mainly in the 15th to 17th centuries: these include the rose window in the upper part of the façade, the Renaissance cupola by Galeazzo Alessi and the beautifully frescoed Lercari chapel. The symbol of St Lawrence (Genoa's patron saint, along with St John the Baptist) is the purse, a fact that prompts much teasing of the Genoese, who are famous for being frugal with money.

The bell tower was created from the right-hand tower in the 16th century.

Black and white striped arches

The rose window was redone in 1869; of the original, from 1476, the symbols of the four Evangelists remain.

★ Sculptures at Main Entrance
Sculptures on medieval church doors introduced the faithful to important doctrinal subjects. Here, fine Romanesque bas-reliefs illustrate Stories from the life of Mary *and the* Tree of Jesse, *on the jambs; and* Christ blessing, the symbols of the Evangelists *and the* Martyrdom of San Lorenzo, *in the lunette.*

The Lions
Two 19th-century lion sculptures flank the main steps. A pair of Romanesque lions can also be seen on the edges of the façade.

Marble pillars

The vault of the presbytery and the apse bears two frescoes by Lazzaro Tavarone (*San Lorenzo and the Church treasury, Martyrdom of the Saint, 1622– 24*); in the apse is a lovely 16th-century wooden choir.

In the right-hand apse, in the Senarega chapel, is a *Crucifix with Mary, John and St Sebastian* by Federico Barocci (1597).

VISITORS' CHECKLIST

Piazza San Lorenzo. **Map** 5 C3.
📞 *010 247 18 31.* ☐ **Church** *8–11:45am, 3–6:45pm.* **Museo del Tesoro** *9am–noon, 3–6pm Mon–Sat; 3–6pm first Sun of month.* 🏛 ♿ 📷 *by appt.* 🚪

Dome by Galeazzo Alessi (1556)

Romanesque blind arches

★ Cappella di San Giovanni Battista
This chapel, dedicated to St John the Baptist, was the work of Domenico and Elia Gagini (mid-1400s). It is richly decorated with marble and topped with flamboyant Gothic detailing. Reliefs on the front of the chapel illustrate the life of the Baptist. Inside, are six wall niches with statues and the stone reliquary that once held the supposed ashes of the saint (see below).

★ MUSEO DEL TESORO
Opened in the 1950s, this unusual museum was the work of Caterina Marcenaro and Franco Albini, and is one of the most elegant of its kind. Built underground near the chancel, the wonderfully atmospheric museum is covered in Promontorio stone, the dark construction material typical of medieval Genoa. Within this charming framework, picked out by spotlights, are displayed objects brought back during the Republic's forays into the Holy Land. Among the highlights are the Sacro Catino, a 9th-century Islamic glass vessel, once believed to be the Holy Grail, used by Christ at the Last Supper; the Croce degli Zaccaria, a 12th-century Byzantine reliquary made of gold and gemstones; the cope of Pope Gelasio, in brocade fabric with gold and silver thread (15th century); and the elaborately embossed silver chest (12th century), which contains the supposed ashes of St John the Baptist, and which is carried in procession through the streets of Genoa on 24 June.

La Croce degli Zaccaria

STAR FEATURES

★ **Cappella di San Giovanni Battista**

★ **Museo del Tesoro**

★ **Sculptures at Main Entrance**

Palazzo Ducale ❷

Piazza Matteotti 9. **Map** 5 C3.
☎ 010 557 40 00. ◯ **Exhibitions**
9am–9pm Tues–Sun. **Shops** daily.
ⓦ www.palazzoducale.genova.it

THIS PALAZZO, constructed during the course of the Middle Ages, was given its name (meaning Doge's Palace) in 1339, when the election of Genoa's first doge, Simon Boccanegra, took place here. It was enlarged to its current size in the late 1500s by Andrea Vannone, a Lombard architect. Further major changes, the work of Neo-Classical architect Simone Cantoni, were made in the late 18th century following a fire. These included the erection of the façade overlooking Piazza Matteotti (another lively, frescoed façade faces Piazza De Ferrari), which features pairs of columns and is topped by statues and trophies.

The palazzo is organized around Vannone's attractive atrium, with a large, elegant, porticoed courtyard at either end. The staircases up to the first floor are lined with frescoes by Lazzaro Tavarone and Domenico Fiasella.

On the upper floor some of the public rooms are very fine: the **doges' chapel** was

Door knocker in the shape of a triton, Palazzo Ducale

frescoed by Giovanni Battista Carlone (1655) with scenes celebrating the glorious history of the city of Genoa; this theme continues in the decoration of the **Sala del Maggior Consiglio** and the **Sala del Minor Consiglio**. The **Salone**, designed by Simone Cantoni, features paintings by Giovanni David (c.1780), among others. Since extensive restoration in 1992, the palace has become a venue for major exhibitions. In addition, there are shops, bars and restaurants (including an expensive rooftop restaurant with panoramic views).

Il Gesù (or Sant'Ambrogio) ❸

Via Francesco Petrarca 1. **Map** 5 C4.
☎ 010 251 41 22. ◯ 10:30am–noon, 4–7pm daily (9:30pm Sun).
◯ with permission.

THIS CHURCH, overlooking Piazza Matteotti, was built by the Jesuits. It was begun in 1589, over the existing church of Sant'Ambrogio, and given the name of il Gesù. The façade, following the original design by Giuseppe Valeriani, was finished only at the end of the 19th century.

The sumptuous Baroque interior consists of a single room topped by a dome.

St Ignatius Exorcising the Devil, by Rubens, Il Gesù

Multicoloured marble decorates the floor, the pilasters and the walls of the side chapels, finished with gilded stuccoes and frescoes by Giovanni Battista Carlone (17th century), on the upper parts of the walls.

The most valuable paintings in the church all date from the 17th century, including works by Guido Reni and a *Crucifixion* by Simon Vouet. There are also works that were commissioned by the Pallavicino family from Peter Paul Rubens: a *Circumcision* (1605) and *St Ignatius Exorcising the Devil* (before 1620), both acknowledged masterpieces and precursors of the Baroque style.

Piazza De Ferrari ❹

Map 6 D4.

THIS PIAZZA, with its large fountain, was created in the late 19th century with the aim of easing the flow of traffic between the Centro Storico and the western side of Genoa. Its design had to accommodate the existing buildings of the Accademia Ligustica di Belle Arti and the Teatro Carlo Felice, both built by Carlo Barabino in the 1820s. The new palazzi built around these two are eclectic in style. The building of the new theatre in 1991 and other more recent alterations, including those of 2001, have given the Piazza De Ferrari a major facelift.

One of the spacious interior courtyards of Palazzo Ducale

Accademia Ligustica di Belle Arti ❺

Via Pertini 4. **Map** 6 D3.
📞 010 538 1226. ⏰ 3–7pm
Tue–Fri. 🎫 by appt. 📷
📷 with permission.
🌐 www.accademialigustica.it

FOUNDED IN 1751 by a group of aristocrats and scholars as a School of Fine Arts (*belle arti*), the Accademia occupies a palazzo built for it in 1826–31 by Carlo Barabino. The museum on the first floor is home to paintings and drawings donated to the academy. Works of art from the 15th to 19th centuries are arranged chronologically: they include works by major Ligurian artists (Gregorio De Ferrari and Bernardo Strozzi among others) and artists who were active in Genoa (such as Perin del Vaga and Anton Raphael Mengs).

Polyptych of St Erasmus by Perin del Vaga

Teatro Carlo Felice ❻

Passo Eugenio Montale 4. **Map** 6 D3.
📞 010 538 11, ticket office 010 589 329 or 010 591 697.
⏰ for performances. 🎫 Mon, by appt. 📷 ♿ 🌐 www.carlofelice.it

THE NEO-CLASSICAL theatre designed in the 1820s by Carlo Barabino was virtually gutted by bombing in 1944, and only parts of the original façade survived. These give way to the modern part of the Teatro Carlo Felice, designed

The ultra-modern stage at the Teatro Carlo Felice

by Ignazio Gardella, Aldo Rossi and Fabio Reinhart in 1991. The new theatre is dominated by a huge square tower pierced by small windows. Four sections of stage area are manoeuvred by a complex, state-of-the-art computerized system, making the theatre one of the most innovative in Europe.

Santo Stefano ❼

Piazza Santo Stefano 2. **Map** 6 E4.
📞 010 587 183. ⏰ 3:30–6:30pm Tue–Sun (Sun am only in Aug).

BUILT AT THE end of the 12th century, the Romanesque church of Santo Stefano stands on the site of a Benedictine abbey. The church underwent major restoration after being damaged in World War II.

The façade features bands of black and white striped marble, typical of Pisan and Ligurian Romanesque, with a main door surmounted by an oculus and a mullioned window. The brick-built apse is particularly lovely, ornamented by blind arches with arcading above. The bell tower and the 14th-century lantern are also constructed in decorative brick.

Inside, in the presbytery, are a *Martyrdom of St Stephen*, a fine work by Giulio Romano (1524), and paintings by various Genoese and Lombard artists, among them Valerio Castello, Gregorio De Ferrari and Giulio Cesare Procaccini.

Museo Civico di Storia Naturale Giacomo Doria ❽

Via Brigata Liguria 9. **Map** 6 F5.
📞 010 564 567. ⏰ 9am–7pm Tue–Fri; 10am–7pm Sat, Sun. 🎫 ♿ 🎫 by appt. 📷 🌐 www.museodoria.it

ESTABLISHED IN 1867 by Marchese Giacomo Doria, its director for more than 40 years, Genoa's Natural History Museum contains important zoological finds, many collected in the 19th century.

On the ground floor there are rooms devoted to mammals and a series of reconstructed animal habitats. Don't miss the Palaeontology Room, with its skeleton of *Elephus antiquus italicus*, an ancient elephant found near Rome in 1941. On the first floor are displays of reptiles, amphibians, birds, butterflies and insects.

The museum does a lot of educational work and has a full calendar of conferences and exhibitions.

Santo Stefano, with its classic combination of black and white marble

Basilica di Santa Maria Assunta in Carignano **9**

Piazza di Carignano. **Map** 3 A4.
[010 540 650. **◯** 7:30–11:30am,
4–6:30pm daily.

THIS FINE Renaissance church, one of the city's most prominent landmarks, was designed for the hill closest to the centre of the city by Galeazzo Alessi, the great Perugian architect. Begun in 1549, it took 50 years to complete.

A monumental flight of steps, designed by Alessi but built in the 19th century, leads up to the broad façade, flanked by two bell towers. Rising above is a high central cupola surrounded by four smaller domes. The elaborate sculptural decoration on the façade, the work of Claude David (18th century), includes a statue of the Virgin Mary over the door and statues of saints Peter and Paul in the side niches. A balcony runs along the roofs and around the central dome, making the most of the church's wonderfully panoramic position.

Inside, the harmonious exterior motif of pilasters with Corinthian capitals continues. As in St Peter's in Rome, the four vast pilasters that support the cupola have niches containing statues: these include *St Sebastian* by Pierre Puget (1620–94). On the second altar on the right is a *Martyrdom of St Blaise* by Carlo Maratta (1625–1713), and in the sixth on the left a famous *Pietà* (c.1571) by Luca Cambiaso. Other paintings, some of which have been adapted to fit the church's particular setting, are by Domenico Fiasella and Guercino. The organ, dating from 1656, is remarkable.

Statue of the Virgin Mary in Santa Maria in Carignano

The two majestic towers of Porta Soprana

Porta Soprana (or di Sant'Andrea) **10**

Via Di Ravecca 47 nero. **Map** 6 D4.
[010 246 53 46. **◯** 9am–noon,
2– 6pm Sat, Sun & hols. **■** weekdays only, groups only, by appt.
◙ with permission.

THIS GATE CORRESPONDS to an opening made in the walls in the 9th century to connect Genoa to the east; the actual structure, however, was part of a ring of walls built in 1155 to defend Genoa from possible attack by Emperor Frederick I, known as Barbarossa *(see p87)*. It is similar to the Porta di Santa Fede, on the other side of the city. Restoration carried out in the 19th and 20th centuries has liberated the historic gate of the structures added to it over the centuries, and exposed the pointed arch flanked by a pair of imposing cylindrical battlemented towers. These are ornamented by delicate arcading and cornicing.

Casa di Colombo **11**

Vico dritto di Ponticello. **Map** 6 D4.
[010 246 53 46.
◯ 9am–noon, 2–6pm Sat, Sun &
hols. **■** (minimum 20 people), by
appt. **◙**

TRADITION, ALMOST certainly of dubious origin, has it that this modest house near Porta Soprana is the place where the world-famous navigator, Christopher Columbus, born in Genoa in 1451, spent his youth.

The house that you visit today is, in fact, an 18th-century reconstruction: the original house was destroyed by cannon fire during a

The supposed birthplace of Christopher Colombus

French bombardment in 1684. Restoration carried out on the building in preparation for the Columbus celebrations of 1992 extended to the adjacent 12th-century **Chiostro di Sant'Andrea** (cloister of St Andrew), all that is left of a Benedictine monastery that was demolished at the beginning of the 20th century.

Museo di Sant'Agostino ⓬

Piazza Sarzano 35 rosso. **Map** 5 C5.
📞 010 251 12 63. ⏱ 9am–7pm Tue–Fri; 10am–7pm Sat, Sun.

www.museosantagostino.it

This 13th-century monastic church was a lucky survivor of World War II bombing, which badly damaged Piazza Sarzano. The façade, with its black and white stripes, is typically Ligurian, while the elegant bell tower is coated with colourful majolica tiles.

Funeral monument of Margaret of Brabant

While the church functions now as an auditorium, the former Augustinian monastery buildings that are adjacent – including the two cloisters (a triangular one, dating from the 14th and 15th centuries, and a rectangular, 18th-century one) – have been skilfully adapted to house the **Museum**. The focus of the collection are the sculptures brought here from sites (including demolished churches) all over the city, but there are also detached frescoes, architectural fragments and examples of Genoese art from the Middle Ages to the 18th century.

There are two particularly important sculptures in the collection. One of these is the remains of the funerary monument of Margaret of Brabant, sculpted in honour of the wife of emperor Henry VII, who died in 1311 while visiting Genoa. The work was sculpted in Pisa in 1313–14 by Giovanni Pisano, one of

the most famous sculptors in Italy at that time. The other is a particularly moving *Penitent Madonna*, by Antonio Canova (1796).

San Donato ⓭

Piazzetta San Donato 10. **Map** 5 C4.
📞 010 246 88 69. ⏱ 8am–noon, 3–7pm daily (Aug: 8am–noon Mon–Fri, Sun; 8am–noon, 3–7pm Sat).
⏺ 16–30 Aug.

The church of San Donato, built during the 12th century, is one of the best examples of Romanesque architecture in Genoa.

The building's most striking and interesting feature, which is characteristic of early Romanesque architecture, is the splendid octagonal bell tower, erected over the church crossing; its three levels (the third is a 19th century addition) are each pierced by windows. The tower was chosen as a model by the designers of the north tower of San Benigno, the so-called "Matitone" (great pencil) in the Porto Antico *(see p44)*.

The façade carries some noticeable features dating from late 19th-century alterations, when the rose

The bell tower of San Donato

window was added, but the main doorway is original and of particular beauty; it incorporates a Roman architrave in the moulding.

On the right-hand side of the church, look out for a shrine with a statue of the *Madonna and Child* (18th century); it is one of many erected in the Centro Storico.

The charming interior has a nave and two aisles, with Corinthian columns and a gallery of windows above; some of the columns are Roman. A *Madonna and Child* (1401) by Nicolò da Voltri is on the altar in the right-hand apse and, in the chapel of San Giuseppe in the left-hand aisle, there is a beautiful panelled triptych by the Flemish painter Joos van Cleve; this depicts an *Adoration of the Magi* (c.1515) in the central panel.

CONTEMPORARY ART AT VILLA CROCE

Villa Croce, surrounded by palms

Via Jacopo Ruffini 3.
📞 010 580 069. ⏱ 9am–7pm Tue–Fri; 10am–7pm Sat, Sun. (free on Sun).

www.museovillacroce.it

The Museo d'Arte Contemporanea, in the 19th-century residential district of Carignano, south of the city centre, is surrounded by a large park overlooking the sea. It occupies a lovely, late 19th-century classical-style villa, which was donated to the city by the Croce family in 1951. The museum currently possesses some 3,000 works, which document in particular Italian graphic arts and abstract art from 1930 to 1980 (including work by Fontana and Licini). There are also examples of work by young Genoese and Ligurian artists. The museum promotes young talent by collecting works, organizing exhibitions and assembling a digital archive of material related to local arts.

Santa Maria di Castello ⓮

Salita Santa Maria di Castello 15.
Map 5 B4. 🄲 *010 246 87 72.*
🄾 **Church** *8am–noon, 3–7pm daily.*
Museum *9am–noon, 3:30–6pm*
Mon–Sat (7pm on Sun).

THIS CHURCH RISES on the site of the Roman *castrum*, or fort, around which the earliest parts of the city were constructed. Among the most illustrious of old Genoese churches, it was built in the 12th century on the site of an earlier place of worship, at a time when Romanesque buildings were appearing all over the city.

In the mid-15th century the church was entrusted to the Dominicans, who added monastic buildings, including three cloisters. The latters' decoration was commissioned by the Grimaldi family (in line with the huge increase in private patronage at that time in Genoa) and turned the complex into a point of reference for artists in the city. In the centuries to come, other aristocratic families commissioned the decoration of the church's side chapels.

The stone façade is crowned by a cornice of blind arches. The central doorway incorporates a Roman architrave, and there are other Roman elements inside: several of the Corinthian capitals which adorn the red granite columns in the nave came from Roman buildings; and in

The Loggia dell'Annunciazione, Santa Maria di Castello

the **Cappella del Battistero** is a sarcophagus of Roman origin.

The apse, the chapels and the dome are the result of changes made from the 15th to the 18th centuries. In the chapel in the left transept is a *Virgin with the saints Catherine and Mary Magdalen and the effigies of St Dominic* by il Grechetto (1616–70). The high altar has a splendid late 17th-century marble sculpture of the *Assumption*.

Among the monastic buildings, the second cloister is of special note. Here, the lower of the two loggias, the **Loggia dell'Annunciazione,** features roundels with *Sibyls* and *Prophets* (15th century) in its vault, and a charming fresco of the *Annunciation* by Justus von Ravensburg, signed and dated 1451.

There is a small **museum**, with works such as *Paradise* and *The Conversion of St Paul* by Ludovico Brea (1513); an *Immaculate Conception*, a wooden sculpture by Maragliano (18th century); and a *Madonna and Child* by Barnaba da Modena (14th century).

Next to the church stands the 12th-century **Torre degli Embriaci**, evidence of the medieval power of the aristocratic Embriaci family, who lived in this quarter.

Porto Antico ⓯

See pp60–61.

Aquarium ⓰

See pp62–3.

The frescoed façade of Palazzo San Giorgio

Palazzo San Giorgio ⓱

Via della Mercanzia 2. **Map** 5 B3.
🄲 *010 24 11.* 🄾 *phone to check opening hours of exhibitions, or ask at the tourist office.* 📷

THIS PALAZZO IS traditionally identified as the place in which Marco Polo was imprisoned following the Battle of Curzola (between the Venetians and the Genoese) in 1298. While here, Polo met a writer from Pisa called Rustichello, with whom he joined forces after their release to write *Il Milione* ("The Travels").

The palazzo is made up of two distinct parts: a medieval part turned towards the city, which was built in 1260 as the seat of the government (the Capitani del Popolo) and later became the Banco di San Giorgio (1407); and a second part, a huge 16th-century extension built to overlook the port. The fresco decoration on the latter's façade (1606–8), by Lazzaro Tavarone, was discovered only during restoration work in the 1990s.

The expansion of the palazzo, which involved major restructuring of the medieval section (later

Detail of the façade of Palazzo San Giorgio

heavily restored in the 1800s), was required because of the rise in power of the Banco di San Giorgio. The bank administered the proceeds from taxes collected by the Republic and also ran the Republic's colonies; it was, in effect, responsible for much of Genoa's prosperity in the 15th century. Today, the palace houses the offices of the harbour authorities.

Inside, the **Salone delle Compere** is decorated with 16th-century statues of the Protettori del Banco (protectors of the bank) and the *Arms of Genoa with the symbols of Justice and Strength* by Francesco De Ferrari (1490–91). The **Sala dei Protettori** features a monumental hearth by Gian Giacomo Della Porta (1554). You can also visit the Manica Lunga, a 128-m (420-ft) long corridor which once served as a dormitory for Benedictine monks, and the Sala del Capitano del Popolo.

Piazza Banchi ⓲

Map 5 B3.

Along harbourside Piazza Caricamento, flanked on one side by Palazzo San Giorgio, runs **Via Sottoripa**. Dating from the 12th century, this charming arcaded street

was designed so that its shops could make the most of their proximity to the buzzing port area. Today, as it did in the past, the street houses various specialist foods shops, and there are snack bars, too.

From here, Via al Ponte Reale leads to **Piazza Banchi**, the commercial core of the city up until the 18th century, and a crucial crossroads of major lines of communication between the city and the port. By the Middle Ages there was already a thriving grain market in the piazza, and money-changers also set up their stalls here, attracting merchants from all over the world; the piazza is named after the money-changers' tables. Later, money-changers and other traders did business in the 16th-century **Loggia dei Mercanti**.

The church of **San Pietro in Banchi**, founded in the 9th century, was destroyed by a fire which damaged the square in 1398, but rebuilding work didn't begin until the 16th century. The project was managed by Bernardino Cantone, who used a form of self-financing which involved the construction and the subsequent sale of several shops at ground level. As a result, the church is raised up on a terrace and is reached by means of a scenic flight of steps. It has a central plan

with an octagonal dome with three pinnacles (four were originally planned). The façade bears frescoes by Giovanni Battista Baiardo (c.1650), which were restored in the 1990s.

The Loggia dei Mercanti, with stalls in front, in Piazza Banchi

Loggia dei Mercanti ⓳

Piazza Banchi. **Map** 5 B3.
☐ *for exhibitions; contact the tourist office for details.*

This elegant Renaissance loggia was built in Piazza Banchi in the late 16th century, to a design by Andrea Vannone, in order to accommodate the work of the city's money-changers. The loggia was a typical element of buildings intended for commerce during the Middle Ages, and there are many examples in the old city.

The loggia in Piazza Banchi is built on a rectangular plan and has a single barrel vault supported by arches resting on paired columns; its openings were glassed in during the 19th century. The exterior features a sculptured frieze (16th century) by Taddeo Carlone, and the interior a fresco of the *Madonna and Child and saints John the Baptist and George* by Pietro Sorri (1556–1621).

In 1855, the loggia became the seat of the first trade Stock Exchange in Italy; it is now used as a site for exhibitions.

Piazza Banchi , overlooked by San Pietro in Banchi

Porto Antico ⓯

THE OLD PORT was the obvious venue for the staging of the Columbus celebrations of 1992, and these provided a perfect opportunity to restore the link between the port, for centuries detached from the rest of the city, with the Centro Storico. This project was undertaken by local architect Renzo Piano, who also transformed the district into an attraction in its own right, by restoring disused buildings such as the 19th-century cotton warehouses – now a multiplex cinema and exhibition centre – and by constructing new works, such as the landmark Bigo and the Aquarium, the design of which includes maritime motifs, emphasizing the history of this district.

Porta del Molo
Also known as Porta Siberia, this gate was built in 1553 by Galeazzo Alessi. It was inserted into the 16th-century walls as a defensive bulwark for the port and as a place for the collection of taxes.

Museo Nazionale dell'Antartide Felice Ippolito is housed in the restored Millo building (1876). This museum features faithful re-creations of animal habitats and also scale models of the Italian base in Antarctica (Baia Terra Nova).

★ **Bigo**
Inspired by the masts of a ship and designed by Renzo Piano, the Bigo features a revolving panoramic lift. From a height of 40 m (130 ft), this offers great views over the port and city.

Boat trips are the only way to reach certain areas otherwise closed to visitors. From the quays of Porto Antico, boats offer guided tours lasting around 45 minutes. The bustle and activity of the port are fascinating and there is a breathtaking panorama of the city from the sea.

La Sfera by Renzo Piano

Built in 2001, "The Sphere" is a futuristic glasshouse containing all sorts of tropical plants, from mangroves to rubber and cocoa trees, as well as numerous types of ferns, some of which are extremely rare. There are butterflies and chameleons, too.

VISITORS' CHECKLIST

Map 5 A2. 🄲 010 248 57 11.
🅆 www.portoantico.it
Museo Nazionale dell'Antartide
🄲 010 254 36 90. ⭘ 10:30am–
6:30pm daily. 🈳 🅆 www.mna.it
⭘ **Boat trips** Alimar. 🄲 010
256 775. Cooperativa Battellieri
🄲 010 265 712. **La Sfera**
⭘ 9:30am–dusk Tue–Sun. 🈳
Città dei Bambini 🄲 010 247
57 02. ⭘ 11:30am–7:30pm
Tue–Sun (last entry 6:15pm). 🈳
🅆 www.cittadeibambini.net
La Lanterna 🄲 010 910 001.
⭘ 10am–7pm Sat, Sun; call to
book other times. **Bigo** ⭘ 10am–
8pm Tue, Wed, Sun; 10am–11pm
Thu, Fri, Sat & public hols. 🈳

La Città dei Bambini is the foremost educational/entertainment centre in Italy, aimed at children. The high-tech hands-on "play and learn" park includes two different routes, aimed at 3–5 year olds and 6–14 year olds.

★ **Aquarium** ⑯
Another work by Renzo Piano, the Aquarium is the largest of its kind in Europe and attracts over one million visitors a year (see pp62–3).

LA LANTERNA

This is the symbol of Genoa, and the oldest working lighthouse in the world. The original lighthouse, dating from the 12th century, was destroyed by Louis XIII's French army. It was rebuilt in its current form, with two superimposed towers, in 1543, and its beam has a reach of 52 km (33 miles). There is a superb view from the top, if you can bear the 375 steps, and a museum is due to open in the fortifications below.

0 metres 100
0 yards 100

STAR SIGHTS

★ **Aquarium**

★ **Bigo**

Aquarium (Acquario) ⑯

THE WORK OF internationally-renowned architect Renzo Piano (co-designer of the Pompidou Centre in Paris), with technical help from American architect Peter Chermayeff, the Aquarium is built within a ship anchored in the port. It is Europe's largest aquarium, with numerous tanks that are viewable from underwater level as well as from above. The aim is to help visitors to discover and marvel at different aspects of the sea and to promote understanding of the extent to which human life is linked to the oceans. There are spectacular reconstructions of diverse ecosystems on the planet, making it possible to observe animals, habitats and ocean floors at close quarters.

The mascot Splaffy

★ Hummingbird Forest
This area re-creates the luxuriant rainforest habitat of the smallest birds in the world. The hummingbird's signature features are its iridescent feathers , long bill and powerful wing-speed.

Level 2

A Coral Reef in Madagascar
This colourful zone is testimony to how coral reefs make a rich and desirable habitat for countless species of fish, from moray eels to angel fish (seen here).

La Grande Nave Blu (Great Blue Ship)
is a real ship, acquired by the Aquarium in 1998. There are 19 tanks in around 2,500 sq m (27,000 sq ft) of exhibition space.

Mediterranean reef

The crocodiles
seen here normally live in various parts of Africa. Visitors can see juveniles of around one and a half years old (preferred by the Aquarium to older animals because they are more lively), but there are also babies, newborns and eggs on show, in a complete reconstruction of the life cycle.

The Forest of Madagascar
reconstructs a tropical forest habitat of this island off the east coast of Africa. A paradise for naturalists, Madagascar teems with plant and animal species found nowhere else.

★ Tactile Tank
One of the most popular attractions, this tank allows people to gently touch skate, gurnard and stingrays. The fish confidently approach the hands held out to stroke them.

★ Shark Tank
*This large tank
houses several
species of shark,
and also the
sharklike ray,
aptly known as
a sawfish* (shown
here).

VISITORS' CHECKLIST

Ponte Spinola. **Map** 5 A2.
📞 *010 234 56 78.* ⏰ *9:30am–
7:30pm (last entry 5:30pm)
Mon–Wed, Fri; 9:30am– 8:30pm
(last entry 6:30pm) Sat, Sun &
hols; 9:30am–10pm (last entry
8:30pm) Thu.* ⬤ *Mon (Nov–
Mar).* 🈳♿🅿🚻♿
🆆 *www.acquariodigenova.it*

Reception

Entrance on
Level 1

Auditorium
(3D films)

Cloakroom

Humboldt penguins,
originally from the coasts of
Chile and Peru and unused
to ice, are housed on level
2 of the Aquarium.

Seal Tank
In July 2001, Penelope (shown
here) *was born thanks to the first
Caesarean section in the world to be
performed on a common seal.
After being cared for and fed by the
Aquarium veterinarians and
biologists, the baby seal was placed
in the display tank with the other
seals for company. Other seals were
born naturally in 2003 and 2004.*

Dolphin Tank
*The Aquarium is proud of its record for breeding
dolphins in captivity. Bonnie, a bottlenosed dolphin
from the Delphinarium in Riccione, has given birth
here twice, in 1994 and 2002. Shown here is
young Achille.*

STAR FEATURES

★ **Hummingbird
Forest**

★ **Shark Tank**

★ **Tactile Tank**

One of the sumptuous rooms in Palazzo Spinola

Palazzo Spinola ⑳

Piazza Pellicceria 1. **Map** 5 B2.
📞 010 247 70 61. ⏰ 8:30am–
7:30pm Tue–Sat; 1–8pm Sun, public
hols. ● 1 Jan, 1 Aug, 25 Dec.
🎫 combined ticket for Palazzo
Spinola & Palazzo Reale. ♿ by appt.
♿ up to the 3rd floor. 📷 on request.
📖 🌐 www.palazzospinola.it

WITH ALL THE elegance and
fascination of an old
aristocratic mansion house,
Palazzo Spinola is richly
frescoed and has sumptuous
furnishings and paintings.
Built in the 16th century by
the Grimaldi family, the
palazzo passed to the Spinola
family in the 18th century,
and they eventually donated
it to the state in 1958.

The first two floors house
the **Galleria Nazionale
di Palazzo Spinola**, in a
manner that is sensitive both
to the building and to the art
collection. The rooms have
been restored to as they were
under the Spinola, with
paintings arranged as though
this were still a private home.
Two important fresco cycles
illustrate the two main phases
in the history of the palazzo.
One, by Lazzaro Tavarone,
illustrates in two rooms
*Exploits and Personalities in
the Grimaldi family* (1614–

1624), while the other
decorates the Galleria degli
Specchi (hall of mirrors) and
salons, the work of Lorenzo
De Ferrari for the Spinola
family (1730–37). The Spinola
donation includes works by
Guido Reni, Anthony van
Dyck and il Grechetto.

The **Galleria Nazionale
della Liguria**, on the third
floor, is reserved for works
which were not part of the
Spinola donation. These
include fine works such as
Antonello da Messina's *Ecce
Homo (c.1474)*, an *Equestrian
Portrait of Gio Carlo Doria*
(1606) by Rubens, and *Justice*,
sculpted by Giovanni Pisano
for the funerary monument of
Margaret of Brabant *(see p57)*.

**Ecce Homo by Antonello da
Messina, Palazzo Spinola**

Santa Maria
delle Vigne ㉑

Vicolo del Campanile delle Vigne 5.
Map 5 C3. 📞 010 247 47 61.
⏰ 8am–noon, 3:30–6:30pm daily.
♿ 📷

THE AREA NOW occupied by
the Piazza delle Vigne was
planted with vines (*vigne*) in
around the year 1000, but
was later engulfed by the
expanding city. The church of
Santa Maria was founded in
the same era, though the only
Romanesque element to have
survived is the bell tower.
The church was otherwise
completely rebuilt in Baroque
style in around 1640, after the
area around the apse had
already been reconstructed
in the 16th century at the
behest of the local Grillo
family. Further changes have
been made since. The façade
(1842) is the work of
Ippolito Cremona.

The interior, with a nave
and two aisles divided by
broad arcades, is bathed in
sumptuous gilding, stucco
and fresco decoration, dating
from different periods. The
presbytery was frescoed in
1612 by Lazzaro Tavarone,
with a *Glory of Mary*; the
aisles and the octagonal

DOOR CARVINGS

Slate ornamental panel showing
St George and the Dragon

A recurrent sight in the Centro Storico are the doorways featuring carvings sculpted from marble or the characteristic black stone of Promontorio (from the Lavagna area). These panels were the product of economic necessity and the scarcity of building space: in the 15th century, noble families were obliged to extend the use of the ground floors of their palazzi in order to accommodate shops, and they therefore wanted to create handsome new doorways that would make their own residences stand out. Famous sculptors (in particular, members of the Gagini family) developed this craft, often producing work of great skill. Among the most common subjects were the triumphs of the commissioning family or holy scenes such as St George killing the dragon. There are some examples in the Museo di Sant'Agostino.

One of the Doria palazzi in Piazza San Matteo

The Romanesque bell tower of
Santa Maria delle Vigne

cupola were painted by various artists from the 18th century to the early 20th century. The church contains paintings by Gregorio De Ferrari, Bernardo Castello and Domenico Piola and a tablet depicting a *Madonna*, attributed to Taddeo di Bartolo (late 14th century).

Piazza
San Matteo ②

Map 5 C3. **Chiesa di San Matteo**
010 247 43 61. 9am–noon, 3–6:30pm daily. donations. outside only.

FROM THE 12th to the 17th centuries this lovely square was the headquarters of the powerful Doria family, which, in common with the other

powerful Genoese dynasties, gathered its political clique in a distinct area of the city. Despite changes to the palazzi facing the square, the piazza has kept its original compact form and a distinct charm, missing from other similar areas.

The buildings bear typical wall coverings of striped black and white marble, characteristic of Gothic civic buildings. Of particular note is **Palazzo di Lamba Doria**, at no. 15, named after the family member who defeated the Venetian fleet at Curzola in 1298; the typical structure of a medieval Genoese palazzo is still in evidence. Also noteworthy is **Palazzo di Andrea Doria**, at no. 17,

which, according to the wishes of the civic senate, was given to the admiral in 1528.

The small church of **San Matteo**, the family place of worship of the Dorias, built in 1125, was rebuilt in the late 13th century in Gothic style. Pilasters divide the black-and-white striped façade into three, corresponding to the aisles. The interior was altered in the 16th century for Andrea Doria, who is buried in the crypt, as is his ancestor Lamba Doria. Giovan Battista Castello, known as il Bergamasco, modified the nave and aisles and painted the nave vault (1557–59), a collaboration with Luca Cambiaso. The statues in the apse niches and the decoration of the presbytery and the cupola (1543–47) are by Angelo Montorsoli.

To the left of the church is a pretty cloister (1308), with pointed arches resting on slim paired columns.

The 14th-century cloister attached to the church of San Matteo

LE STRADE NUOVE

W ALKING AROUND THE district known as Le Strade Nuove (or "new streets") – along Via Balbi and Via Garibaldi in particular – you are drawn back to the era of the 16th and 17th centuries, when Genoa dominated much of Europe in the field of finance. The "Genoese Century", or golden age, lasted from 1528 to 1630, when the power of several families was at its height. They poured their legendary wealth into new buildings and art commissions. The Centro Storico was not touched since they preferred to build anew –

Decorative frieze on the façade of Palazzo Doria Tursi

and magnificently – alongside, adapting Renaissance designs to the uneven terrain. The artist Rubens held the palazzi on Via Garibaldi in such high esteem that he made detailed drawings for a 1622 publication. The palazzi typically have loggias and hanging gardens, designed to disguise the steep slopes, and are the work of several architects; foremost among them Galeazzo Alessi. He found an ideal model in the Palazzo Doria Pamphilj (built in 1529 for Andrea Doria), which continued to inspire the palaces built for the Balbi family in the 17th century.

SIGHTS AT A GLANCE

Historic Buildings
Albergo dei Poveri **9**

Historic Streets and Squares
Piazza della Fontana
  Marose **1**
Via Balbi **10**
Via Garibaldi **3**

Museums and Galleries
Galata Museo del Mare **14**
Galleria di Palazzo Bianco **6**
Museo di Arte Orientale
  Edoardo Chiossone **2**
Palazzo Rosso pp72–5 **5**

Palazzi
Palazzo Doria Pamphilj
  or del Principe **15**
Palazzo dell'Università **11**
Palazzo Doria Tursi **4**
Palazzo Reale **12**

Churches
San Giovanni di Pré **13**
San Siro **7**
Santissima Annunziata
  del Vastato **8**

KEY

▦	Street-by-Street *pp68–9*
ℹ	Tourist information
P	Parking
FS	Railway station
M	Underground

0 metres   500

0 yards   500

◁ **The opulent palazzi lining Via Garibaldi, evidence of the glorious "Genoese Century"**

Street-by-Street: around Via Garibaldi

W HEN VIA GARIBALDI WAS laid out in the mid-16th
century, it was the first of the "new streets", and
was known as La Strada Nuova. The mansions lining
the street are wonderfully preserved, with sumptuous
interiors, and often contain exceptional decoration or
fine art collections, the fruits of shrewd collecting.
Among the palazzi open to the public are Palazzo
Doria Tursi (the largest in the street), now the town
hall, and Palazzo Bianco and Palazzo Rosso, which
both house excellent art galleries. Not far away is the
church of San Siro, richly decorated in the 16th and
17th centuries and the first cathedral of Genoa. Beyond
Piazza della Fontana Marose, the
attractive square at one end of
Via Garibaldi, is the Edoardo
Chiossone museum *(see
p70)*, a rare collection
of oriental art that was
assembled in the 19th
century.

**Santissima Annunziata
del Vastato, Palazzo Reale,
Palazzo Doria Pamphilj**

★ **Palazzo Rosso**
*The city's largest art
gallery has treasures such
as portraits by Van Dyck
and Genoese works
from the 16th to the
18th centuries* ❺

0 metres   50

0 yards   50

San Siro
*Genoa's ancient
cathedral probably
dates from the 4th century. There are no
traces of its origins, however, due to a fire
that destroyed it in the late 16th century.
The reconstruction was undertaken by the
Theatine Order (see p76), which turned it
into a temple resplendent with marble inlay
and frescoes* ❼

PIAZZA
MERIDIANA

VIA SAN SIRO

VIA CAIROLI

VIA DELLA MADDALENA

VICO ANG

★ **Palazzo Bianco**
*This gallery reopened in 2004 following
major upgrading work to coincide with
Genoa's year as European City of Culture.
The collection includes a large number of
Genoese works, as well as some important
Flemish paintings, such as a* Venus and
Mars *by Rubens, shown here* ❻

Palazzo Doria Tursi
*Three times the length of
the other mansions in via
Garibaldi, this 16th-century
palazzo has an exquisite
courtyard, with a double
staircase leading up to an
arcaded loggia.* ❹

LOCATOR MAP
See Street Finder, maps 2, 5 & 6

Via Garibaldi
*Now pedestrianized,
this street transports
you back to the golden
age of the Genoese
aristocracy in the 16th
and 17th centuries.
The monumental
façades loom high
above you as you
walk beneath* ❸

Palazzo Podestà
was begun in 1563.
The façade is a
delightful example of
Genoese Mannerism.

Palazzo Doria
has a lovely Baroque
façade dating from
1563–67.

KEY

‑ ‑ ‑ ‑ Recommended route

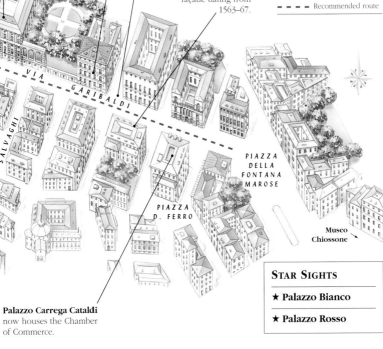

VIA GARIBALDI

VIA SALVAGHI

PIAZZA
DELLA
FONTANA
MAROSE

PIAZZA
D. FERRO

Museo
Chiossone

Palazzo Carrega Cataldi
now houses the Chamber
of Commerce.

STAR SIGHTS

★ **Palazzo Bianco**

★ **Palazzo Rosso**

Piazza della Fontana Marose ●

Map 6 D2.

THIS SQUARE owes its name to an ancient fountain *(fonte)*, which was recorded in a 13th-century document but destroyed in the 19th century. The piazza is attractive and free of traffic, but has an "assembled" look, the result of numerous changes in the layout and of the variations in street level.

Among the palazzi facing onto the square, the main one, at no. 6, is **Palazzo Spinola "dei Marmi"**, built in the mid-15th century and so-called because of its typically elegant covering of black and white striped marble (*marmo*). The palazzo's design had to adapt to the extremely uneven terrain and pre-dates the building of the palazzi in Via Garibaldi.

The only building in the piazza contemporaneous with the buildings on Via Garibaldi is **Palazzo Interiano Pallavicini** (no. 2), which was constructed in 1565 by Francesco Casella.

Museo di Arte Orientale Edoardo Chiossone ●

Villetta Di Negro, Piazzalle Mazzini 4. **Map** 6 D2. 010 542 285. 9am–1pm Tue–Fri; 10–7pm Sat, Sun. public hols. ground floor. www.museochiossonegenova.it

GENOA'S MUSEUM of Oriental Art is set within the **Parco della Villetta Di Negro**, which was designed as a garden of acclimatization for exotic plants by the nobleman Ippolito Durazzo at the beginning of the 19th century. The gardens are still planted with the original mix of Mediterranean and exotic plants. The museum is housed in the villa at the top of the park, which was built in

Colour woodblock print, early 19th century, Museo Chiossone

1971, as a replacement for an earlier villa destroyed during World War II.

What is one of Europe's foremost collections of oriental art is named after Edoardo Chiossone (1833–98), a Genoese painter and engraver who, from 1875–98, ran the Printing Bureau of the Ministry of Finance in Tokyo, designing banknotes for the Japanese government. He also became a respected portrait painter at the Japanese court, as well as an avid collector of oriental art.

Edoardo Chiossone bequeathed his collection of around 15,000 pieces to Genoa's Accademia Liguistica, where he had trained. These pieces, some of which are exceedingly rare, even in the Far East, include paintings, prints, lacquerware, enamels, sculptures, ceramics, textiles, and an exceptional collection of Samurai armour. Specific works include a *Seated Buddha*, a lacquered wood Japanese sculpture, from the Kamakura period; and Ukiyoe paintings, a genre which flourished in Japan from the middle of the 17th century, including works by the masters Harunobu, Shunsho and Utamaro.

Sculpture at the Museo Edoardo Chiossone

Via Garibaldi ●

Map 5 C2.

THE FRENCH WRITER, Madame de Staël (1766–1817) was so struck by the magnificence of this street that she called it *Rue des Rois* (street of kings). For the Genoese it was simply "la Strada Nuova delli Palazzi" (the new street of mansions). Its construction resulted from the creation of an oligarchy by the Genoese admiral Andrea Doria, supported by a few wealthy families devoted to lucrative commercial and financial activity. In the mid-16th century, these families abandoned the old town, where space was severely restricted, and created this handsome residential street.

The entrance to Palazzo Lercari Parodi on Via Garibaldi

Designed by the treasury architect Bernardino Cantone, the palazzi were erected between 1558 and 1583. In the first section, you can see how the entrances to the palazzi run in parallel on both sides of the street, a sign of the planning involved in the layout. (The vast Palazzo Doria Tursi interrupts this symmetry.) Today, the palazzi are occupied mainly by offices, banks and museums.

At no. 1 is **Palazzo Cambiaso**, which fronts onto both Via Garibaldi and Piazza della Fontana Marose, creating a clever continuity between the two spaces. Nearby, at no. 3, is **Palazzo**

Lercari Parodi (1571–78). Originally, this palazzo had loggias open to both the exterior and the interior, but today these are closed. The interior is unusual in that the rooms around the courtyard housed the servants' quarters while the public rooms were on the first floor; the opposite arrangement was more common.

At no. 4 stands **Palazzo Carrega Cataldi** (1561), by Bernardo Cantone and G. Battista Castello; its façade is a delightful fusion of frescoes and stuccowork.

At no. 7 stands lovely **Palazzo Podestà**, also built by Cantone and Castello. The façade has rich stucco decoration, echoed by an innovative interior with an oval atrium and a garden.

Palazzo Doria Tursi ❹

Via Garibaldi 9. **Map** 5 C2.
📞 010 275 80 98. 🕐 9am–7pm Tue–Fri, 10am–7pm Sat, Sun.

CONSTRUCTED FOR Nicolò Grimaldi (so rich that he was nicknamed "monarca" by his fellow citizens), this

The grand interior courtyard of Palazzo Doria Tursi, with its lovely clock tower

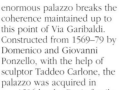
Genoa's coat of arms on the façade of Palazzo Doria Tursi

enormous palazzo breaks the coherence maintained up to this point of Via Garibaldi. Constructed from 1569–79 by Domenico and Giovanni Ponzello, with the help of sculptor Taddeo Carlone, the palazzo was acquired in 1596 by the Doria family, in whose hands it remained until 1848, when it was bought by Emperor Vittorio Emanuele I and became the seat of the town council.

The façade, with its imposing entrance, is distinctive for the varied colours of the stone: a mixture of white marble, local pink Finale stone and slate tiles. A high plinth unites the central section with two airy side loggias; the latter were built in the late 16th century for the Doria but they blend in so neatly with the whole façade that they may have been part of the original design.

Inside is one of the most magnificent courtyards in Genoa, with a grand staircase that splits elegantly into two after the first flight. The clock tower was added in 1820. Inside, the rooms flow harmoniously through the palazzo despite the uneven ground. Previously private rooms were opened up to the public as a museum in 2004. The highlights of the collection, which includes decorative and applied arts, coins and ceramics, are a 1742 violin owned by Nicolò Paganini, and various manuscripts relating to Christopher Columbus, including three signed letters.

Palazzo Rosso ❺

See pp72–5.

***Ecce Homo** (1605) by Caravaggio in Palazzo Bianco*

Galleria di Palazzo Bianco ❻

Via Garibaldi 11. **Map** 5 C2.
📞 010 557 20 13.
🕐 9am–7pm Tue–Fri, 10am–7pm Sat, Sun. 🅿 ✓ ♿ 🏪
🌐 www.museopalazzobianco.it

PALAZZO BIANCO, at the end of Via Garibaldi, was built in the mid-16th century for the Grimaldi family. It was altered in 1714 for Maria Durazzo Brignole Sale, Duchess of Galliera, who introduced a new white façade, perhaps to distinguish it from the nearby Palazzo Rosso, the first home of the Brignole family.

In 1888 the palazzo and its art collection, including collections assembled by later occupants of the palazzo, were donated to Genoa by a later Duchess of Galliera (who also donated the Palazzo Rosso to the city).

The gallery offers an exhaustive tour of Genoese painting as well as many great European paintings from the 13th to the 18th centuries. Genoese artists represented include Luca Cambiaso, Bernardo Strozzi, Giovan Battista Castiglione, known as il Grechetto, and Alessandro Magnasco, whose famous *Trattenimento in un Giardino di Albaro* (1735) is here.

There is also an important core of Flemish paintings, with works by Gérard David, Van Dyck and Rubens, as well as paintings by Murillo, Filippino Lippi, Caravaggio and Veronese.

Palazzo Rosso ❺

THIS PALAZZO, which owes its name to the reddish colour of its exterior (*rosso* means red), is the last of the sumptuous mansions on Via Garibaldi, and one of the most important noble residences in Genoa. It was built by Pierantonio Corradi for the Brignole Sale family in the 1670s, then at the height of its power; the two main floors were intended for the art collector brothers Gian Francesco and Ridolfo, and their heirs. When the Duchess di Galliera, Maria Brignole Sale De Ferrari, gave the palace to the city in 1884, she included its rich art collection. Palazzo Rosso was damaged during World War II, but Franco Albini's restoration in the 1950s successfullly recaptured the majesty of the original building. Inside, the frescoes and gilt and stucco work are as much to be admired as the art. See pp74–5 for a detailed description of the exhibits.

Ceiling frescoes by Gregorio De Ferrari in Room 12 were destroyed by bombs that fell in 1942.

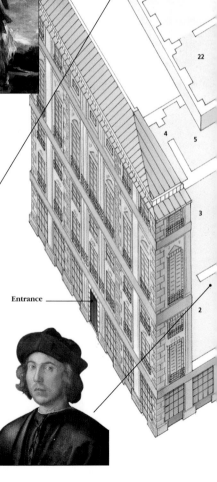

★ **Portraits by Van Dyck**
Fine portraits of the Brignole Sale family by Van Dyck in Room 13 include this picture of Anton Giulio, which pictures the 22-year-old frozen in a pose hitherto reserved for sovereigns, a superb affirmation of his social status.

★ ***Allegory of Spring* by Gregorio De Ferrari**
When Gregorio De Ferrari painted this allegory (1686–7) in the Sale delle Stagioni, he used the scene in which Venus seduces Mars. This masterpiece of Baroque "illusionism" was the fruit of the collaboration between a great artist, De Ferrari, and artists skilled in perspective and stuccowork.

Entrance

Portrait of a Young Man by Albrecht Dürer
This work, dated 1506, was produced during the Nuremberg artist's second trip to Italy. In abandoning the traditional sideways profile, the subject is brought into more direct contact with the onlooker.

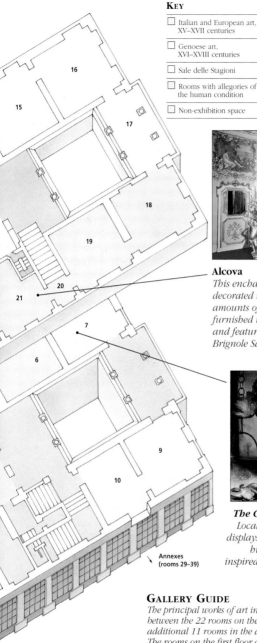

KEY

☐ Italian and European art, XV–XVII centuries

☐ Genoese art, XVI–XVIII centuries

☐ Sale delle Stagioni

☐ Rooms with allegories of the human condition

☐ Non-exhibition space

Alcova
This enchanting 18th-century room is decorated with frescoes enclosed by lavish amounts of gilt and stuccowork. It is furnished with a large bridal bed (c.1780) and features pastel portraits of the Brignole Sale family.

The Cook by Bernardo Strozzi
Local artist Strozzi (1581–1644) displays exceptional virtuosity with his brushwork in this canvas, inspired by Flemish models and the naturalism of Caravaggio.

GALLERY GUIDE
The principal works of art in Palazzo Rosso are distributed between the 22 rooms on the two main floors (there are an additional 11 rooms in the annexes to the main building). The rooms on the first floor contain works by Guido Reni and Guercino, as well as by Genoese artists including Bernardo Strozzi. On the second floor, the magnificently decorated rooms are a big attraction, particularly the Sale delle Stagioni, along with the portraits of Brignole Sale by Anthony Van Dyck. The gallery also has the finest library of art history in Liguria, as well as an education centre (centro didattico), which organizes activities for children. Note that the arrangement of paintings and objects was being reorganized at the time of going to press.

Annexes
(rooms 29–39)

STAR FEATURES

★ **Allegory of Spring**

★ **Portraits by Van Dyck**

Exploring Palazzo Rosso

THE MAIN MUSEUM takes up two floors, and occupies rooms which are still decorated with antique furniture, sculptures, mirrors and porcelain. On the upper floor (the only one to have been lived in) are rooms frescoed by the great painters of the 17th century in Liguria, magnificent examples of Baroque decoration. The paintings of the Brignole Sale family, which form the core of the art collection, are primarily works by Italian and Flemish masters and the Genoese school, reflecting the taste prevalent in the centuries during which the collection was formed. Palazzo Rosso combines beautifully and seamlessly the role of a noble residence with that of a gallery of art assembled by a family of Genoese patricians.

The intense *St Sebastian* by Guido Reni, on display in Room 4

ROOMS 2–6: ITALIAN AND EUROPEAN PAINTING, 15–17TH CENTURIES

THE COLLECTION of paintings was assembled by the Brignole Sale family, whose intelligent acquisitions and commissions lasted for more than two centuries. The marriage between Giovan Francesco Brignole Sale and Maria Durazzo strengthened the collection with works belonging to the Durazzos.

Due to changes made in 2004 to coincide with Genoa's role as City of Culture, some paintings may no longer be in the location described here.

Room 1 has a fine *Portrait of Maria Brignole Sale* (1856), one of many family portraits. In Room 2, as well as a noted *Portrait of a Youth* (1506) by Albrecht Dürer, is a *Portrait of a Man* (15th century); once attributed to Pisanello, this is

now thought to be by Michele Giambono or Gentile da Fabriano. The *Madonna and Child, St John the Baptist and Mary Magdalen* (1520–22) by Palma il Vecchio is a beautiful work, featuring enchanting landscapes and a lovely use of colour.

Room 3 is dedicated to works of the Venetian school from the 16th century, including works by Paolo Veronese and Tintoretto, the great artists of the second half of the 16th century in Venice. One of the finest works is *Judith and Holofernes* by Paolo Veronese. The Venetian style enjoyed huge success in Italy and across Europe in the second half of the 17th century (when the Brignole began collecting in grand style). Other works in Room 3 are by Paris Bordone and Alessandro Bonvicini (also known as il Moretto).

Room 4 has 17th-century paintings of the Emilian school, mainly from Bologna. Among the highlights is an *Annunciation* on copper by Ludovico Carracci, a key figure in the Bolognese school along with his cousins Agostino and Annibale. Among his pupils was Guido Reni, whose *St Sebastian* (1615–16) reveals his ability to depict a range of emotions through measured, classical painting. The works of Giulio Cesare Procaccini are also of interest.

Room 5 contains works by Guercino (1591–1666), documenting the notable success that the artist achieved in Genoa. The fine *Dying Cleopatra* was bought by one of the Durazzo family in 1648 and added to the Brignole collection in the 18th century. By the same artist is *God the Father with Angel* (c.1620), once part of a great altar painting entitled *Vestizione di San Guglielmo*, now in the Pinacoteca Nazionale di Bologna, and the *Suicide of Catone Uticense* (1641).

Room 6 is devoted to 17th-century Neapolitan and Roman painting, including a *Rest on the Flight to Egypt* (1680) by Carlo Maratta, and several works by Mattia Preti, including *The Resurrection of Lazarus* (1630–40), which employs a most dramatic use of light and shade.

ROOMS 7–10: GENOESE PAINTING FROM THE 16–18TH CENTURIES

THESE ROOMS document the richness and high quality of the works produced by the Genoa school during the city's so-called golden age, a period of great economic and cultural fervour which lasted from the 16th to the 18th centuries.

Room 7 is dedicated to local artist Bernardo Strozzi (1581–1644). His paintings range from the youthful *Carità* to two devotional

Judith and Holofernes by Paolo Veronese, displaying great mastery of colour

paintings depicting *St Francis* and magnificent works from his mature phase: such as a *Madonna with Child and San Giovannino*, showing the clear influence of Caravaggio, and *The Cook*, showing a Flemish influence.

In Room 9 are paintings by Sinibaldo Scorza (1589–1631) and Giovan Battista Castiglione, known as il Grechetto (1610–65). Scorza was primarily a painter of landscapes and animals, while il Grechetto, a hugely talented draughtsman and engraver, dealt with pastoral themes. He was a brilliant interpreter of biblical scenes: *his Flight of the family of Abraham* (1630s) is a good example.

Room 10 is dedicated to Genoese artists of the 17th and 18th centuries, including Gioacchino Assereto, Giovanni Bernardo Carbone and Carlo Antonio Tavella, specialists in depictions of idyllic landscapes.

Geronima Brignole Sale and her daughter Aurelia, by Van Dyck

ROOMS 12–17: ROOMS OF THE FOUR SEASONS AND LOGGIAS

ROOM 12 originally bore frescoes of the *Myth of Phaethon* by Gregorio De Ferrari. They were destroyed during World War II, however, and are recorded only in preparatory drawings. His work does survive, however, in the subsequent rooms. Frescoes on the ceiling in the next four rooms (13–16), completed in 1687–89, depict the Allegories of the Four

Loggia delle Rovine (or Loggia di Diana), frescoed by Piola

Seasons: *Spring* and *Summer* are by Gregorio De Ferrari, and *Autumn* and *Winter* by Domenico Piola (assisted by perspective painters Enrico and Antonio Haffner). These superb works use complex iconography to exalt the glory of the Brignole Sale family, taking the form of illusionistic art that weaves together fact and fiction by superimposing stuccoes over frescoes.

This decorative cycle culminates in the Loggia delle Rovine (or Loggia di Diana) by Paolo Gerolamo Piola.

Fine portraits are displayed in these same rooms. The works by Van Dyck (highlights include the portraits of *Anton Giulio Brignole Sale, Paolina Adorno Brignole Sale* and *Geronima Brignole Sale and her daughter Aurelia*), were commissioned in the first half of the 17th century by Gio Francesco Brignole. It was the first significant demonstration of the economic power that the family had acquired.

ROOMS 18–22: ROOMS WITH ALLEGORIES OF HUMAN LIFE

THESE ROOMS WERE frescoed in 1691–92 by Giovanni Andrea Carlone, Bartolomeo Guidobono, Carlo Antonio Tavella and Domenico Parodi. The paintings depict the allegories of the *Life of Man* (Room 18), the *Liberal Arts* (19) and *Youth in Peril* (22).

Room 21, Alcova, is a delightful space, decorated and furnished in full 18th-century style: delicate perspective wall paintings by Andrea Leoncino adorn the walls and the ceiling. The bridal bed was made by Gaetano Cantone in 1783.

ROOMS 29–39: ANNEXES (COINS, WEIGHTS AND MEASURES, AND CERAMICS)

The pieces on display in the annexes were gained both through acquisitions and donations. Note that at the time of going to press only the ceramics were on display, owing to restoration work. The numismatic collection includes 6th–2nd century-BC coins; Roman coins (Republican and Imperial and from the Eastern Empire); coins from the Genoese mint dating from the 12th to 19th centuries, plus coins from mints in Liguria, elsewhere in Italy and Genoese colonies. The Ceramics Collection possesses superb majolica, porcelain and china from Italy and Europe (15th–19th centuries), with many pieces from the manufacturer Ginori and the Venetian firm of Geminiano Cozzi (Room 36) and Meissen and Sèvres (Room 37). From the latter comes *Amore Minaccioso*, a fine piece of unglazed porcelain (or biscuit) by French sculptor Etienne Falconet. China includes English objects made by Josiah Wedgwood. In Room 38, 18th-century Italian majolica (plates from Pavia and from Castelli d'Abruzzo) dominates; in 39 are 16th-century pieces from Faenza, Deruta and Montelupo.

Ceramic plate manufactured in Italy

San Siro ❼

Via San Siro 3 . **Map** 5 B2.
📞 010 246 16 74.
🕐 8am–noon, 3–7pm daily.

A CHURCH OF ancient
foundation, San Siro was
mentioned in documents in
the 4th century. It was
Genoa's cathedral until the
9th century, when that title
passed to San Lorenzo.
Following a fire in 1580,
San Siro was reconstructed
under the supervision of the
Theatines, an order of Italian

**The richly decorated interior of the church
of San Siro, once Genoa's cathedral**

monks established to oppose
the Reformation by raising the
tone of piety in the Roman
Catholic church. The church's
current appearance dates
from this period, though the
façade was the work of Carlo
Barabino (1821).

Inside, there are three
broad aisles with frescoes and
stuccoes by Giovanni Battista
and Tommaso Carlone
respectively (second half of
the 17th century). In the
presbytery, adorned with
multicoloured marbles, is a
monumental high altar in
bronze and black marble, a
fine work by Pierre Puget
(1670). Also of interest in the
church is an *Annunciation*
by Orazio Gentileschi (1639).
Several side chapels were
decorated by Domenico
Fiasella, Domenico Piola and
Gregorio De Ferrari, who also
painted the canvases in the
church sacristy.

Santissima Annunziata del Vastato ❽

Piazza della Nunziata 4 . **Map** 5 B1.
📞 010 246 55 25. 🕐 7–11:30am,
4–6:30pm Mon–Fri; 7:30am–12:45pm,
4:30–6:45pm Sat, Sun. 📷 not during
services.

T HE NAME OF THIS church
combines the two names,
one past and one present, of
the square that it looks onto.
Now Piazza della Nunziata,
the square was originally
Piazza del Vastato, a
name derived from
guastum or *vastinium*:
these terms referred
to the fact that the
district, which was not
enclosed within the
city walls, was free
from the restrictions
which could prevent its
use by the military.

The original church
dates from 1520, but it
was rebuilt in the 16th
and 17th centuries for
the powerful Lomellini
family. The façade has
two bell towers, with a
19th-century pronaos
(portico).

The rich interior
decoration is thought
to be the work of the
brothers Giovanni and Giovan
Battista Carlone in 1627–28,
involving other important
artists such as Gioacchino
Assereto, Giovanni Andrea
Ansaldo and Giulio Benso
over the ensuing decades.
The central nave is
dedicated to glorifying
the divinity of Christ
and of the Virgin Mary.
In the vaults of the
transepts, frescoes by
Giovanni Carlone
depict the *Ascension*
and *Pentecost*; the
Assumption of Mary
in the cupola was
painted by Andrea
Ansaldo and later
restored by Gregorio
De Ferrari.

In the side aisles are
frescoed scenes from
the Old and New
Testaments. The
frescoes in the
presbytery and the

apse *(Annunciation and
Assumption)*, by Giulio
Benso, are placed within
a grandiose painted
architectural framework.

Albergo dei Poveri ❾

Piazzale Brignole 2. **Map** 2 E1.

T HE GRANDIOSE white façade
of the vast Albergo dei
Poveri, with the Genoa city
coat of arms at the centre,
dominates your vision as you
approach along Via Brignole
De Ferrari. One of Italy's
earliest charitable institutions,
providing food, lodging and
medical care for the poor and
sickly, it was established in the
1600's under the patronage of
Emanuele Brignole.

The former poorhouse, an
emblem of the munificence
of the city's nobility, is laid
out around four courtyards,
with a church at the centre.
Works of art housed here
include paintings by Giovan
Battista Paggi, Pierre Puget
and Domenico Piola. The
building has been taken over
recently by the University of
Genoa, but may be open to
the public in the future.

Nearby are the **Salita
di San Bartolomeo del
Carmine** and the **Salita San
Nicolò**, perfectly preserved
narrow uphill streets (*creuze*)
that were once in the
outskirts but have now been
absorbed into the city centre.

**The imposing façade of the Albergo
dei Poveri**

The internal courtyard of one of the majestic palazzi on Via Balbi

Via Balbi ❿

Map 2 E2.

THIS STREET, leading from Piazza della Nunziata, was one of the original Strade Nuove. Created in 1602 by Bartolomeo Bianco for the powerful Balbi family, its building was the result of a deal between the Balbi and the government, which ostensibly aimed to improve traffic flow in the area. (Ironically, Via Balbi is often clogged with traffic, though efforts are being made to rectify this.) By 1620, seven palazzi had been built, creating the Balbi's very own residential quarter. Sadly, none of the palazzi are open to the public.

At no. 1, **Palazzo Durazzo Pallavicini** (1618), one of the many residences to have been designed by Bianco, has a lovely atrium and a superb 18th-century staircase. **Palazzo Balbi Senarega**, another Bianco work at no. 4, is now a university faculty. Inside are fine frescoes by Gregorio De Ferrari.

Palazzo dell'Università ⓫

Via Balbi. **Map** 2 E2. 010 209 91. ◷ 7am–7pm Mon–Fri; 7am–noon Sat.

PERHAPS THE MOST famous building on Via Balbi, this palazzo was built as a Jesuit college in 1634–36 to a design by Bartolomeo Bianco. It has

functioned as the seat of the University of Genoa since 1775. Today it houses the rectorate and several faculties. Like the palazzi in Via Garibaldi (especially Palazzo Doria Tursi), this palazzo has the familiar succession of atrium, raised courtyard and hanging garden. The courtyard, with paired columns, is beautiful and airy. In the **Great Hall** (Aula Magna) there is a series of six statues personifying the theological and cardinal virtues by Giambologna (1579).

The **Biblioteca Universitaria** (university library), occupies the adjacent former church of saints Gerolamo and Francesco Saverio: the apse, with some fine frescoes by Domenico Piola, has been transformed into a reading room.

Palazzo Reale ⓬

Via Balbi 10. **Map** 5 A1. 010 271 02 36. ◷ 9am–1:30pm Tue, Wed; 9am–7pm Thu–Sun. ● 1 Jan, 1 May, 25 Dec. combined ticket valid for Palazzo Reale and Palazzo Spinola. www.palazzorealegenova.it

CONSTRUCTED FOR the Balbi family in 1643–55, this fine palazzo was rebuilt for Eugenio Durazzo only 50 years later. Its new designer,

Vase on display in Palazzo Reale

Carlo Fontana, opted for a Baroque mansion, modelled on a Roman palazzo. The building acquired its present name in 1825, when it became the Genoa residence of the royal House of Savoy.

Fontana's internal courtyard is striking: a combination of delightful architecture in red and yellow and fine views over the port.

The superb mosaic pavement in the garden came from a monastery.

The palazzo's magnificent rooms, decorated in the 18th and 19th centuries by the Durazzo family and by the Savoys, now form part of the **Galleria Nazionale**. They contain furniture, furnishings and tapestries, along with frescoes, paintings and sculpture. The 18th-century rooms include the lavish and breathtaking Galleria degli Specchi (hall of mirrors), with a ceiling frescoed by Domenico Parodi. Rooms created by the Savoys include the Sala del Trono (throne room), Sala delle Udienze (audience chamber) and the Salone da Ballo (ballroom). The most valuable works of art in the museum include paintings by Luca Giordano, Van Dyck, Bernardo Strozzi, il Grechetto and Valerio Castello; and sculptures by Francesco Schiaffino and Filippo Parodi.

The splendid Galleria degli Specchi in Palazzo Reale

Loggias on Piazza della Commenda

San Giovanni di Pré and La Commenda ⓫

Piazza della Commenda 1.
Map 2 D2. **Ⓒ** *010 265 486.*
Ⓓ Upper church *8am–12:30pm,
3–7pm Mon–Sat; 7:30am–1pm,
3–7pm Sun.* **Lower church** *By appt
only.* **Ⓞ** *on request.*

A STONE'S THROW from the main railway station, the church of San Giovanni di Pré was founded in 1180 by the Knights of the Order of St John. The originally Romanesque church was largely rebuilt in the 14th century. The bell tower, adorned with a pyramidal spire, is original and very attractive.

The main church consists, in fact, of two churches, one above the other. The lower one, which was always intended for public worship, has three aisles with cross vaults. The upper one was used by the Knights of the Order and opened to the public only in the 18th century. To do this, the church had to be re-oriented in the opposite direction, an entrance made in the apse and a second, artificial apse created from the opposite end. The upper church is similar in style to the other, though it is larger. Heavy columns support Gothic arches between the aisles and ribbed vaults, the bare stone

making the interior very atmospheric. There are paintings by Giulio Benso, Bernardo Castello and Lazzaro Tavarone.

La Commenda, next door, was founded by the Knights of St John in the 11th century to provide lodgings for pilgrims waiting to sail to the Holy Land; it also functioned as a hospital. Its portico, topped by two loggias, faces onto Piazza dell Commenda. The complex was rebuilt in the 16th century, but restoration work in the 1970s revived its Romanesque appearance. Exhibitions and cultural events are held here.

A short walk eastwards, along Via di Pré (derived from "prati", meaning fields, a reminder of how rural this area once was), brings you to the **Porta dei Vacca** (or **Santa Fede**), a Gothic arch (1155) much altered by the addition of subsequent buildings.

Galata Museo del Mare ⓬

Calata De Mari 1, Darsena.
Map 2 D3. **Ⓒ** *010 234 5655.*
Ⓓ *Nov–Feb: 10am–6pm Tue–Sun;
Mar–Oct: 10am–7:30pm daily
(10am–10pm Fri in Aug).*
Ⓑ Ⓥ Ⓚ Ⓟ Ⓞ Ⓛ
Ⓦ *www.galatamuseodelmare.it*

COMPLETED IN 2004 and intrinsic to the revival of Genoa's port area, this major new museum of the sea is the largest museum of its kind in the Mediterranean. The complex combines 16th-century and Neo-Classical architecture with a stylish glass, wood and aluminium structure. It is located in the Darsena port area, alongside the Stazione Marittima and the historic Galata shipyards

The museum illustrates Genoa's longstanding relationship with the sea, from the Middle Ages to the

present. The star exhibit and focal point is a beautifully restored 16th-century Genoese galley, eye-catching behind its glass veil, lit up at night and visible across the whole bay. As well as a fine display of maps and sailing instruments, the museum's 20 rooms house an original 17th-century launching berth and a reconstructed 17th-century pirate ship, which visitors can board.

Fully interactive, the museum enables visitors to taste life at see at first hand: you can even experience what it is like to cross the Cape Horn in a storm.

**The magnificent Fountain of Neptune, in
the gardens of Palazzo Doria Pamphilj**

Palazzo Doria Pamphilj or del Principe ⓭

Piazza del Principe. **Map** 1 C1.
Ⓒ *010 255 509.*
Ⓓ *10am–5pm Tue–Sun.* **Ⓔ** *1 Jan,
Easter, 1 May, Aug, 25 Dec.*
Ⓖ Ⓣ *book ahead.* **Ⓚ** *entrance on
Via San Benedetto 2.* **Ⓘ Ⓕ**
Ⓦ *www.palazzodelprincipe.it*

CONSTRUCTED BY Andrea Doria when he was at the height of his political power, this palazzo was conceived as a truly magnificent, princely residence, a demonstration of the admiral's power. It is still owned by the Doria Pamphilj family.

The building was begun in around 1529 and incorporated several existing buildings. When Charles V came as a

ANDREA DORIA

This portrait of Andrea Doria (1468–1560), painted by Bronzino after 1540, and now in Palazzo Doria Pamphilj, is fitting: posing, despite his advanced years, in a heroic attitude, semi-nude, as the god of the sea, Neptune. Two fundamental themes in his life are concentrated in this work: the sea and the arts. A member of one of the most powerful families in Genoa, he did not, however, have an easy life. He made a successful career through warfare: initially serving the pope, then the king of France and, finally, emperor Charles V. A soldier and admiral of huge talent, he was one of the few to defeat feared pirates operating in the Mediterranean, to such an extent that he gained the deep respect of the Genoese, who declared him lord of the city in 1528. From this position of power he established an aristocratic constitution which lasted until 1798. He spent many years in his palazzo, built with the help of some of the great artists of the Renaissance.

Andrea Doria as Neptune by Bronzino

guest in 1533, the decoration was largely complete. The principal artist involved was Perin del Vaga (c.1501–47), a pupil of Raphael summoned to Genoa by Andrea Doria.

A marble entrance by Silvio Cosini gives way to an atrium, decorated with frescoes (1529) by Perin del Vaga showing *Stories of the kings of Rome* and *Military Triumphs*. On the upper floor, between the public rooms, the **Loggia degli Eroi** has a stuccoed ceiling by del Vaga and Luzio Romano. Along the internal wall, frescoes by del Vaga depict 12 ancestors of the Doria family. Following lengthy restoration work in the loggia, the splendour of the frescoes' original colours has been greatly revived. The

Salone dei Giganti has a ceiling fresco by del Vaga showing *Giants struck by Jove* (1531). Fine tapestries depicting the *Battle of Lepanto*, in the **galleria**, were made in Brussels in 1591 to a design by Luca Cambiaso.

As well as bringing new life to the palazzo's decoration, restoration work has also made it possible for the public to visit the private apartments of Andrea Doria and his wife.

Around the palazzo, from the water's edge to Monte Granarolo to the rear, there was an enchanting garden,

Detail from the Fontana del Tritone

much altered in the 19th and 20th centuries to make way for a section of railway line and several road junctions. Damage during World War II didn't help, and there is now a project to return the garden to its 16th-century appearance. The garden's two main landmarks are the **Fontana del Tritone** by Montorsoli (a pupil of Michelangelo) and the **Fontana di Nettuno** by Taddeo Carlone, both made in the 16th century.

The nearby **Stazione Marittima**, a 1930s departure point for transatlantic liners, was created out of the Doria's private quay.

The beautifully restored frescoes by Perin del Vaga in the Loggia degli Eroi

FURTHER AFIELD

One of the cats fed by Boccadasse's fishermen

GENOA SPRAWLS westwards and eastwards from the city centre, taking in the Circonvallazione a Monte (mountain by-pass) and the old city walls and forts, as well as the towns annexed to the city with the creation of Greater Genoa in the 1920s. From Voltri, on the Riviera di Ponente to the west, to Nervi, on the Riviera di Levante to the east (the limits of Genoa's administrative territory), the steep landscape and beautiful coastline conceal all kinds of surprises: from the splendid 19th-century park of Villa Durazzo Pallavicini, at Pegli, to the sanctuaries just above Genoa, famous for their nativity scenes and the focus of pilgrimages. Genoa's city walls, which circle the regional capital some distance from the centre, date from the 17th century and feature magnificent fortresses, still in a perfect state of preservation. Then there are medieval jewels such as the church of San Siro di Struppa, standing alone among vineyards and gardens. One sight that should not be missed is the Neo-Classical cemetery at Staglieno, regarded as one of Genoa's major attractions.

East of the city centre, the residential district of Albaro is full of graceful villas set into an urban context, while Boccadasse is a picturesque, well-preserved fishing village, popular with visitors and locals alike. Nervi is a famous bathing resort with beautiful Art Nouveau buildings, a municipal park created out of the gardens of three villas, and the Passeggiata Anita Garibaldi, one of the loveliest coastal walks in Italy.

SIGHTS AT A GLANCE

Historic Buildings
Castello D'Albertis **6**
City Walls
 and Fortresses **9**

Residential Districts
Albaro **12**
Boccadasse **13**
Nervi **14**

Pegli **2**
Voltri **1**

Churches and Sanctuaries
Basilica di San Francesco
 di Paola **4**
San Bartolomeo degli
 Armeni **8**
San Siro di Struppa **11**
Santuario della Madonnetta **7**
Santuario di Oregina **5**

Parks and Gardens
Parco Durazzo Pallavicini **3**

Cemeteries
Cimitero di Staglieno **10**

KEY

☐ Central Genoa
☐ Greater Genoa
═ Motorway
▬ Main road
═ Minor road
— Railway line
— Walls
⛴ Ferry terminal
✈ Airport

0 kilometres 5

0 miles 5

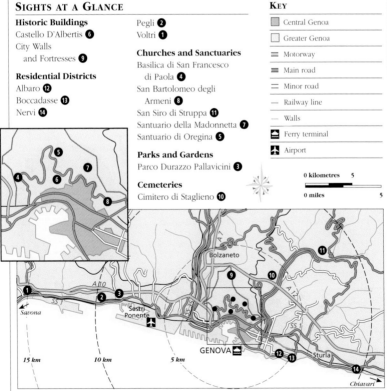

◁ **The Egyptian obelisk overlooking one of the pools at the Parco Durazzo Pallavicini in Pegli**

The Villa Brignole Sale, surrounded by an English garden, at Voltri

Voltri ❶

Road Map D3.
🚉 Genoa–Savona line. 🚌

O NE OF THE MOST important towns in Greater Genoa, Voltri is more or less a continuation of the periphery of the city. The main sight of interest here is the **Villa Brignole Sale**, also called the Villa della Duchessa di Galliera. Originally built in the 17th century, what you see was largely created in the 18th century. The palace became the home of Maria Brignole Sale, Duchess of Galliera, in 1870. Her most striking contribution was the creation of an English-style garden, complete with pine trees, holm oaks and a deer park. The park extends for over 32 ha (80 acres) and is scattered with romantic follies and farmhouses. While the villa, with its lavish interior, is not open to the public, the grounds are a public park.

On the left of the villa, in a beautiful panoramic position, stands the **Sanctuary of Nostra Signora delle Grazie**. The Duchess of Galliera had it restored in Gothic style. She was buried here in 1888.

Pegli ❷

Road Map D3. 🚉 🚌

A NNEXED, LIKE other nearby towns, to the city of Genoa in 1926, Pegli owes its fame to the aristocracy of Europe. From the end of the 19th century onwards, this was the aristocrats' preferred

holiday place; it was also a popular retreat for the Genoese. Two villas hint at its former elegance.

Villa Durazzo Pallavicini, surrounded by a splendid park bursting with fanciful pagodas, arches and other follies *(see pp84–5)*, is the home of the **Museo Civico di Archeologia Ligure**. Objects from the paleontological, prehistoric, Etruscan and Roman eras are displayed alongside the collection of antique vases given to the city in 1866 by Prince Otto of Savoy. Among the more interesting finds are tools from the caves at Balzi Rossi *(see p169)* and the earliest known statue-stele from Lunigiana (c.3000 BC).

The 16th-century Villa Centurione Doria, featuring frescoes by Lazzaro Tavarone, is now home to the **Museo Civico Navale**. This traces Genoa's seafaring history using a fascinating array of objects. These include a portrait of Christopher Columbus by Ghirlandaio, models of three caravels, ship instruments such as astrolabes, and a famous view of Genoa by De Grassi, dating from 1481.

🏛 **Museo Civico di Archeologia Ligure**
Via Pallavicini 11. 📞 *010 698 10 48.*
🕐 *9am–7pm Tue–Fri, 10am–7pm Sat, Sun & public hols.* 🈺 ♿ 🚻 ⬛
🌐 *www.museoarcheologicogenova.it*
🏛 **Museo Civico Navale**
Piazza C Bonavino 7.
📞 *010 696 98 85.* 🕐 *9am–1pm Tue–Fri; 10am–1pm Sat.* 🈺 ♿
🌐 *www.museonavale.it*

Parco Durazzo Pallavicini ❸

See pp84–5.

Ex votos in the Basilica di San Francesco di Paola

Basilica di San Francesco di Paola ❹

Piazza San Francesco di Paola, 4.
Map 1 C1. 📞 *010 261 228.* 🚌 *32, 35.* 🕐 *7:30am–noon, 3:30–6pm daily.* ♿ 📷

T HIS SANCTUARY IS at one extreme of the so-called Circonvallazione a Monte, the charming but tortuous panoramic road which snakes across the slopes just above the city. From the church courtyard, built on a rocky outcrop which dominates the district of Fassolo, visitors can enjoy a marvellous view of Genoa's Porto Antico, which

Overlooking Pegli, with the airport in the background

can be reached via a brick-paved road lined with the stations of the Cross.

Dating from the early 16th century, the basilica took on an important role during the following century, when its patrons included powerful families such as the Doria, the Balbi and the Spinola. Also known as the Sanctuary of Sailors, the church contains numerous mariners' ex votos. Stuccoes and multicoloured marble embellish the spacious interior, and the side chapels contain some important works of art. In the third chapel on the right is a *Nativity* by Luca Cambiaso (1565), while the chapel at the end of the left aisle contains a *Washing of the Feet* signed by Orazio De Ferrari. Anton Maria Maragliano, one of the most active sculptors in Liguria in the 17th century, was responsible for the wooden statue of the Virgin Mary in the apse.

Detail from the funerary monument of Alessandro de Stefanis

Santuario di Oregina ❺

Salita Oregina 44. **Map** 2 D1.
📞 *010 212 024.* 🚌 *39, 40.*
🕐 *8am–noon, 4–7pm daily.* 📷

THE HISTORY OF this sanctuary is linked with worship of the Madonna di Loreto. It stands at the top of a flight of steps, preceded by a tree-filled square, in a gorgeous panoramic position looking over the city and the sea beyond.

A group of monks singled out this area, which still had a strongly rustic character at the time, as a place of hermitage in 1634. They immediately built a simple chapel, but this was taken over by the Franciscan Friars Minor in the following year.

The sanctuary, as it appears today, was built in 1650-55, with further modifications being made in 1707,

including the addition of a dome and changes to the façade, some of which echoed motifs already used inside the church. The upper part of the façade features pilasters, Corinthian columns, a large window and a curvilinear pediment with stuccoes, following the dictates of Ligurian Baroque churches in hilly areas.

Inside the sanctuary, as well as a valuable painting by Andrea Carlone (1639–97), a *St Joseph with Baby Jesus* on the left-hand altar, there are mementoes of the era of the Risorgimento, including the funerary monument of Alessandro de Stefanis, a local hero who died in 1848, and, in the parish office, a case with flags of subalpine, Ligurian and Lombard peoples. The church is also famous for its *Nativity (presepe)*, which contains figures dating from the 1700s.

Castello D'Albertis ❻

Corso Dogali 18. **Map** 2 E1.
📞 *010 272 38 20/34 64.* 🚌 *39, 40.*
🕐 *Oct–Mar: 10am–5pm Tue–Sun; Apr–Sep: 10am–6pm Tue–Sun.* ♿
🌐 *www.castellodalbertisgenova.it*

THIS FORTRESS, built in just six years, from 1886 to 1892, occupies a striking position on the bastion of

Montegalletto, not far from the city centre. The man behind the building was the captain Enrico Alberto D'Albertis, a curious figure who was an explorer as well as a courageous navigator. He was passionate about the project and employed a group of four architects, under the leadership of Alfredo D'Andrade, the great exponent of the Neo-Gothic revival of that time.

One of the most emblematic symbols of revivalism in Genoa, Castello D'Albertis stands out for the forcefulness of the complex: from its mighty 16th-century base to its battlemented towers; the terracotta cladding echoes a style used in similar Genoese Romanesque monuments.

The captain bequeathed the building to the town council in 1932, together with the ethnographic collections that are now on display in the **Museo Etnografico** that now occupies the castle. Among items left by the captain are several sundials (made by D'Albertis himself), nautical instruments and geographical publications, as well as arms from that era. The museum also received a donation of finds from the American Committee of Catholic Missions in 1892. This included Native American costumes, crafts and jewellery and terracotta pieces, masks, stone sculptures and vases dating from the Mayan and Aztec civilizations. Other acquisitions include objects from South-East Asia, Oceania and New Guinea.

An aerial view of the impressive Castello D'Albertis

Parco Durazzo Pallavicini ❸

THE MAN RESPONSIBLE FOR transforming the gardens of the Villa Durazzo Pallavicini was Michele Canzio, set designer at Genoa's Teatro Carlo Felice *(see p55)*. Between 1837 and 1846 he created a splendid English-style garden, following the romantic fashion of the time. He was commissioned by Marchese Ignazio Alessandro Pallavicini, who inherited the villa from his aunt Clelia Pallavicini Durazzo. She was passionate about plants and had begun a botanic garden here in the late 18th century. Today, more than 100 varieties of exotic species, including tropical carnivorous plants, are grown here. The park covers around 11 ha (27 acres).

One of the four Tritons around the Temple of Diana

STAR FEATURE

★ **Temple of Diana**

Cappelletta della Madonna

Mausoleum of the captain

The 14th-century castle stands on the top of the hill, well concealed among trees. Squarely constructed around a circular, battlemented tower, the castle was conceived as the house of an imaginary lord of the time. The interior features fresco and stucco decoration, as do most of the other buildings in the park. The castle, sadly, is not open to the public.

Swiss chalet

Frieze on the Temple of Flora

THE PARK AS A STAGE SET

As a set designer, it is perhaps not surprising that Michele Canzio saw the park as a stage for a historical fairy tale, whose story unwinds en route through the grounds and evokes musings on the mystery of existence. The narrative, typical of a romantic melodrama, consists of a prologue and three acts of four scenes each. The prologue is made up of the Gothic Avenue and the Classic Avenue, while the first act, Return to Nature, develops through the hermitage, a pleasure garden, the old lake and the spring. The second act, representing the Recovery of History, passes from the shrine of the Madonna to the Swiss chalet and on to the captain's castle and the tombs and mausoleum of the captain. The third and final act, Purification, takes in the grottoes, the big lake, a statue of Flora (the goddess of flowers) and her charming temple, with a small square ("remembrance") surrounded by cypresses and a stream.

The Chinese Pagoda

The pagoda roof is adorned with little bells and sculpted dragons. This fun and exotic construction, one of the most charming in the entire park, is built on the lake and can be reached across a double iron bridge.

The Triumphal Arch bears an inscription in Latin which invites the onlooker to forget city life and become immersed in the appreciation of nature. The reliefs and statues were by Gian Battista Cevasco.

Temple of Flora

This feminine, octagonal building could not be dedicated to anyone other than a goddess, the ancient protectress of the plant kingdom. Located just south of the lake, and surrounded by box hedges, the temple is a sign of the renewed interest in the Classical Greek and Roman periods that was so influential in the 19th century.

Turkish kiosk

Coffee house

★ Temple of Diana

This circular Ionic-style temple, dedicated to the Graeco-Roman goddess of hunting, stands in a wonderful position at the centre of the lake. A statue of Diana, the work of Gian Battista Cevasco, poses elegantly beneath the dome, while four tritons stand guard in the water around the temple.

Paving at the Santuario della Madonnetta

Santuario della Madonnetta ❼

Salita della Madonnetta, 5. **Map** 2 F1.
📞 010 272 53 08. 🚇 Zecca–Righi
funicular. 🚌 33. 🕐 9am–noon,
3–7pm daily (4–6pm in summer).

L YING AT THE END of a
creuza, one of Liguria's
distinctive steep narrow
streets, paved with brick,
this sanctuary is one of
the highlights along the
Circonvallazione a Monte.

The complex Baroque
building was erected in 1696
for the Augustine Order. The
delightful area paved with
black and white pebbles
outside dates from the 18th
century. On one side a niche
contains a marble sculpture of
a Pietà by Domenico Parodi.

The interior is also
charming, with a light-filled
central chamber in the form
of an irregular octagon linked
to the presbytery by two side
staircases. Another ramp leads
beneath the presbytery down
to the so-called "scurolo", an
underground chamber on
whose altar stands a revered
statue of the Madonnetta

(17th century), from
which the sanctuary
takes its name; it is
the work of Giovanni
Romano. In the chapel
alongside is a wooden
Pietà (1733), by Anton
Maria Maragliano.

The sanctuary's
crypt houses some of
Genoa's best-loved
nativity scenes
(presepi), of particular interest
because of their faithful
reproduction of parts of the
old city centre. The wooden
figures were carved mainly
in the 17th and 18th
centuries, including some by
Maragliano and others by the
Gagini, a hugely talented
family of sculptors originally
from Lombardy.

In the sacristy you can see
an Annunciation (1490)
attributed to Ludovico Brea, a
native of Nice who was active
in Liguria from around 1475
to 1520 (see p159).

San Bartolomeo degli Armeni ❽

Piazza San Bartolomeo degli
Armeni 2. **Map** 6 F1.
📞 010 839 24 96. 🚌 33.
🕐 8:30–11:30am, 3–6:30pm
daily. 📷

T HIS CHURCH was
founded in 1308
by Basilian monks
(followers of St Basil)
and then passed to
the Barnabites,
who rebuilt
it in 1775 and are

the current occupants. The
church is almost completely
enclosed by a 19th-century
building, but still has its bell
tower, dating from 1300.

San Bartolomeo owes its
fame to the fact that it is home
to the relic of Santo Volto
(Holy Face), a piece of linen
with an image of the face of
Jesus Christ. People also call it
"Santo Sudario", or "Mandillo"
(handkerchief in the local
dialect). This relic was given
to Leonardo Montaldo, doge
of Genoa, in 1362 by the
Constantinople emperor
Giovanni V Paleologo, in
return for military assistance.
The doge, in turn, gave the
relic to the Basilian monks.
Much of the decoration inside
the church relates to the
tradition of the relic.

The Santo Volto itself is set
against a background of
gold and silver filigree (a
masterpiece of Byzantine
goldsmithery), with ten
embossed tiles describing the
origins of the portrait and later
episodes in its history.

**Triptych depicting the Madonna and
Saints in San Bartolomeo, 1415**

**Nativity scene at the Santuario della
Madonnetta**

THE NATIVITY SCENES TRADITION

The spread of the cult of the nativity scene (presepe) may
date back to the Jesuits, who were particularly active in
Genoa in the first half of the 17th century. Although the
tradition was not as strong here as in Naples, it was
nonetheless very popular. During the 17th and 18th
centuries, aristocratic houses assembled presepi but kept
them in private family chapels. The scenes were
eventually made public and bourgeois families of the late
19th century and early 20th century became accustomed
to making special visits to the presepi at Christmas.
Today, it is possible to follow the 19th-century custom
all year round. Several churches still display nativity scenes, including the Madonnetta and
Oregina sanctuaries. Typical figures, usually carved from wood, sometimes made of
coloured wax or plaster, included those of a young, smiling peasant girl, an old peasant
woman with a grotesque expression, and a lame beggar (lo zoppo); the latter became a
famous symbol of poverty and need.

The most valuable work of art is the triptych on the high altar, *Madonna and Saints*, by Turino Vanni (1415).

City Walls and Fortresses **9**

Parco Urbano della Mura.
🚉 *Genova–Casella line.* 🚌 *40, 64.*
🚡 *Zecca–Righi funicular (terminus).*
📋 *organized by Cooperativa DAFNE (010 247 39 25).*

GENOA'S DEFENSIVE walls have been rebuilt or moved several times over the centuries. Traces remain of the 1155 and 1536 walls, but the impressive 13-km (8-mile) triangle of walls that still encloses the city dates from the 1600s. These fortifications, which became known as La Nuova Mura ("the new wall"), were designed in part by Bartolomeo Bianco, and became one of the city's outstanding features. Major alterations had to be made to the walls in the 1800s, after attacks by Austrian troops made clear their inadequacy; most of the forts along their length date from this period.

The best way to explore the old walls is to drive along the scenic Strada Nuova Mura, which begins at Piazza Manin, north of the Centro Storico, and follows the line of what remains of the 17th-century walls (and which also defines the boundaries of the Parco Urbano delle Mura). Piazza Manin itself is home to the

fanciful **Castello Mackenzie** (1896–1906), the work of Gino Coppedè, which embraces medieval, Renaissance and even Art Nouveau influences.

Travelling along the line of the walls in an anti-clockwise direction, you reach **Forte Castellaccio**, mentioned in the 13th century but rebuilt in the 16th century by Andrea Doria and again altered in the 1830s; within its ring of bastions is the Torre della Specola, where condemned men were once hanged.

Forte Sperone juts out on the top of Monte Peralto, at the apex of the triangle. Originally 16th-century, the massive citadel you see today was built in 1826–27 by the House of Savoy.

Inland from Forte Sperone, off the line of the city walls, lies **Forte Puin** (accessible by train from the Genoa–Casella line), completed in 1828. Its square tower is one of the key landmarks in the Parco Urbano delle Mura. Polygonal **Forte Diamante**, the furthest inland of the forts, is in a high and delightful position. Dating from 1758, it has survived almost intact.

Back along the walls, **Forte Begato** has a rectangular layout, with robust buttresses supporting bastions from which there are fine views. **Forte Tenaglia**, which dominates the Valle del Polcevera, was first recorded in the 16th century. Its horn-shaped structure, acquired in the 19th century, was badly damaged in World War II.

The funerary monument to Giuseppe Mazzini at Staglieno

Cimitero di Staglieno **10**

Piazzale Resasco 1.
📞 *010 870 184.* 🚌 *12, 14, 34, 48.*
🕐 *7:30am–4:50pm daily.*
⛔ *1 Jan, Easter Monday, 1 May, 24 Jun, 15 Aug, 8 Dec, 26 Dec.*
🌐 *www.cimiterodistaglieno.it*

THIS VAST AND extraordinary monumental Neo-Classical cemetery on the bank of the River Bisagno, northeast of the city centre, was designed by Carlo Barabino, but he died before the grand project was carried out (1844–51).

Containing a great panoply of grandiose and exuberant monuments to the dead, the cemetery fills an area of 160 ha (395 acres), hence the shuttle bus, which ferries people around.

In a dominant position, on the side of the hill, stands the circular Cappella dei Suffragi, adorned with statues by Cevasco, sculptor of the statues in the Parco Durazzo Pallavicini (*see pp84–5*). Other works of note include the colossal 19th-century marble statue of *Faith* by Santo Varni, and, probably the best-known monument at Staglieno, the tomb of Giuseppe Mazzini, the great philosopher of the Risorgimento. Also buried here, in the Protestant section, is the wife of Lord Byron, Constance Mary Lloyd.

Two wooded areas – the broad Boschetto Regolare and an area of winding paths known as the Boschetto Irregolare – enhance the atmosphere of the place.

Aerial view of Forte Diamante, along the line of the old city walls

San Siro di Struppa ⓫

Via di Creto 64.
📞 010 809 000. 🚌 12, 14.
🕐 summer: 8am–8pm daily; winter: 8am–6:30pm. ♿ 📷

THIS ABBEY CHURCH sits in an isolated position among gardens and rows of vines in the district of Struppa, the most northeasterly part of Genoa. Mentioned in 13th-century documents, it was built around 1000 and named after the bishop of Genoa, San Siro, who was born here in the 4th century. From the late 16th century onwards, the church was tampered with periodically, by the end of which its early Romanesque appearance had greatly suffered. Separate projects to restore the building, carried out in the 1920s and 1960s, have restored San Siro to its original form, including the decorative masonry in grey sandstone and the pavement of black and white pebbles outside the church.

Wooden statue of San Siro, 1640

The façade, pierced by a rose window, is divided by pilasters into three sections

Polyptych of San Siro (1516), San Siro di Struppa

that correspond to the three interior aisles. Above is a bell tower, with three-mullioned windows at the top.

Inside, traces of the original fresco decoration are still visible, and the columns in the nave feature interesting capitals. On the wall in the right-hand aisle is an almost jaunty, heavily gilded wooden statue of *San Siro*, dating from 1640 and much restored. The high altar is modern, but notice the front part, which was the architrave of a door from a 16th-century palazzo in Genoa.

The splendid *Polyptych of San Siro* (depicting the saint enthroned, eight scenes from his life and the Virgin and Child) dates from 1516. It is possibly the work of Pier Francesco Sacchi and hangs in the left-hand aisle.

Albaro ⓬

Road Map D3. 🚌

ALBARO WAS ONE OF the towns annexed to the city in 1926. It marks the start of the eastern, Levante zone of Greater Genoa, an almost unbroken succession of settlements rich in both artistic and historical interest, extending as far as Nervi. The scenic Corso d'Italia road hugs the coast along the way.

Since the Middle Ages, Albaro has been a popular spot for Genoa's high nobility to build their country houses. It remains the residential district par excellence of the city. Though now rather over-developed, it boasts a series of beautiful suburban villas. One of these is the 16th-century **Villa Saluzzo Bombrini**, also known as "il Paradiso". Its charming Renaissance garden features in *Trattenimento in un Giardino di Albaro* (1735), the famous painting by Alessandro Magnasco, now in Palazzo Bianco (*see p71*).

Villa Saluzzo Mongiardino, dating from the early 18th century, played host to the English poet Lord Byron in 1823. **Villa Giustinani Cambiaso** (1548) is the work of the great Renaissance architect Galeazzo Alessi, and was highly influential at the time. Set in an elevated position, surrounded by

---

The Casella train crossing a viaduct

THE CASELLA TRAIN

🚉 **Genova–Casella**
Via alla Stazione per Casella 15, Genova. 📞 010 837 321.
🌐 www.ferroviagenovacasella.it 🚌 33.

First opened in 1929, the Genova–Casella line is one of the few narrow-gauge railway tracks remaining in Italy. It takes around 55 minutes to make the 24-km (15-mile) journey from Piazza Manin in Genoa to the Apennine hinterland. The route passes through forests, over viaducts and through tunnels and reaches its highest point (458 m/1,503 ft) at Crocetta, the ancient border of the Genoese Republic; Casella, at 410 m (1,345 ft), is the head of the line. This mountain railway follows a steep gradient and is known as the "tre valli", after three valleys, the Val Bisagno, Val Polcevera and Valle Scrivia. The small stations along the way (Trensasco, Campi, Pino, Torrazza, Sardorella, Vicomorasso and Sant'Olcese) are starting points for walking and biking trails (bikes can be hired at the stations), and have trattorias eager to feed hungry travellers. You can choose to travel either in a modern or period carriage; either way, you should book.

The Villa Luxoro at Nervi, home to the
Museo Giannettino Luxoro

extensive grounds, it now
houses the university's faculty
of engineering. Inside are
decorative reliefs which are
reminiscent of Classicism and
Roman Mannerism. Two
frescoes by the Bergamo artist
Gian Battista Castello and
Luca Cambiaso embellish the
upstairs loggia.

Boccadasse ⓭

Road Map D3. 🚌

A T THE START of the Riviera
di Levante, but still within
Greater Genoa, Boccadasse is
a fishing village which has
managed to retain its
picturesque charm. The

houses, their façades
painted in lively
colours, are tightly
packed around the
small harbour. This
is one of the most
popular destinations for
the Genoese, who
come for day trips,
especially at the
weekends. It has also
become very popular
with tourists, for whom
Boccadasse has the air
of a place where time
has stood still.

Nervi ⓮

Road Map D3. 🚉 🚌
W www.nervi.ge.it

N ERVI WAS, from the second
half of the 19th century, a
major holiday destination for
the European aristocracy,
especially the English. These
days it is better known for its
international dance festival,
held in the summer.
 The town's seaside location,
gardens and art are the main
attractions. A path called the
Passeggiata Anita Garibaldi,
created for Marchese Gaetano
Gropallo in the 19th century,
offers one of the most
beautiful panoramas in Italy,
with views along Nervi's own

rocky shore and, beyond, the
entire Riviera di Levante as
far as Monte di Portofino.
The 2-km (1-mile) path
passes the 16th-century Torre
Gropallo, which was later
modified by the Marchese in
Neo-Medieval style.
 In the town, the gardens
of three villas have been
combined to form a single
park, planted with exotic
or typically Mediterranean
species and extending over
9 ha (22 acres).

Portrait of Miss Bell, by
Boldini, Raccolta Frugone

The first of these, Villa
Gropallo, houses the town
library, while Villa Serra
contains the **Raccolta d'Arte
Moderna**, a gallery with a
fine gathering of Ligurian
paintings from the last two
centuries. Villa Grimaldi
Fassio houses the **Raccolta
Frugone**, with mainly
figurative works from the
19th and 20th centuries.
 The **Museo Giannettino
Luxoro** has three paintings by
Alessandro Magnasco, but is
best known for its decorative
arts, including ceramics, clocks
and nativity scene figures.

🏛 **Raccolta d'Arte Moderna**
Villa Serra, Via Capolungo 3.
📞 010 557 47 39.
🕐 10am–6pm Tue–Sun. ♿
🏛 **Raccolta Frugone**
Villa Grimaldi, Via Capolungo 9.
📞 010 322 396. 🕐 9am–7pm
Tue–Fri; 10am–7pm Sat, Sun. ♿ 📷
🏛 **Museo Giannettino
Luxoro**
Villa Luxoro, Viale Mafalda
di Savoia 3. 📞 010 322 673.
🕐 9am–1pm Tue–Fri, 10am–1pm Sat.
📷 📷 with permission. 🛅

The picturesque fishing village of Boccadasse

STREET FINDER

HE ATTRACTIONS described in the Genoa section of this guide, as well as the city's restaurants and hotels (listed in the Travellers' Needs section), all carry a map reference, which refers to the six maps in this Street Finder. The page grid below shows which parts of Genoa are covered by these maps. A complete index of the names of streets and squares marked on the maps can be found on the following pages. In addition, the maps show other sights and useful institutions (including ones not mentioned in this guide), including post offices, police stations, hospitals, bus stations and railway termini, sports grounds, public parks, and the principal places of worship in the Ligurian capital. The medieval part of Genoa is made up of an intricate web of narrow streets and alleys, and therefore maps 5 and 6 feature an enlarged map of the Centro Storico, in order to help visitors orientate themselves within this complicated labyrinth.

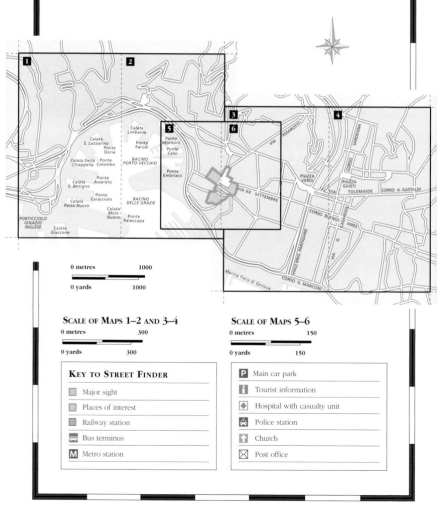

SCALE OF MAPS 1–2 AND 3–4

| 0 metres | 300 |
| 0 yards | 300 |

SCALE OF MAPS 5–6

| 0 metres | 150 |
| 0 yards | 150 |

KEY TO STREET FINDER

▦	Major sight
▦	Places of interest
▦	Railway station
▦	Bus terminus
M	Metro station

P	Main car park
ℹ	Tourist information
✚	Hospital with casualty unit
🚓	Police station
✝	Church
✉	Post office

Streetfinder Index

A

Accademia Ligustica
di Belle Arti 3 A2, 6 D3
Accinelli (Salita) 2 F2
Acquasola (Spianata dell') 3 B2
and 6 F3
Acquaverde (Piazza) 2 D2
Acquidotto (Passo dell') 6 F1
Acquidotto (Salita) 5 C1
Acquidotto (Vico) 5 C1
Adorno (Vico degli) 5 B1
Adorno Cattaneo (Palazzo) 2 E2,
5 A1
Adua (Via) 1 C2
Agnello (Piazza dell') 5 B2
Agnello (Vico) 5 B2
Alabardieri (Vico) 5 C4
Albaro 4 E5
Albaro (Via) 4 E4
Albergo dei Poveri 2 E1
Albero d'Oro (Via dell') 4 E2
Albertazzi Alberto (Via) 1 A4
Alessi Galeazzo (Piazza) 3 A3,
6 E5
Alessi Galeazzo (Via) 3 A3
Alghero (Via) 3 A4
Alimonda Gaetano (Piazza) 4 D3
Alizeri Federico (Via) 1 B2
Almeria (Via) 2 D1
Alpini d'Italia (Via) 2 D2
Antonini Paolo (Via) 3 C3
Aquarium (Acquario) 2 E3, 5 A2
Arancio (Vico dell') 6 D3
Archi (Via degli) 3 B3, 6 E5
Archimede (Largo) 3 C3
Archimede (Via) 3 C3
Arcivescovato (Salita) 5 C3
Arco Trionfale dei Caduti 3 C5
Arecco Bartolomeo (Via) 3 C1
Argento (Vico dell') 5 B1
Argonne (Via) 4 D5
Armellini Carlo (Corso) 3 B1
Armenia (Via) 4 D3
Arsenale di Terra (Via) 2 D2
Artoria (Piazza) 4 D1
Ascensore (Galleria) 5 C2
Asiago (Via) 3 C1
Asilo Davide e Delfina
Garbarino (Via all') 1 B2
Aspromonte (Viale) 3 A4
Assarotti (Via) 3 B1, 6 E2
Assereto (Ponte) 1 C4
Assereto (Via) 6 D5
Avezzana (Via) 2 D1
Ayroli (Via) 4 D1

B

Bacigalupo Nicolò (Via) 3 A1,
6 E2
Balbi Piovera Giacomo (Via) 2 E2,
5 A1
Baliano (archivolto) 5 C4
Baliano (Via) 3 A3, 6 D5
Balilla (Via) 6 E3
Baltimora Giardini 2 F5, 6 D5
Banchi (Piazza) 2 F3, 5 B5
Banchi (Via) 5 B3
Banderali Riccardo (Via) 3 B4
Bandiera (Piazza) 2 E2, 5 A1
Barabino Carlo (Via) 3 B4
Barbareschi Gaetano (Via) 1 A2
Bari (Via) 1 C1
Barili Anton Giulio (Via) 4 F5
Barisone (Piazza) 5 B4
Barnaba (Salita inferiore) 2 E1
Barnabiti dei (Vico) 5 B2
Baroni Eugenio (Via) 3 C5
Basadonne (Via) 5 B4
Bassi Ugo (Corso) 2 E1
Bastioni (Salita dai) 1 A2
Battisti Cesare (Via) 4 D5
Battistine (salite delle) 3 A1, 6 D2
Beccari Odoardo (Via) 3 C5
Belimbau (Palazzo) 5 B1
Bellucci Dino (Via) 2 E2
Bensa (Via) 5 B1
Bernardine (Via delle) 3 B4
Bersaglieri d'Italia (Via) 2 D2
Bertani Agostino (Via) 3 A1, 6 D1
Bertora Giovanni (Via) 6 F1
Bettolo Giovanni (Calata) 1 B5
Bettolo Giovanni (Via) 1 B5
Bianchetti (Via) 5 B1
Bianchi Madre Rosa (Via) 4 F2
Bianchi (Via) 4 D4
Bianco (Palazzo) 5 C2
Biglia Giuseppe (Via) 3 A4
Biscotti (Vico) 5 C4
Bixio Nino (Galleria) 3 A2, 6 D2
Bixio Nino (Via) 3 A4
Blelè Vincenzo (Via) 4 F2
Boccan (Via) 2 D2
Boccanegra (Vico) 5 C2

Boccanoro (Vico) 5 C5
Boccardo Gerolamo (Calata) 2 E4,
5 A4
Boccardo Gerolamo (Via) 6 D4
Bocchella (Via) 4 F4
Boetto Pietro Cardinale (Via) 5 C4
Bologna (Via) 1 B1
Bonanni Carlo (Via) 1 C1
Bonifacio (Via) 4 D1
Borghese Giorgio (Scalinata) 4 D4
Borgo degli Incrociati
(Passo al) 3 C2
Borgo degli Incrociati
(Via al) 3 C2
Borgo Pila (Piazza) 3 C3
Borsa (Palazzo) 3 A3, 6 D4
Bosco Bartolomeo (Via) 3 A2,
6 D1
Bosio Carlo (Via) 4 E5
Bottai (Vico dei) 5 A4
Bottaro (Viale) 6 D1
Bozzano Pietro (Via) 4 E2
Bracelli (Passo) 3 B3
Brera (Via) 3 B3
Brigata Bisagno (Viale) 3 C4
Brigata Liguria (Viale) 3 B3
Brigate Partigiane (Viale) 3 B5
Brignole Piazzale 2 E2
Brignole Emanuele (Vico) 5 C2
Brignole Sale Antonio (Via) 6 D2
Buenos Aires (Corso) 3 C3
Buonvicini (Via) 1 A2
Buozzi Bruno (Via) 1 C2
Byron Giorgio (Via) 4 E4

C

Cadore (Via) 4 D5
Cadorna Luigi (Via) 3 C3
Caduti Via Fani (Rampa di) 2 E4,
5 B3
Caffa (Via) 4 D3
Caffaro (Via) 3 A1, 6 D1
Cagliari (Via) 4 D1
Cairoli (Via) 2 F3, 5 B1
Calatafimi (Via) 6 E2
Caldetto (Salita) 1 C1
Calvi (Ponte) 2 E3, 5 A2
Calvi (Vico) 5 B2
Cambiaso (Palazzo) 3 A2, 6 D2
Cambiaso (Piazzetta) 2 F3, 5 C2
Cambiaso (Viale) 4 D2
Cambiaso (Viale) 4 F4
Cambio (Vico) 5 C2
Camelie delle Grazie (Vico) 5 B4
Camionabile (Viadotto della) 1 A4
Camionale (Piazzale della) 1 A3
Campanile delle Vigne
(Vico) 5 C3
Campetto (Piazza) 5 C3
Campetto (Via) 2 F4
Campetto (Vico) 5 C3
Campo (Piazza del) 5 B2
Campo (Via del) 2 E3, 5 B1
Campo (Vico del) 5 B1
Campo di Santa Sabina
(Piazzetta del) 2 E2, 5 B1
Campo Terzo (Vico del) 5 C4
Campopisano (Via) 5 C5
Campopisano (Vico) 5 C5
Campopisano
Superiore (Via) 5 C5
Canale Giuseppe
Michele (Via) 4 F2
Canevari (Via) 4 D1
Canneto il Curto (Via di) 2 F4,
5 B3
Canneto il Lungo (Via di) 2 F4,
5 B3
Cannoni (Vico dei) 5 C4
Cantore Antonio (Via) 1 A3
Cappellini Vincenzo (Via) 4 F5
Cappuccine (Mura delle) 3 B4
Cappuccini (Piazza dei) 6 E1
Caprettari (Via) 5 B3
Carabaghe (Via) 5 C4
Caracciolo (Ponte) 4 D1
Carbonara (Corso) 2 F2
Carbonara (Salita di) 2 F2
Carcassi Claudio (Via) 3 B2, 6 F3
Carducci Giosuè (Via) 6 D4
Caricamento (Piazza) 2 E3, 5 B2
Carignano (Piazza di) 2 F5
Carità (Vico della) 4 D1
Carloforte (Piazza) 4 D1
Carlone (Via) 5 C3
Carmagnola (Vico) 6 D3
Carrozzino (Via) 3 C2
Cartai (Vico) 5 B3
Casa di Colombo 6 D4
Casa di Mazzini (Via alla) 5 B1
Casacce (Via delle) 3 A2, 6 E4
Casana (Vico della) 5 C3
Casareggio (Vico) 5 C5
Casaregis Giuseppe (Via) 4 D4
Casoni (Vico chiuso) 5 C4
Casoni Filippo (Via) 4 E2
Cassa di Risparmio (Via) 6 D3
Cassai (Via dei) 5 B3
Castagna (Vico) 5 C4
Castelfidardo (Ponte) 4 D2
Castelletto (Scalinata) 5 C1
Castelletto (Spianata di) 2 F3, 5 C1
Castello (Via) 3 B3
Castoro (Via del) 4 D1

Cataldi Bombrini (Via) 4 E4
Cattaneo (Piazza) 5 B4
Cattaneo Grillo (Piazza) 5 B4
Causa Francesco (Via) 4 E4
Cavalieri di Vittorio Veneto
Piazza 3 C5
and 2 E1
Cavalletto (Piazza) 3 B3
Cavallino (Passo) 4 D4
Cavallino (Passo) 4 D4
Caviglia Enrico (Viale) 3 C3
Cavigliere (Vico delle) 5 B1
Cavour (Piazza) 2 E4, 5 B4
Cebà (Via dei) 6 D3
Cecchi Antonio (Via) 3 C4
Cellini (Scalinata) 4 E2
Cellini (Via) 4 E2
Cembalo (Vico) 2 D2
Centro Congressi 2 D4, 5 A3
Centurione Adamo (Via del) 1 C1
Ceppi di Bairolo Angelo
(Via) 1 C2
Cera (Vico) 5 B3
Cesarea (Via) 3 B3, F5
Chiabrera (Via) 5 B4
Chiaffarino Carlo (Piazzetta) 5 B1
Chiappella (Calata delle) 1 B3
Chiappella (Via della) 1 B3
Chiesa della Maddalena
(Vico della) 5 C2
Chiesa delle Vigne (Vico) 5 C3
Chiossone David (Via) 2 F4, 5 C2
Chiusa (Via) 1 A4
Chiuso (Portico) 1 B2
Cicala (Vico) 5 B2
Cimella (Vico) 5 A4
Cinque Dicembre (Via) 6 E4
Cinque Lampade (Vico) 5 B3
Cinque Santi (Vico dei) 2 D1
Cipresso (Via del) 1 C1
Cipro (Via) 3 C4
Citerni Carlo (Via) 3 C5
Coccagna (Salita di) 6 D5
Coccagna (Vico di) 6 D5
Cocito Leonardo (Via) 4 D5
Colalanza (Vico) 5 B3
Col Dino (Via) 1 A3
Colle (Passo del) 5 C5
Colle (Via del) 3 A3
Colli (Fosso dei) 3 A3, 6 D5
Colombo (Piazza) 3 B3, 6 F4
Colombo (Ponte) 1 C3
Colombo Cristoforo
(Galleria) 3 A3, 6 E5
Colombo Cristoforo (Via) 3 B3,
6 F4
Colombo G. (Via) 5 C4
Combattenti Alleati
(giardino) 3 A1, 6 E1
Commenda (Piazza) 2 D2
Compere (Piazza) 5 B3
Concenter (Calata) 1 A5
Conservatori del Mare (Via) 5 B2
Consolazione (Via della) 3 B3,
6 F4
Corallo (Vico del) 3 B2
Coro della Maddalena
(Vico dietro il) 5 C2
Coro delle Vigne
(Vico dietro il) 5 C3
Corridoni Filippo (Via) 4 F3
Corrieri (Vico) 5 B3
Corsica (Via) 3 A4
Corvetto (Piazza) 3 A2, 6 E2
Costa Lorenzo (Via) 2 F1
Cravero Enrico (Via) 3 C5
Crimea (Via) 4 E3
Croce Bianca (Via della) 5 B1
Crocetta (Via della) 3 C1
Crosa di Vergagni (Via) 5 C1
Cuneo (Via) 4 F4
Cuneo (Vico) 5 A1
Curletto (Vico chiuso) 3 B2, 6 D3
Curtatone (Via) 6 F2
Curti Stefanino (Via) 4 D5

D

D'Albertis (Castello) 2 E1
D'Albertis GB (Via) 4 E2
D'Annunzio Gabriele (Via) 5 C5
D'Aste Ippolito (Via) 3 B3, 6 F5
Da Novi Paolo (Piazza) 3 C3
Da Vinci Leonardo (Piazza) 4 F5
Dalla Chiesa Carlo Alberto
(giardini) 4 F5
Dante (Piazza) 3 A3, 6 D4
Dante (Via) 3 A3, 6 D4
Darsena 2 E3, 5 A1
Darsena (Calata) 2 D1
Darsena (Piazza) 5 A1
Dassori Francesco (Via) 4 E3
De Albertis Eduardo (Via) 1 B2
De Amicis Edmondo (Via) 3 B2
De Cardi (Vico) 5 B3
De Ferrari Brigata (Via) 2 E2
De Ferrari Raffaele (Piazza) 3 A2,
6 D4
De Franchi (Piazza) 5 B2
De Gatti (Vico) 5 B1
De Marini (Piazza) 5 B3
De Marini (Vico) 5 B3
De Paoli Giuseppe (Via) 4 D2
Denegri (Vico) 5 B3
Di Robilant Marina (Via) 4 F2
Diaz Armando (Via) 3 B4

Dieci Dicembre (Via) 2 D1
Digione (Via) 1 B2
Dinegro (Piazza) 1 B3
Dodici Ottobre (Largo) 6 D3
Dodici Ottobre (Via) 3 A2, 6 E3
Dogali (Corso) 2 E1
Domoculta (Vico) 6 D3
Don Luigi Orione (Via) 4 D1
Donaver Federico (Via) 4 E1
Donghi (Via) 4 F2
Doria (Palazzo) 2 F3, 5 C2
Doria (Ponte) 1 C3
Doria Andrea (Via) 1 C2
Doria or del Principe
(Palazzo) 1 C2
Dragone (Vico del) 5 C5
Droghieri (Vico dei) 5 B2
Duca (Vico del) 3 C3
Duca D'Aosta (Viale) 3 C3
Ducale (Palazzo) 2 F4, 5 C3
Duomo 2 F4, 5 C3
Durazzo Marcello (Via) 3 B1

E

Embriaco (Ponte) 2 F3, 5 A3
Erbe (Piazza delle) 2 F4, 5 C4
Erbe (Via delle) 5 C4

F

Faenza (Via) 1 A1
Falamonica (Vico) 5 C3
Famagosta (Salita di) 2 E2
Fanti d'Italia (Via) 2 D2
Faralli Vannucci (Piazza) 3 A3,
6 D5
Fasce Giuseppe (Via) 4 E3
Fasciuole (Vico delle) 5 B2
Fassolo (Via di) 1 C1
Fate (Vico delle) 5 C4
Fava Greca (Salita) 5 C5
Ferradini Spartaco (Piazza) 3 C1
Ferrara (Via) 1 A1
Ferreira Pedro (Piazza) 2 D1
Ferretto (Piazza) 4 E1
Ferretto Arturo (Via) 4 E1
Ferro (Piazza del) 5 C2
Ferro (Vico del) 5 C2
Ferro (Vico inferiore del) 5 C2
Ferro (Vico superiore del) 6 D2
Ferruccio Francesco (Viale) 3 C4
Fiascaie (Vico) 5 C3
Fiasella Domenico (Via) 3 B5,
6 F5
Fico (Vico del) 2 F4, 5 C4
Fieno (Vico del) 5 C4
Fiera Internazionale
di Genova 3 A5
Fieschi (Passo) 6 D5
Fieschi (Via) 3 A3, 6 D5
Fieschine (Salita delle) 3 C2
Filo (Vico del) 5 C3
Finocchiaro Aprile Camillo
(Via) 3 C4
Fiodor (Via) 3 A4
Firenze (Corso) 2 E1
Firpo (Piazza) 4 D1
Firpo Attilio (Piazzetta) 3 C2
Fiume (Via) 3 B3
Foglia (Via) 3 C5
Foglie Secche (Vico) 5 A1
Foglietta (Via) 5 B4
Fondaco (Salita del) 5 C3
Fontane (Via delle) 2 E2, 5 A1
Fontana Marose
(Piazza della) 3 A2, 6 D2
Forlì (Via) 1 B1
Fornetti (Vico) 5 B3
Formiche (Vico chiuso) 5 B1
Fornaro (Via) 5 C2
Forni (Piazza dietro i) 5 C1
Fortuna (Vico del) 5 B1
Foscolo Ugo (Via) 6 F4
Fossatello (Piazza) 5 B2
Fossatello (Via) 5 B2
Francia (Passo) 1 A4
Francia (Via di) 1 A3
Franzone (Palazzo) 6 D3
Frate Oliviero (Via) 5 B3
Fregoso (Piazza) 5 B1
Fregoso (Vico del) 5 B3
Frugoni Innocenzo (Via) 3 B3,
6 F5
Fucine (Vico) 6 D3
Fumo (Vico) 5 B4

G

Gadda (Calata) 2 D4
Gagliardo Lazzaro (Via) 1 B2
Galata (Via) 3 B2, 6 F4
Galera (Via) 5 C2
Galilei Galileo (Corso) 4 D2
Galimberti Tancredi (Via) 3 A4
Galliera (Corso) 4 D2
Gandolfi Francesco (Viale) 4 F4
Garaventa Lorenzo (Via) 3 A3,
6 E4
Garibaldi (Vico dei) 5 C3
Garibaldi Giuseppe
(Galleria) 2 F3, 5 C2
Garibaldi Giuseppe (Piazza) 6 D3
Garibaldi Giuseppe (Via) 2 F3,
5 C2

Gastaldi Aldo (Corso)   4 E3
Gattagà Maddalena (Via)   5 C2
Gaulli Giambattista (Via)   4 F1
Gavotti Antonio (Via)   3 A4
Gelsa (Vico chiuso)   5 A4
Gesù e Maria (Salita)   1 C1
Giaccone (Calata)   1 B5
Giacometti Paolo (Via)   4 D2
Giannini (Vico)   5 B2
Giardino (Largo)   3 C1
Gibello (Vico)   5 B3
Ginevra (Via)   3 A4
Giordana Carlo (Via)   1 B1
Giuseppina (Via della)   1 B1
Giusti (Piazza)   4 D2
Giustiniani (Piazza)   5 B4
Giustiniani (Via dei)   2 F4, 5 B4
Giustiniani (Vico)   5 B4
Gobbi (Salita)   2 E1
Gobetti Piero (Via)   4 E2
Goito (Via)   4 A1, 6 E2
Gorrini Fratelli (Passo)   3 B1, 6 E1
Gramsci Antonio (Via)   2 E2, 5 A1
Granarolo (Salita di)   1 C1
Granarolo Principe
  (funicolare)   1 C1
Granello (Via)   3 B3, 6 F5
Grazie (archivolto delle)   5 B4
Grazie (bacino delle)   1 C4
Grazie (Calata)   2 E5, 5 B5
Grazie (Mura delle)   2 F5, 5 B4
Grazie (Piazza delle)   5 B4
Grazie (Via delle)   5 B4
Greci (Piazza)   5 C3
Greci (Vico)   5 C3
Grenchen (Via)   6 E2
Grimaldi (Piazza)   5 C2
Gropallo (lungoparco)   3 C1
Gropallo (parco)   3 C1
Gropallo (Via)   3 B2
Gruber (parco)   3 A1
Gruber (Villa)   6 E1
Guarchi (Vico)   5 B4
Guardiano (molo)   2 E5
Guerrieri Filippo (scalinata)   4 D5
Guidobono Bartolomeo (Via)   2 E1

I

Iacopo da Varagine
  (Funicolare)   5 B2
Ilva (Via)   3 C4
Imperia (Via)   3 C2
Imperiale (Palazzo)   2 F4, 5 C4
Imperiale (Via)   4 F2
Imperiale (Viadotto)   4 F2
Incarnazione (Salita della)   5 A1
Indoratori (Vico degli)   2 F4, 5 C3
Inglese Ignazio (Porticciolo)   1 A5
Innocenzo IV (Via)   3 A4
Interiano G. (Via)   6 D2
Invrea (Piazza)   5 C3
Invrea (Via)   3 C3
Invrea (Vico)   5 C3
Isola (Vico dell')   5 C3

K

Kassala (Via)   2 E1
Kennedy John Fitzgerald
  (Piazzale)   3 B5
King Martin Luther (Piazzale)   3 C5

L

La Lanterna   1 A5
Lagaccio (Via del)   1 C1
Lanata Gian Battista (Via)   3 B2
Lanfranconi L. (Via)   3 B4
Lanterna (Largo)   1 A5
Largo (Vico)   5 A1
Lavagna (Piazza)   5 C2
Lavagna (Vico)   5 C2
Lavandaie (Piazza)   6 D4
Lavatoi (Vico)   5 A4
Lavezzi (Vico)   5 C4
Lavinia (Via)   4 D5
Leccavela (Piazza)   5 B4
Leone (Vico chiuso del)   5 B2
Leopardi (Piazza)   4 E4
Lepre (Piazza)   5 C2
Lepre (Via)   5 C2
Lepre (Vico della)   5 C2
Lercari (Scalinata)   6 D1
Lercari (Via)   2 D2
Libarna (Vico)   3 C4
Libertà (Via della)   3 C4
Limbania (Calata)   2 D2
Liri Alberto (Via)   4 D5
Lodola (Passo)   2 D1
Loggia Spinola (Vico)   6 D2
Lomellini (Via)   5 B1
Lomellini Sofia (Via)   2 F3
Luccoli (Piazza)   6 D3
Luccoli (Via)   2 F3, 5 C3
Lugo (Via)   1 B1
Lurago Rocco (Via)   5 C2
Luxoro (Vico dei)   5 B4

M

Macaggi Giuseppe (Via)   3 B4, 6 F5
Macellari (Vico dei)   2 E2
Macelli di Soziglia (Via dei)   5 C2
Maddalena (Piazza della)   5 C2
Maddalena (Via della)   2 F3, 5 C2
Maddaloni (Via)   3 C4
Madonna (Vico della)   5 B2

Madonnetta (Salita)   2 F1
Madre di Dio (Via)   2 F5, 5 C5
Maestri dei Lavoro (giardini)   2 F2
Magenta (Corso)   3 A1, 6 E1
Magnaghi Gian Battista (Via)   3 C5
Malapaga (Mura)   2 E4, 5 A4
Malatti (Vico)   5 A4
Malinverni Carlo (Via)   2 D1
Mallone (Vico)   5 C2
Malta (Via)   3 B3, 6 F5
Mameli Goffredo (Galleria)   4 D4
Mameli Goffredo (Via)   3 A1, 6 E1
Mandraccio (Calata del)   2 E4
          5 A3
Manin (Piazza)   3 A3
Manunzio Aldo (Via)   4 F2
Manzoni Alessandro (Piazza)   4 D2
Maragliano Anton Maria
  (Via)   3 B3, 6 F5
Marchi Giulio (Piazzetta)   2 F1
Marchini Ettore (Via)   4 E1
Marconi Guglielmo (Corso)   3 C5
Marina (Mura della)   5 C5
Marina (Via della)   2 F5, 5 C5
Marina d'Italia (Via)   2 D1
Marina Fiera di Genova   3 A5
Marinella (Calata)   2 E4, 5 A3
Mario Alberto e Jessie (Via)   4 E2
Marsala Distacco di (Piazza)   4 D2
Marsala (Piazza)   3 A1, 6 E2
Martinez Giovanni (Piazza)   4 E2
Martiri di Cefalonia (Via)   4 F4
Maruffo (Piazzetta)   5 B4
Mascherona (Salita)   5 B4
Mascherona (Via di)   2 F4, 5 B4
Mascherpa Luigi (Via)   3 C5
Massa Don Giacomo
  (scalinata)   4 D5
Matteotti (Piazza)   2 F4, 5 C2
Mazzini Giuseppe (Galleria)   6 D3
Mele (Vico delle)   5 B3
Melegari (Via)   1 A3
Mentana (Corso)   3 A4
Merani (Piazza)   4 D5
Merani (Via)   4 D4
Mercanzia (Via della)   5 B3
Meridiana (Piazza)   5 C2
Metellino (Piazza)   5 A1
Meucci Antonio (Via)   6 D4
Mezzagalera (Vico di)   5 C4
Migliorini (Via)   6 D3
Milano (Via)   1 B3
Milazzo (Via)   3 B4
Milite Ignoto (Scalinata)   3 B4
Mille (Ponte dei)   2 D3
Minetti Vincenzo (Via)   1 C2
Mira (Via)   3 C5
Miramare (Via)   2 F5
Misericordia (Salita)   6 F3
Mojon (Via)   3 B2, 6 F3
Molini (Salita)   5 B1
Molo (Mura del)   5 A4
Molo (Via del)   2 E4, 5 A4
Molo Nuovo (Calata)   1 C5
Molo Vecchio (Calata al)   2 D4
Monache Turchine
  (Salita alle)   5 C1
Monachette (Vico)   2 D2
Mongiardino (archivolto)   5 C4
Montagnola (Salita)   6 D5
Montagnola della Marina
  (Salita della)   5 C5
Montaldo Luigi (belvedere)   5 C1
Montallegro (Via)   4 F4
Monte Cengio (Via)   3 C2
Monte di Pietà (Via)   6 D3
Monte Galletto
  (Scalinata chiusa di)   2 D1
Monte Galletto (Via di)   2 E1
Monte Grappa (Corso)   3 C1
Monte Grappa (Via)   2 D2
Monte Zovetto (Via)   4 F4
Montebello (Salita di)   2 E2
Montello (Via)   3 C1
Montesano (Via)   4 D4
Monte Suello (Via)   4 D4
Montevideo (Via)   4 D3
Monumento "G. Mazzini"   3 A2,
          6 E2
Morando (Vico)   5 B3
Morcento (Via)   6 D4
Morchi (Piazza)   5 B2
Morchi (Vico)   5 B2
Moresco Giacomo (Via)   4 D2
Morin Costantino (Via)   3 C5
Moro Aldo (Strada
  Sopraelevata)   1 C2, 5 A1
Moronsini (Ponte)   2 E3, 5 A2
Multedo (Salita)   3 B1
Mura degli Angeli
  (di sotto le)   1 A1
Mura di Porta Murata   1 A1
Murette (Passo delle)   5 C5
Murette (Vico sotto le)   5 C5
Museo d'Arte Orientale
  Eduardo Chiossone   6 D2
Museo Civico di Storia
  Naturale Giacommo Doria   6 F5

N

Napoli (Via)   2 D1
Negri Renato (Piazza)   5 C5
Negrone (Palazzo)   6 D2
Neve (Salita della)   2 D1

Neve (Vicolo della)   5 C3
Nizza (Via)   4 D4
Noce (Salita della)   4 F2
Noce (Vico della)   5 B3
Noli (Vico)   6 D5
Nostra Signora del Monte
  (Salita nuova di)   4 E2
Nostra Signora del Monte
  (Salita vecchia di)   4 F1
Nostra Signora del Monte
  (Santuario di)   4 F1
Notari (Vico)   5 C4
Novaro Michele (Via)   4 D2
Nunziata (Piazza della)   2 E2, 5 B1
Nuovo (Ponte)   4 D1
Nuovo (Vico)   5 A1

O

Oche (Piazza delle)   5 C3
Oderico Nicolò (Via)   4 E4
Odero Attilio (Via)   3 C5
Odessa (Via)   4 D3
Odino Gian Carlo (Viale)   3 A1,
          6 D1
Olio (Vico dell')   5 C3
Oliva (Vico)   5 B3
Olivette (Passo)   4 D1
Olivieri Angelo (Via)   4 D3
Ombroso (Vico)   5 B1
Opera Pia (Vial del')   4 E3
Oratorio (Via)   4 F1
Orefici (Via degli)   5 C3
Oregina (Salita)   2 D1
Orfani (Via)   4 D1
Oristano (Via)   4 D2
Oro (Vico dell')   5 B1
Orso (Salita del)   4 E1
Orso (Vico del)   4 E1
Orti (Vico)   3 C3, 5 B3
Orti di Banchi (Piazza)   5 C4
Orto (Vico dell')   4 D1
Orto (Vico del')   5 B2
Orto botanico   2 E2
Ospedale (Galleria)   3 B4
Osservatorio (Via)   2 D1
Ozanam (Passo)   6 D3

P

Pace (Via della)   6 F4
Pacifici (Largo)   6 F1
Padre Santo (Viale)   6 E2
Paganini (Corso)   1 C2
Pagano (Via)   1 C2
Paggi (Via)   4 F3
Palazzi Goffredo (Viale)   4 E3
Palazzo dello Sport   3 B5
Palazzo di Giustizia   3 A2, 6 E3
Paleocapa (Ponte)   2 D5
Paleocapa (Via)   2 E1
Palermo (Piazza)   4 D4
Palestro (Via)   3 A1, 6 E2
Palla (Via)   5 A4
Pallavicini (Salita)   6 D5
Pallavicino (Palazzo)   6 D2
Pallavicino T (Palazzo)   6 D2
Palmaria (Via)   3 B3
Pammatone (Via di)   3 A2, 6 E3
Pantaleo Spinola (Palazzo)   6 D2
Pantera (Salita)   4 F2
Paolucci Raffaele (Via)   3 C5
Papa (Piazzetta del)   1 C2
Papa (Vico del)   5 B4
Pareto (Passo)   3 C4
Pareto Lorenzo (Via)   4 D4
Parini (Via)   4 E5
Parmigiani (Vico dei)   6 D3
Parodi (Palazzo)   2 F3, 6 D2
Parodi (Ponte)   2 D3
Passo Nuovo (Calata)   1 B5
Pastengo (Via)   3 A1, 6 E1
Paverano (Via)   4 E1
Pavone (Via)   3 C2
Pece (Vico)   5 B4
Pelletier Rosa Virginia (Via)   4 E5
Pellicceria (Vico di)   5 B2
Pellicceria (Piazza inferiore)   5 B2
Pellicceria (Vico superiore di)   5 B2
Pellico Silvio (Via)   3 B4
Pellizzari (giardini)   2 E1
Pendola Tomaso (Via)   4 E2
Pepe (Via del)   5 C2
Perani (Via)   3 B3, 6 F5
Perosio Ettore (Via)   4 F4
Pertinace (Via)   2 F1
Peschiera (Via)   3 B2, 6 F2
Peschiere (Palazzo delle)   3 B2
  and   6 F2
Pescio Amedeo (Via)   1 A2
Pestarino Isidoro (Piazzale)   1 B1
Petrarca Francesco (Via)   5 D4
Piaggio (Via)   2 F1, 6 E2
Piaggio Martin (Via)   3 A1
Piave (Via al)   4 D5
Piccapietra (Piazza)   3 A2, 6 D3
Pietraminuta (Passo)   2 E2
Pinelli (Piazza)   5 B2
Pinelli Laura (Via)   5 B2, 6 D4
Pirandello Luigi (Via)   4 D2
Pisacane (Via)   3 C4
Podestà (Corso)   3 A3, 6 E5
Podestà (Palazzo del)   2 F3, 5 C2
Pollaioli (Piazza)   5 C3
Pollaioli (Salita)   5 C3
Polleri (Via)   2 F2, 5 B1

Polo Marco (Via)   2 F1
Pomino (Vico)   5 C2
Pomposa (Via)   1 A1
Ponte (Via)   6 F4
Ponte Calvi (Via al)   5 B2
Ponte Monumentale   3 A3, 6 E4
Ponte Reale (Via al)   5 B3
Ponterotto (Via del)   4 D1
Ponticello (Vico del)   6 D2
Ponza (Via)   2 D1
Porta degli Archi (Via)   6 E4
Porta del Molo (Piazzetta)   2 E4,
          5 A3
Porta del Molo Siberia   5 A3
Porta Nuova (Vico)   5 C2
Porta Soprana (Via di)   2 F4, 5 C4
Porta Vecchia (Via)   5 C2
Portafico (Salita)   5 B3
Portello (Piazza)   3 A5
Portello (Piazza del)   6 D2
Portello (Via del)   6 D2
Portello (Vico inferiore)   6 D2
Porto Franco (Calata)   2 E3
Porto Franco (Calata)   1 A4, 5 A3
Porto Vecchio   5 A3
Portoria (Piazza)   3 A2, 6 E3
Posta Vecchia (Piazza)   5 C2
Posta Vecchia (Via)   5 C2
Posta Vecchia (Vico della)   5 C2
Pozzo (Vico del)   5 A1
Pozzo Francesco (Via)   4 D4
Prato (Mura del)   3 B4
Prè (Via di)   2 E2, 5 A1
Prefettura   6 E2
Preve Mario (Via)   2 F1
Principe (Piazza)   1 C2
Principe (stazione)   2 D2
Prione (Salita)   5 C4
Provvidenza (Salita della)   2 D1

Q

Quadrio Maurizio (Corso)   2 F5,
          5 B5
Quattro Canti di San
  Francesco (Via ai)   5 C2
Quattro Novembre (Viale)   3 A2,
          6 E3
Questura   3 C4

R

Ragazzi (Vico)   5 C3
Raggi (Vico chiuso)   5 B2
Raggi Giambattista (Piazza)   3 C2
Raggio Edilio (Via)   2 F2, 5 B1
Raibetta (Piazza della)   5 B3
Rana (Vico chiuso della)   5 B2
Rapalli (Via)   2 D1
Ratti Giuseppe (Via)   1 B2
Ravasco Eugenia (Via)   2 F5, 5 C5
Ravecca (Via di)   5 C5
Ravenna (Via)   1 B1
Re Magi (Salita)   5 C5
Reale (Palazzo)   2 E2, 5 A1
Reggio Tommaso (Via)   5 C3
Repetto Alessandro (Via)   4 E2
Revelli Beaumont Paolo (Via)   4 E2
Riboli Eduardo Giovanni
  Battista (Via)   4 D4
Ricci Federico (Via)   4 F4
Ricci Vincenzo (Via)   3 B2
Righetti Renzo (Via)   4 F5
Rigola Rinaldo (Via)   4 E1
Rimassa Alessandro (Via)   3 C5
Rivale (Via del)   3 C4
Rivoli (Via)   3 A4
Rocca (Piano di)   2 E2
Roccatagliata Ceccardi
  Ceccardo (Via)   3 A3, 6 D4
Rodi (Via)   4 F4
Roma (Via)   3 A2, 6 D3
Romagna (Via)   1 C1
Romagnosi (Piazza)   4 D1
Romairone (Galleria)   1 A4
Romani Felice (Via)   3 B2
Rondinella (Passo)   5 C1
Rondinella
  (Salita superiore della)   5 B1
Rosa (Vico della)   5 B2
Rosario (Vico)   5 B2
Rosina Tito (giardini)   2 F2
Roso (Piazza inferiore del)   5 A1
Roso (Vico inferiore del)   5 A1
Roso (Vico superiore del)   5 A1
Rosselli Carlo Nello (Via)   4 E5
Rossetti Raffaele (Piazza)   4 F4
Rossi (giardini)   2 F1
Rosso Cesare (Via)   4 F5
Rosso (Palazzo)   2 F3, 5 C2
Rotonda Calata   2 E3, 5 A2
Rovere (Vico della)   5 C3
Rubattino Raffaele (Via)   2 D2
Ruffini Jacopo (Via)   3 A4
Ruspoli Eugenio (Via)   3 C5

S

Sacramentine (Viale delle)   4 E4
Saffi Aurelio (Corso)   3 A5
Sale (Vico del)   5 B4
Salumi Calata   2 E3, 5 A2
Salute (Vico)   5 C2
Saluzzo (Via)   4 D4
Salvaghi (Vico)   5 C2
Salvago Paride (Via)   2 F1
San Bartolomeo (Piazza)   6 F1

San Bartolomeo degli Armeni (Via) 3 B2, 6 F2
San Bartolomeo del Fossato (Via) 1 A2
San Benedetto (Via) 1 C2
San Benigno (Calata) 1 B4
San Benigno (Piazzale) 1 A4
San Benigno (Via) 1 B3
San Bernardo (Piazza) 5 C4
San Bernardo (Via di) 2 F4, 5 B4
San Bernardo (Vico) 5 C4
San Biagio (Vico) 5 B4
San Cosimo (Vico dietro il coro di) 5 B4
San Donato (church) 2 F4, 5 C4
San Donato (Via di) 2 F4, 5 C4
San Donato (Vico) 5 C4
San Fermo (Via) 1 B3
San Filippo (Piazza di) 5 B1
San Filippo (Vico di) 5 B1
San Fortunato (Vico) 1 A4
San Francesco (Salita) 5 C2
San Francesco da Paola (Largo) 1 C2
San Francesco da Paola (Salita) 1 C2
San Francesco d'Assisi (Piazza) 3 A4
San Fruttuoso (Via) 4 E2
San Genesio (Vico) 5 B3
San Gerolamo (Salita di) 2 F2, 5 C1
San Gerolamo (scalinata) 6 D2
San Gerolamo (Vico) 2 F2
San Gerolamo (Salita superiore) 2 F2
San Giacomo (Via) 3 A4
San Giacomo della Marina (Piazza) 5 B3
San Giorgio (Palazzo) 2 F3, 5 B3
San Giorgio (Piazza) 5 B4
San Giorgio (Via) 5 B4
San Giorgio (Vico) 5 B4
San Giovanni (Salita) 2 D2
San Giovanni di Pré (church) 2 D2
San Giovanni il Vecchio (Piazzetta) 5 C3
San Giuliano (Via) 4 F5
San Giuseppe (Largo) 6 E3
San Gottardo (Via) 6 E5
San Lazzarino (Calata) 1 C3
San Lazzaro (rampa) 1 B3
San Leonardo (Piazza) 6 E5
San Leonardo (Salita) 6 E5
San Leonardo (Via) 3 A3
San Lorenzo (Piazza) 5 C3
San Lorenzo (Via) 2 F4, 5 B3
San Luca (Piazza) 5 B2
San Luca (Via) 2 F3, 5 B2
San Luca d'Albaro (Via) 5 B2
San Marcellino (Vico) 5 B2
San Marco (church) 2 E4, 5 A4
San Marino (Via) 1 B1
San Matteo (church) 2 F4, 5 C3
San Matteo (Piazza) 5 C3
San Matteo (Salita) 5 C3
San Matteo (Vico) 5 C3
San Nazzaro (Via) 4 E5
San Niccolò (Salita) 2 F1, 5 C1
San Nicolosio (discesa) 5 C1
San Pancrazio (Piazza) 5 B2
San Pancrazio (Via) 5 B2
San Pancrazio (Via a destra) 5 B2
San Paolo (Salita) 2 D2
San Pasquale (Vico) 5 C2
San Pietro dei Banchi (church) 2 F4, 5 B3
San Pietro della Foce (Via) 3 C5
San Pietro della Porta (Vico) 5 B3
San Raffaele (Vico) 5 B2
San Rocchino Inferiore (Salita) 3 A1, 6 E2
San Rocchino Superiore (Salita) 6 F1
San Rocco (quartiere) 1 C1
San Rocco (Salita) 1 C1

San Salvatore (Vico chiuso di) 5 C5
San Sebastiano (Via) 3 A2, 6 D3
San Sepolcro (Vico) 5 B3
San Silvestro (Piazza) 5 C5
San Silvestro (Salita) 5 B5
San Simone (Salita inferiore) 2 F1
San Simone (Salita superiore) 2 F1
San Siro (church) 2 F3, 5 B2
San Siro (Via) 2 F3, 5 B2
San Teodoro (quartiere) 1 B2
San Teodoro (Piazza) 1 C2
San Tomaso (Passo) 2 D1
San Vincenzo (Via) 3 B3, 6 F4
San Vincenzo (Vico) 6 F4
San Vito (Via) 4 D5
Sanguineti (Largo) 5 B3
Sanità (Calata) 1 C5
Sanità (Via della) 1 B3
Sansone (Via dei) 3 A3, 6 E5
Sant'Agata (Ponte) 4 D2
Sant'Agnese (Via) 5 B1
Sant'Agostino (church) 2 F4, 5 C5
Sant'Agostino (stradone) 2 F4, 5 C5
Sant'Ambrogio or del Gesù (church) 2 F4, 5 C4
Sant'Andrea (Chiostro) 6 D4
Sant'Andrea (Piano di) 6 D4
Sant'Andrea (Porta di) 6 D4
Sant'Anna (Funicolare di) 3 A1, 6 D1
Sant'Anna (Salita inferiore) 3 A1, 6 D1
Sant'Antonio (Vico inferiore) 5 A1
Sant'Ignazio (Vico) 6 E5
Sant'Ugo (Via) 2 D1
Santa Catarina (Salita) 6 D2
Santa Chiara (Mura di) 3 B4
Santa Chiara (Via) 3 A3, 6 E5
Santa Consolata (Via) 2 D2
Santa Croce (Piazza di) 5 B6
Santa Croce (Via di) 2 F4, 5 B5
Santa Fede (Piazza) 5 A1
Santa Fede (Via) 5 A1
Santa Maria Assunta in Carignano (church) 3 A4
Santa Maria degli Angeli (Piazza) 5 C2
Santa Maria dei Servi (Largo) 3 C5
Santa Maria del Carmine (church) 2 E2
Santa Maria della Sanità (Salita) 3 A1, 6 E1
Santa Maria delle Vigne (church) 2 F3, 5 C3
Santa Maria di Castello (church) 2 F4, 5 B4
Santa Maria di Castello (Salita) 5 B4
Santa Maria di Castello (Via di) 1 F4, 5 B4
Santa Maria Immacolata (church) 3 B1, 6 F2
Santa Maria in Passione (Piazza) 5 B4
Santa Maria in Via Lata (Piazza) 3 A3, 6 D5
Santa Maria in Via Lata (Salita) 3 A3, 6 E5
Santa Maria in Via Lata (Via) 6 E5
Santa Maria Maddalena (church) 5 C2
Santa Rosa Vicolo 5 B4
Santa Sabina (Vico superiore) 5 B1
Santa Sabina (Piazzetta del campanile di) 5 B1
Santa Teresa (Salita) 2 D2
Santa Zita (Via) 3 C3
Santa Zita (Via privata) 3 C4
Santi Giacomo e Filippo (Via) 3 A2, 6 E2
Santo Stefano (church) 3 A3, 6 E4
Santo Stefano (Piazza) 6 E4
Santo Stefano (Via) 3 A3, 6 E4

Sapri (Via) 2 D1
Sardegna (Corso) 4 D2
Sarzano (Piazza di) 2 F5, 5 C5
Sassi (Salita dei) 2 F5
Sauli (Piazza) 5 B4
Sauli (Viale) 3 B2, 6 F3
Sauli seconda (Via) 5 B4
Sauli (Vico) 5 B4
Savelli Rodolfo (Via) 4 E1
Savona (Via) 3 C4
Savonarola Gerolamo (Piazza) 4 D4
Scienza (Vico della) 5 C2
Scimmia (Vico) 5 B1
Scio (Piazza) 4 D4
Scogli (Via) 4 F3
Scorza Sinibaldo (Via) 2 E1
Scuole Pie (Piazza delle) 5 B3
Scuole Pie (Via) 5 B3
Scurreria (Via) 5 C3
Scurreria la Vecchia (Via) 5 C4
Seminario (Via del) 6 E4
Senarega (Piazza) 5 B3
Serra (Ponte) 4 D1
Serra (Via) 3 B2, 6 F3
Serra (Vico) 5 C3
Serra Gerace (Palazzo) 5 B2
Serriglio (Piazza) 5 B2
Serriglio (Vico) 5 B2
Seta (Salita della) 5 B5
Sirena (Via della) 4 F5
Siria (Via) 3 C5
Sivori Francesco (Via) 2 E1
Smirne (Via) 4 D3
Solari Stanislao (Piazza) 4 E1
Solferino (Corso) 3 A1, 6 E1
Soprana (Porta) 3 A3, 6 D4
Sopranis Raffaele (Piazza) 1 B2
Sottile (Vico) 5 C3
Soziglia (Piazza) 5 C3
Soziglia (Via) 2 F3
Spada (Vicolo) 6 D2
Spallanzani Lazzaro (Via) 1 B1
Speranza (Vico della) 6 D2
Spianata di Castelletto (Salita alla) 5 C1
Spinola (Palazzo) 2 F3, 5 B2
Spinola (Ponte) 2 E3, 5 A2
Spinola (Vico) 5 C2
Spinola Gerolamo (Via) 2 E1
Spinola Pessagno (Palazzo) 6 D2
Squarciafico (Vico) 5 C3
Staglieno (Vico) 3 C4
Stampa (Piazza) 5 B3
Stampa (Vico) 5 B3
Statuto (Piazza dello) 5 A1
Stazione per Casella (Via alla) 3 C1
Stella (Piazza) 5 B4
Stella (Vico) 6 D2
Stoppieri (Vico degli) 5 B4
Strozzi Bernardo (Via) 2 F1

T
Talamone (Via) 1 C1
Targa Carlo (Via) 2 F2, 5 B1
Tartaruga (Vico della) 5 B2
Tassorelli (Via dei) 4 F4
Tavella Carlo Antonio (Via) 2 E1
Teatro (Passo del) 6 D3
Teatro Carlo Felice 3 A2, 6 D3
Teatro Nazionale (Vico del) 5 C5
Teodosia (Via) 4 D3
Terralba (Piazza) 4 E2
Terralba (scalo merci) 4 F3
Terralba (Via) 4 E3
Terrapieni (Salita ai) 3 C1
Terrapieni (Salita superiore ai) 3 C1
Tessitori (Piazza dei) 5 C4
Testadoro (Vico) 6 D3
Thaon de Revel Paolo (Viale) 3 C3
Tolemaide (Via) 3 C3
Tollot (Via) 3 B2

Tommaseo (Piazza) 4 D4
Torino (Corso) 3 C4
Torre degli Embriaci 2 F4, 5 B4
Torre degli Embriaci (Salita) 5 B4
Torre delle Vigne (Via) 5 C3
Torretta Gerolamo (Salita della) 5 C1
Torti (Passo) 4 E2
Torti Giovanni (Via) 4 E2
Toselli Pietro (Via) 4 D2
Tosse (Salita) 6 F4
Tre Re Magi (Piazzetta) 5 C5
Tre Re Magi (Vico) 5 C5
Trebisonda (Via) 4 D4
Trento (Via) 4 D5
Trieste (Via) 4 D5
Tripoli (Via) 4 F3
Trogoletto (Vico del) 5 C2
Turati Filippo (Via) 2 E4, 5 B4
Tursi Municipio (Palazzo) 2 F3, 5 C2

U
Umiltà (Vico dell') 5 C3
Untoria (Vico di) 5 B1
Uso di Mare (Via) 5 C3

V
Vacca (Porta dei) 2 E3, 5 A1
Vacchero (Piazza) 5 B1
Vallechiara (Via) 5 B1
Valletta Cambiaso (parco) 5 B1
Valoria (Piazza) 5 C4
Valoria (Vico) 5 C4
Valoria Inferiore (Vico) 5 C4
Vannucci Atto (Via) 3 B5
Varese (Via) 3 B2
Varese Carlo (Via) 4 D2
Varni (Viale) 3 C2
Vegetti (Vico) 5 C4
Vele (Vico delle) 5 A4
Veneroso (Piazza) 5 C4
Veneroso (Vico) 5 C4
Venezia (Via) 1 B2
Venti Settembre (Via) 3 A3, 6 D4
Venticinque Aprile (Via) 3 A2, 6 D3
Ventotene (Via) 2 D1
Verdi Giuseppe (Piazza) 3 C3
Vernazza (Via) 6 D4
Vernazza Ettore (Via) 3 A2
Vespa (Via) 4 D4
Viale Salvatore (Salita) 6 E4
Vigne (Piazza delle) 5 C3
Vigne (Via delle) 5 C3
Vigne (Vico delle) 5 C5
Vignola Francesco (Salita) 4 D5
Villa di Negro (parco) 3 A1, 6 D2
Villa Glori (parco) 3 A4
Villa Goffredo (Piazza) 2 F2, 5 C1
Villa Imperiale 4 E2
Villa Serra (Museo del Teatro Stabile) 3 B2, 6 F3
Villetta (salita) 2 F5
Vinelli Francesco (Via) 4 D1
Virtù (Vico delle) 5 B4
Vitale Vito (Via) 4 E2
Vittoria (Piazza della) 3 B3
Vivaldi Francesco (Via) 2 D2
Volta Alessandro (Via) 3 B4
Volturno (Via) 3 C4

Z
Zara (Via) 4 E5
Zecca (Largo della) 2 F3, 5 B1
Zecca Righi (funicolare) 2 F2, 5 C1
Zerbino (Mura dello) 3 C1
Zerbino (Piazza dello) 3 C1
Zingari (Calata degli) 1 C3
Zingari (Mura degli) 2 D2

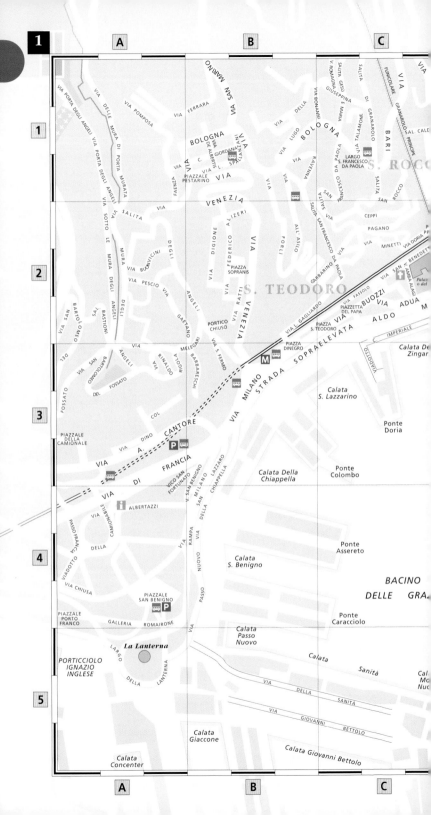

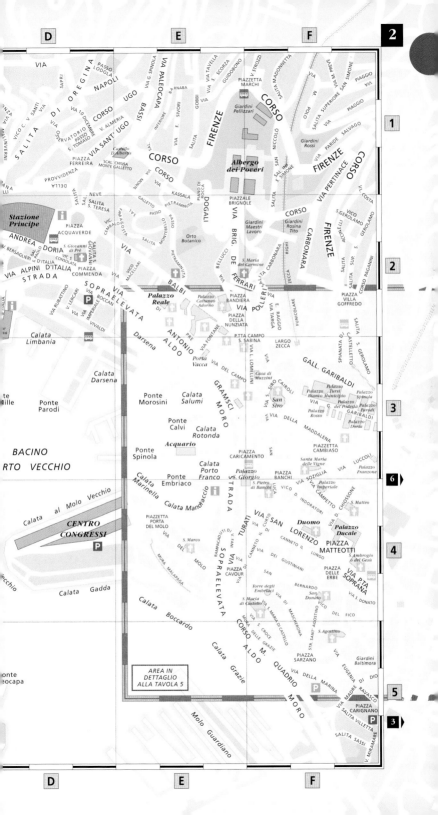

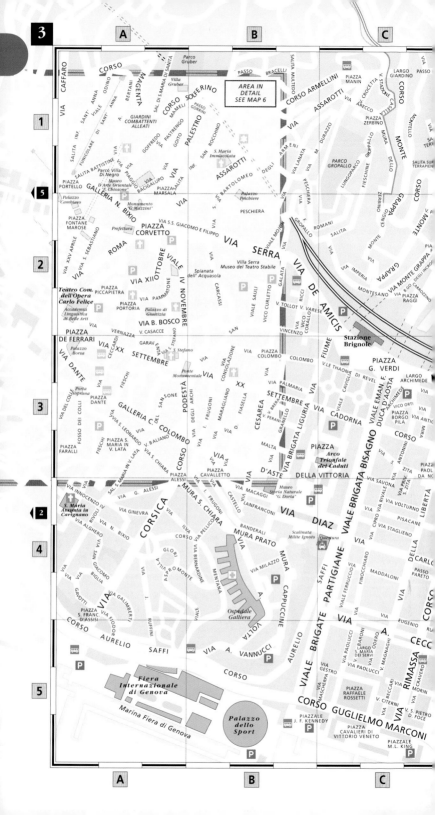

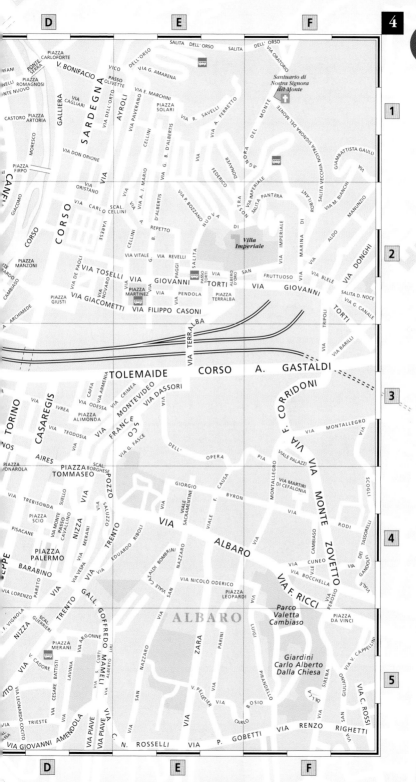

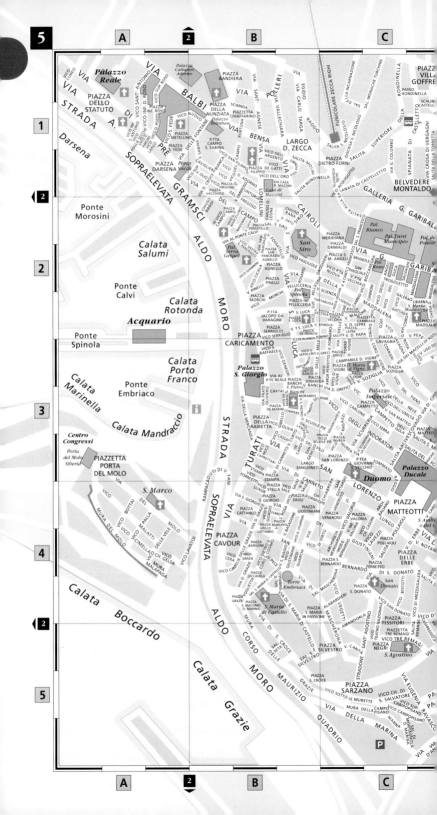

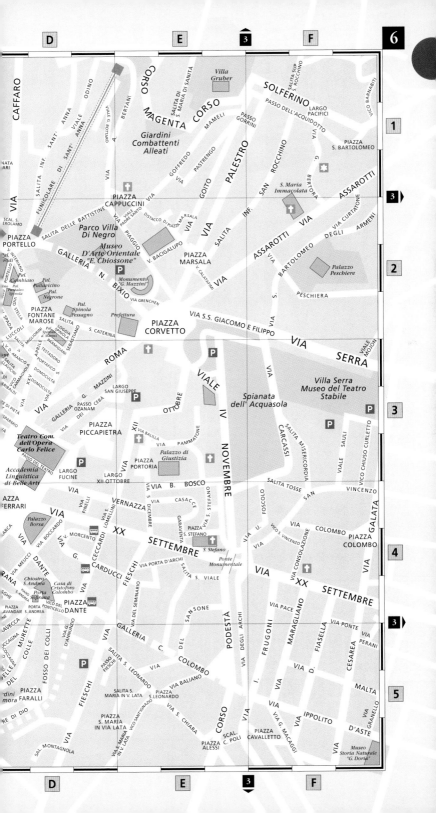

THE ITALIAN RIVIERA AREA BY AREA

THE ITALIAN RIVIERA AT A GLANCE 102-103
THE RIVIERA DI LEVANTE 104-129
THE RIVIERA DI PONENTE 130-171

The Italian Riviera at a Glance

LIGURIA IS ONE of the smallest regions in Italy in terms of its area. As well as dramatic landscapes, both along the coast and in the mountains behind, the region has a rich cultural history. Genoa, the Ligurian capital, lies midway along the coast. To the east of the city lies the Riviera di Levante (which includes La Spezia, a provincial capital), bordering the regions of Tuscany and Emilia-Romagna. To the west is the Riviera di Ponente, which meets the border with France, and has two more provincial capitals, Savona and Imperia. Liguria's long, rocky coast is often superbly picturesque, particularly in the Cinque Terre and the headland of Portofino, both on the Riviera di Levante. Punctuating the shores are seaside resorts which are buzzing with life in summer, as well as towns of historic interest such as Albenga and Bordighera. The often forested and mountainous hinterland (the so-called *entroterra*) is also home to some fascinating medieval towns, such as Pieve di Teco, Pigna and Dolceacqua.

Albenga (see pp148–51) *shelters within its historic centre some of the oldest and most significant monuments in the region, such as the cathedral of San Michele* (above) *and the Early Christian baptistry.*

The town of Cervo (see p153) *clings to a peak and is overlooked by the lovely parish church of San Giovanni Battista (1686–1734). This fine example of Ligurian Baroque has a great concave façade embellished with stuccoes.*

THE RIVIERA DI
PONENTE
(see pp130–171)

The Casino (see p164) *in San Remo is an example of the Art Nouveau style so popular in the heyday of this wonderful and old-fashioned seaside resort. San Remo is also known for its Festival of Italian Song.*

The town of Portofino (see pp110–11) *is packed with tall, narrow, pastel-coloured houses gathered around a small harbour. This is one of the most appealing sites in the entire region, on one of Italy's most famous stretches of coastline.*

Luni (see p127), *close to the border with Tuscany, is an important archaeological site with a large Roman amphitheatre. It is also the source of these prehistoric statue-stelae.*

THE RIVIERA DI LEVANTE
(see pp104–129)

0 kilometres   20

0 miles   20

The church of San Pietro (see p120) *at Portovenere stands on a rocky promontory overlooking the sea. The striped church dates from the 6th century.*

THE RIVIERA DI LEVANTE

HOUGHTS TURN, INEVITABLY, *when considering this part of the world, to the great poets who have lauded it, including the romantic poets Percy Bysshe Shelley and Lord Byron; there is even a gulf named in their honour. These poets and other writers have celebrated the enchantment of the Riviera di Levante, the gentleness of the climate, the colourful flowers and the beautiful coves.*

This stunningly beautiful area genuinely deserves their praise. The often beautifully positioned coastal resorts and villages are truly delightful, the result of the combined efforts of man and nature. The contrast between the sea and the steep mountains immediately behind adds to the fascination, which only increases as you head inland, into the jagged valleys and ravines where villages cling to hilltops.

The Riviera di Levante is home to a number of chic resorts – including Portofino, Santa Margherita Ligure and Rapallo – once the haunt of European, and particularly English aristocrats, but now frequented mainly by Italians. Tourism has thrived in this area since the 1800s, though this formidable success has meant the arrival of mass tourism and, with it, inevitably, over-development in some areas and periods of overcrowding (both on the beaches and the roads). But what may seem like high-season chaos to some, is liveliness and fun to others.

Largely in response to the effects of increased development, including pollution and erosion, nature reserves, national parks and other protected areas have been founded both along the coast (such as the Cinque Terre) and inland, and are a vital contribution to the conservation of this precious landscape.

The way of life in the interior is a world away from the bustling scene on the coast. Steep valleys, formed by the rivers Magra, Vara and Aveto, cut deep into the landscape and are carpeted with dense forest. There is a serious problem of population decline in some areas (a problem common to all parts of the Italian Apennines), but village communities do survive in the hinterland, dependent mostly on agriculture.

Green shutters and flower-filled balconies, a feature of Ligurian houses

◁ **The church of San Pietro at Portovenere, in a lovely position by the sea**

Exploring the Riviera di Levante

THIS SLIM TONGUE OF LAND starts just south of
Genoa and runs as far as the easterly region of
Lunigiana. Dotted along the coast are famous
beaches and pretty resorts, from Camogli, Rapallo
and Portofino in the west to Portovenere in the east.
The inland mountains and valleys are less visited,
but shelter attractive towns of both historical and
architectural interest, such as Varese Ligure and
Sarzana, and the archeological ruins at Luni; walks
through chestnut woods reveal the contrast with
the exuberant Mediterranean flora of the
coast. Important monuments in the
region include the forts of Sarzana, the
churches of San Salvatore dei Fieschi
and Sant'Andrea di Borzone and the
abbey of San Fruttuoso, examples of
the magnificent Romanesque and
Gothic architecture which
developed in the 3rd and 4th
centuries in the region.

SEE ALSO

• *Where to Stay* pp178–81
• *Where to Eat* pp190–94

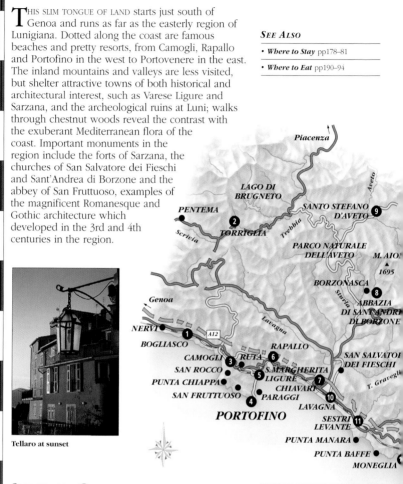

Tellaro at sunset

**Fishing boats at Manarola, one of
the villages in the Cinque Terre**

SIGHTS AT A GLANCE

Abbazia di Sant'Andrea di Borzone **8**
Ameglia **25**
Bocca di Magra **26**
Bogliasco **1**
Bonassola **14**
Camogli **3**
Campiglia **17**
Castelnuovo di Magra **28**
Chiavari **7**
The *Cinque Terre* (pp118–9) **16**
Fiascherino and Tellaro **23**
Palmaria, Tino and Tinetto **19**
La Spezia (pp124–5) **25**
Lavagna **10**
Lerici **22**
Levanto **15**
Luni **27**
Moneglia **13**
Montemarcello **24**
Portofino Peninsula (pp110–11) **4**
Portovenere **18**
Rapallo **6**
San Terenzo **21**
Santa Margherita Ligure **5**
Santo Stefano d'Aveto **9**
Sarzana (pp128–9) **29**
Sestri Levante **11**
Torriglia **2**
Varese Ligure **12**

The seafront at La Spezia, the easternmost city on the Riviera di Levante

KEY

━━ Motorway

━━ Major road

━━ Minor road

— River

⋈⋈ Railway line

···· Ferry route

GETTING AROUND

The main communication routes in the Riviera di Levante are the A12 (the motorway linking Livorno with Genoa) and the A15, linking Parma to La Spezia. Running the length of the coast is the Via Aurelia (Strada Statale 1). Numerous roads link the coast to the hinterland, often travelling through spectacular landscapes. The Genoa–Livorno railway line provides train links, with regional and local train services connecting all towns and villages, with the important exception of Portofino. Efficient coach services ensure daily links between all the towns on the coast and those inland. In high season, there are also ferry services running between the key centres along the coast between Portofino and La Spezia, including the Cinque Terre, as well as to the most popular offshore islands.

Typically painted façades in Bogliasco

Bogliasco ➊

Genoa. **Road Map** D4. 🏛 *4,600.*
🚆 🚌 **ℹ** *Via Aurelia 106, 010 347
04 29.* 🎪 *Festa Patronale della
Madonna del Carmine (Jul); Festa
Patronale della Madonna della
Guardia (Aug).*

O N THE APTLY NAMED Golfo
di Paradiso east of Genoa,
Bogliasco is an elegant
residential and tourist town
with a few small beaches.
It retains the look of a
traditional fishing village,
though, with painted houses
arranged prettily around the
mouth of the River Bogliasco
(crossed by a medieval bridge
known as the Ponte Romano).
The town is dominated by
the 1,000-year-old **Castello**,
a defensive tower built by the
Republic of Genoa. To the
west, high up on a cliff, is the
18th-century parish church,
with a terrace of black and
white pebbles in front. The
Oratory of Santa Chiara
(15th century) is also of note.
Inside are several traditional,
highly ornate, processional
crosses, among them one by
Maragliano (1713).

Torriglia ➋

Genoa. **Road Map** D3. 🏛 *2,300.*
🚆 *Genoa.* 🚌 **ℹ** *Ente Parco
d'Antola, Via Nostra Signora della
Provvidenza 3, 010 944 931.*
🎪 *Presepe di Pentema (Dec–Jan).*

T HIS SMALL SUMMER holiday
resort is distinguished
by its position among the
forested Antola mountains. In

the Roman period it was a
significant commercial centre,
located as it was at an
important crossroads on the
main route between Genoa
and Emilia-Romagna.
The town is overlooked
by the imposing ruins of a
medieval **castle**. Built by the
Malaspina family, it was later
occupied by the Fieschi
family and, from the second
half of the 16th century, by
the Doria dynasty.

ENVIRONS: two pleasant trips
can be made from Torriglia.
The first is to **Pentema**, about
6 km (4 miles) north of the
town along a winding road.
Having crossed a totally
unspoilt landscape of hills
and mountains covered in
dense forest, you reach one
of the loveliest villages inland
from the Riviera di Levante.
Pentema consists of a handful
of houses scattered on a sun-
facing hill, with a church at
the top. The houses, set on
terraces, are identical, all very
simple and with chalet-style
roofs. The village streets are
still paved with river stones,
or simply earth.
Absolute silence seems to
reign at the wonderfully
peaceful **Lago del Brugneto**,
some 8 km (5 miles) east of
Torriglia. An artificial basin
created as a reservoir for
Genoa, the lake lies within
the **Parco Regionale del
Monte Antola** and is entirely
surrounded by hills and
mountains. A scenic walking
trail snakes around the shores
of the lake: some 13 km
(8 miles) long, the walk takes
about six hours to complete.

Camogli ➌

Genoa. **Road Map** D4. 🏛 *5,900.*
🚆 🚌 **ℹ** *Via XX Settembre 33,
0185 771 066.* 🆆 *www.camogli.it*
🎪 *Sagra del Pesce (second Sun in
May).*

A N OLD FISHING AND seafaring
village on the Golfo di
Paradiso, Camogli is named
after the women (*moglie*)
who ran the town while their
husbands were at sea. It has
an enchanting medieval heart,
with tall, narrow houses
(some are over six storeys
high) crowded around the
harbour and along the maze
of alleys and steps behind.
A small promontory, known
as the "Isola" (island) because
it was once separated from
the mainland, is home to the
**Basilica di Santa Maria
Assunta**, founded in the 12th
century but much modified.
It has a Neo-Classical façade
and a 17th-century pebbled
courtyard. The interior is
richly decorated: the vault in
the central nave has a fresco
by Francesco Semino and
Nicolò Barabino, and the
high altar has a sculpture of
the Virgin Mary by Bernardo
Schiaffino (18th century).
On a cliff overlooking the
sea stands **Castel Dragone**,
medieval but much altered.
The **Museo Marinaro Gio
Bono Ferrari**, at the end of
the seafront, documents a
glorious period in Camogli's
history that seems almost
unthinkable today: namely,
the 18th and 19th centuries,
when Camogli supplied a
fleet of some 3,000 merchant
ships under contract to the

The seafront at Camogli with the "Isola" in the background

The seafront at Santa Margherita Ligure

major European states; they even fought with Napoleon. Camogli's fishing fleet today is tiny by comparison.

The museum contains models of ships, navigational instruments and also paintings of ships (often by the ships' owners), which served as ex votos. The cloister next to the sanctuary of **Nostra Signora del Boschetto**, just outside Camogli, is also full of sailors' ex votos.

If you are in the area in May, don't miss the famous Sagra del Pesce, when vast numbers of fish are cooked in a giant frying pan (see p28).

🏛 **Museo Gio Bono Ferrari**
Via GB Ferrari, 41. 📞 0185 729 049.
🕐 9am–noon Mon, Thu, Fri; 9am–noon, 3–6pm Wed, Sat, Sun & hols (4–7pm Jun–Sep).

Portofino ❹

See pp110–13.

Santa Margherita Ligure ❺

Genoa. **Road Map** E4. 🏠 10800.
🚉 🚌 Via XXV Aprile 2/B, 0185 287 485. 🌐 www.apttigullio.liguria.it
📅 Nostra Signora della Rosa (Jul).

BUILT ALONG AN INLET on the Golfo del Tigullio, Santa Margherita is a lively resort with a beautiful harbour and grand hotels and villas. The lavish rococo church of Santa Margherita d'Antiochia gave the town its name.

Santa Margherita emerged in its own right only in the 19th century, when it was created out of the two villages of Pescino and Corte. It soon became a popular destination among the (mainly British) holidaying elite.

The hill between the two old villages has been transformed into the public **Parco di Villa Durazzo**. The villa at the top, begun in the mid-16th century, still has its original furnishings as well as an art collection. The large Italian-style garden offers lovely views of the city and the sea.

At the foot of the hill, in the district known as Corte, is the 17th-century church of the Cappuccini, with a 15th-century wooden cross.

Rapallo ❻

Genoa. **Road Map** E4.
🏠 29,300. 🚉 🚌
ℹ️ Lungomare Vittorio Veneto 7, 0185 230 346.
🌐 www.apttigullio.liguria.it
📅 Mostra Internazionale dei Cartoonists (Nov–Dec); Festa della Madonna di Montallegro (Jul).

RAPALLO ENJOYS a gorgeous position on the Golfo del Tigullio and is perhaps the best-known resort along the Riviera di Levante. It has a large marina, swimming pool, sailing, tennis and riding schools, as well as an 18-hole golf course.

The climate was a big draw for aristocrats from the 19th century, as can be seen from the Art Nouveau cafés and hotels lining **Lungomare Vittorio Veneto**. Max Beerbohm (1872–1956), the English wit and critic, was a resident for many years.

In the centre, the parallel streets Via Venezia, Via Mazzini and Via Marsala define the medieval "borgo murato" (walled village), so-named because of the way the buildings are closely packed together. Historic monuments include the old parish church of Santo Stefano (mostly 17th century) and the adjacent 15th-century civic tower, and the medieval Ponte di Annibale (Hannibal's bridge), with a single-span arch of 15 m (49 ft).

From Piazza Pastene, on the seafront, you can reach the **Castello**, built in 1551 on a cliff to defend the settlement against pirate raids. There is also a highly enjoyable funicular ride up to the **Santuario di Montallegro** (16th century), from where there are superb views of the coast and sea.

Villa Tigullio is home to the **Museo del Merletto**, a museum of lace with more than 1,400 pieces from the 16th to 19th centuries.

The castle at Rapallo, a defensive structure dating from 1551

Among these are lace clothing, lace for furnishing, and several 18–19th century pillows. There is also a collection of designs.

ENVIRONS: just east of Rapallo, **Zoagli** is a small resort which still feels like a fishing village despite being bombed in World War II.

🏛 **Museo del Merletto**
Villa Tigullio, Parco Casale.
📞 0185 633 05.
🕐 3–6pm Tue, Wed, Fri, Sat; 10–11:30am Thu, Sun. 📷

Portofino Peninsula ④

Tᴴɪs HEADLAND EXTENDS for around 3 km (2 miles) out to sea and separates the Paradiso and Tigullio gulfs. The southern part, hot and dry, has high cliffs that enclose gorgeous inlets hidden in the Mediterranean maquis; on the northern side, woods of chestnut trees dominate. The small area is extraordinarily rich botanically, and its favourable position has drawn human settlements since antiquity: *Portus Delphini* (the bay was, and still is, known for its large dolphin population) was an important settlement in the Roman era. Today, the peninsula is dotted with impossibly picturesque hamlets and villages, including the world-famous port and celebrity mecca of Portofino. There are also magnificent walks to be done, as well as all kinds of maritime sports, including some great diving.

A splendid view of the rocky coast close to Portofino

Camogli
(see p108)

San Fruttuoso

Cristo degli Abissi
This bronze statue by Guido Galletti was lowered into the sea at San Fruttuoso in 1954, a symbol of the attachment of the Ligurian people to the sea. Every year, on the last Sunday in July, garlands of flowers are given to the statue in memory of those who have lost their lives at sea. Divers pay homage to the statue at all times of the year.

★ **San Fruttuoso**
A symbol of the Italian heritage and conservation organization FAI, to which it has belonged since 1983, San Fruttuoso is a delightful village with houses grouped around a Benedictine abbey, built by the Doria family in the 1200s . It is dominated by the church's octagonal bell tower. Alongside is the cloister and mausoleum of the Doria family. San Fruttuoso is accessible only by boat or on foot: it is 30 minutes by boat from Camogli, for example, or 75 minutes' walk from Portofino.

Paraggi

In Paraggi, a short distance from Portofino, multicoloured houses are gathered around a small sandy cove, with terraces rising up the mountain behind. Nowadays, the once-flourishing trades of fishing and olive-pressing have given way to tourism. The views from here are beautiful.

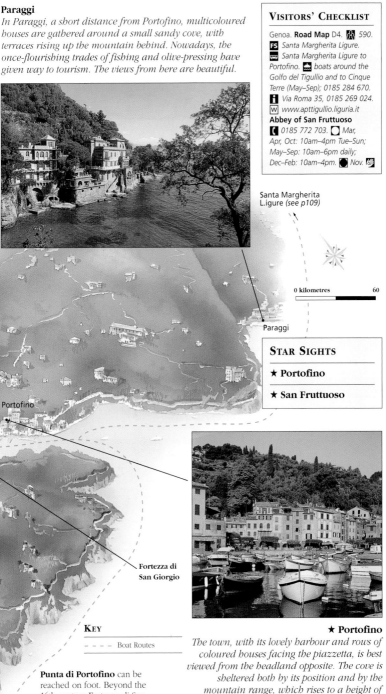

Santa Margherita
L.igure (see p109)

0 kilometres   60

Paraggi

VISITORS' CHECKLIST

Genoa. **Road Map** D4. 590.
Santa Margherita Ligure.
Santa Margherita Ligure to Portofino. boats around the Golfo del Tigullio and to Cinque Terre (May–Sep); 0185 284 670.
Via Roma 35, 0185 269 024.
www.apttigullio.liguria.it
Abbey of San Fruttuoso
0185 772 703. Mar, Apr, Oct: 10am–4pm Tue–Sun; May–Sep: 10am–6pm daily; Dec–Feb: 10am–4pm. Nov.

STAR SIGHTS

★ **Portofino**

★ **San Fruttuoso**

Portofino

Fortezza di
San Giorgio

KEY

– – – Boat Routes

Punta di Portofino can be reached on foot. Beyond the 16th-century Fortezza di San Giorgio, known as "Castle Brown", is the lighthouse and the Madonnina del Capo statue.

★ Portofino

The town, with its lovely harbour and rows of coloured houses facing the piazzetta, is best viewed from the headland opposite. The cove is sheltered both by its position and by the mountain range, which rises to a height of 600m (1,970 ft) and forms a 3-km (2-mile) long cliff behind the town. While small, the port still has space for 300 mooring berths.

View of Portofino's unmistakeable little harbour ▷

Chiavari ⓻

Genoa. **Road Map** E4.
👥 28,200. 🚉 🚌
🛈 Corso Assarotti 1, 0185 325 198.
ⓦ www.apttigullio.liguria.it
🎭 Festa patronale di Nostra Signora dell'Orto (2 Jul).

The abbey of Sant'Andrea di Borzone, in a stunning position

ONE OF THE principal cities in Liguria, Chiavari stands on an alluvial plan on the eastern shores of the Golfo del Tigullio and on the west bank of the Entella torrent. Called Clavarium, ("key to the valleys") by the Romans, the town was once known for its old crafts, particularly ship-building, chair-making and macramé. Nowadays, tourism is the most important source of income. The marina has space for some 450 boats.

The ruins of a necropolis, dating from the 8th–7th centuries BC, now held in the local archaeological museum, demonstrate that the area was inhabited by the Liguri Tigulli people in the pre-Roman era. The fortified town of Chiavari dates from 1178, when the Genoese expanded into the Riviera di Levante in their struggle to counter the power of the Fieschi family (arch rivals of the Doria dynasty).

The heart of Chiavari is Piazza Mazzini, around which the arcaded streets of the old city are laid out. One of these, Via dei Martiri della Liberazione, is a straight alleyway known as a "*carruggiu dritu*"; it was

The old centre of Chiavari, with its characteristic arcaded streets

occupied by the bourgeoisie from the 14th century. This street, Via Rivarola and Via Ravaschieri have porticoes made of the local slate.

The cathedral, **Nostra Signora dell'Orto**, has 17th-century origins but many alterations were carried out in the 19th–20th centuries. The interior, richly decorated with gilded stucco and marble inlay, contains works by Orazio De Ferrari and Anton Maria Maragliano. The parish church of San Giovanni Battista was founded in 1182 but was rebuilt in 1624.

In the outskirts, at Bacezza, is the 15th-century **Santuario della Madonna delle Grazie**, from where there is a lovely view stretching from Portofino to Sestri Levante. Inside is a 16th-century cycle of frescoes by Teramo Piaggio and Luca Cambiaso.

Abbazia di Sant'Andrea di Borzone ⓼

Via Abbazia 63, Borzonasca. **Road Map** E3. 🚉 Chiavari. 🚌 ℂ 0185 340 056. ⏰ until sunset daily. ♿ 📷

THE LOVELY abbey of Sant'Andrea di Borzone can be reached along a winding road that runs eastwards from the centre of Borzonasca, an inland town some 16 km (10 miles) from Chiavari.

Standing in splendid isolation, Sant'Andrea is one of the oldest Benedictine

settlements in Italy. It was founded in the 12th century by the monks of San Colombano in Bobbio (in Emilia-Romagna) and donated in 1184 to the Benedictines of Marseille, who reclaimed the land and used it for cultivation. The monks undertook a programme of terracing and irrigation: even today, despite the fact that the woods have begun to encroach, the remains of dry stone walls can still be seen along the paths. The abbey was rebuilt in the 13th century, at the behest of the Fieschi counts, but has managed to retain its original Romanesque look.

The church, with a square bell tower, is built of brick and stone. It has a single nave and a semicircular apse, and a cornice of terracotta arches. Several cloister columns survive from the old monastery. In the presbytery is a polyptych dating from 1484, by an unknown Genoese artist, and a slate tabernacle from 1513.

Santo Stefano d'Aveto ⓽

Genoa. **Road Map** E3. 👥 1,250. 🚌
🛈 Piazza del Popolo 6, 0185 880 46.
ⓦ www.apttigullio.liguria.it and www.parks.it
🎭 Cantamaggio (2 May).

SITUATED IN AN almost Alpine-looking hollow, dominated by Monte Maggiorasca, Santo Stefano is both a summer and a winter holiday resort. It is a popular centre for cross-country skiing. In summer, you can enjoy the simple pleasure of strolling around the pretty historic centre, with its winding alleys and small squares.

Close to the village are the isolated, imposing ruins of **Castello Malaspina**, built by the local nobles in the 12th century, and subsequently passed to the Fieschi and Doria families.

The Val d'Aveto was formed by the Aveto torrent, which carves out an upland plain southwest of the town, where pastures are enclosed by mountains covered in forests of silver fir, Norway spruce, and beech and ash trees. Much of this is now part of the **Parco Naturale Regionale dell'Aveto**.

From Santo Stefano, you can reach Monte Aiona, the tallest peak in the park at 1,700 m (5,576 ft), along trails that show off the beauty of this wild, unspoilt area. Note that the western slopes form part of the **Riserva Naturale delle Agoraie** and are open only to those doing scientific research.

Another area of interest is the great forest of Le Lame, where there are marshes and small lakes of glacial origin. The icy cold water has perfectly preserved some 2,500-year-old fir trunks, which can be seen lying on the bottom of Lago degli Abeti.

San Salvatore dei Fieschi, Lavagna

Lavagna ⑩

Genoa. **Road Map** E4.
🚶 12,900. 🚆 ℹ️ *Piazza della Libertà 48/A, 0185 395 070.*
🌐 *www.apttigullio.liguria.it*
🎉 *Torta dei Fieschi (7–14 Aug).*

T HE TOWN OF LAVAGNA lies across the Entella from Chiavari, to which it is linked by several bridges, including the fine medieval Ponte della Maddalena.

In the Middle Ages this coastal town was a stronghold of the local Fieschi counts. Historically, its prosperity has been due largely to the local slate quarries. Nowadays, the town depends more on its beach and marina, which has space for more than 1,500 yachts.

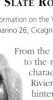
Logo of the Parco Naturale dell'Aveto

The town's medieval heart developed inland from the sea, from what is now Via Nuova Italia. Historic monuments include the church of **Santo Stefano**, dating from the 10th century, but rebuilt in 1653, when a Baroque staircase and asymmetrical bell towers were added; the imposing 17th-century Palazzo Franzone, now the town hall; and the church of **Santa Giulia di Centaura** (1654), reached along a scenic road from Viale Mazzini and with panoramic views along the coast.

ENVIRONS: a short drive or 30 minutes' walk inland from Lavagna lies the village of San Salvatore di Cogorno, from where you can reach the **Basilica di San Salvatore dei Fieschi**, one of the most important Romanesque-Gothic monuments in Liguria. It was commissioned in 1245 by Ottobono Fieschi, the future Pope Hadrian V and nephew of Pope Innocent IV (another Fieschi), who made it a basilica in 1252. The building lies in a particularly lovely setting, on the top of a hill surrounded in olive groves, and surrounded by ancient buildings, among them the ruined 13th-century Palazzo dei Conti Fieschi.

The church is dominated by a powerful square tower which rises over the crossing. It has cornices of blind arches and four-mullioned windows, and is crowned with a tall spire with four pinnacles. The upper façade features alternating bands of marble and slate, and a large rose window. The marble and slate striped bands are repeated inside the rather austere interior, and slate is used elsewhere, too, in the form of tiles in the transept and presbytery.

🏛️ **Basilica di San Salvatore dei Fieschi**
Piazza Innocenzo IV, San Salvatore di Cogorno. 📞 *0185 380 245.*
🕐 *8am–noon, 1:30–6pm daily (7pm in summer)..*

Sestri Levante **⓫**

Genoa. **Road Map** E4.
🏠 *19,000.* FS 🚌 **🛈** *Piazza Sant'Antonio 10, 0185 457 011.*
w *www.apttigullio.liguria.it*
🎭 *Premio letterario per la fiaba Hans Christian Andersen (end May).*

A T THE FAR WESTERN point of the Golfo del Tigullio, Sestri Levante is one of the liveliest resorts on the coast.

Fishing boats on the Baia del Silenzio at Sestri Levante

It clusters around a rocky peninsula known as the "Isola". In the heart of the old town, the most interesting monuments are the **Basilica of Santa Maria di Nazareth** by Giovan Battista Carlone (1604–16); **Palazzo Durazzo Pallavicini** (17th century), now the town hall; and the lovely Romanesque church of **San Nicolò dell'Isola** (12th century).

Of much greater appeal altogether, however, is the wonderful Grand Hotel dei Castelli *(see p181)*, at the tip of the peninsula. Built in the 1920s on the site of an old castle, the hotel has a magnifi-cent park overlooking two bays: the sandy **Baia delle Favole**, named after Hans Christian Andersen, who stayed here in 1833 (*favole* means fairy tales), is now rather built up; but the small-er and more secluded **Baia del Silenzio**, framed by multi-coloured houses and dotted with fishing boats, is utterly charming. Also in the grounds is the tower where Marconi

carried out some of his radio experiments in 1934.

Back in the old town, the **Galleria Rizzi** has paintings, sculptures, ceramics and furniture collected by the local Rizzi family. The paintings include works by Giovanni Andrea De Ferrari and Alessandro Magnasco.

🏛 **Galleria Rizzi**
Via dei Cappuccini 4. **📞** *0185 413 00.* ☐ *Apr–Oct: 10:30am–1pm Sun; May–Sep: 4–7pm Wed, (mid-Jun–Sep: 9:30–11:30pm Fri, Sat).* 🖼

Varese Ligure **⓬**

La Spezia. **Road Map** E4.
🏠 *2,500.* 🚌 *from Sestri Levante.*
🛈 *Via Portici 19, 0187 842 094 (in high season).*
w *www.aptcinqueterre.sp.it*

T HIS PRETTY, INLAND summer resort was, for centuries, an important market town and stopping place on the route north to Parma, in Emilia-Romagna. After the decline in traffic across the mountains in the 19th century, it acquired the rural role the town still has today. Agriculture is the main trade.

Varese Ligure was a possession of the Fieschi family, who obtained it in fief from Emperor Frederick 1 (Barbarossa) in 1161. They built the rather splendid 15th-century castle. This stands in a piazza which was once the market square, around which the so-called **Borgo Rotondo** was built: almost perfectly circular, with a continuous screen of buildings, this ring of shops and houses around the market was an ingenious

defensive idea dreamt up by the Fieschis. Charming to look at, the multicoloured façades are supported by arches and porticoes. The 16th-century **Borgo Nuovo**, which grew up alongside, features aristocratic palazzi dating from the 16th to 19th centuries, a long, affluent period for the town.

Nearby, crossed by a medieval bridge, is the River Crovana. This is one of the tributaries of the Vara, whose valley, the **Val di Vara**, extends for more than 60 km (37 miles) and has a varied landscape, among the best preserved in the region. The upper reaches of the river flow through wonderful mountain scenery, among woods of beech and chestnut, interspersed by meadows where cows and horses graze; elsewhere there are scenic stretches where the river is confined between rocks. Towards the coast the valley widens and the river flows through the Parco Naturale Regionale di Montemarcello-Magra *(see p126).*

Moneglia **⓭**

Genova. **Road Map** E4.
🏠 *2,700.* FS 🚌
🛈 *Corso Longhi 32, 0185 490 576.*
w *www.prolocomoneglia.it*
🎭 *Mostra-Mercato dell'Olio d'Oliva (mid-Apr).*

T HE TOWN once known as Monilia faces a small gulf which interrupts the high, jagged cliff extending between Sestri Levante and Deiva Marina. Moneglia is a typical fishing town, with picturesque *carruggi* and

View of the unusual Borgo Rotondo in Varese Ligure

The beach at Moneglia in summer, crowded with tourists

slate roofs, and a thoroughly gentle pace.

Long years of loyalty to the Republic of Genoa have left many traces: among them, the **Fortezza Monleone**, dating from 1173, and the 16th-century **Castello di Villafranca**, on the slopes above the town centre.

The striped parish church of **Santa Croce** (1726) has a *Last Supper* by Luca Cambiaso, the great 16th-century artist who was born in Moneglia. Inside, there are also two links from the chain that once closed the gates of Pisa, trophies from the battle of Meloria *(see p38)*, in which the Monegliese helped Genoa to defeat Pisa.

There is lots of scope for swimming at Moneglia, especially beneath the cliffs, and you can go on lovely walks through the maquis west towards Punta Baffe and Punta Manara, or through hillside villages and scenic vineyards towards the Bracco mountain pass.

Bonassola ⑭

La Spezia. **Road Map** E4. 🏛 *1,000.*
🚉 🚌 ℹ️ *Via Fratelli Rezzano, 0187 813 500.* 🌐 *www.prolocobonassola.it*
🎭 *Madonna del Rosario (first weekend in Oct).*

BUILT AROUND A COVE, in a splendid spot, Bonassola was selected by the Genoese in the 13th century as the site for a naval base.

These days, Bonassola has no marina, but it is not difficult to land small boats here. The town also has a wide beach, mostly pebbles, and the sea bed is varied and suited to dives of medium difficulty.

Sights of interest include the parish church of **Santa Caterina** (16th century), with sumptuous Baroque decoration and numerous ex votos, evidence of the busy seafaring lives of the inhabitants. The tiny church of **Madonna della Punta**, built on a cliff jutting out over the sea to the west of the village, is the focus of a popular sunset walk.

Several old villages in the vicinity are worth exploring, either on foot or by car. One path, following a route through vineyards and olive groves, takes walkers the 9 km (6 miles) to **Montaretto**, known for its production (albeit limited) of good white wine.

Santa Croce bell tower, in Moneglia

Levanto ⑮

La Spezia. **Road Map** E4. 🏛 *5,800.*
🚉 ℹ️ *Piazza Mazzini, 0187 808 125.* 🌐 *www.aptcinqueterre.sp.it.*
🎭 *Festa del mare (24–25 Jul).*

OVER THE YEARS, Levanto has been a centre for trade, agriculture and, most recently, tourism: it has a long and lovely beach. The small town is divided into Borgo Antico, the

medieval district around the church of Sant'Andrea and the hill of San Giacomo, and the Borgo Nuovo, which grew up in the 15th century on the nearby plain. In the medieval district is the lovely Loggia del Comune (13th century), the Casa Restani, with a 13th–14th-century portico, a castle (privately owned) and a stretch of the old town walls, dating from 1265.

The principal monument is the parish church of **Sant' Andrea**, a lovely example of Ligurian Gothic. The façade is striped with white marble and local serpentine (a softish green stone), with a finely carved rose window. Serpentine is also used in the capitals of the columns in the nave. Works of art inside include two canvases from a polyptych by Carlo Braccesco (1495) depicting *Saints Augustine and Jerome* and *Saints Blaise and Pantaleon*. In the ex-oratory of the church is a **Museo Permanente della Cultura Materiale**, which reconstructs various aspects of the rural and seafaring life of the Riviera di Levante.

Among vestiges of Levanto's more recent past are several important palazzi (often with painted façades) dating from the 17th and 18th centuries, when many Genoese noble families chose to build their summer residences here: **Palazzo Vannoni**, facing on to Piazza Cavour, is the most important one.

🏛 **Museo Permanente della Cultura Materiale**
Piazzetta Massola 4.
📞 *0187 817 776.*
🕐 *Jul, Aug: 9–11pm Tue–Sun; at other times by request.* 📷

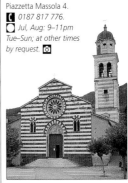
Sant'Andrea in Levanto

The Cinque Terre ^⑯

Tᴿᴬɴsʟᴜᴄᴇɴᴛ sᴇᴀ and cliffs plunging into the water; towns clinging to rocky slopes, and terraces dug into the contours of the mountains directly behind the coast. These are the Cinque Terre (Five Lands), today a national park encompassing some 20 km (12 miles) of coast and the immediate hinterland. A UNESCO World Heritage site, this is a place where the relationship between man and the environment is preserved in miraculous equilibrium. The five small towns on the coast that give the area its name are Monterosso al Mare, Vernazza, Corniglia, Manarola and Riomaggiore. The coastal paths are great for both walking and horse riding *(see p201)*, and you can go diving, too. Access is primarily by foot, boat or train (rather than car), and note that accommodation gets very booked up in high season.

Monterosso al Mare ①
For Italians, the words of writer Eugenio Montale (1896–1981), who holidayed here as a child, capture the atmosphere of Monterosso. Alongside the old town is the popular tourist area of Fegina, with a sandy beach.

LEVANTO

PIGNONE

PIGNONE

S.Antonia
Semaforo

0 kilometres   1

0 miles   1

The Terraces ②
The steep-sided landscape of the Cinque Terre is an extraordinary example of an architectural landscape. The terraces sculpted out of the mountain slopes have been used primarily to cultivate olives and vines (from which the highly coveted Sciacchetrà fortified wine – *see p187* – is made).

Vernazza ③
With its colourful houses clustered around an inlet, Vernazza is the only town in the Cinque Terre to have a harbour; this is known to have been in use in antiquity. The port has made Vernazza the richest village in the area, while the combination of the surroundings and architectural grace also make it the prettiest place in the Cinque Terre.

Corniglia ④

This town, built high on a ridge, 100 m (320 ft) above a beautiful and sheltered beach, was called Cornelia by the Romans. The beach has a history almost totally separate from that of the town above, which has always been an agricultural centre. The local vineyards produce limited quantities of white Cinque Terre and Sciacchetrà wine.

VISITORS' CHECKLIST

La Spezia. **Map** E–F4. **FS**
i **Corniglia** station, 0187 812 523; **Manarola** station, 0187 760 511; **Monterosso al Mare** station, 0187 817 059; **Riomaggiore** station, 0187 760 091; **Vernazza** station, 0187 812 533. Compulsory Carta Cinque Terre gives access to transport, paths and maps.
W www.aptcinqueterre.sp.it.
W www.parconazionale5terre.com

Manarola ⑥

Clinging to a cliff overlooking the sea, the village of Manarola makes a striking sight with its compact, coloured houses.

The Strada dei Santuari ⑤

This tortuous path across often cultivated land is cut into the mountainside and links the five coastal towns. It can be covered on foot, by bicycle or on horseback, and offers superlative views.

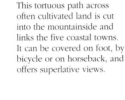

Menhir di M. Capri ●

Volastra

● Groppo

KEY

━━ Coastal Tour route

━━ Mountain route

══ Other roads

── Railway

── River

─ ─ Ferry

Via dell'Amore ⑦

Constructed in the 1920s, the Via dell'Amore (Path of Love) traces a route from Manarola to Riomaggiore. The path, cut into the steep cliffs, is just 2 km (1 mile) long and easy to walk, but is scenic, thrilling and justifiably renowned.

Riomaggiore ⑧

The headquarters of the national park, Riomaggiore has two rows of tall narrow houses and lots of seafood restaurants. You can go diving off nearby Punta di Montenero.

The church in the pretty medieval village of Campiglia

Campiglia ⓱

La Spezia. **Road Map** F5. *150.*
La Spezia. *from La Spezia.*
APT Cinque Terre, 0187 770 900.
www.campiglia.net and
www.tramontidicampiglia.it

THIS RURAL VILLAGE, founded in the Middle Ages and occupying a precipitous position near the coast only a short distance from La Spezia, is fascinating and magical.

Campiglia was built on an old mule road along the ridge between Portovenere and Levanto, and it is still a great starting point for walks. The most beautiful, and hardest, walk is along CAI (Italian Alpine Club) path no. 11. This takes you through the spectacular terrain of the **Tramonti**, a continuation of the Cinque Terre with terraces of vines, until you descend a steep flight of 2,000 steps, as far as the small beach of Punta del Persico: the landscape open to the sea is genuinely breathtaking.

Portovenere ⓲

La Spezia. **Road Map** F5.
4,600. *La Spezia.*
Piazza Bastreri 7, 0187 790 691.
www.portovenere.it *Festa della Madonna Bianca (17 Aug).*

PORTUS VENERIS (the port of Venus) was fêted for its beauty as far back as Roman times. Nowadays, its beauty and cachet even rival those of Portofino.

Lying at the base of the rocky cliff that fringes the western side of the Golfo della Spezia, Portovenere looks like a typical fortified fishing village, with rows of gaily painted houses on the slope down to the harbour. Behind is a maze of narrow alleys and vaulted staircases, populated by Portovenere's famous cats.

At the tip of the headland, in a superb position, is the striped church of **San Pietro**, built in 1277 in honour of the patron saint of fishermen. It incorporates elements of a 6th-century, Early Christian church and has a small Romanesque loggia, open to the sea.

Also worth visiting is **San Lorenzo**, a short walk up an alley from the harbour. This beautiful Romanesque church was built in the 12th century, but reworked in the Gothic and Renaissance eras. It has a wonderfully rustic font inside.

If you keep going (it's a steep climb), you reach the 16th-century **castello**. Built by the Genoese, this is a grandiose example of military architecture, and also offers fantastic views. It is linked to the town by a line of walls with square towers. The remains of various medieval fortifications are still visible around Portovenere.

Le Grazie, along the winding route north from Portovenere to La Spezia, is another place of great beauty. Monte Muzzerone nearby is hugely popular among free-climbers. The village itself is home to the church of Santa Maria delle Grazie (15th century), and the 16th-century monastery of the Olivetans. By the inlet of Varignano, nearby, is a ruined **Roman villa** (2nd to 1st centuries BC), with a mosaic pavement and a small museum, known as the **Antiquarium**.

Castello
0187 791 106.
8:30–11am Mon–Sat.
Antiquarium del Varignano
Le Grazie. *0187 790 307.*
on request.

The church of San Pietro at Portovenere, overlooking the sea

Palmaria, Tino and Tinetto ⓳

La Spezia. **Road Map** F5.
from La Spezia or Portovenere for Isola Palmaria, 0187 732 987.
IAT Portovenere, 0187 790 691.

LIGURIA'S ONLY archipelago once formed part of the headland of Portovenere.

The largest island, **Isola Palmaria,** is divided from the mainland by just a narrow channel. It is covered in dense vegetation on one side, and has steep cliffs and caves on the other. In the past, Portor marble, a valuable black stone used in some

The harbour at Portovenere, with its characteristic painted houses

The island of Palmaria, the largest in the Ligurian archipelago

buildings in Portovenere, was quarried here, which has partially disfigured the island. Palmaria is a popular among the locals, who come for day trips, but the island's appeal can't compete with that of the mainland.

The much smaller islands of Tino and Tinetto are in a military zone. Access to **Tino** is allowed only on 13 September, for the Festa di San Venerio. There is a ruined 11th-century abbey, built on the site of a chapel where the hermit saint lived in solitude. The island lighthouse guides ships into the gulf.

Tinetto is an inhospitable rock, but the rich sea beds make this a popular diving area. The ruins of two religious buildings confirm the earliest known Christian presence in the area (5th century).

La Spezia ⑳

See pp124–5.

San Terenzo ㉑

La Spezia. **Road Map** F5.
FS *La Spezia.* ☐ ⬛ *Lerici, 0187 967 346.*

SAN TERENZO LIES on the northern side of the Golfo della Spezia, overlooking the pretty bay of Lerici. Once a small group of fishermen's houses clustered on the shore, San Terenzo was a favourite among certain 19th-century poets, including Percy Bysshe Shelley. (Casa Magni, the last home Shelley shared with his wife Mary, is nearby.) Today, sadly, the village is suffering from the effects of mass tourism.

Sights to visit include a castle on a rocky promontory nearby; the church of Santa Maria Assunta; and Villa Marigola, with lovely gardens.

Lerici ㉒

La Spezia. **Road Map** F5.
🚶 *12,000.* FS *La Spezia.* ⬛
🛈 *Via Biaggini 6, 0187 967 346.*
🎭 *festa di Sant'Erasmo (Jul).*

IN THE MIDDLE AGES Lerici was a major port, and enjoyed both commercial and strategic importance. Today, it is a

The port of Lerici, dominated by an imposing castle

popular tourist town, but one that manages to still feel like a working community with a strong identity.

The old centre is dominated by the **Castello**, the most important example of military architecture in the region. Built by the Pisans in the 13th century to counter a Genoese fort at Portovenere, it was taken by Genoa shortly afterwards; they enlarged it in the 15th century. It is still in a remarkably good state, with its pentagonal tower and massive walls. There is an archaeological museum inside.

Below the castle is the lovely (and sandy) Baia di Maralunga, good for a swim.

⚓ Castello and Museo
Piazza San Giorgio. 📞 *0187 969 042.*
☐ *mid-Oct–mid-Mar: 10:30am–12:30pm Tue–Fri; 10:30am–12:30pm, 2:30–5:30pm Sat, Sun, public hols; mid-Mar–Jun, Sep–mid-Oct: 10:30am–1pm, 2:30–6pm Tue–Sun; Jul–Aug: 10:30am–12:30pm, 6:30pm–midnight Tue–Sun.* ⬤ *Mon.* 🎫

THE GULF OF POETS

It was the Italian playwright Sem Benelli who first described the Gulf of Lerici as the "Gulf of Poets" in 1919. It is an evocative and romantic epithet, and not inaccurate given the personalities who came here in the 19th and 20th centuries: including Percy Bysshe Shelley (who drowned at sea en route to La Spezia from Livorno, in 1822, and was cremated at Viareggio) and his wife Mary (author of *Frankenstein*), Lord Byron, DH Lawrence and Virginia Woolf. The gulf still has strong appeal today and attracts

artists and intellectuals, mainly Italians. As a consequence a "cultural park" has been established, called the Parco Culturale Golfo dei Poeti, joining similar parks dedicated to Eugenio Montale, in the Cinque Terre, and in the Val di Magra and Terra di Luni. For more information contact the tourist office APT Cinque Terre-Golfo dei Poeti in La Spezia *(see p207).*

Shelley

The Castello di San Terenzo seen at night ▷

La Spezia ⑳

One of the cannons on the seafront at La Spezia

THE PORT OF LA SPEZIA has been important since antiquity as a trading centre for produce from all over the world, especially spices (*la spezia* means spice in Italian). In the 13th century, the Fieschi family transformed what had been a fishing village into a fortress surrounded by walls. The city expanded and a second defensive ring was built in the 1600s. This city was lauded by poets in the 19th century, and attracted generations of European travellers, drawn by La Spezia's elegance and attractive position on the gulf. The city, and its role, changed radically after 1861, when the Savoy government began construction of a naval base. Today, traces of the distant past are tucked away amid the sprawling metropolis. The naval base and port are still thriving.

⚓ Arsenale Militare and Museo Navale

Viale Amendola 1. **[** 0187 783 016. **○** Sep–Jun: 8:30am–6pm Mon–Sat, 10:15am–3:45pm Sun; Jul–Aug 8:30am–1pm Mon–Sat, 8:30am–1:15pm Sun. **●** 1 Jan, 15 Aug, 8, 24–26 Dec. 🅿 🔲 📷 no flash.

In exile on St Helena, Napoleon, tracing a portrait of the Italian peninsula, wrote of La Spezia that "it is the most beautiful port in the universe; its defence by land and by sea is easy... maritime institutions would be sheltered here". It was not Napoleon, however, who transferred the naval base from Genoa to La Spezia, but the Savoy government under Camillo Cavour.

Construction of the colossal site began in 1861. The city inevitably expanded as a result of the building of the base, and from 1861 to 1881 the number of inhabitants tripled. Badly damaged by bombing in World War II and further damaged by German troops, who occupied the site between 1943 and 1945, the base was reconstructed with meticulous care.

The structure today shows how the designer, colonel Domenico Chiodo, responded carefully to the practical requirements: the workshops are located close to the

Figurehead, Museo Navale

entrance for the convenience of the workers, the general warehouse and offices are placed at the centre of the entire complex, and so on. The predominant style is Neo-Classical. It is possible to visit parts of the base, including the old workshops, sailmakers' yards, masonry docks and the swing bridge.

The **Museo Tecnico Navale della Marina Militare** is one of Italy's oldest and most important naval museums. The core of its collection dates back to the 16th century, and was started by Emanuele Filiberto of Savoy, who gathered mementoes from the Battle of Lepanto (1571). Models help to illustrate the history of the port; there is also a fine collection of anchors (around 120 different ones) and a good display of 28 figureheads from old sailing ships.

🏛 Museo Amedeo Lia

Via Prione 234. **[** 0187 731 100. **○** 10am–6pm Tue–Sun. **●** 1 Jan, 15 Aug, 25 Dec. 🅿 ♿ 📷 🚫

This excellent and award-winning museum, opened in 1996, is based around the works donated by Amedeo Lia and his family. It is housed in part of the ancient church and monastery of the monks of San Francesco da Paola, restored for the purpose. The museum includes paintings and miniatures, medieval ivory, Limoges enamels, medals and numerous archaeological finds from excavations around the Mediterranean basin.

Paintings are the collection's most significant element: indeed, the 13th-century and 14th-century paintings form one of the finest private collections in Europe.

Besides fine works by Paolo di Giovanni Fei, Pietro Lorenzetti, Sassetta and Lippo di Benivieni, there are two 16th-century highlights: a presumed *Self Portrait* (1520) by Pontormo, painted, unusually, using tempera on terracotta, and a *Portrait of a Gentleman* (1510) by Titian.

The 17th-century paintings by followers of Caravaggio are also worth seeking out, as are the Venetian views by Canaletto, Bellotto, Marieschi and Guardi. There are also bronzes from the 16th and 17th centuries.

Self Portrait by Pontormo, Museo Amedeo Lia

♣ Castello di San Giorgio

Via XXVII Marzo. **[** 0187 751 142. **○** see Museo Archeologico.

The oldest architectural vestige of centuries past, the Castello di San Giorgio occupies a commanding position overlooking the city. The imposing fortification was commissioned by the Fieschi family in the 13th century, though what you see today dates from a reconstruction that took place

Castello di San Giorgio, home to the Museo Archeologico

in the 14th century, and from defence work carried out in the 17th century. Following major restoration work, the castle is now home to the Museo Civico Archeologico.

⌂ Museo Civico Archeologico Ubaldo Formentini

Castello di San Giorgio, Via XXVII Marzo. **⦿** 0187 751 142.
⦿ summer: 9:30am–12:30pm, 5–8pm daily; winter: 9:30am–12:30pm, 2–5pm. ⦿ Tue (except hols), 1 Jan, 24, 25 Dec. ⦿ ⦿ ⦿ ⦿
w www.castagna.it/sangiorgio
This museum was established in the 19th century as a home for the many archaeological finds and fossils discovered in the city environs, mainly as a

result of excavation work carried out when the naval base was being built.

Some of these finds provide evidence of the first human settlements in the Lunigiana area: coins and ceramics dating from the prehistoric, Etruscan and Roman eras are among the objects found near the ancient city of Luni (*see p127*). Also of interest are paleolithic finds from the Grotta dei Colombi on the island of Palmaria.

The most significant section of the museum is, however, the collection of statue-stelae, sculptures in sandstone dating from the Bronze and Iron ages, depicting in stylized form warriors grasping weapons and figures of women. Although typical art of the Lunigiana, their function and signifi-cance are unclear.

♙ Chiesa Santa Maria dell'Assunta

Piazza Beverini.
⦿ 9:30–11am, 3–5:30pm daily.
This 14th-century church has been modified more than once. Its appearance today, with its black and white façade, owes

Statue-stele at the Museo Archeologico

much to reconstruction after the war. It contains a *Coronation of the Virgin*, a glazed terracotta relief by Andrea Della Robbia and a *Martyrdom of St Bartholomew* (16th century) by Luca Cambiaso.

♙ Pieve di San Venerio

This charming parish church dates from the 11th century, although excavations carried out in the last century have revealed much earlier, even Roman, origins. The façade is decorated with a two-mullioned window and is flanked by a bell tower. The interior has two aisles, the older of which ends, unusually, in two apses.

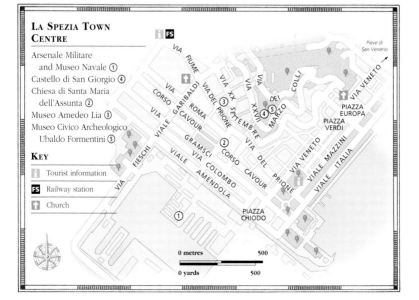

LA SPEZIA TOWN CENTRE

Arsenale Militare and Museo Navale ①
Castello di San Giorgio ④
Chiesa di Santa Maria dell'Assunta ②
Museo Amedeo Lia ③
Museo Civico Archeologico Ubaldo Formentini ⑤

KEY

⦿ Tourist information
⦿ Railway station
⦿ Church

0 metres 500
0 yards 500

A picturesque alley in Tellaro

Fiascherino and Tellaro ㉓

La Spezia. **Road Map** F5.
🏠 800. 🚉 La Spezia. 🚌
ℹ️ Lerici, 0187 967 346.
🅦 www.aptcinqueterre.sp.it
🎭 Natale Subacqueo (24 Dec).

THESE TWO pretty fishing villages of painted houses lie next to each other, just south of Lerici. Both face small bays, with verdant hills behind.

Tiny **Fiascherino** has a lovely beach, and the cliffs conceal enchanting coves accessible only by boat. The writer DH Lawrence lived in the village from 1913–14.

Thanks to its position on the cliffs high above the sea, medieval **Tellaro** has preserved its original features almost intact, though the instability of the rock itself has caused some damage. The oldest part is built on a promontory that marks the furthermost limit of the Riviera di Levante: the tall houses here had to be built on different levels in order to accommodate the terrain. The village's extremely narrow streets are linked by flights of steps and tunnels. The Baroque church of San Giorgio overlooks the sea, while the Oratory of In Selàa has a lovely courtyard, which also faces the water.

Montemarcello ㉔

La Spezia. **Road Map** F5. 🏠 4,600.
🚉 La Spezia. 🚌 ℹ️ Via Nuova 48, 0187 691 071 (seasonal). **Parco N R Montemarcello-Magra**, Via Paci Agostino 2, Sarzana, 0187 600 324.
🅦 www.parcomagra.it
🅦 www.aptcinqueterre.sp.it

THIS TOWN on the eastern fringes of the Golfo della Spezia offers fantastic views, both west towards the gulf and east towards the Versilia coast.

Montemarcello doesn't share the structure common to hilltowns: lacking the traditional concentric arrangement, it is instead laid out on a square network, echoing the layout of the original Roman military camp, or *castrum*. The houses in the oldest part, still partially enclosed by the remains of the town walls, are painted in the bright colours usually seen in coastal towns, an anomaly in a mountain village. Indeed, the street layout and the architectural style of the houses give Montemarcello a particular and unusual atmosphere, more akin to an elegant holiday resort than a rural village. As such, it has become a discreet haven for Italian intellectuals and artists – a situation that has, in effect, saved Montemarcello from attempts at major development.

The landscape around the town is delightful: this is the southern tract of the **Parco Naturale Regionale Montemarcello-Magra**, Liguria's only river park, which offers great opportunities for walks, with several marked walking trails. The park extends from the summit of the eastern headland of the Golfo della Spezia as far as the plain of the river Magra. In the southern stretches, near Bocca di Magra, the vegetation and the wildlife are typically Mediterranean, while in the northern part of the park cultivated fields and wetlands alternate.

Logo of the Parco di Montemarcello

Ameglia ㉕

La Spezia. **Road Map** F5. 🏠 4,500.
🚉 Sarzana, Santo Stefano Magra.
🚌 ℹ️ Via Fabbricotti, Bocca di Magra, 0187 608 037.
🅦 www.comune.ameglia.sp.it
🎭 Carnevale Amegliese (Feb).

ALTHOUGH IT IS NOT far from the mouth of the river Magra, Ameglia still has the look of a hill town. Tall, narrow houses are packed together around a hilltop where a castle once stood. Its ruins include a round tower and parts of the original walls; the main part was replaced in the Renaissance period by the Palazzo del Podestà, later the Palazzo Comunale (town hall).

From the summit, alleys extend in concentric circles, broken up by small squares. The piazza in front of the church of Santi Vincenzo e Anastasio is lovely, with views over the lower Lunigiana and the Apuan Alps. The church has a 16th-century marble door.

Bocca di Magra ㉖

La Spezia. **Road Map** F5. 🏠 4,300.
🚉 Sarzana, Santo Stefano Magra.
🚌 ℹ️ Via Fabbricotti, 0187 608 037.

ORIGINALLY a fishing village at the mouth (*bocca*) of the river Magra, this town manages to keep a grip on its heritage, despite its new role as a tourist resort. In addition to numerous holiday homes,

A glimpse of Montemarcello

The ancient Roman amphitheatre at Luni

there is a small beach, a spa and a well-equipped marina.

The coast here is very different from that of the Cinque Terre and the Golfo della Spezia: it is near here that the low-lying, sandy stretch, known as the Versilia coast, begins.

The appeal of Bocca di Magra, which stems largely from its combined seaside and riverside location, was not lost on writers, poets and other demanding holidaymakers, who were attracted to Bocca in the first half of the 20th century, just as they were to other towns in the area.

Nearby are the remains of a **Roman villa** dating from the 1st century AD. It is built on sloping terraces on the cliff, in a panoramic position above the mouth of the river.

Luni ②

Via Luni 37, Ortonovo (La Spezia). **Road Map** F5. 〓 📞 0187 668 11. **Site and museum** 🕘 9am–7pm Tue–Sun. ● 25 Dec, 1 Jan, 1 May.

T HE ROMAN COLONY of *Portus Lunae* was founded in 177 BC in an effort to counter the native Ligurians. Its role as an important port grew as Luni became a major channel for the shipping of marble from the nearby Apuan Alps (known as Luni marble) to all corners of the Roman empire.

Luni's prosperity faltered during the early centuries of the Middle Ages, due to the tailing-off of the marble trade, with full-blown decline accompanying the silting-up of the harbour. (The coast is now 2 km/1 mile away.) In

1204, the bishopric was moved to nearby Sarzana, and soon, all that was left of Luni was its name, which had also given the surrounding area its title, the Lunigiana.

The archaeological site at Luni is the most important in northern Italy. Surrounded by walls, the city was built to a perfectly regular layout, with the public buildings equally neatly placed. A great temple and several prestigious houses stood near the huge, marble-paved Forum. Nearby was the Capitolium, a temple dedicated to Jove, Juno and Minerva, encircled by a marble-edged basin and with a flight of steps in front. Remains of these buildings are still visible.

Nearby was the Casa dei Mosaici, with an atrium in Corinthian style surrounded by rooms with mosaic floors; some of these 3rd–4th century AD mosaics survive. The vast Casa degli Affreschi was built around a garden and had numerous rooms with fine floors and frescoes. Inside the walls there are also the ruins of the Early Christian basilica of Santa Maria, including the remains of three early Romanesque apses and the base of a bell tower.

Outside the walls is the amphitheatre, built in the Antonine era (1st–2nd centuries AD) and the scene of bloody gladiatorial fights. The lower section of stepped seats, as well as part of a covered portico, survives. The complex system of steps and corridors that led to the seating is still visible.

On the site of the Forum is an **archaeological museum**, with displays of

Imperial-era marble statues, busts, fragments of frescoes, jewellery, tools, stamps and ceramics.

Castelnuovo di Magra ②

La Spezia. **Road Map** F5. 🏠 8,000. 🚉 Sarzana, Santo Stefano Magra. 🚌 ℹ Via Aurelia 241, 0187 693 306. 🎭 Corteo Storico "A Pace de Dante" (end Aug).

I T SEEMS PROBABLE that the origins of this inland town coincided with the decline of nearby Luni and the abandonment of the port by its inhabitants.

Castelnuovo, built on a hilltop in view of the mouth of the River Magra, is spread out attractively along a ridge, with the church at one end and the bishop's palace (a 13th-century castle) at the other. Linking these two landmarks is Via Dante, lined with handsome palazzi with elegant façades. Sections of the old town walls and two 15th-century towers are still visible.

The church at one end of Via Dante is **Santa Maria Maddalena**, built in the late 16th century but with a 19th-century façade. The marble columns inside are thought to have come from Santa Maria Assunta at Luni. Inside is a *Calvary* by Brueghel the Younger.

Between Castelnuovo and Luni, up a very winding road, is **Nicola**, a pretty medieval hilltop village centred around the church of Santi Filippo e Giacomo.

Nicola, near Castelnuovo

Sarzana ㉙

T<small>HIS</small> <small>LIVELY</small> agricultural and commercial centre has a splendid historic centre which has remained almost intact, despite being bombed during the war. Built by the River Magra and on the Via Francigena, the main land route between Rome and northern Europe, Sarzana was of strategic importance both under the Romans and in the Middle Ages. It is no surprise that such a desirable town was fought over at length by its most powerful neighbours, including Pisa and Florence, until in 1572 the town became a stable possession (and the easternmost outpost) of the Republic of Genoa. A sophisticated town, Sarzana has a famous antiques market and great shops.

Statue of the *Procellaria* in Piazza Matteotti

Church of Sant'Andrea
This ancient Romanesque church has a sober stone façade with an unusual 16th-century door decorated with caryatids.

PIAZZA MATTEOTTI

VIA BONAPARTE

VIA MA

VIA FIASELLA

VIA MAZZINI

VIA ROSSI

PIAZZA CALANDRIN

VIA DEI GIARDINI

PIAZZA NICOLO

Piazza Matteotti, with its distinctively tapered corner

★ **Cathedral**
The cathedral of Santa Maria Assunta, begun in 1204 after the transfer of the bishopric from Luni to Sarzana, was completed in the 15th century and modified in the 17th century. The 14th-century door, the finely carved marble rose window and the bell tower are all enchanting. Inside are two marble altarpieces (mid-1400s) by Leonardo Riccomanni.

LA FORTEZZA DI SARZANELLO

Just north of Sarzana, the Fortress of Sarzanello rises on a hill in an excellent strategic position from which to control the lower Lunigiana. Built for Castruccio Castracani, a lord of Lucca, in around 1322, it was altered in later centuries, including in 1493, when it was restored by the Florentines. The fortress is built on a triangular plan and has three cylindrical corner towers. Access is over a bridge, which straddles a deep moat.

VISITORS' CHECKLIST

La Spezia. **Road Map** F4–5.
🏛 20,000. 🚊 🚌 🛈 Piazza
San Giorgio, 0187 620 419.
🌐 www.aptcinqueterre.sp.it
🌐 www.sarzana.com
🗓 "Soffitta in Strada", crafts
and antiques market (3–22 Aug).

KEY

 Recommended route

★ Cittadella

This imposing fortress was built by Lorenzo the Magnificent, the powerful Medici ruler of Florence, from 1488–92. It is built on a rectangular plan with six round towers and a moat. The 16th-century walls were constructed by the Genoese.

| 0 metres | 50 |
| 0 yards | 50 |

VIA CASTRUCCIO

VIA FIASELLA

PIAZZA CITTADELLA

VIA MAZZINI

STAR SIGHTS

★ Cathedral

★ Cittadella

Via Mazzini corresponds to the ancient Via Francigena, which links the Neo-Classical Porta Romana and Porta Parma.

The Cross of Maestro Guglielmo, the work of a Tuscan artist, dated 1138, can be seen in the Cathedral. A key work, it was a prototype for the crucifixes painted in Tuscany and Umbria in the following two centuries.

Sarzanello

THE RIVIERA DI PONENTE

ITH THE CAPITAL CITY OF *Genoa at one end and Ventimiglia, on the border with France, at the other, the Riviera di Ponente extends for around* 150 km (93 miles). *There is spectacular scenery in the interior, and the coast is so green and lush that it is divided, fittingly, into the Riviera delle Palme (of palm trees) and the Riviera dei Fiori (of flowers).*

Any visitor to this area cannot fail to appreciate the mild climate of the coast, which has been exploited in the past for the cultivation of citrus fruits and is now used in the growing of cut flowers and house plants, adapting customs as well as the landscape in the creation of a new industry. Liguria is now one of the most important flower-growing areas in the world. It is no coincidence that San Remo, one of the main towns along this coast, is known as the "città dei fiori", or city of flowers. Olives are the other major crop, particularly around Imperia.

Like the Riviera di Levante, the Riviera di Ponente became a favourite holiday destination among the European aristocracy, particularly the British and the Russians, from the late 19th century. Hotels and Art Nouveau villas are still in evidence almost everywhere.

The western part of Liguria also has a rich history, evoked by numerous atmospheric towns and villages. You need head only a short distance inland to discover fascinating medieval towns which are in stark contrast to the touristy coastal towns. Traces of the Romans can also be found both on the coast and in the interior, such as the five Roman bridges in the Parco del Finalese (in whose limestone caves paleolithic utensils and burial tombs have been found), or the excavations of Albintimilium, ancient Ventimiglia.

In between excursions, as well as spending time on the beach or swimming in the sea, visitors can relax and breathe fresh clean air in one of the region's parks: such as the Parco Naturale del Monte Beigua, above Savona, with trees and plants of tremendous variety and numerous animal species.

Triora, in the hinterland behind Imperia, also known as the "village of witches"

◁ Palm trees in the gardens of Villa Ormond in San Remo

Exploring the Riviera di Ponente

T HE TWO PROVINCIAL CAPITALS on the Riviera di
Ponente are Savona and Imperia. San Remo,
with its grand Art Nouveau architecture, is the main
holiday resort. New developments have spoilt the
coast closest to Genoa, but there are many
interesting places to visit elsewhere along the coast:
these range from Noli, with its church of San
Paragorio, one of the key monuments of Ligurian
Romanesque, and Albenga, with its well-preserved
historic centre and its Early Christian baptistry, to the
splendid English gardens at Villa Hanbury, close to
the French border, and the nearby caves at Balzi
Rossi, a fascinating prehistoric site. In the hinterland,
the delightful medieval village of Dolceacqua is
especially worth a visit, as is Triora, famous for a
witch trial held here at the end of the 16th century.
The luxuriant vegetation and mild climate make this
part of the Ligurian coast a pleasure to explore.

Villa Hanbury, near Ventimiglia

SIGHTS AT A GLANCE

Alassio ⑮
Albenga (pp148–51) ⑭
Albisola Superiore ③
Albissola Marina ④
Andora ⑯
Balzi Rossi ㉙
Bergeggi ⑥
Bordighera ㉗
Borgio Verezzi ⑩
Cervo ⑰
Dolceacqua (pp166–7) ㉖
Dolcedo ⑳
Finale Ligure ⑨
Villa Hanbury
    (pp170–71) ㉚
Grotte di Toirano
    (pp146–7) ⑬
Imperia (pp154–7) ⑫ ⑲
Loano ⑫
Noli ⑧
Parco Naturale del
    Beigua ②

Pietra Ligure ⑪
Pieve di Teco ⑱
Pigna ㉕
San Remo ㉔
Savona (pp136–9) ⑤
Spotorno ⑦
Taggia ㉒
*Tour of the Armea and Crosia
    Valleys (pp160–61)* ㉓
Triora ㉑
Varazze ①
Ventimiglia ㉘

SEE ALSO

• *Where to Stay* pp181–3

• *Where to Eat* pp194–7

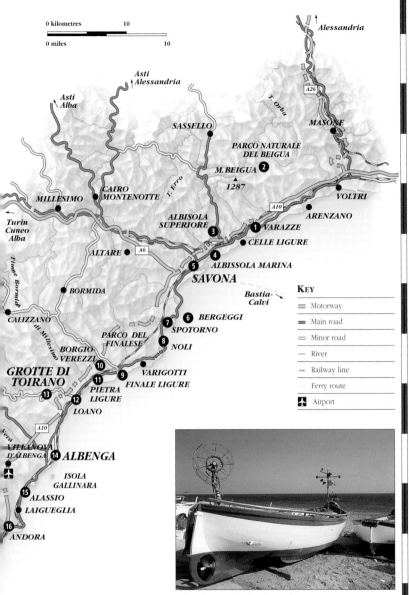

0 kilometres   10

0 miles   10

Alessandria

Asti
Alessandria

Asti
Alba

SASSELLO

MASONE

PARCO NATURALE
DEL BEIGUA

M.BEIGUA **2**
▲
1287

VOLTRI

MILLESIMO

CAIRO
MONTENOTTE

T. Erro

T. Orba

A26

ARENZANO

A10

ALBISOLA
SUPERIORE
3

1 VARAZZE

CELLE LIGURE

Turin
Cuneo
Alba

ALTARE ● *A6*

4

5 ALBISSOLA MARINA

SAVONA

Bastia-
Calvi

BORMIDA

Fiume Bormida

CALIZZANO

6 BERGEGGI

7

SPOTORNO

PARCO DEL
FINALESE

8 NOLI

BORGIO-
VEREZZI

10

9 VARIGOTTI

GROTTE DI
TOIRANO

11

FINALE LIGURE

13

12 PIETRA
LIGURE

LOANO

A10

Vena

VILLANOVA
D'ALBENGA **14** ALBENGA

ISOLA
GALLINARA

15 ALASSIO

LAIGUEGLIA

16

ANDORA

KEY

═══ Motorway

▬▬▬ Main road

═══ Minor road

── River

╍╍╍ Railway line

⋯⋯ Ferry route

✈ Airport

Fishing boats on the beach at Noli

GETTING AROUND

The main communication routes along the Riviera di Ponente are the A10, the motorway between Genoa and Ventimiglia, and the SS1, or Via Aurelia (once a Roman road), which runs parallel to the motorway at sea level, passing by all the main towns. The roads leading into the interior are narrow and twisting, although they do pass through very beautiful countryside. The A6, the motorway from Savona to Turin, gives access to Altare, Carcare and other towns located inland from the Riviera delle Palme. Regional, inter-regional and intercity trains connect Genoa and Ventimiglia (with up to 15 trains a day). It is also possible to get around using coaches, particularly if heading inland; the provincial coach companies operate a good network of services.

Varazze ❶

Savona. **Road Map** C3.
👥 14,000. 🚂 🚌
ℹ️ Corso Matteotti 54, 019 935 043.
🌐 www.inforiviera.it
🎭 Processione e Corteo Storico di Santa Caterina da Siena (30 Apr); Festa del Mare (early Aug).

AT THE EASTERN end of the Riviera di Ponente, Varazze is a major seaside resort, complete with a beach and palm-shaded promenade.

The town's name derives from the Roman name of *Varagine* ("trees"), though it was later known as *Ad Navalia* ("At the shipyards"). Both names were appropriate since much of the local wood was used for boat-building. The town was the birthplace of Jacopo da Varagine, a famous 13th-century friar and writer, and later a saint.

In the old centre, sights of interest include the church of **Sant'Ambrogio**, dating from 1535. Remaining from an earlier 14th-century construction is an imposing brick bell tower in the Lombard style, complete with a spire. The Neo-Renaissance façade, in Finale stone, was built in 1916. The courtyard was paved in beach pebbles, laid out in a pretty geometrical design. The façade of an earlier, Romanesque church dedicated to Sant'Ambrogio has been incorporated, curiously, into the **town walls**, an impressive work dating from the 12th century.

Built in 1419, but much modified since, the church of **San Domenico** is famous as the home of the silver urn containing the remains of

The Romanesque church of Sant'Ambrogio at Varazze

Jacopo da Varagine. There is also a polyptych (16th century) depicting *Blessed Jacopo and other saints*, by Simone da Pavia, and a 12th-century fresco, probably of the Sienese school, with a *Madonna delle Grazie*. A cannon ball, fired from a French ship in 1746, is embedded in the church façade.

From San Domenico you can go on a lovely seafront walk along disused railway tracks; various paths en route cut inland up to Monte Beigua.

ENVIRONS: Celle Ligure, 4 km (2 miles) west of Varazze, is a small fishing village with twisting *carruggi* (narrow streets) and a wall of hills behind. The tradition of painting the houses bright colours began so that sailors could make them out while still at sea.

The **Deserto di Varazze**, 9 km (6 miles) inland from Celle Ligure, is another lovely spot. It is a simple 17th-century hermitage associated with the barefoot Carmelite friars, surrounded by a dense wood.

Parco Naturale del Beigua ❷

Genoa/Savona. **Road Map** C3.
🚂 🚌 ℹ️ Ente Parco del Beigua, Corso Italia 3, Savona, 019 841 873 00. 🌐 www.parks.it

THIS DENSELY forested park covers an area of 17,000 ha (42,000 acres) and runs from the border with Piemonte down to the coast, east of Varazze. It is the biggest of the region's three national parks. and takes its name from Monte Beigua (1,300 m/4,265 ft), which is accessible by road. The grassy plain at the mountain summit

The seafront at Varazze

provides a platform for great views stretching for miles in all directions, and is a starting point for numerous walks.

The park's rocky heart is composed of ophiolites, also known as "green rocks" (mainly serpentine) – metamorphic rocks deriving from changes which occurred in the original igneous rock. Prehistoric axes found in this area are on display, along with other prehistoric utensils, at the Museo Civico Archeologico in Pegli, near Genoa (see p82). Prehistoric as well as more recent graffiti have also been discovered in Monte Beigua.

The flora and fauna in the park are very varied. In terms of the plant life, there are vast numbers of beeches, and the Alpine aster (*Aster alpinus*) is also common; drosera (*Drosera rotundifolia*), an insect-eating carnivorous plant, can be found in the wetland area known as the Riserva del Laione. And there is the scented daphne (*Daphne cneorum*), too, whose characteristic pink flowers have been chosen as the symbol of the park.

The wildlife is varied, too, and includes foxes, badgers, weasels, wild boar and roe

Scented daphne, symbol of the Parco del Beigua

deer. Two endemic species of amphibian – *Salamandrina terdigitata* and *Triturus vulgaris meridionalis* – have also been seen, here at their westernmost limit. From the southern slopes you can also see migratory birds in spring.

The park headquarters is in Sassello, a pretty town on the park's western fringes.

The remains of an Imperial-era Roman villa at Albisola Superiore

Albisola Superiore ❸

Savona. **Road Map** C3.
🏛 *12,000.* 🚉 🚌 🛈 *IAT Albisola Marina, Corso Ferrari, Albisola Marina, 019 400 20 08.*
🅆 *www.inforiviera.it*

KNOWN TO THE Romans as Alba Docilia, Albisola consists, in fact, of two parts: Albissola Marina, on the coast, and Albisola Superiore, a short way inland. The different spelling of Albisola perhaps indicates the towns' wish to reinforce their separation, but since the 15th century they have both enjoyed fame for their ceramics, made from the local clay and typically decorated in blue and white.

Albisola's ancient heritage can be seen in traces of a vast Roman **villa**, occupied from the 1st to 5th centuries AD. The parish church of **San Nicolò** was reconstructed in 1600 in the shadow of the castle, now in

Ceramic plate from Albisola

ruins. The Baroque wooden statues inside were carved by Maragliano and Schiaffino. A 17th-century oratory stands alongside.

Within a large park, adorned with fountains and statuary, stands **Villa Gavotti**, built in 1739–53 for the last doge of Genoa, Francesco Maria Della Rovere, replacing a 15th-century building. The sumptuous interior contains stuccoes by the Lombard school and local ceramics.

The villa is now home to the **Museo della Ceramica Manlio Trucco**, which is devoted to ceramics from the 16th century onwards. Displays include work by artists from Albisola and elsewhere in Liguria, as well as tools of the trade.

🏛 **Museo della Ceramica Manlio Trucco**
Corso Ferrari 191. ☎ *019 482 741.*
🕐 *Oct–May: 3:30–7pm Tue–Fri, Wed & Sat 10am–12:30pm, 10am–7pm Sat; Jun–Sep: 6–10:30pm Tue–Sat, 10am–12:30pm Wed & Sun.*

Albissola Marina ❹

Savona. **Road Map** C3. 🏛 *5,600.*
🚉 🚌 🛈 *IAT Albissola Marina, Corso Ferrari, 019 400 20 08.*
🅆 *www.inforiviera.it*
🎨 *Mostre Nazionali di Ceramica d'Arte (biennial, next in Jun 2006).*

SEPARATED FROM Albisola Superiore since 1615, this coastal town is also known as Borgo Basso (or "lower town"). Like its neighbour, Albissola Marina has prospered historically thanks to its ceramics industry, but it is also now a well-known seaside resort.

Of interest in the old town is the **Forte di Sant'Antonio**, known as the Castello, built in 1563 against a Saracen invasion, and **Piazza della Concordia**, attractively paved with concentric circles of black and white pebbles, in front of the parish church.

The unmissable sight is the handsome 18th-century **Villa Faraggiana** (named after its last owner, who gave it to the town in 1961), formerly Palazzo Durazzo. The lavishly furnished interior includes some lovely local majolica tiles, while the delightful gardens feature grottoes and statuary, including nymphs and sculptures of the god Bacchus and goddess Diana.

On **Lungomare degli Artisti**, the mosaic paving dating from 1963 was created with works by contemporary painters and sculptors, among them the artists Lucio Fontana and Aligi Sassu.

🏛 **Villa Faraggiana**
Via Salomoni 117–119.
☎ *019 480 622.*
🕐 *Mar–Sep: 3–7pm daily.* ♿
🅆 *www.villafaraggiana.it*

The 18th-century Villa Faraggiana at Albissola Marina

Savona ⑤

ONE'S FIRST IMPRESSION OF Savona tends to be of a sprawling and industrial port. Yet this thriving, untouristy city has a lovely historic centre. Savona (the name derives from the Ligurian tribe of the Sabates) is the largest town on the Riviera di Ponente, and a provincial capital. Its history has always been linked with that of Genoa: the rivalry between the two has existed since ancient

Majolica jar, Pinacoteca

times, when, during Hannibal's Punic wars, Savona sided with Carthage, and Genoa with Rome. The port (destroyed by the Genoese in 1528) was rebuilt only in the 1800s. It was heavily bombed in World War II. There is lots to see here. The Fortezza del Priamàr, a symbol of the city, is now a vast museum complex; you can stroll around the medieval centre and port; or explore the arcades and the Art Nouveau palazzi in Via Paleocapa, jewels of 19th-century architecture.

The imposing bulk of the Fortezza del Priamàr

Ⅲ Il Priamàr
Piazza Chabrol 1. 019 811 520.
 summer: 8:30am–1pm, 6:30–
11:30pm Mon–Sat; winter: 8:30am–
1pm Mon–Sat (closes 6:30pm Thu).
Pinacoteca Civica
 as for Il Priamàr.
Museo Sandro Pertini
 8:30am–1pm Mon–Sat.
 public hols.
Civico Museo Storico-Archeologico
 019 822 708. Jun–Sep:
10am–noon, 5–7pm Tue–Sat; Oct–
May: 10am–noon, 3–5pm Tue–Sat.
Museo Renata Cuneo
 by request only.
The Roman writer Livy records the building of an early fortress here. Today's fort was built on the site of the first Savona settlement (destroyed by the Romans following the war against Hannibal) in the 16th century, in a bid by Genoa to establish its hold over the port. It wasn't completed until 1680. During the 19th century, the Priamàr (derived from *pietra*

sul mare, or "stone above the sea") was used as a prison: Giuseppe Mazzini, a key figure in the Risorgimento, was imprisoned here in 1830–31. Now restored, it houses some of Liguria's most important museums, but is also well worth a visit as a work of military architecture.

You enter across the San Giorgio bridge. To your left is the keep, from which you can reach, via ramps and embankments, the Bastione dell'Angelo and Bastione di San Carlo, and then the so-called Cavallo Superiore, from which there are stunning views over the city.

Palazzo della Loggia, between the Angelo and San Carlo bastions, houses three museums. The most important of these is the **Pinacoteca Civica**, on the third floor, which is dedicated to works by Ligurian artists from the Middle Ages to the

20th century. Highlights here include *Crucifixions* by Donato de' Bardi and Giovanni Mazone, active in the 14th and 15th centuries. There is also a lovely polyptych (another part of which is in the Paris Louvre) by Mazone: *Christ on the Cross between the Marys and St John the Baptist* (1460s).

Many painters from the 17th and 18th centuries, active both in Genoa and in Savona, are represented: such as Fiasella, Robatto, Guidobono, Brusco, Ratti, Agostino and Bozzano. Of the contemporary art, Eso Peluzzi's works from the 1920s stand out.

A room dedicated to ceramics (12th–20th centuries) includes a particularly fine majolica jar decorated with historical scenes (including *St George and the Dragon*), as well as vases.

The middle floor is taken up by the **Museo Sandro Pertini**, with around 90 works by modern artists from the late Italian president's collection. Names represented here include De Chirico, Guttuso, Manzù, Morandi, Arnaldo and Giò Pomodoro, Sassu and Sironi; some works, including those of Henry Moore and Joan Miró, bear a dedication.

On the first floor is the **Civico Museo Storico-Archeologico**. The focus of the displays here is the original Savonese settlement, with finds mostly gathered from other (Roman or pre-Roman) collections, as well as items discovered in the city environs, including both objects and documents.

Palazzo Pavoni on Via Paleocapa

Crucifixion by Donato de' Bardi,
an early painting on canvas

Ceramics, amphorae and
funerary objects from the
Bronze and Iron ages are
on display, along with
medieval weaving tools,
ornamental objects and eating
and drinking vessels.

Well worth seeking out
are the superb Arab- and
Byzantine-influenced ceramics
and the multicoloured and
Savona majolica (typically
coloured blue and white).
There are also cooking
pots and metal, bone and
glass objects from local
excavations, as well as a
5–6th-century burial ground.

The San Bernardo bastion,
reached via underground
passages, houses the **Museo
Renata Cuneo**. Two floors
house works by this Savona
sculptor, who was active for
virtually the whole of the
20th century: they include
29 plaster figures, 50
sculptures and more than 150
drawings. Highlights include
The Shell and *Ecce Homo*. At
the bastion entrance are two
bronzes: *Man Sleeping* and
Summer.

🏛 Torre del Brandale
Piazza del Brandale.

The old port is one of the
most attractive parts of the
city, not so much for the
mass of boats that
moor here but for the
backdrop of medieval
towers.

Dating from the 12th
century, the Torrre
del Brandadlei one
of the most
interesting of
Savona's old towers.
It owes its name to
the flagstaff on top,
commonly known
as the "brandale".
Inside, traces of
frescoes from the

**The Torre del
Brandale**

same era can be seen, while
on the façade there is a
ceramic relief, entitled
Apparition: first carved in
1513, what you see today
dates from the 1960s.

The tower's great bell
is known to the Savonesi
as "*a campanassa*" – a
name used by a local
history association
which has its
headquarters in
the adjacent
Palazzo degli
Anziani, formerly
the seat of the
podestà. Built in
the 14th century,
its façade dates
from the 1600s.

VISITORS' CHECKLIST

Road Map C4. 🏛 69,000.
FS ☐ ℹ *Corso Italia, 157 r,
019 840 23 21.*
ⓦ *www.inforiviera.it*
ⓐ *savona@inforiviera.it*
🎭 *Good Friday procession,
Pasqua Musicale Savonese;
Concorso Nazionale della
Ceramica d'Arte (biennial ceramics
fair shared with Albissola Marina;
next in 2006); Confuoco (Sun
before Christmas.*

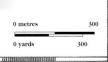

KEY

ℹ Tourist information
⛪ Church
P Parking

SAVONA TOWN CENTRE

Cattedrale di Nostra Signora
Assunta ⑧
Chiesa di Sant'Andrea ⑤
Il Priamàr ①
Nostra Signora di
Castello ⑨
Oratorio del Cristo
Risorto ⑦
Palazzo Della Rovere ⑥
Piazza Salineri ③
Torre del Brandale ②
Torre di Leon Pancaldo ④

0 metres 300
0 yards 300

🏛 Piazza Salineri

The heart of mercantile trading in the Middle Ages, thanks to its position by the sea, this lovely square still has traces of its former splendour, especially in the streets opening on to it: Via Orefici and Via Quarda Superiore.

Two interesting towers rise up above the piazza: the Ghibellina (dated 1200) and the tower of the Aliberti (1100). Nearby stands the dilapidated 16th-century Palazzo Martinengo, which bears a curious conundrum. Five proverbs have been muddled up to create a word game, and the onlooker is invited to reconstruct the sayings.

🏛 Torre di Leon Pancaldo

Piazza Leon Pancaldo.
This small tower at one end of the harbour (by the cruise ship terminal) is the last remnant of the 14th-century walls. It is dedicated to the Savona-born navigator who accompanied Magellan on his voyages to the Americas, and who died on the Rio della Plata in 1537.

The tower features an effigy of the *Madonna della Misericordia*, patron saint of the city, dated 1662. Beneath it is a verse by the local poet Gabriello Chiabrera, dedicated to the Madonna: "In mare irato/In subita procella/Invoco Te/Nostra benigna stella", unusual

Fishing boats in the harbour, with the Torre del Brandale behind

because the words are the same in both Italian and Latin. In English it reads: "In this raging sea, this sudden storm, I beseech thee, oh guiding star."

🏛 Chiesa di Sant'Andrea

Via Paleocapa. ☎ 019 851 952.
🕐 8:30am–noon, daily.
The lovely arcaded Via Paleocapa, Savona's main shopping street, runs inland from the Torre di Leon Pancaldo. Notice the lovely Palazzo dei Pavoni at no. 3, designed by Alessandro Martinengo.

A short distance along the street, a broad flight of steps leads up to the church of Sant'Andrea. This was built at the beginning of the 18th century as the Jesuit church of Sant'Ignazio, on the site of a medieval church. It has an elegant façade, while inside there is an *Immaculate Conception* (1749) by Ratti and a *Madonna (1500s)* by Defendente Ferrari. In the sacristy is an icon of *St Nicholas* from Constantinople, and a *Madonna della Misericordia (1800s)*, sculpted by Antonio Brilla.

🏛 Oratorio del Cristo Risorto

Via Paleocapa. ☎ 019 838 63 06.
🕐 4–7pm Mon–Sat; 8:30am–noon Sun.
Further along Via Paleocapa, this oratory was reconstructed in the early 17th century as part of an existing convent of Augustinian nuns, the Santissima Annunziata. The façade is typical of many

The Torre di Leon Pancaldo, known as the "Torretta"

Baroque buildings in the region, which have richly painted architectural decoration instead of more sculptural motifs.

The interior, where chapels face onto a single room with a barrel vault, is charming. Liberally adorning the place are 18th-century trompe l'oeil frescoes and stuccoes, which create a wonderfully illusionistic background.

Traditionally, the high altar is attributed to Francesco Parodi, but he may have been responsible only for the design; in the presbytery, the powerful statue of *Christ Arisen* (Cristo Risorto), to whom the oratory is dedicated, is by an unknown artist. The organ dates from 1757, and there are also some fine 15th-century carved choir stalls.

Maragliano's *Annunciation* (1722), the *Addolorata* (1795) by Filippo Martinengo and the *Deposition* (1866) by Antonio Brilla are three processional floats for which the oratory is famous. (Many churches in Savona have floats featuring scenes from the Passion which go onto the streets on Good Friday.)

🏛 Palazzo Della Rovere

Via Pia 28.
The ancient Via Pia, which begins near the oratory, is one of the most charming streets in the old city. Hemmed in and full of shops of every description, its medieval layout has lost none of its original fascination.

At the far end of Via Pia, at no. 28, is Palazzo Della Rovere, now the police headquarters. This fine palace, begun in 1495, was designed by Giuliano da Sangallo (one of the architects of St Peter's in Rome) for Cardinal Giuliano Della Rovere, later Pope Julius II.

Statue of the *Assumption* on the cathedral

It became the property of the Spinola family and then, in 1673, was acquired by the Order of the Poor Clares. The nuns covered up the magnificent interior decoration with plaster and renamed it Palazzo Santa Chiara. (At one stage it was the Napoleonic prefecture.)

With its façade divided into three storeys with pilasters, its two-tone marble cladding, and its vast courtyard, this palazzo is a clear example of Tuscan architecture, a rarity in the region. Only a very few of the splendid original frescoes are now visible inside.

🔒 Cattedrale di Nostra Signora Assunta

Piazza del Duomo.
Museo del Tesoro della Cattedrale
🆔 *019 825 960.* ⬜ *by request: 4–5:30pm Tue, Sat; 9:30–11:30am Thu.*

This church was built in the late 16th century to replace the old cathedral of Santa Maria del Castello, which had been demolished (along with other buildings) to make space for the Priamàr fortress. Many of the contents of the old building were transferred to the new, including the splendid baptismal font, made from a beautifully carved Byzantine capital, and a late 15th-century marble *Crucifixion;* both are found in the central nave, behind the façade.

The imposing marble façade dates from the late 19th century and features, above the central door, an *Assumption* by the Carrara artist, Cibei (1706–84). Inside, the three aisles are divided by imposing columns and flanked by chapels. The frescoes in the central nave, like those of the presbytery and the transept, were produced between 1847 and 1951; the walls and the cupola (dated 1840) were decorated between 1891 and 1893.

In the presbytery is a masterpiece by Albertino Piazza, *Enthroned Madonna with Child and saints Peter and Paul,* and *Presentation of Mary at the Temple,* a marble relief dating from the 16th century. Also in the presbytery stand the splendid wooden choir stalls, dated 1515. Commissioned and financed by the Republic of Savona and Cardinal Giuliano Della Rovere for the first cathedral, they were removed from their original setting and then remodelled for the new semicircular apse.

In one of the chapels in the left-hand aisle is a notable fresco of the *Madonna della Colonna (early 15th century),* originally on a column in the Franciscan monastery on whose site the current cathedral was constructed. Also of note is the pulpit of the Evangelists (1522).

To the left of the presbytery there is access to the **Museo del Tesoro della Cattedrale,** a treasury museum with works from different sources. The core of the collection dates from the first half of the 14th century. Other works include a polyptych, *Assumption and Saints,* by Ludovico Brea (1495), a *Madonna and saints* by Tuccio d'Andria (1487), and an *Adoration of the Magi* (early 16th century) by the Master of Hoogstraeten.

In the cloister alongside the church are 21 marble statues of saints. At the far end is Savona's own **Cappella Sistina,** built in 1481 for another Della Rovere pope, Sixtus IV (for whom the Sistine Chapel in the Vatican was built), as a resting place for his parents. The interior of the chapel was transformed in the 18th century, when rococo decoration in the form of multicoloured stucco was introduced. The marble tomb of Sixtus IV's parents (1483) is on the left-hand side.

🔒 Nostra Signora di Castello

Corso Italia. 🆔 *019 804 892.*
⬜ *Sun am, for Mass.*

This small oratory is almost hidden from view on Corso Italia, a long street of elegant shops which, along with Via Paleocapa, was the most important road built during the expansion of Savona in the 19th century. It houses one of the finest paintings in the city – a late 15th-century polyptych of the *Madonna and Saints,* by the Lombard artist Vincenzo Foppa, completed by Ludovico Brea (one of Liguria's most active painters at that time).

The oratory also contains what is claimed to be the world's tallest processional float, a *Deposition* built by Filippo Martinengo in 1795.

***Adoration of the Magi* by the Master of Hoogstraeten, Museo del Tesoro**

The Ponte della Gaietta at Millesimo

ENVIRONS: Heading inland from Savona the first place of interest, about 14 km (9 miles) from the coast, is **Altare** in the Apennines. This town has been famous for the production of glass since at least the 11th century (before Murano glass from Venice came onto the scene.) The **Museo del Vetro e dell'Arte Vetraria** houses both antique and modern examples, as well as objects from the local school of engraved glass, and documents and books related to the subject, some as much as 800 years old. The displays include some splendid vases in blue crystal decorated in pure gold.

Also in the town is the church of the Annunziata (late 15th century), with a bell tower belonging to an earlier Roman building, and the late 17th-century Baroque church of Sant'Eugenio, whose façade is flanked by two bell towers. On the nearby hill of Cadibona is the Forte Napoleonico della Bocchetta, built in the late 18th century.

Nine km (6 miles) beyond Altare, on the left bank of the River Bormida di Spigno, lies **Cairo Montenotte**, important historically because Austro-Piemontese troops were defeated here by Napoleon Bonaparte in 1796.

Within the town, a large tower, called the Torrione, and the ogival Porta Soprana are all that remain of the original circle of 14th-century walls. On the hill overlooking the village are the ruins of an old castle, also dating from the 14th century and belonging originally to the Del Carretto family, local lords during the Middle Ages.

The parish church of San Lorenzo, with a tall bell tower, dates from 1630–40, though it was modified later. Local gastronomic specialities are fruit-flavoured amaretti and black truffles, best tasted with a glass of the local Dolcetto wine.

Millesimo, 27 km (17 miles) from Savona, is a charming hill town and the main centre in the upper Valle Bormida. It retains well-preserved traces of the late Middle Ages. The ruined castle (1206), on the edge of the town, dominates from on high, and once belonged to the Del Carretto family; the castle, like the town, later passed to the Spanish, and eventually ended up in the hands of the House of Savoy.

The central **Piazza Italia**, much of it arcaded, is very pretty; the so-called **Torre**, now the town hall, dates from around 1300 and was a Del Carretto residence.

The most striking monument in the town is the **Ponte della Gaietta**, whose simple design, complete with watch tower, dates from the 12–13th centuries.

🏛 **Museo del Vetro e dell'Arte Vetraria**
Oratorio di San Sebastiano, Piazza di San Sebastiano, Altare. 📞 019 584 734. ⏰ 3–6pm Tue; 9:30am–12:30pm Thu; 10am–noon, 3–5pm Sat. ♿ 🚻

Bergeggi ❻

Savona. **Road Map** C4.
🚶 1,200. 🚉 🚌 🛈 Pro Loco, Via Aurelia 1, 019 859 777 (seasonal).
🌐 www.inforiviera.it

THIS SMALL BUT BUSY coastal resort lies in a lovely spot on the slopes of Monte Sant'Elena. Records of a settlement on this site date back to Roman times. Its strategic position and its defences enabled the town to fend off Saracen raids in the 10th and 11th centuries. In 1385, Bergeggi became the seat of a colony of deportees set up by the Republic of Genoa, which governed the town at that time.

The town is distinctive for its houses with roof terraces overlooking the sea, and famous for its Claudio restaurant, which serves some of the best (and dearest) seafood on the entire Riviera.

Traces of the Middle Ages can be seen in two look-out towers, the **Torri di Avvistamento**, at the top of the town; the parish church of **San Martino** dates from the early 18th century.

Coat of arms on the Porta Soprana, Cairo Montenotte

The ruins of two ancient churches, a monastery and a tower can be seen on the nearby island of **Bergeggi**, an important religious centre in the Middle Ages. Now uninhabited, and also a nature reserve, the island is covered in thick vegetation. The entrance to a cave, 37 m

Bergeggi rooftops, with Bergeggi island in the background

The arching beach overlooked by the resort of Spotorno

(121 ft) long and 17 m (23 ft) wide, is visible at sea level. There are boats to Bergeggi from Savona and Finale Ligure in high season.

Spotorno ❼

Savona. **Road Map** C4.
🏠 4,300. 🚉 🚌 ℹ️ Piazza Matteotti 6, 019 741 50 08.
🖥 www.inforiviera.it and www.comune.spotorno.it
🎭 Festival del Vento (end Mar–early Apr); Rassegna Nazionale di Musica Etnica (Jul & Aug).

DESPITE THE growth of tourism in this part of the region, which has transformed Spotorno into a large resort, the historic nucleus of this town has not lost the appearance of a Ligurian fishing village, with buildings scattered along the waterfront. There is a good and popular beach.

Once the possession of the bishops of Savona, and later of the Del Carretto family, Spotorno was destroyed by neighbouring Noli in 1227.

At the centre of the old town, focused around Via Mazzini and Via Garibaldi, rises the 17th-century parish church of the **Assunta**. Inside, the chapels feature frescoes by artists such as Andrea and Gregorio De Ferrari, Domenico Piola and Giovanni Agostino Ratti.

There is more to see at the **Oratorio della Santissima Annunziata**, which contains works by the Genoese school (17th century) and a wooden sculpture by Maragliano (18th century), as well as curious maritime ex votos. Above the town are the ruins of the 14th-century **castello**.

Noli ❽

Savona. **Road Map** C4.
🏠 2,900. ℹ️ Corso Italia 8, 019 749 90 03. 🖥 www.inforiviera.it
🎭 Regatta Storica dei Rioni (first or second Sun in Sep).

THIS IS ONE OF the best preserved medieval towns in the entire region. Its good fortune began in 1097, when it assisted in the first Crusade, thereby setting itself up to become a maritime power. In the early 13th century Noli allied itself with Genoa, and fought at her side against Pisa and Venice.

In the old town, the narrow alleys with suspended arches between the houses are reminiscent of the Centro

The castle on Monte Ursino at Noli, with its tall central tower

Storico in Genoa. Several of the once-numerous medieval towers survive. On Corso Italia, Noli's main street, look out for the 13th-century Torre Comunale and, next door, the **Palazzo Comunale** (15th century); the loggia that forms part of this palace recalls the arcades that once lined the Corso Italia.

The **Cattedrale di San Pietro** is medieval beneath its Baroque shell. Inside, the apse contains a *Madonna enthroned with Child, angels and saints*, a polyptych by the school of Ludovico Brea (late 1400s). Also of note is the altar, which incorporates a Roman sarcophagus.

The wooden cross in the church of San Paragorio

The key monument in Noli is, however, the church of **San Paragorio**, one of the finest examples of Romanesque in Liguria, originally built in the 11th century and beautifully restored in the late 19th. Blind arches and pilasters decorate the façade, adorned with exotic majolica. On the left are several Gothic tombs in Finale stone.

Inside, the church has three aisles with semicircular apses, also Romanesque. Highlights include a vast wooden cross (Romanesque), a 12th-century bishop's cathedra in wood, fragments of 14th-century frescoes, and a marble pulpit.

On the slopes of Monte Ursino rise the ruins of a 12th-century **castello**. Battlemented walls connect the castle to the town below.

The small island of Bergeggi, a tiny natural oasis a short distance from the coast ▷

Finale Ligure 🟨

Savona. **Road Map** C4. 🏛 *13,000.*
FS 🚌 🅿 *Pro Loco, Via San Pietro
14, Finale Marina, 019 681 019.*
W *www.inforiviera.it and
www.comunefinaleligure.it*
🎉 *Festa dell'Assunta at Finalpia
(15–20 Aug); historic re-enactment of
the exploits of the Marchesi Del
Carretto (Aug–Sep).*

FINALE LIGURE consists of the three separate communities of Pia, Marina and Borgo, united in 1927 to form one of the main towns on the Riviera di Ponente. Finale Marina, the buzzing resort overlooking pebbly beaches, with a smattering of smart 16th–18th century palazzi, is the newest part, while nearby Finale Pia and Finalborgo, just inland and protected from the worst of the new development along the coast, grew up in the Middle Ages.

Finale Pia, across the river Sciusa from Finale Marina, developed around the church of **Santa Maria di Pia**, which is the most important monument in the town and was first documented in 1170. The rococo-style façade dates from the 18th century, and the interior is also Baroque. The bell tower is medieval. The grandiose 16th-century Benedictine abbey next door contains some coloured terracottas by the Tuscan Della Robbia school (15th–16th centuries).

The most interesting of the three villages is Finalborgo, whose old centre remains almost intact within its 15th-century walls. Elegant houses and palazzi abound, many now housing shops, small cafés and restaurants. (Finalborgo is famous for its basil, so pasta with pesto is a speciality here and should not be missed.)

The bell tower of San Biagio

The church of **San Biagio** dates largely from the 17th century, but retains its Gothic bell tower, the symbol of Finalborgo. Inside is a marble pulpit by Schiaffino, a fine example of Genoese Baroque.

The ex-convent of **Santa Caterina**, founded in 1359, is home to the **Civico Museo del Finale**, which exhibits archaeological finds from prehistoric times to the Middle Ages, including Roman-era objects.

One of the best examples of Ligurian Baroque is the basilica of **San Giovanni Battista** in Finale Marina. Its façade is flanked by two bell towers, and inside there is a wooden *Crucifixion* by Maragliano (18th century).

🏛 **Civico Museo del Finale**
Chiostri di Santa Caterina, Finalborgo.
📞 *019 690 020.* ⏰ *Jul; Aug:
10am–noon, 4–7pm Tue–Sun (10pm
Wed, Fri); Sep–Jun: 9am–noon,
2:30–5pm Tue–Sun.* 🎟

THE PARCO DEL FINALESE

Limestone rock with reddish veining is found in abundance in the hinterland behind Finale, and forms an amphitheatre of cliffs that is the focus of the Parco del Finalese. Some 20 million years old, the cliffs are riddled with caves in which evidence of paleolithic life has been found. To reach the area, take the road to Manie, which runs inland from Finale Pia. Fans of freeclimbing will find the upland plain of Le Manie an absolute paradise. There are traces of Roman and even pre-Roman roads in this area. A Roman road, the Via Julia Augusta, ran through the tiny Val Ponci, just north of Manie, and you can still see the remains of five Roman bridges, some of which are in excellent condition.

Grotto in the Parco del Finalese

ENVIRONS: **Varigotti**, some 6 km (4 miles) up the coast towards Noli, is almost impossibly pretty, with its colourful houses and a truly gorgeous setting overlooking a broad sandy beach. The fishermen's houses, painted in all shades of ochre and pink, are of particular interest since they date from the 14th-century settlement founded by the Del Carretto, a local dynasty all-powerful in the Middle Ages.

On Capo di Varigotti, you can see the ruins of the Byzantine-Lombard fortifications (Varigotti was originally a Byzantine settlement, destroyed in the 7th century by the Lombards), as well as the remains of a castle built by the Del Carretto. North of the old town is the church of San Lorenzo Vecchio, of medieval origin. It stands in a dramatic position, facing a precipice jutting over the sea.

Typical fishermen's houses on the beach at Varigotti

Borgio Verezzi ⑩

Savona. **Road Map** C4.
🏛 *2,200.* FS 🚌 🛈 *Via Matteotti 158, 019 610 412 (seasonal).*
Ⓦ *www.inforiviera.it and www.comuneborgioverezzi.it*
🎭 *open-air and classic theatre seasons (summer): www.festivalverezzi.it*

T HIS TOWN IS FORMED by the two distinct centres of Borgio, on the coast, and Verezzi, on the slope above. The medieval heart of Borgio has remained virtually intact: old cobbled streets alternate with gardens and orchards, rising up to the 17th-century parish church of **San Pietro**.

Piazza Sant'Agostino in Borgio Verezzi

Near the cemetery is the pretty medieval church of **Santo Stefano**, with a bell tower of decorative brick.

A winding scenic road leads up to Verezzi. Of the four groups of houses which make up the village, all on different levels, the best preserved is Piazza, which still displays some Saracen influence. At the centre stands the church of **Sant'Agostino** (1626). There is a view over the sea from one side of the pretty church square.

ENVIRONS: the nearby **Grotte di Valdemino** are well worth a visit: inside these limestone caves are stalactites so slim that they vibrate at the sound of a voice, as well as magical underground lakes. Fossils of saber-tooth tigers, cave bears and elephants have been discovered here.

🦴 **Grotte di Valdemino**
Via Battorezza. 🄲 *019 610 150.*
⭘ *May–Sep: 9–11:30am, 3–5:30pm Tue–Sun. Oct–Apr: guided tours Tue–Sun (6 daily).* ⬤ *25 Dec, 1 Jan.*
♿ 📷 *with permission.*

Pietra Ligure ⑪

Savona. **Road Map** B4.
🏛 *9,400.* FS 🚌 🛈 *Via Gio Batta Montaldo 2, 019 629 003.*
Ⓦ *www.inforiviera.it*
🎭 *Processione di San Nicolò, (8 Jul); Confoëgu (24 Dec).*

T HIS BEACH resort takes it name from the rocky outcrop to the northeast of the old town (*pietra* means stone), where a fortified site stood in the Byzantine era. The medieval town grew up around the base of the **castello**, a Genoese stronghold which underwent alterations in the 16th century and again in later centuries. The so-called **Borgo Vecchio** was planned on a regular layout with five streets running parallel to the coastline. As you stroll along these streets today, notice how both medieval houses and 16–17th century palazzi rub shoulders, an unusual architectural combination which resulted from partial reconstruction in the 16th century. In Piazza XX Settembre, not far from the sea, stands the 18th-century church of **San Nicolò di Bari**, its façade flanked by two bell towers.

ENVIRONS: just inland, high up above Pietra Ligure, is the village of **Giustenice**, from where there are superb views over the coast. This former Del Carretto stronghold lost its castle in the 15th century.

The medieval castle dominating Pietra Ligure

Loano ⑫

Savona. **Road Map** B4. 🏛 *11,000.*
FS 🚌 🛈 *Corso Europa 19, 019 676 007.* Ⓦ *www.inforiviera.it and www.cai.loano.com (information on walking in Loano and Finalese area).*
🎭 *Carnevalöa, Liguria's largest carnival (in summer); re-enactment of Battle of Loano (Sep).*

E VER SINCE ROMAN times, Loano has been a desirable place to live. It has been the property of, among others, the bishops of Albenga, the Doria family and the Republic of Genoa. (It was also the site of Napoleon's first victory in Italy.) These days Loano is an extremely pleasant town with an extensive beach.

The most interesting building is the 16th-century **Palazzo Comunale**, built for the Doria family. Its austere appearance is softened by balconies and loggias, while a gallery links it to a watch tower (1602). A beautiful Roman mosaic pavement is housed here, and in the palazzo's central hall is the **Civico Museo Naturalistico**, whose collection includes 400 species of bird from both Italy and Europe.

In a lovely spot in the hills above Loano is the **Convento di Monte Carmelo**, founded in 1603 by the Doria. The complex includes a church full of Doria tombs and the Casotto, a Doria residence.

🏛 **Civico Museo Naturalistico**
Piazza Italia 2. 🄲 *019 675 694.*
⭘ *on request.*

Grotte di Toirano ⓭

Logo of the Grotte di Toirano

THESE CAVES, a real wonder of nature, are among the most beautiful in Italy. They are situated in the karst area of the Val Varatella, between Albenga and Pietra Ligure. Discovered by young researchers and speleologists from Toirano in 1950, these subterranean caves, full of broad caverns, stalactites and stalagmites of all sizes and rare crystal formations, are reminiscent of images of hell. Of prime importance is the beautiful Grotta della Bàsura ("Cave of the Witch" in Ligurian dialect), where traces of Paleolithic man and also the extinct cave bear have been found. The caves are also the habitat of the largest ocellated lizards in Europe. The site, which can be toured in around an hour and a half, is undoubtedly one of the greatest attractions of the Riviera di Ponente.

The Antro di Cibele
offers the extremely rare spectacle of rounded concretions, spherical even, which have been shaped by rhythmical but continuous fluctuations in the water level.

★ Sala dei Misteri
Various traces of prehistoric man are still visible in this part of the Grotta della Bàsura. The balls of clay hurled at the cave walls were probably concerned with propitiatory rites or hunting ceremonies.

①

Sala Morelli
The route within the Grotto della Bàsura starts in this room. A little further ahead is the Torre di Pisa (left), an impressive central stalagmite formed when water ceased to flow on the cave floor.

Entrance

In the Bear Cemetery
you can see footprints of *Ursus spelaeus* (cave bear).

★ Salotto
Venturing further into the cave system, you reach the area known as the Salotto ("drawing room"). Here, stalactites, stalagmites and wall concretions create a truly fairytale environment, mirrored in the waters of an underground pool, with light playing off the surfaces.

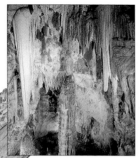

Sala del Pantheon

This cavern contains a stalagmite which reaches the great height of 8m (26 ft) and which, in its vast scale and visual impact, evokes images of Dante's Inferno. Aragonite flowers cover it like a light dusting of sugar on a biscuit.

VISITORS' CHECKLIST

Toirano (Savona). **Road Map** B4.
🚌 🛈 *Piazzale Grotte, Toirano.*
📞 *0182 980 62.*
⭕ **Caves and Museo Etnografico Toirano** *Oct–Jun: 9:30am–12:30pm, 2–5pm; Jul, Aug: 9:30am–12:30pm, 2–5:30pm.* 🖼 ☑ 🖥 🅿
Ⓦ *www.toirano.it and www.toiranogrotte.it*

In the Corridoio delle Colonne evidence of ancient earthquakes can be seen in the fracture lines which split numerous formations in half.

★ Grotta di Santa Lucia Inferiore

This cave shows no human or animal traces but contains beautiful and rare crystallized deposits, including these aragonite flowers.

KEY

① Grotta della Bàsura

② Grotta di Santa Lucia Inferiore

③ Grotta di Santa Lucia Superiore (open only 13 Dec for patron saint's day)

④ Grotta del Colombo (closed to the public)

STAR FEATURES

★ Grotta di Santa Lucia Inferiore

★ Sala dei Misteri

★ Salotto

The Landscape

Toirano is in the high Val Varatella, characterized by steep-sided walls of karst rock. There are lovely views of the landscape from the road leading to the caves.

Street-by Street: Albenga ⓮

I̶N THE PROVINCE OF SAVONA, Albenga is one of the Riviera di
Ponente's most important cities. It owes its fame not only to
its historic centre, one of the best-preserved in Liguria, but also
to the mildness of its climate and the fertility of the surrounding
plain, which has been under cultivation since the Roman era
and produces a wide range of fruit and vegetables. The Roman
town of *Albingaunum* was founded on the
site of a port built by the Ingauni, a
Ligurian tribe. For centuries, Albenga's
prosperity depended on the River Centa,
but its role as a major sea power
declined after Genoa asserted itself,
and following the silting-up of the
port. A long avenue links the
old city to the coast, now a short
distance away.

Porta Molino
is the largest of
the gates in the
city walls.

Porta Torlaro
*A solid bastion
called Il Torracco,
once used as a
prison, projects
from the northwest
corner of the city
wall. Alongside is
17th-century
Porta Torlaro.*

**Lengueglia Doria Tower
and House** lie at the end of
Via Ricci. The tower dates
from the 13th century, while
the brickwork house was built
in the 15th century.

Via Bernardo Ricci,
lined with intact or
restored medieval
houses, is Albenga's
most picturesque
long street. In the
Roman era it formed
part of the main road
or *decumanus
maximus*, as did its
continuation Via
Enrico d'Aste.

Loggia dei Quattro Canti
*Set at the corner of Via Ricci and Via Medaglie
d'Oro, this loggia features one rounded arch and
one ogival arch and dates from the transitional
period between the Romanesque and Gothic styles.
In the Middle Ages, it served to increase visibility
and ease the traffic flow at the crossroads.*

★ Baptistry
*This is the only example of late
Roman architecture left intact in
Albenga. Built by the general
Costanzo in the early 5th century,
the baptistry is the foremost Early
Christian monument in Liguria.*

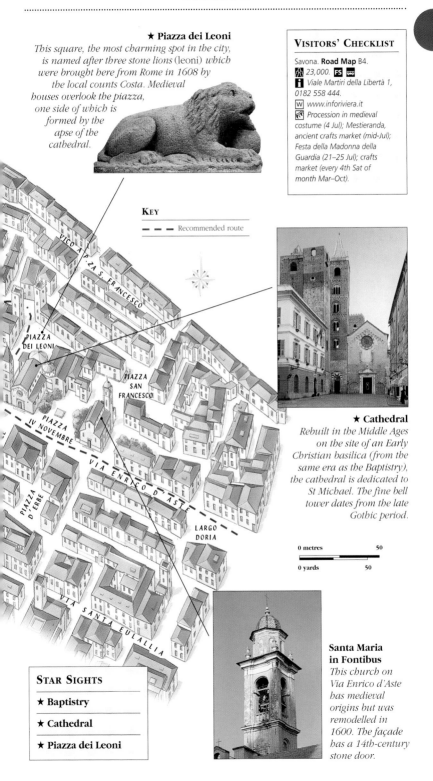

★ **Piazza dei Leoni**
This square, the most charming spot in the city, is named after three stone lions (leoni) *which were brought here from Rome in 1608 by the local counts Costa. Medieval houses overlook the piazza, one side of which is formed by the apse of the cathedral.*

VISITORS' CHECKLIST

Savona. **Road Map** B4.
23,000. FS
Viale Martiri della Libertà 1,
0182 558 444.
www.inforiviera.it
Procession in medieval costume (4 Jul); Mestieranda, ancient crafts market (mid-Jul); Festa della Madonna della Guardia (21–25 Jul); crafts market (every 4th Sat of month Mar–Oct).

KEY

– – – Recommended route

PIAZZA DEI LEONI

VICO A.P.ZA S. FRANCESCO

PIAZZA SAN FRANCESCO

PIAZZA IV NOVEMBRE

PIAZZA D'ERBE

VIA ENRICO D'ASTE

LARGO DORIA

VIA SANTA EULALLIA

★ **Cathedral**
Rebuilt in the Middle Ages on the site of an Early Christian basilica (from the same era as the Baptistry), the cathedral is dedicated to St Michael. The fine bell tower dates from the late Gothic period.

0 metres 50
0 yards 50

Santa Maria in Fontibus
This church on Via Enrico d'Aste has medieval origins but was remodelled in 1600. The façade has a 14th-century stone door.

STAR SIGHTS

★ Baptistry

★ Cathedral

★ Piazza dei Leoni

Exploring Albenga

Detail of the Baptistry mosaics

IN THE OLD HEART OF Albenga, with its superb collection of medieval piazzas, palazzi and churches, the streets are set at intersecting right angles, reflecting the grid layout of the *castrum* (or military camp) of the early Roman town. With its plethora of red-brick tower-houses, some still standing proud, some now much reduced, and many now restored, the historic centre of Albenga is utterly delightful. This rare example of a medieval city built on Roman foundations is undoubtedly one of the top places to visit in the whole of Liguria and should not be missed. There are two excellent museums, the Museo Navale Romano and the Civico Museo Ingauno, but a stroll along Via Enrico d'Aste, Via Bernardo Ricci and Via Medaglie d'Oro is sufficient to appreciate the beauty of the place.

Medieval fresco in the loggia of Palazzo Vecchio del Comune

in the central nave, an enormous 19th-century organ, and the Carolingian crypt.

Roman amphorae at the Museo Navale in Palazzo Peloso Cepolla

🏛 Palazzo Peloso Cepolla

Piazza San Michele.
Museo Navale Romano
📞 0182 512 15. ⏰ *winter: 10am–12:30pm, 2:30–6pm Tue–Sun; summer 9.30am–12:30pm, 3:30–7:30pm Tue–Sun.* 🎫 🔲
Originally made up of several buildings – the medieval part of the palazzo came to light only recently – the Palazzo Peloso Cepolla was unified in a single late Renaissance building in the 17th century. The building is dominated by a Romanesque tower.

The palazzo is home to the **Museo Navale Romano**. Its most important finds include more than 1,000 amphorae, vases and other objects found on board the wreck of a Roman ship which sank off the coast of Albenga in the 1st century BC.

Pharmacy jars from the hospital of Albenga, dating from between 1500 and 1700, are made of the white and blue pottery typical of Savona and Albisola.

⛪ Cathedral of San Michele

Piazza San Michele.
⏰ *7:30am–8pm daily.*
Overlooking Albenga's lovely main square, the cathedral is the old seat of both civil and religious authority. It has been remodelled several times since its construction in the Middle Ages (on the site of an Early Christian church), but remnants of the Romanesque building survive: including blind arches in the lower part of the façade, and elements of the apse. The fine bell tower, rebuilt in the late 14th century, is Gothic, but its base of large stone blocks is Romanesque.

The interior was returned to its simple 13th-century form by restoration work carried out in the 1960s. Highlights inside include a fresco of the *Crucifixion with Saints* (1500), the 19th-century frescoes

🏛 Palazzo Vecchio del Comune

Via Nino Laboglia 1.
Civico Museo Ingauno
📞 0182 512 15. ⏰ *winter: 10am–12:30pm, 2:30–6pm Tue–Sun; summer: 9:30am–12:30pm, 3:30–7:30pm Tue–Sun.* 🎫 🔲
This building dates from the early 14th century and, with the contemporaneous Torre Comunale, forms a truly impressive medieval complex. The cathedral tower, the Torre Comunale and the tower of the Palazzo Vecchio itself are known as "Preghiera" (prayer), "Governo" (government) and "Giustizia" (justice) respectively.

The side of the palazzo facing Via Ricci has the great Loggia Comunale (1421), built of brick and with sturdy round pillars supporting the heavy arches. On the rear façade, facing the Baptistry, are decorative Ghibelline (swallowtail) battlements and a steep double staircase. At the top of the tower is a big bell known as the *campanone*, cast in 1303.

The Palazzo Vecchio del Comune houses the **Civico Museo Ingauno**, with finds from around Albenga, dating from the pre-Roman era to the Middle Ages. Objects include mosaics, tomb-stones, sculptures and Roman ceramics. Make sure you carry on right to the top floor, from where there is a lovely view of the city.

Decoration on the façade of the cathedral

🔒 Baptistry

Piazza San Michele. ◯ *combined ticket with the Museo Ingauno.*

Albenga's most important monument is also the only remaining evidence of the Early Christian era in the whole of Liguria. It is thought to have been founded by Constantius, general to the emperor Honorius, in the 5th century. Restoration work in the 20th century returned the building to its original appearance.

Unusually, the Baptistry takes the form of an irregular decagon outside and a regular octagon inside. There is a niche in each of these eight sides, with columns of Corsican granite topped by Corinthian capitals supporting the arches above. The entrance to the Baptistry is through one of these niches, while others function as windows; two of the latter feature beautiful sandstone transennas. In another niche, part of its original blue and white mosaic decoration is still visible.

On the altar niche is a *Trinity and the apostles*, a 5–6th century mosaic in Byzantine style; in another is a Romanesque fresco of the *Baptism of Christ*. The Baptistry also contains some interesting medieval tombs with Lombard-style reliefs, and at the centre is an octagonal font for total immersion baptisms, with traces of 5th-century frescos.

The cupola dates from the 19th century: its predecessor, possibly the original, was dismantled prior to that, probably in error.

ISOLA GALLINARA

Riserva Naturale Regionale dell'Isola Gallinara 【 *0182 541 351 (comune di Albenga).* Ｗ *www.parks.it*

This island lies just off the coast between Albenga and Alassio. Its name derives from the hundreds of wild hens (*galline*) that used to be resident here. It was also once inhabited by hermit monks: St Martin of Tours found refuge here in the 4th century and Benedictine monks later founded an abbey, which was destroyed in the late 15th century; its ruins are still visible. At the top of the island stands the Torre di Vedetta, a tower built by the Republic of Genoa in the 16th century. Isola Gallinara is now a nature reserve and can be visited only on special tours. Boat trips (including for diving) leave from Alassio.

🔒 Palazzo Vescovile

Piazza San Michele.

Museo Diocesano d'Arte Sacra
【 *0182 502 88.* ◯ *10am–noon, 3–6pm Tue–Sun.*

This palazzo, whose principal façade faces the Baptistry, is an assembly of medieval buildings, rebuilt in the 16th century. The oldest wing, to the far right, dates from around 1000, while a 12th-century tower rises from the left-hand corner. On Via Ricci, typically Genoese black and white striped decoration, dating from the 15th century, is still visible.

The Palazzo Vescovile is now home to the **Museo Diocesano d'Arte Sacra**, where visitors can admire precious church furnishings, illuminated manuscripts, Flemish tapestries, silverware and some fine works of art, including *Martyrdom of St Catherine* by Guido Reni, a *Last Supper* by Domenico Piola and an *Annunciation* by Domenico Fiasella, all painted in the 17th century.

ENVIRONS: a short distance south of Albenga, interesting archaeological ruins of the Roman town of *Albingaunum* can be seen, including an amphitheatre, aqueduct, various other buildings and a funerary monument known as "il Pilone"; there are also traces of Roman road, thought to have been part of the Via Julia Augusta (*see p144*).

Around 10 km (6 miles) west of the city, **Villanova d'Albenga** (close to the international airport) is well worth a visit. This fortified settlement, laid out in the 13th century to provide extra protection for Albenga, has a polygonal layout and outer walls reinforced with square towers. The alleys through the town are charming, full of atmosphere and the scent of the abundant flowers that the locals use to adorn their windows and doorways.

The interior of the Baptistry, with the remains of a font at its centre

The famous "Muretto" of Alassio, in front of Caffè Roma

Alassio ⓯

Savona. **Road Map** B4. 🏛 *11,300.* 🚉 🚌 ℹ️ *Piazza della Libertà 5, 0182 647 027.* Ⓦ *www.inforiviera.it and www.alassiovirtuale.com* 📅 *Election of "Miss Muretto" (late Aug); Premio Alassio Centolibri; a literature prize (summer).*

A BEACH OF beautifully fine sand, which extends for some 4 km (over 2 miles) and slopes almost imperceptibly down to the sea, makes Alassio the undisputed queen of the Riviera delle Palme. In the 19th century, it became a favourite holiday destination among the English, who came here and built splendid villas with gardens. Many of these, including some Art Nouveau gems, have since been turned into hotels.

Local legend has it that the town's name derives from Adelasia, daughter of Holy Roman Emperor Otto I of Saxony, who came here in the 10th century; (Alassio is still very popular with German visitors). Originally a fishing village, in the Middle Ages it became the property of Albenga and, later, of Genoa. The Roman road Via Aurelia still passes through it.

The typically Ligurian character of Alassio can be seen in the long *carruggio* (narrow street) that runs parallel with the sea, hemmed in by 16th–17th-century houses and modern shops: this is

Via XX Settembre, known as the "Budello", and the heart of the town's commercial life. From here, narrow streets known locally as *esci* fan out, leading to the seafront.

At the corner of Via Dante and Via Cavour, **Caffè Roma** has been a popular meeting place since the 1930s. In the 1950s, the café's owner had the idea of making ceramic tiles out of the autographs of famous visitors to Caffè Roma, to hang on the wall of the garden opposite. The **Muretto** now bears the signatures of many famous personalities, including Ernest Hemingway, Jean Cocteau and Dario Fo.

Alassio's most signficant monument is the parish church of **Sant'Ambrogio**. Founded in the 1400s, it has a 19th-century façade, an early 16th-century bell tower and a Baroque interior.

ENVIRONS: from Alassio, you can go on a lovely (but steep) panoramic walk along the route of an old Roman road, the start of an archaeological walk that runs all the way to Albenga. In 45 minutes you can reach Capo Santa Croce, where a small 13th-century church of the same name overlooks the sea.

At the southern end of the bay of Alassio lies **Laigueglia**, a civilized seaside resort with a well-preserved and picturesque old centre. Of Roman origin, it became an important centre for coral

The round tower in Laigueglia

fishing in the 16th century. A round tower, known as the **Torrione circolare** (1564), the only bastion remaining of three which once protected Laigueglia from pirates, is the oldest building in the village. The church of **San Matteo** has two bell towers with bright, majolica-covered cupolas, a delightful example of Ligurian Baroque.

On the ridge between Laigueglia and Andora is **Colla Micheri**, a hamlet whose houses were restored and made into a home by Thor Heyerdahl, the Norwegian navigator and ethnologist famous for his epic journey by raft from Peru to Polynesia in 1958; he died here in 2002.

Santi Giacomo e Filippo church, Andora

Andora ⓰

Savona. **Road Map** B4. 🏛 *6,500.* 🚉 🚌 ℹ️ *Via Aurelia 122/a, Villa Laura, 0182 681 004.* Ⓦ *www.inforiviera.it* 📅 *Estate Musicale Andorese, festival of classical music in church of Santi Giacomo e Filippo (Jul, Aug).*

T HE LAST COASTAL town at the western end of the Riviera delle Palme, Andora groups together several communities, including Marina di Andora on the coast. Founded perhaps by the Phocaeans, from Asia Minor, several centuries BC, Andora later belonged to the Romans, who built a bridge over the River Merula. The ten-arched **Ponte Romano** visible today dates, in fact, from the Middle Ages. The old Roman road goes up to the ruins of **Andora Castello**, in a lovely spot at the top of the hill. Built by the Marchesi di Clavesana in around 1000, this fortified complex must have been impressive in its heyday. Through the castle gate is the lovely church of **Santi Giacomo e Filippo**, founded in around 1100 and once part of the castle's defences. Entirely built out of stone from nearby Capo Mele, the church façade is adorned with Gothic cornices and arches. Inside, there are great round columns and octagonal pilasters of bare stone.

Another church within the castle, San Nicolò, is of proto-Romanesque origins.

Museo Etnografico, Cervo

Cervo ⑰

Imperia. **Road Map** B5.
🏠 1,300. **FS** 🚌 **ⓘ** IAT, Piazza Santa Caterina 2, 0183 408 197.
🌐 www.rivieradeifiori.org
🎵 Festival Internazionale di Musica da Camera, chamber music festival (nine evenings Jul, Aug).

THIS VILLAGE, perched on a hill between Capo Cervo and the mouth of the River Cervo, signals the beginning of the province of Imperia. Once the property of the Del Carretto and then the Doria families, from the 14th century Cervo came under Genoese domination and followed that city's fortunes.

Nowadays, Cervo is an extremely pretty resort, with houses painted in white and pale shades of yellow overlooking a shingle beach. Dominating the village is a 12th-century **castello**, which belonged to the Marchesi di Clavesana and was a control point along the Via Aurelia in the Middle Ages. The site is now occupied by the **Museo Etnografico del Ponente Ligure**, which features reconstructions of life at sea and on land, together with original rooms from a local house.

Facing the sea is the attractive parish church of **San Giovanni Battista**, with its distinctive concave, stucco-embellished façade that

features a stag (cervo in Italian). Begun in 1686, it is a fine example of Ligurian Baroque. The bell tower and the interior, which is decorated with frescoes and stuccoes, both date from the 18th century. The latter contains a St John the Baptist, a 17th-century work in multicoloured wood by Poggio, and an 18th-century Crucifixion attributed to Maragliano.

Also in the town there are several interesting 17th–18th-century palazzi. These include **Palazzo Morchio**, now the town hall, and **Palazzo Viale**, which has 18th-century porticoes.

🏛 Museo Etnografico del Ponente Ligure
Piazza Santa Caterina 2. **【** 0183 408 197. **⊙** 9am–12:30pm, 3–7pm daily (Jul, Aug: 4:30–10pm).

Pieve di Teco ⑱

Imperia. **Road Map** B4.
🏠 1,450. **FS** Imperia Oneglia. 🚌 **ⓘ** Comunità Montana Alta Valle Arroscia, Via San Giovanni Battista 1, 0183 362 78. 🎪 Mercatino dell'Antiquariato e dell'Artigianato, antiques and craft market (last Sun of month).

HEADING INLAND, almost as far as the border with Piemonte, you reach the busy market town of Pieve di Teco. Founded in 1293, the town belonged, like many others in the area, to the Marchesi di Clavesana and subsequently (from the late 14th century)

to Genoa. The town is known for its hand-made walking boots.

Two squares mark either end of the arcaded and typically medieval **Corso Ponzoni**, the heart of the town. On either side, craft workshops alternate with the palazzi of well-to-do families.

The porticoes on Corso Ponzoni

The oldest part of Pieve di Teco is focused around the 15th-century church of **Santa Maria della Ripa**. Also of interest is the late 18th-century collegiate church of **San Giovanni Battista**, which contains several important paintings, including a St Francis de Pauul attributed to Luca Cambiaso (16th century), and a Last Supper by Domenico Piola (17th century).

The 15th-century **Convento degli Agostiniani** has the largest cloister (which is also one of the prettiest) in the whole region.

Not far from the town, a lovely medieval hump-backed bridge straddles the River Arroscia.

The medieval bridge over the Arroscia, close to Pieve di Teco

Imperia ⑲ – Oneglia

Coat of arms of the Museo dell'Olivo, Imperia

O NE OF FOUR PROVINCIAL capitals in Liguria, Imperia lies at the centre of the coastal strip known as the Riviera dei Fiori. It consists of the two centres of Oneglia and Porto Maurizio, united in 1923 by Mussolini. People like to say that he chose the name Imperia out of arrogance, but it derives from the River Impero, which divides the two centres. Historically rivals, the two cities seem to share as little as possible (there are two harbours, two railway stations, even two dialects). Imperia is fascinating because of its split personality.

The name Oneglia probably derives from a plantation of elms *(olmi)*, on which the town was originally built. Oneglia was recorded in documents as far back as 935, when it was destroyed by the Saracens. From the 11th century it was owned by the bishops of Albenga, but they sold it to the Doria family in 1298. (The great admiral, Andrea Doria, was born here in 1466.) The House of Savoy claimed ownership for a time, but Oneglia, along with Porto Maurizio, passed into the hands of the Genoese republic in 1746. The House of Savoy returned in 1814, and made Oneglia the provincial capital. In 1887, an earthquake caused severe damage to the town.

The Port
East of the mouth of the River Impero, the port of Oneglia (Porto di Levante) is dedicated largely to commercial trade, in particular the trade in olive oil (the town has a museum devoted to olive oil); there is

also a vast pasta factory on the seafront. The port, whose appearance dates mainly from the period of Savoy rule, is the centre of activity in Oneglia. In the summer (from mid-June to mid-September), look out for boats offering to take you out to sea to watch whales and dolphins – a great experience.

⛴ Calata Giovan Battista Cuneo
This characteristic quay building faces the harbour, its traditional arcades perfectly designed to shelter fishmongers, trattorias and fishermen's houses. When the boats of Oneglia's fishing fleet return from their trips out on the open sea, an auction of fresh fish is held here, usually around the middle of the afternoon. The fish trade is vital to the local economy. The local bars and restaurants are always entertaining places to while away the time.

⛪ Collegiata di San Giovanni Battista
Piazza San Giovanni.
📞 0183 292 671. 🕐 8am–noon, 3–7pm daily.
This church stands in the piazza of the same name, right at the heart of Oneglia's shopping district. It was built from 1739–62 in late Baroque style, though the façade was finished only in 1838. The fresco decoration inside also dates from the 19th century.

Look out for the marble tabernacle (to the left of the presbytery), which dates from 1516 and is attributed to the Gagini school; various saints are represented here and, in the lunette, *Christ arising from the Tomb.* Also of interest are the wooden choir stalls; the lovely *Madonna del Rosario* (in the first chapel in the left-hand aisle), attributed to the school of the 18th-century sculptor Maragliano; and *St Clare drives out the Saracens* (1681), a moving work painted by Gregorio De Ferrari, a native of Porto Maurizio, though he spent much of his time in Genoa.

The Madonna del Rosario

⛪ Chiesa di San Biagio
Piazza Ulisse Calvi.
📞 0183 292 747. 🕐 7:45am–noon, 4–6:30pm daily.
This church, dated 1740, has a sober façade and a Baroque bell tower. The spacious, light-filled interior is shaped, curiously, in an oval and ends in a choir.

The church contains various works of art, among them a *Gloria di San Biagio* (Glory of St Blaise) by Bocciardo, visible in the apse, and a wooden *Crucifixion* by the school of Maragliano on the right-hand altar.

⛪ Via Bonfante
From Piazza San Giovanni, the pedestrian street of Via San Giovanni leads north to Via Bonfante, Oneglia's main shopping street. This is a wonderful place for a stroll, and for soaking up the atmosphere of the town.

The multicoloured, arcaded houses of Calata Giovan Battista Cuneo

Piazza Dante, at the heart of Oneglia

Beneath Via Bonfante's 19th-century arcades you can find all manner of art galleries and shops (including designer boutiques), as well as cafés that manage to tempt even the hardiest passers-by inside.

🏛 Piazza Dante
At the end of Via Bonfante is the central Piazza Dante, the real heart of Oneglia, also known locally as the "Piazza della Fontana" (square of the fountain).

A busy crossroads, the piazza is surrounded by neo-medieval palazzi: among the most interesting of these is the ex-**Palazzo Comunale,** at no. 4, built in the 1890s in an eclectic mix of styles.

🏛 Museo dell'Olivo
Via Garessio 11. [0183 295 762.
W *www.museodellolivo.com*
🕐 9am–12:30pm, 3:30–7pm
Mon–Sat. 📷 ♿

Housed in an old olive oil mill, the Museo dell'Olivo was opened by the Fratelli Carli, owners of just one of the many local producers of olive oil that compete for market share in the region.

One part of the museum traces the history of olive cultivation, starting with the Roman period, when the oil was used more for medical and cosmetic purposes than as a food; little bottles, used to store oil as perfume or medicine, are on display. There is also a reconstruction of the hold of a Roman ship,

which shows how amphorae full of olive oil were stacked ready for transportation.

The main section, complete with audiovisual aids, is dedicated to explaining the production of olive oil: on display are all sorts of mills, presses, machines for filtering oil, and containers for storing and for transporting it.

The visit concludes with a visit to an oil mill that is still being used by the Fratelli Carli company.

Reconstruction of the hold in a Roman ship with its cargo of oil

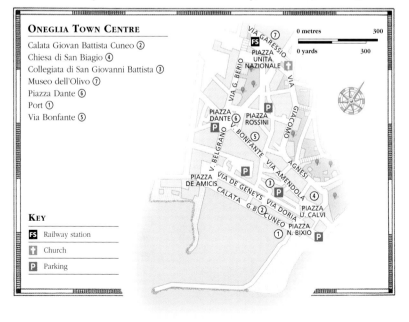

ONEGLIA TOWN CENTRE

Calata Giovan Battista Cuneo ②
Chiesa di San Biagio ④
Collegiata di San Giovanni Battista ③
Museo dell'Olivo ⑦
Piazza Dante ⑥
Port ①
Via Bonfante ⑤

KEY

FS	Railway station
🏛	Church
P	Parking

Imperia - Porto Maurizio

Plaque dedicated to San Maurizio

WHILE ONEGLIA represents the more modern, commercial side of Imperia, Porto Maurizio is its old heart, with its long porticoes, 16th-century bastions and Baroque churches. The quarter of Parasio, the medieval part of town with narrow alleys in typically Ligurian style, is focused around the cathedral. The two most important museums in Imperia are also found here. Porto Maurizio has two coastal districts, known as Borgo Foce and Borgo Marino.

The second town forming the city of Imperia has a history that is very similar to, and yet different from, that of Oneglia. Porto Maurizio, on the west side of the mouth of the River Impero, has kept more traces of its earlier history than Oneglia, which developed primarily in the 18th and 19th centuries. Indeed, its Centro Storico, largely a monument to the Genoese golden age, remains almost intact.

Porto Maurizio fell into Genoese hands in 1797, and in 1805 was annexed, along with Genoa, to France during the Napoleonic era. Restored to the Ligurian Republic in 1814, it was united for the first time with Oneglia as part of the Kingdom of Sardinia, and in 1860 was absorbed into the Kingdom of Piemonte, under whose rule it remained until union with Oneglia in 1923.

The Port
Also known as the Porto di Ponente (to distinguish it from Oneglia's Porto di Levante), the port is protected by two piers. With its floating landing stages, the harbour is reserved for holiday yachts and contrasts sharply with Oneglia's commercial port.

🔒 Duomo
Piazza del Duomo. ☎ 0183 619 01.
⬤ 7am–noon, 3–7pm daily.

As you take in the majestic bulk of the Duomo di San Maurizio, it should come as no surprise that this is the

The interior of Porto Maurizio's Duomo

largest church in Liguria. It was built between 1781 and 1838 by Gaetano Cantoni in Neo-Classical style to replace the old parish church of San Maurizio, which had been demolished.

The impressive façade features eight Doric columns, culminating in a drum flanked by two solid bell towers, which form a portico. A lantern crowns the great cupola. Beneath the portico are statues that once belonged to the old parish church.

The impressive interior, built on a Greek cross plan, contains a rich array of 19th-century canvases and Neo-Classical-style frescoes, the work of painters mostly from Liguria and Piemonte. Highlights among these include a *Predica di San*

Francesco Saverio, attributed to De Ferrari. In the third chapel on the left, there is a fine wooden cross by the school of Maragliano, while the second chapel on the right contains a statue of the *Madonna della Misericordia*, (1618), which also came from the demolished San Maurizio.

🏛 Pinacoteca Civica
Piazza del Duomo. ☎ 0183 608 47.
⬤ 4–7pm Wed, Sat (also 9–11pm in Jul & Aug).

Also on Piazza del Duomo is the entrance to the Pinacoteca Civica, the municipal art gallery. On display here are collections derived from legacies and various donations, but exhibitions of local work are held here, too.

Works by Barabino, Rayper, Frascheri and Semino, among others, form part of the Rebaudi collection, which includes 19th-century Ligurian and Genoese works.

🏛 Museo Navale Internazionale del Ponente Ligure
Piazza del Duomo 11. ☎ 0183 651 541. ⬤ 3–7pm Wed, Sat (also 9–11pm in Jul & Aug).

Imperia's naval museum is one of the most interesting institutions in the city, unmissable for anyone with an interest in seafaring, though the exhibition space is somewhat cramped.

The museum is subdivided into various sections and includes dioramas and models of ships. Most visitors enjoy the section that deals with life on board ship the most. There are also displays of various documents and other mementoes relating to the seafaring tradition along the Riviera di Ponente.

🚻 Parasio
The old palace of the Genoese governor was known in the local dialect as "Paraxu" (the Ligurian for Palatium, as in Palatine Hill, in Rome);

Model of a diving suit, Museo Navale

Parasio, the old city, set above Porto Maurizio

translated into Italian, this became Parasio, the name now given to Porto Maurizio's medieval district. The governor's palace was built on the top of the hill, in Piazza Chiesa Vecchia, now at the heart of the medieval district and only a short walk from the Piazza del Duomo, along Via Acquarone.

After a long period of real neglect and decline, Parasio has in recent years been the subject of an ambitious restoration project, financed mainly by foreign investors. Visitors cannot truly claim to have seen Imperia unless they have strolled around and climbed these charming and steep streets, lined with handsome palaces and churches, including the

convent of Santa Chiara and the Oratorio di San Leonardo. In Via Acquarone, look out for striking **Palazzo Pagliari** (1300–1400), with an entrance portico with ogival arches.

🏛 Oratorio di San Leonardo

Via Santa Caterina.
📞 0183 627 83. ⬤ 9am–noon, 3–7pm. ⬤ 1st Mon of the month.
In the southern part of Parasio, looking out towards the sea, this oratory (1600) is dedicated to Imperia's official patron saint. Inside is a lovely work, *Our Lady of Sorrows and souls in Purgatory*, by Gregorio De Ferrari (1647–1726).

St Leonard (1676–1751) was born in the house standing next to the oratory.

🏛 Convento di Santa Chiara

Via Santa Chiara 9. 📞 0183 627 62.
Church ⬤ 7am–noon, 3:30–7pm Mon–Sat (from 9am Sun & hols).

The principal reason to visit these buildings, which date from 1300 (modified in the 18th century), is to see the splendid arcade behind the convent, from which there is a fantastic view of the sea, and which is used to stage classical concerts in summer.

Inside the church is a *San Domenico Soriano and Madonna*, the work of Domenico Fiasella, and a *Madonna with Child and Santa Caterina da Bologna* by Sebastiano Conca.

🏛 Chiesa di San Pietro

Salita San Pietro. 📞 0183 603 56.
⬤ 6pm Sat for mass.

This Parasio church stands on the same level as a loggia overlooking the sea. Founded in 1100, it was built on the ruins of the old town walls. A medieval lookout tower forms the base of the round bell tower.

The façade, dating from 1789, is lively, with paired columns supporting three arches. Inside, a pictorial cycle on the *Life of St Peter* is attributed to Tommaso and Maurizio Carrega (late 1700s).

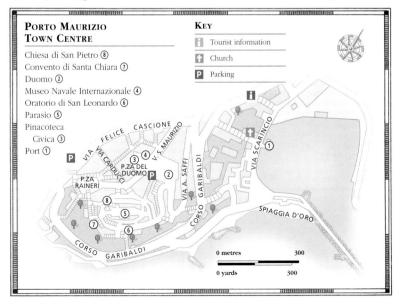

PORTO MAURIZIO TOWN CENTRE

Chiesa di San Pietro ⑧
Convento di Santa Chiara ⑦
Duomo ②
Museo Navale Internazionale ④
Oratorio di San Leonardo ⑥
Parasio ⑤
Pinacoteca
   Civica ③
Port ①

KEY

🛈 Tourist information

🏛 Church

🅿 Parking

0 metres 300
0 yards 300

The church of the Assunta, Triora

Dolcedo ⑳

Imperia. **Road Map** B4–5.
🚶 *1,200.* 🚆 *Imperia.* 🚌 ℹ️
Comune, 0183 280 004. 🎪 *La
Mongolfiera, traditional country
festival (1st Sun, Sep), organic market
(3rd Sun of month).*

SITUATED IN THE hinterland
behind Porto Maurizio,
in the Prino valley, is Dolcedo
a mountain village with
stone-paved mule tracks and
watermills along the banks of
the river, evidence of an olive
oil tradition dating back to
the 1100s; the local olive
groves are among the most
famous in the region.

There are no less than five
bridges across the river. The
oldest, known as **Ponte
Grande**, was built in 1292 by
the Knights of St John.

The parish church of **San
Tommaso** overlooks a small
piazza, paved in the Ligurian
style in black and white
pebbles. This Baroque jewel
was built in 1738.

Triora ㉑

Imperia. **Road Map** A4. 🚶 *500.*
🚆 *San Remo.* 🚌 ℹ️ *Pro Loco,
Corso Italia 7, 0184 944 77.*
🌐 *www.comune.triora.im.it*
🎪 *Processione del Monte (2nd Sun
after Easter), Festa della Madonna
della Misericordia (1st Sun in Jul).*

THE OLD MEDIEVAL village of
Triora, an outpost of the
Republic of Genoa, lies
near the head of the Valle
Argentina. With the Ligurian
Alps rising up behind, this is
a truly enchanting place.

Also known as the
"paese delle streghe"
(village of witches),
Triora is famous above
all for the witchcraft
trials, held here between
1587 and 1589. The
unique and popular
**Museo Etnografico
e della Stregoneria** is
devoted to the story of
these trials.

The centre of Triora
still preserves much
evidence of the village's
medieval origins, with
little alleys, narrow streets
and houses huddled together
around small squares. Of
seven original gates, the only
survivor is **Porta Soprana**,
with a rounded arch. Nearby
is the Fontana Soprana, the
oldest fountain in the town.

The one sight not to miss is
the collegiate church of
Assunta. It was originally
Romanesque-Gothic and still
retains the old bell tower and
main door, though the façade
is Neo-Classical. Inside
(reduced to a single aisle in
1770) there are several
notable works of art,
including several by Luca
Cambiaso; but chief among
them is an exquisite painting
on a gold background of the
Baptism of Christ (1397), by
the Sienese artist Taddeo di
Bartolo. It is the oldest
known painting of its type in
the Riviera di Ponente.

There is also a delightful
church, of **San Bernardino**,
just outside Triora; its interior
is virtually smothered in
15th-century frescoes.

🏛 **Museo Etnografico
e della Stregoneria**
Corso Italia 1. 📞 *0184 944 77.*
🕐 *3–6:30pm Mon–Fri, 10:30am–
noon, 3–6:30pm Sat, Sun.* 🎫

ENVIRONS: about 10 km
(6 miles) beyond Triora, just a
stone's throw from the French
border, is the tiny village of
Realdo. It is set in a stunning
position, teetering on a rocky
cliff at 1,065 m (3,500 ft)
above sea level, with some of
Liguria's highest peaks as a
backdrop. The houses have a
distinctly Alpine look and the
few inhabitants speak in old
Provençal.

Taggia ㉒

Imperia. **Road Map** A5.
🚶 *14,000.* 🚆 🚌 ℹ️ *Via Boselli,
Arma di Taggia, 0184 437 33.*
🌐 *www.rivieradeifiori.org and
www.taggia.it*
🎪 *Corteo Storico dei Rioni (4th Sun
in Feb); Festa della Maddalena (3rd
Sun in Jul); antiques market (last
weekend of month).*

LYING CLOSE TO THE mouth
of the Valle Argentina is
Taggia, whose 16th-century
walls conceal a fascinating
medieval village. One of the
most impressive sights is the
medieval bridge across the
Argentina, with 16 arches of
which two are Romanesque.

Via Soleri, the heart of
the old centre, is flanked by
porticoes with black stone
arches and many fine old
buildings. The Baroque parish
church of **Santi Giacomo e
Filippo** is lovely, but
Taggia's most important
monument is the **Convento
di San Domenico**. Built
between 1460 and 1490, it is
considered to have the best
collection of works by the
Liguria-Nice school. Its
masterpieces include five
works by the French artist
Ludovico Brea.

It is worth popping down to
Arma di Taggia, the small
resort on the coast. It has a
lovely beach, as well as several
hotels and restaurants.

🏛 **Convento di San
Domenico**
Piazza Beato Cristoforo.
📞 *0184 476 254.* 🕐 *9am–noon,
3–6pm Mon–Sat.* 🎫

**The arcaded Via Soleri in Taggia,
with its black stone arches**

Ludovico Brea

O F THE MANY FOREIGN artists working in Liguria, and in particular on the Riviera di Ponente, between the mid-15th century and the mid-16th century, Ludovico Brea (1443–c.1523) is the best documented.

Pietà by Ludovico Brea, in Taggia

Born in Nice, Brea became a painter in his native city and was probably influenced by the artistic trends emanating from Avignon. Cultural exchange, encouraged by trade between Liguria and the South of France – a depot for goods from northern Europe – was lively at that time, and it was not unusual for Flemish paintings, or the artists themselves, to find themselves in the Ligurian area. Thus, Ludovico Brea was able to learn from and be influenced by works from different schools of painting and absorb a variety of cultural elements. Of northern European styles, he was particularly interested in Flemish art, but was also fascinated by the miniatures found in medieval manuscripts. Brea was extremely adept at understanding the taste of his Ligurian patrons, a skill that enabled him to work in Italy for many years.

After producing some early work in his native city, Brea transferred to Liguria. Traces of his various moves and of his life in general at that time are scant, and generalizations about his artistic influences are usually made by looking at his later work. While in Liguria, you may also come across the work of Ludovico's brother, Antonio, and his son, Francesco.

THE ARTIST AT WORK

Ludovico Brea did most of his work in three Ligurian cities: in Genoa, where his works can be seen in the gallery of Palazzo Bianco (a *St Peter* and *Crucifixion*) and in the church of Santa Maria di Castello (*Conversion of St Paul* and *Coronation of the Virgin*); in Savona, where there are works in the oratory of Nostra Signora di Castello (*Madonna and Saints*), in the Cathedral treasury (*Assunta and Saints*, detail shown left) and in the Pinacoteca Civica (*Christ on the Cross between the Madonna and St John the Evangelist*); and in Taggia, with works in the Convento di San Domenico and the adjacent museum. All three paintings illustrated below can be seen in Taggia.

The **Madonna del Rosario**, *which dates from 1513 and is also in San Domenico in Taggia, features a landscape background of some depth. A lightening sky looms in the background.*

The **polyptych** *dedicated to Santa Caterina da Siena (1488), has an astonishing gold background, against which the figures emerge in an almost surreal fashion.*

The **Baptism of Christ** (1495) *is a polyptych in San Domenico, in Taggia, in the chapel on the left of the presbytery, and is the only work complete with its frame and predella.*

Tour of the Armea and Crosia Valleys ㉓

One of the
colourful murals
in Apricale

THIS ITINERARY FOLLOWS a route which can be covered easily in a day. It takes the visitor to some of the most picturesque villages in the far west of the Riviera del Ponente, on the slopes of the hinterland behind the strip between San Remo and Bordighera. Interesting though the coastal towns are, this part of the Ligurian interior also has a great deal to offer visitors. Here you will find ancient towns and villages which grew up along the old salt routes, often very close to the border with France. Set among green hills which rise rapidly to become mountains, many of these ancient centres have managed to preserve their old appearance and atmosphere, despite the passing of time.

Apricale ③

At the heart of this medieval village, set in a panoramic position, is Piazza Vittorio Emanuele, with the parish church of the Purificazione di Maria, the Oratory of San Bartolomeo and some castle ruins. Apricale (from *apricus*, which means "facing towards the sun") is also known as the "artists' village", because of the modern murals painted on the façades of the old houses.

Perinaldo ④

At the top of Val Crosia, this village was the birthplace of Italy's greatest astronomer, Gian Domenico Cassini (1625–1712), discoverer of asteroids and moons and famous for his work for Louis XIV; a museum in the Palazzo del Comune is dedicated to him. The parish church of San Nicolò dates from 1495.

Vallecrosia Alta ⑤

Set among fields of flowers and vineyards which produce Rossese, one of Liguria's most prized wines, this town is the older twin of the modern seaside village of Vallecrosia, just west of Bordighera. In the medieval quarter is the church of San Rocco. Nearby, at Garibbe, there is an unexpected Museum of Song and Sound Reproduction.

PIGNA

PIGNA

R. Bonda

Isolabonana •

③

④

T. Nervia

T. di Vallecrosia

⑤

NICE

• *Ventimiglia*

• *Bordighera*

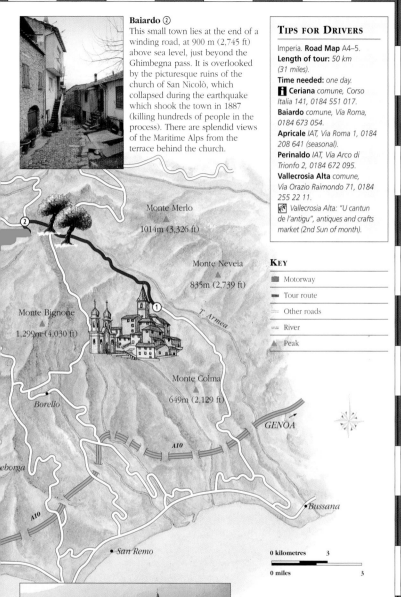

Baiardo ②

This small town lies at the end of a winding road, at 900 m (2,745 ft) above sea level, just beyond the Ghimbegna pass. It is overlooked by the picturesque ruins of the church of San Nicolò, which collapsed during the earthquake which shook the town in 1887 (killing hundreds of people in the process). There are splendid views of the Maritime Alps from the terrace behind the church.

TIPS FOR DRIVERS

Imperia. **Road Map** A4–5.
Length of tour: *50 km (31 miles).*
Time needed: *one day.*
🛈 **Ceriana** *comune, Corso Italia 141, 0184 551 017.*
Baiardo *comune, Via Roma, 0184 673 054.*
Apricale *IAT, Via Roma 1, 0184 208 641 (seasonal).*
Perinaldo *IAT, Via Arco di Trionfo 2, 0184 672 095.*
Vallecrosia Alta *comune, Via Orazio Raimondo 71, 0184 255 22 11.*
🛍 *Vallecrosia Alta: "U cantun de l'antigu", antiques and crafts market (2nd Sun of month).*

KEY

🛤 Motorway

▬ Tour route

═ Other roads

═ River

▲ Peak

Monte Merlo

1014m (3,326 ft)

Monte Neveia

835m (2,739 ft)

T. Armea

Monte Bignone

1,299m (4,030 ft)

①

Monte Colma

649m (2,129 ft)

Borello

GENOA

A10

eborga

A10

•Bussana

• San Remo

0 kilometres   3

0 miles   3

Ceriana ①

This pretty mountain-top village lies in the Valle Armea, 12 km (7 miles) north of San Remo. Built in the Middle Ages on the site of a Roman villa, Ceriana's old centre is still encircled by perfectly preserved walls. Walking around the narrow streets and alleys, you can enjoy unexpected glimpses of the surrounding countryside.

San Remo ㉔

Imperia. **Road Map** A5. 🚶 *59,000.*
🚆 🚌 ℹ️ *APT Riviera dei Fiori,
Largo Nuvoloni 1, 0184 590 59.*
🌐 *www.rivieradeifiori.org*
🎭 *Festival della Canzone Italiana
(late Feb or early Mar); Milano–San
Remo cycle race (Sat following
19 Mar); Rally di San Remo (early Oct).*

D EFINED, in the eyes of
many Italians, by its
thriving flower industry and
its Festival of Italian Song,
San Remo is also one of the
Italian Riviera's best-known
and most atmospheric resorts.

The city is divided into
three distinct areas: Corso
Matteotti and around (the
heart of the shopping district),
La Pigna (the old town), and
the west end of the seafront,
which was the heart of the
resort during its heyday.

Tourism, mainly English,
boomed in San Remo from
the mid-1800s to the early
1900s, a period of great
expansion when all manner
of grand hotels and villas
were built, including various
Art Nouveau palazzi. There
is no better Belle Epoque
monument than the splendid
and still-thriving **Casinò
Municipale**, built by Eugenio
Ferret in 1904–06.

Another unmistakable San
Remo landmark, with its
onion domes, is the **Russian
Orthodox Church**, built in
the 1920s. The Russians were
almost as passionate about
San Remo as the
English, and the
seafront **Corso
Imperatrice** was
named in honour of
Maria Alexandrovna,
wife of Czar Alexander
II and a frequent visitor
to San Remo. This
seafront boulevard
is a favourite place to
stroll, and provides a
wonderful taste of the
old aristocratic resort.

Beyond **Lungomare
Vittorio Emanuele II** and
Lungomare delle Nazioni,
where the streets are broken
up by lawns, the road
continues to the modern
marina, Portosole, and the old,
or town, port.

At the end of Corso Trento
e Trieste, beyond the **Giardini
Ormond**, stands **Villa
Nobel**, where the famous
Swedish scientist lived
and where he also
died in 1896.

The other part of
San Remo that no
one should miss
is its medieval
"città vecchia",
fortified in the 11th
century in order to
keep out the Saracens.
The area is known as
La Pigna, or pine
cone, because of
its layout: the
maze of alleys,
steps, arches and covered
walkways spread out in
concentric circles from the
top of the hill.

The main monuments,
including the cathedral
and the Oratorio
dell'Immacolata
Concezione (1563), are
found in the central
Piazza San Siro. The
Cathedral of San Siro,
founded in the 12th
century, has two fine
side doors featuring
bas-reliefs in the lunette:
the one on the left,
which dates from the
12th century, represents
the *Agnello pasquale*, or
paschal lamb. Inside,
there are three aisles and
three apses, extended in
1600. There are good
works of art including a
15th-century *Crucifixion*.

San Remo's famous casino

At the top of La Pigna is the
sumptuous **Santuario di
Nostra Signora della Costa**,
remodelled in the 1630s.
There is a fine pebble mosaic
outside and four statues by
Maragliano on the high altar.

As well as shops, there are
some interesting palazzi on
Corso Matteotti. One of
these is Palazzo Borea
d'Olmo, a curious mix of
Mannerism and Baroque.
As the **Museo Civico**,
it houses a mix of
archaeological
finds, Garibaldian
relics and 18th-
and 19th-century
paintings.

Finally, for an insight
into the local flower
trade, visit San Remo's
famous wholesale
flower market,
which lies just east
of the city centre
in the Armea valley.

Statue of *Spring*, on the
San Remo seafront

🏛 **Museo Civico**
Corso Matteotti 143.
📞 *0184 531 942.*
🕐 *9am–noon, 3–6pm Tue–Sat.*

ENVIRONS: About 10 km
(6 miles) east of San Remo
is the suburb of **Bussana
Nuova** and, beyond,
Bussana Vecchia, one of the
most charming spots on the
Riviera di Ponente.

Destroyed by the 1887
earthquake, which left only
the bell tower of the Baroque
church of **Sacro Cuore**
intact, Bussana Vecchia was
partially restored in the 1960s,
when an artists' colony
moved in. They opened up
studios and crafts workshops,
but took care to change the
original appearance of the
village as little as possible.

The harbour at San Remo

◁ **The little church of Sant'Ampelio, in Bordighera**

Pigna ㉕

Imperia. **Road Map** A4.
🏠 1,015. 🚊 Ventimiglia. 🚌
ℹ Comune, Piazza Umberto I,
0184 241 016.

SITUATED IN THE foothills of
the Maritime Alps in the
Alta Val Nervia, some 40 km
(25 miles) north of San Remo,
Pigna is a fascinating place;
its form is reminiscent of the
eponymous district in San
Remo. Strolling around the
narrow streets, known as
chibi, you can understand
how the medieval town
was built, with the houses
grouped defensively on
concentric streets.

Among a number of fine
churches, the most important
is the church of **San Michele**,
founded in 1450. A splendid
white marble rose window,
perhaps the work of Giovanni
Gagini from the early 1500s,
adorns the façade. Inside, the
Polyptych of St Michael is a
monumental work by the
Piemontese
artist Canavesio
(1500s), in which
the influence of
the Brea brothers
(see p159) is
evident. Also by
Canavesio are
the frescoes
portraying *The
Passion of Christ*
housed in the
small church of **San
Bernardo**, within the
cemetery. Other places of
interest are the ruins of the
church of **San Tommaso**,
and **Piazza Castello**, with
lovely views over the village
of Castel Vittorio.

The rose window at San
Michele, Pigna

Dolceacqua ㉖

See pp166–7.

Bordighera ㉗

Imperia. **Road Map** A5.
🏠 11,300. 🚊 🚌 ℹ Via Vittorio
Emanuele II 172-174, 0184 262 322.
🌐 www.rivieradeifiori.org
🎭 Bordighera Città dell'Umorismo,
a festival of humour (late Apr–early
May).

A FAMOUS PAINTING BY
Monet called *A View of
Bordighera* is evidence of the
historic fame of this sunny
and lively resort. As was the
case elsewhere on the
Riviera, Bordighera was
particularly popular with the
British. Here, too, you find
Art Nouveau palazzi (many
converted into hotels or
apartments), and a popular
seafront boulevard – the
Lungomare Argentina, with
Capo Sant'Ampelio at the far
end. The beach is good
and often busy, and
there are palm trees
wherever you look.
The **Biblioteca
Museo Clarence
Bicknell** was
founded by one of
Bordighera's many
British visitors, a
vicar, botanist and
archaeologist.
Bicknell's library-
cum-museum houses
Roman funerary objects and,
more interestingly, casts of
rock drawings and a vast
photographic archive of
ancient graffiti from the
nearby Vallée des Merveilles
in France.

Plaque welcoming people to
Seborga, near Bordighera

There is a handful of sights of
historic interest. By the sea,
on Capo Sant'Ampelio, is
the Romanesque church of
Sant'Ampelio, with an 11th-
century crypt; it stands on the
spot where Ampelio (a hermit
who later became a saint),
once lived.

More centrally, look out for
the 17th-century church of
Santa Maria Maddalena,
with a fine early 16th-century
marble sculpture on the
high altar, attributed to the
workshop of Domenico
Parodi. In nearby Piazza De
Amicis there is a marble
fountain (1783) featuring a
statue of Magiargiè, a slave to
the Spanish Moors who died
in Bordighera.

For a quiet but interesting
interlude, go to the **Giardino
Esotico Pallanca**, which has
more than 3,000 species of
cacti and succulents.

🏛 **Biblioteca Museo
Clarence Bicknell**
Via Bicknell 3. 📞 0184 263 694.
🕐 9:30am–1pm, 1:30–4:45pm
Mon–Fri. ⬤ public hols.
🌵 **Giardino Esotico
Pallanca**
Via Madonna della Ruota 1.
📞 0184 266 347. 🕐 winter:
2–5pm Mon, 9am–5pm Tue–Sun;
summer: 9am–12:30pm, 2:30–7pm
daily. 🎫 🌐 www.pallanca.it

ENVIRONS: In a lofty position
about 12 km (7 miles) north
of Bordighera is the ancient
village of **Seborga**, which,
along with its 350 inhabitants,
enjoys the unexpected title of
"principality". Thanks to an
historical anomaly, the town
was able to elect its own
sovereign, Giorgio I, in 1963,
and pass a constitution, which
was renewed in 1995. They
have their own currency, the
luigino (Seborga's first mint
was set up by Benedictine
monks in 1660), and print their
own stamps, and cars carry
SB on their licence plates.

Cactus in the tropical garden of Pallanca at Bordighera

Dolceacqua **26**

Inscription with the words of Monet

A QUIRK OF FATE: this delightful medieval village is, despite its name (which means "fresh water"), home to one of the most prized and famous red wines in Italy, Rossese, a favourite with Napoleon and Pope Julius III. Overlooked by the imposing but not overbearing mass of the ruined Castello dei Doria, the village spreads out on the slopes of the mountain and is reminiscent of one of Liguria's traditional *presepi* (nativity scenes) when seen from above. The River Nervia divides Dolceacqua into two. On one side is the older part, known as Borgo, while the newer district on the right is called Terra. The artist Claude Monet, who loved this area, painted the castle and described the old bridge which links the two quarters as a "jewel of lightness".

★ Church of San Giorgio
Across the river from the old village, the 13th-century church of San Giorgio has the remains of a Romanesque bell tower, and a ceiling with interesting painted beams. In the crypt is a Doria family tomb.

★ Ponte Vecchio
This light and elegant bridge has a single ogee arch with an impressive span of 33 m (110 ft). Built in the 15th century, the bridge links the two quarters of Terra and Borgo, separated by the River Nervia.

Monument to the "Gombo"
This modern work is dedicated to Pier Vicenzo Mela, a local man who was the first to use an olive press (gombo) to extract oil, in the 1700s.

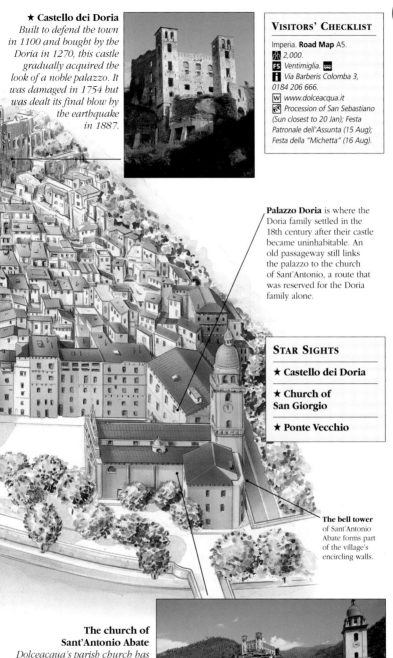

★ **Castello dei Doria**
Built to defend the town in 1100 and bought by the Doria in 1270, this castle gradually acquired the look of a noble palazzo. It was damaged in 1754 but was dealt its final blow by the earthquake in 1887.

Palazzo Doria is where the Doria family settled in the 18th century after their castle became uninhabitable. An old passageway still links the palazzo to the church of Sant'Antonio, a route that was reserved for the Doria family alone.

STAR SIGHTS

★ **Castello dei Doria**

★ **Church of San Giorgio**

★ **Ponte Vecchio**

The bell tower of Sant'Antonio Abate forms part of the village's encircling walls.

The church of Sant'Antonio Abate
Dolceacqua's parish church has in front of it a broad square paved with pebbles, in the Ligurian tradition. The church dates from 1400, but was altered in the Baroque era. Inside there is a lovely polyptych painted by Ludovico Brea.

Ventimiglia ㉘

Imperia. **Road Map** A5.
🏘 *26,000.* FS 🚌
ℹ️ *Via Cavour 61, 0184 351 183.*
w *www.rivieradeifiori.org and
www.ventimiglia.it*
🎭 *Corteo Storico, historical
procession (1st or 2nd Sun in Aug,
odd years); Battaglia di Fiori (summer).*

VENTIMIGLIA is the last major
town on the Riviera di
Ponente before the French
border. It is a perfect
synthesis of the characteristics
of towns along this part of the
coast, and, more generally,
of all coastal towns in the
region: a place where past
and present seem to co-exist
quite happily, where Roman
ruins rub shoulders with the
latest tourist facilities.

A frontier town par
excellence (its history is
studded with numerous
disputes with nearby France
over the national border
lines), Ventimiglia straddles
the Roia and the Nervia
valleys, among the most
beautiful in the Ligurian Alps.
Nearby are marvels of nature
such as the Grotte dei Balzi
Rossi and the gardens of Villa
Hanbury *(see pp170–71).*

The River Roia divides
Ventimiglia into two: the
medieval part on a hill to the
west, and the modern town
on the coastal plain to the
east. Traces of the era of
Roman domination, which
followed rule by the Liguri
Intemelii people, can be seen
at **Albintimilium**, on the
eastern periphery of the new
town. Clearly visible from the
flyover on the Via Aurelia, the
ruins consist of a stretch of
the *decumanus maximus* (or

**View of the apse of the Cattedrale
dell'Assunta, Ventimiglia**

main street), a few houses
and the great baths (the
source of the lovely Mosaico
di Arione, now in front of the
hospital). More important
than any of these, however, is
the small **Theatre**, the most
significant Roman monument
in Liguria. Dating from the
early 3rd century BC, the
theatre could seat more than
5,000 spectators. Ten levels of
steps in the lower section,
made from Turbia stone, are
still well preserved, while
the western entrance gate is
practically intact. Various
finds discovered at the site
are on display in the nearby
**Museo Archeologico
Gerolamo Rossi**, in the Forte
dell'Annunziata in town.

Via Garibaldi (also known
as "la piazza") is the main
street through the cobbled
and charming *centro storico*.
There are some fine palazzi
here, some with hanging
gardens to the back opening
onto the upper floors, in the
16th-century tradition. Among
the most important buildings
are the Palazzo Pubblico,

the Loggia del Magistrato
dell'Abbondanza, and the
Neo-Classical former Teatro
Civico. This houses the
Civica Biblioteca Aprosiana,
the oldest public library in
Liguria (founded in 1648)
with a fine collection of rare
books and manuscripts.

At the heart of Via Garibaldi
is the imposing bulk of the
Cattedrale dell'Assunta.
This was built in place of
an 8th-century Carolingian
chuch in the 11th and 12th
centuries, and has been
modified at intervals since:
the façade is Romanesque, for
example, while the portico,
added in 1222, is Gothic. The
bell tower, constructed on a
12th-century base, was rebuilt
in the Baroque era and
remodelled once again in
the 19th century.

**Marble cover of a funerary urn,
1st century AD**

Inside, there is not much to
see, though in the crypt you
can see parts of the old
medieval church, as well as
some pre-Roman sculptures.

Adjoining the Assunta is
the octagonal **Baptistry**
(11th century); this contains
a wonderful font dating from
the 12th–13th centuries.

Continuing along Via
Garibaldi, past another
couple of churches, you
eventually reach Porta Nizza.
From here, following Via
della Torre and Via Appio,
you reach Piazza Colletta
and the lovely Romanesque
church of **San Michele**. The
unimpressive façade is 19th-
century, but the main body of
the church, of which only the
central nave survives, dates
from the 11th century; the
bell tower, apse and vault are
from the 12th century. Inside
is an interesting 11th-century

The Roman theatre in Ventimiglia, dating from the 3rd century AD

Overlooking the town of Ventimiglia

crypt, incorporating various Roman materials, including columns used in the high altar.

From Porta Nizza, you can also climb up west of the old city to the ruins of three medieval forts, a reminder of the battles once fought over Ventimiglia. One of these, the **Castel d'Appio**, built by the Genoese in the 13th century, occupies the site not only of a Roman military camp *(castrum)* but also of an early Ligurian defence post. There are marvellous views of the Riviera from here.

The modern, eastern part of Ventimiglia, complete with seaside promenades, is a shopping mecca and is very popular with the French. The streets are busy at weekends and on Fridays, when people from the surrounding area flood in for the weekly market.

♙ Albintimilium
Corso Genova. **[]** *refer to the tourist office.* **◻** *summer: 3–6pm Sat, Sun.*
🏛 Museo Archeologico Gerolamo Rossi
Via Verdi 41. **[]** *0184 351 181.*
◻ *9am–12:30pm, 3–5pm Tue–Sat; 10am–12:30pm Sun.* ▨ **[]**

Balzi Rossi ㉙

Grimaldi di Ventimiglia (Imperia).
Road Map A5.

THIS PREHISTORIC SITE, one of the most famous in the western Mediterranean, lies about 10 km (6 miles) west of Ventimiglia, below the village of Grimaldi and just a stone's throw from the Italy-France frontier. It consists of nine

caves, which have been explored at various times since the 19th century. The name of Balzi Rossi (meaning "red rocks") derives from the reddish colour of the precipitous limestone cliffs.

This atmospheric place has yielded fascinating evidence of human settlement in this part of Liguria, going back as far as the Paleolithic age. The area was probably chosen because of the favourable natural conditions, including the warm climate and the proximity of the sea. There is a walkway connecting some of the caves, some of which you are also allowed to enter.

Numerous stone and bone instruments, fossil remains of animals, and various

Necklace found in the Triple Tomb

ornamental and artistic objects have been discovered in the caves, in particular in the Grotta del Principe, slightly removed from the other caves and also the largest. Of greatest interest are the many tombs, which provide a few tangible snippets of information about the people who lived here some 240,000 years ago. They were undoubtedly among the most sophisticated of any people then living in Europe.

The most famous of these tombs, known as the **Triple Tomb**, was discovered in Barma Grande cave in 1892. Today, it is on display in the **Museo Preistorico dei Balzi Rossi**, founded by the Englishman Sir Thomas Hanbury *(see p170)* in 1898. To the sides are two male individuals, a boy on the left and a man over 2 m (6 ft) tall on the right. At the centre is a girl of around 16 years old. Funerary objects, such as sea shells, pendants of worked bone, deer teeth and necklaces fashioned out of fish vertebrae, traditionally accompanied the deceased.

The museum also has on display a reproduction of the only figure engraved in a naturalistic style to be discovered at Balzi Rossi. Found in the Grotta del Caviglione, it is the profile of a shortish, stocky horse, 40 cm (16 in) long and 20 cm (8 in) high. It is known as the **Przewalskii Horse**; a few rare examples of the breed survive in Mongolia.

Also on display are stone instruments, animal skeletons and small statues.

🏛 Grotte e Museo Preistorico dei Balzi Rossi
Ponte San Ludovico, Via Balzi Rossi 9.
[] *0184 381 13.*
◻ *9am–12:30pm, 2–6pm Tue–Sun.* **[]** *hourly.* ▨

One of the nine Balzi Rossi caves

Villa Hanbury ③

Oriental bronze bell

THIS SPLENDID botanical garden was founded in 1867 by Sir Thomas Hanbury, a rich English businessman, and his brother Daniel, a botanist, with the help of the eminent German botanist Ludovico Winter. Sir Thomas was passionate about Liguria, and saw the opportunity that its warm climate provided: the exotic plants that he brought back from his travels, particularly those from hot, dry areas such as Southern Africa and Mexico, he was able to acclimatize to co-exist with the local flora. By 1898, the garden included more than 7,000 plant species. The gardens were left to decay during much of the 20th century but are now being coaxed back to their former glory by the University of Genoa.

Agave
Aloes and agaves, particular favourites of Sir Thomas, are planted among the rocks to re-create the desert habitat from whence they came.

★ Dragon Fountain
Encircled by papyruses, warm-climate plants which have acclimatized well here, this fountain has an ancient and rather mysterious air. Sitting on the rim is a dragon, an echo of Sir Thomas's beloved Far East.

Temple of the Four Seasons
This is one of many temples that Sir Thomas had built around the gardens, in line with late 19th-century taste. Its classical style is evocative of an Italian Renaissance garden.

STAR FEATURES

★ **Dragon Fountain**

★ **The Villa**

The Terraces
In this part of the garden the plants are grouped so as to form "themed gardens". There are wonderful views from the Pavilion.

VISITORS' CHECKLIST

Corso Montecarlo 43, La Mortola Inferiore (Imperia). **Road Map** A5.
☎ 0184 229 507.
FS *Ventimiglia.*
◯ *Nov–Mar: 10am–4pm Thu–Tue; Apr–mid-Jun: 10am–5pm daily; mid-Jun–Sep: 9am–6pm daily; Sep–Oct: 10am–6pm.* 🎫
W *www.amicihanbury.it*

The Viale dei Cipressi (avenue of cypresses) is one of the most charming parts of the garden, with its lines of tall trees, a familiar sight in the Italian countryside.

★ **The Villa**
The original palazzo was built in the 14th century and extended in the 17th. In the 1930s, Mussolini held a notorious meeting with General Franco here. The villa now houses offices and is not open to the public, but you can enjoy the lovely views over the gardens and down to the sea from the villa's loggia.

TRAVELLERS' NEEDS

WHERE TO STAY 174-183
WHERE TO EAT 184-197
SHOPPING 198-199
OUTDOOR ACTIVITIES 200-201
ENTERTAINMENT 202-203

WHERE TO STAY

L IGURIA HAS LONG been popular with holiday-makers and therefore has a long tradition of providing a wide range of accommodation, particularly on the coast. Along both the Riviera di Levante and the Riviera di Ponente, with their collection of renowned resorts, visitors will find an almost uninterrupted string of sumptuous hotels and family-run *pensioni*, which are open virtually all year round. Genoa, sandwiched between the two rivieras, has accommodation to suit all tastes and budgets both in the Centro Storico and in the immediate vicinity.

In general, visitors tend to stay on the coast and make day trips inland. If you want to try out the increasingly popular option of *agriturismo*, which means staying on a farm, you should head into the Ligurian hinterland. Camping is another option, which you can do either inland or along the coast.

Logo of the Grand Hotel Diana in Alassio

HOTEL CATEGORIES AND PRICES

I N LIGURIA, HOTELS are classified according to the Italian national system. The categories go from one up to five stars, that is, from budget accommodation to luxury hotels. In general, you can expect services to be of a good standard, but the best value for money is generally found in the three-star category. Note that hotels in the lower categories may not accept credit cards.

Prices vary according to the season, rising in the (admittedly long) high season and during major festivals and cultural events.

BOOKING

I N A POPULAR REGION like Liguria the low season tends to be limited to relatively short periods, such as mid-winter. High season, obviously, is the summer, when Liguria's long coastline and beaches attract big crowds. Anyone planning to visit the region in the summer is strongly advised to book accommodation well in advance. In most cases a fax or an e-mail will suffice to confirm a booking.

HOTELS

A REGION WHICH depends to a large extent on tourism for its economy, Liguria has a well-developed network of hotels, with generally good facilites. The one exception on the coast is the Cinque Terre, where accommodation tends to be fairly simple.

Most of the coastal resorts can offer hotels in all the five categories. A list of hotels, including family-run *pensioni*, with prices, can be obtained from the regional tourist

Holidaymakers on the beach at Monterosso

(APT) offices *(see opposite)* or from the local offices in the larger resorts *(see p207).*

AGRITURISMO AND BED & BREAKFAST

A GRITURISMO (or farm holidays), have become a popular alternative form of accommodation, particularly for people who love the outdoors or who want to choose from activites such as fishing or horse riding. Staying in a rural farm also provides a chance to escape from the hubbub of the coast.

The *agriturismo* formula, which can be found in other regions of Italy, is simple: working farms offer rooms (including self-catering options) and authentic home-made food, as well as other facilities, ranging from a

Comfortable public rooms at the Hotel Royal in San Remo

◁ **Colourful houses, typical of coastal Liguria, and beach huts**

The seafront at Bordighera, lined with hotels

children's play area to a swimming pool. The options range from the small family-owned farm, able to accommodate just a handful of people, to the grander, less traditional places that offer greater comfort and a wider range of facilities.

At all of the farms, however, you can expect genuinely good food, based on local ingredients, in many cases grown or made by the owners themselves, whether in the form of fruit and vegetables, home-reared meat or home-made cheese. It is usually possible to buy the farm produce, too.

Bed & breakfast accommodation, also available in Liguria, is generally comfortable and inexpensive. This type of lodging is found mainly in the larger cities and in the principal coastal resorts – rarely in the interior. Unlike on farms geared to *agriturismo*, meals are not provided.

Tourist signs

CAMPING

CAMPING IN Italy does not have as big a following as in some other European countries, so you may have to search quite hard for a camp site to suit your needs. Even so, most of the Riviera resorts have at least one site that can accommodate tents, camper vans or caravans. Many camp sites are situated close to the sea, some with private beaches reserved for camp residents. Sites are usually clean and well-cared for and in reasonably natural surroundings. Coastal sites are often particularly busy in August, so be sure to book in advance. And, since camping is not necessarily a cheap option in Italy, always check the rates.

Note that there are strict regulations as to where camper vans can be parked.

A list of camp sites can be obtained from any regional tourist (APT) office.

SELF-CATERING

BESIDES THE option of self-catering on an *agriturismo* farm or camp site, there are also self-catering apartments available for rent. These can be found primarily in the largest seaside resorts along the riviera, and may well suit families with young children

better than a hotel. Again, the accommodation listings provided by the many tourist (APT) offices should provide the names, addresses and phone numbers of the various agencies which deal with short-term lets. In addition, the tourist literature should also include details and phone numbers of private individuals who offer apartments for rent.

A Casa di Roby, a bed & breakfast in Moneglia

DIRECTORY

APT Cinque Terre e Golfo dei Poeti
Viale Mazzini 47,
La Spezia.
📞 0187 770 900.
FAX 0187 770 908.
W www.aptcinqueterre.sp.it
@ info@aptcinqueterre.sp.it

APT Genova
Stazione Principe,
Genova.
📞 010 246 2633.
FAX 010 581 408.
W www.apt.genova.it
@ aptgenova@apt.genova.it

APT Riviera Ligure delle Palme
Viale Gibb 26,
Alassio.
📞 0182 647 11.
FAX 0182 644 690.
W www.inforiviera.it
@ aptpalme@inforiviera.it

APT Riviera dei Fiori
Largo Nuvoloni 1,
San Remo.
📞 0184 590 59.
FAX 0184 507 649.
W www.rivieradeifiori.org
@ aptfiori@rivieradeifiori.org

APT Tigullio
Via XXV Aprile 4,
Santa Margherita Ligure.
📞 0185 292 91.
FAX 0185 290 222.
W www.apttigullio.liguria.it
@ infoapt@apttigullio.liguria.it

Agenzia Regionale per la Promozione Turistica "In Liguria"
Piazza Matteotti 9,
Genova.
📞 010 530 82 01.
FAX 010 595 85 07.
W www.turismo.liguriainrete.it

Choosing a Hotel

These hotels have been selected across a wide price range for their good value, facilities and location. They are listed by region and then by price. Use the colour-coded thumb tabs, which indicate the areas covered on each page, to guide you to the relevant section. For map references, see the Genoa Street Finder on pages 94–9 or the road map inside the back cover.

		Rooms	Credit Cards	Garden or Terrace	Parking	Restaurant

GENOA

Il Centro Storico: *Colombo*   € | 26 | ● | ■ | | |
Via Porta Soprana 27. **Map** 2 F4 or 6D4. **(** and **FAX** *010 251 36 43.*
W www.hotelcolombo.it
This hotel, perfectly located on a pedestrian street close to the cathedral, is very friendly and very popular. The rooms are clean and individually decorated. Wonderful roof terrace with views down to the port.

Il Centro Storico: *Veronese*   €€ | 19 | ● | | ● | |
Vico Cicala 3. **Map** 5 B2. **(** *010 251 07 71.* **FAX** *010 251 06 39.*
W www.hotelveronese.com
In the heart of the old town, and just a stone's throw from the old port and the Aquarium. Rooms are comfortable, well-equipped and quiet. ▤ 🐾

Il Centro Storico: *Palazzo Cicala*   €€€ | 6 | ● | | | |
Piazza San Lorenzo 16. **Map** 5 C3. **(** *010 251 88 24.* **FAX** *010 246 74 14.*
W www.palazzocicala.it
In a wonderfully central location, facing the cathedral and in a buzzing area, this old aristocratic home has been transformed into a stylish hotel with all mod cons, an eclectic mix of modern and antique furniture, and great views. High ceilings, stucco and DVD, PC and Internet access in every room. No hotel facilities, however, and no breakfast provided. ▤

Il Centro Storico: *Bristol Palace*   €€€€€ | 133 | ● | | ● | ▨ |
Via XX Settembre 35. **Map** 6 D-E4. **(** *010 592 541.* **FAX** *010 561 756.*
W www.hotelbristolpalace.com
Genoa's most fascinating hotel, close to Brignole Station, occupies a palazzo with typical Belle Epoque rooms. The public rooms, including a congenial English bar, are airy and full of atmosphere. An imposing staircase leads to the upper floors, where spacious and elegant rooms are furnished in keeping with the era. ▤ ♿

Le Strade Nuove: *Acquaverde*   €€ | 27 | ● | | ● | ▨ |
Via Balbi 29/6. **Map** 2 E2. **(** *010 265 427.* **FAX** *010 246 48 39.*
W www.hotelacquaverde.it
This hotel, recently refitted, occupies three floors in an old palazzo in Via Balbi, one of Genoa's oldest and most prestigious streets. Four of its rooms have a kitchenette and can be used for self-catering. ▤ 🐾 ♿

Le Strade Nuove: *Agnello d'Oro*   €€ | 30 | ● | | ● | |
Via Monachette 6. **Map** 2 D2. **(** *010 246 20 84.* **FAX** *010 246 23 27.*
W www.hotelagnellodoro.it
Just a short distance from Piazza del Principe, this tranquil hotel occupies a former Doria residence, dating from the 17th century. Rooms are simple but well cared for, and offer good value for money. The rooms on the top floor have great views, as does the hotel's lovely terrace.

Le Strade Nuove: *Vittoria & Orlandini*   €€ | 41 | ● | ▨ | ● | ▨ |
Via Balbi 33. **Map** 2 E2. **(** *010 261 923.* **FAX** *010 246 26 56.*
W www.vittoriaorlandini.com
A pretty Ligurian house alongside Palazzo Reale, this hotel has an inner courtyard and a pleasant interior, decorated with plants and the odd antique. Rooms are spacious and you can enjoy lovely views over the old city while you have breakfast. ▤ 🐾

Le Strade Nuove: *Astoria (Golden Tulip)*   €€€ | 69 | ● | | ● | |
Piazzale Brignole 4. **Map** 2 E2. **(** *010 873 316.* **FAX** *010 831 73 26.*
W www.hotelastoria-ge.com
The Hotel Astoria occupies a large Neo-Classical building in the heart of the city. Much of the original, elegant design survives inside, most obviously in the public areas. Guest rooms have all the usual facilities, including satellite TV and minibar. ▤ 🐾

		Rooms	Credit Cards	Garden or Terrace	Parking	Restaurant
Price categories are for a standard double room for one night including tax, service charges and breakfast: € under 85 euros €€ 85–125 euros €€€ 125–175 euros €€€€ 175–225 euros €€€€€ over 225 euros	**CREDIT CARDS** Hotels which accept the main credit cards. **GARDEN OR TERRACE** Hotel in a park or garden or with a terrace with panoramic views. **PARKING** Garage or parking facilities for guests, either within the hotel or nearby. **RESTAURANT** Hotel with a particularly good restaurant which is also open to non-residents.					

LE STRADE NUOVE: *Europa* €€€

Vico Monachette 8. **Map** 2 D2. ☎ 010 256 955. ℻ 010 261 047.
W www.pangea.it/europa

Very close to the Stazione Principe, the Europa has a pretty roof terrace with panoramic views over the port area. Rooms are comfortable There is a cocktail bar. ▤ 🛏

Rooms	Credit Cards	Garden or Terrace	Parking	Restaurant
38	●	▨	●	

LE STRADE NUOVE: *Metropoli (Best Western)* €€€

Piazza della Fontana Marose. **Map** 5 D2. ☎ 010 246 88 88. ℻ 010 246 86 86.
W www.bestwestern.it/metropoli_ge

An elegant three-star hotel situated close to Via Garibaldi. Rooms are tastefully decorated and have good facilities. Attractive public rooms and good breakfast buffet. ▤ 🛏

Rooms	Credit Cards	Garden or Terrace	Parking	Restaurant
48	●		●	

LE STRADE NUOVE: *Savoja Majestic* €€€€

Via Arsenale di Terra 5. **Map** 2 D2. ☎ 010 261 641. ℻ 010 261 883.
W www.hotelsavoiagenova.it

This large hotel occupies a late 19th-century palazzo near the Stazione Principe. Rooms are very spacious and well furnished. The public spaces, including the restaurant and bar, are all very pleasant and welcoming. ▤ 🍴 ♿ 🛏

Rooms	Credit Cards	Garden or Terrace	Parking	Restaurant
120	●		●	●

LE STRADE NUOVE: *Britannia (Ramada)* €€€€

Via Balbi 38. **Map** 2 E2. ☎ 010 269 91. ℻ 010 246 29 42. W www.britannia.it

The Britannia is a snazzy, modern hotel with rooms equipped with videos, safes and links with pay-TV. Fantastic views from the top floor and good facilities including a pool table, sauna, gym and snack bar. ▤ 🍴 🛏

Rooms	Credit Cards	Garden or Terrace	Parking	Restaurant
97	●		●	

LE STRADE NUOVE: *City (Best Western)* €€€€€

Via San Sebastiano 6. **Map** 3 A2. ☎ 010 55 45 or 800 820 080. ℻ 010 586 301.
W www.bestwestern.it/city_ge

In a road off the central Via Roma, this four-star hotel combines functionality and comfort. Elegant decor and excellent buffet breakfast. Rooms have everything you need, with particularly well-equipped bathrooms. ▤ 🍴 🛏

Rooms	Credit Cards	Garden or Terrace	Parking	Restaurant
66	●		●	●

FURTHER AFIELD (CENTRAL GENOA): *Assarotti* €€

Via Assarotti 40 C. **Map** 6 E2. ☎ 010 885 822. ℻ 010 839 12 07.
W www.hotelassarotti.it

In the 19th-century part of the city, beyond Via Roma, this hotel has comfortable rooms with satellite TV. Free internet access in foyer. ▤ 🛏

Rooms	Credit Cards	Garden or Terrace	Parking	Restaurant
25	●		●	

FURTHER AFIELD (CENTRAL GENOA): *Bellevue* €€€

Salita della Provvidenza 1. **Map** 2 D1. ☎ 010 246 24 00. ℻ 010 265 932.

Close to the Stazione Principe, this is a smart, modern hotel with sound-proof windows, minibar and colour TV (with national and European stations). Adjacent garage, large terrace with good views and meeting rooms, but no restaurant. ▤ 🛏

Rooms	Credit Cards	Garden or Terrace	Parking	Restaurant
38	●	▨	●	

FURTHER AFIELD (CENTRAL GENOA): *Moderno Verdi (Golden Tulip)* €€€€

Piazza G. Verdi 5. **Map** 3 C3. ☎ 010 553 21 04. ℻ 010 581 562.
W www.modernoverdi.it

In a reconstructed Liberty-style palazzo that dominates the large Piazza Giuseppe Verdi, next to the Brignole railway station. Good welcome and service. Don't miss the library. ▤ 🛏

Rooms	Credit Cards	Garden or Terrace	Parking	Restaurant
87	●		●	●

FURTHER AFIELD (CENTRAL GENOA): *Starhotel President* €€€€

Via Corte Lambruschini 4. **Map** 3 C3. ☎ 010 52 27. ℻ 010 553 18 20.
W www.starhotels.it

A large, modern building opposite the Stazione Brignole, and not far from the trade fair area, this is Genoa's top hotel. Built in the 1990s, the Starhotel combines functionality with comfort and luxury throughout, from the spacious rooms to the grand public areas and the gourmet La Corte restaurant. ▤ 🍴 🛏 ♿

Rooms	Credit Cards	Garden or Terrace	Parking	Restaurant
191	●		●	●

	Price categories		ROOMS	CREDIT CARDS	GARDEN OR TERRACE	PARKING	RESTAURANT

Price categories are for a standard double room for one night including tax, service charges and breakfast:

€ under 85 euros
€€ 85–125 euros
€€€ 125–175 euros
€€€€ 175–225 euros
€€€€€ over 225 euros

CREDIT CARDS
Hotels which accept the main credit cards.

GARDEN OR TERRACE
Hotel in a park or garden or with a terrace with panoramic views.

PARKING
Garage or parking facilities for guests, either within the hotel or nearby.

RESTAURANT
Hotel with a particularly good restaurant which is also open to non-residents.

Hotel	€	Rooms	Credit Cards	Garden or Terrace	Parking	Restaurant
FURTHER AFIELD (OUTER GENOA): *La Capannina*	€	32	●		●	

Via Tito Speri 7. **Road Map** D3. ☎ *010 317 131.* FAX *010 362 26 92.*
W www.lacapanninagenova.it
In the eastern residential district of Albaro, this is a quiet hotel close to the sea. Rooms are simple. The top-floor rooms have a private terrace, and the hotel has its own large terrace with lovely views, too. 目 ♥

| **FURTHER AFIELD (OUTER GENOA):** *Tirreno Al Mare* | €€ | 35 | ● | | ● | |

Via dei Mille 17. **Road Map** D3. ☎ *010 389 342.* FAX *010 386 342.*
W www.hoteltirrenogenova.it
A perfect place for anyone in search of tranquillity, comfort and elegance. The Tirreno is situated by the sea in the residential quarter of Sturla, just east of Albaro, with beaches and genteel nightlife nearby. Access to tennis courts, swimming pools and a sports ground. 目 ♥

| **FURTHER AFIELD (OUTER GENOA):** *Torre Cambiaso* | €€€ | 48 | ● | ▨ | ● | ▨ |

Via Scarpanto 49, Pegli. **Road Map** D3. ☎ *010 665 055.* FAX *010 697 30 22.*
The building occupied by the hotel since the 1980s was once a lookout tower for the Saracens; over the years it has been a villa (in the 15th century), then a small castle (in the 19th century) and then a monastery (in the 1920s). Some rooms still have their original frescoes and the occasional antique. 目 ♨ ♣ ♥ ♿

| **FURTHER AFIELD (OUTER GENOA):** *Villa Pagoda* | €€€€ | 17 | ● | ▨ | ● | ▨ |

Via Capolungo 15, Nervi. **Road Map** D3. ☎ *010 372 61 61.* FAX *010 321 218.*
W www.villapagoda.it
This 19th-century villa sits alongside the great gardens of Nervi, east of the city. Attractive rooms with lovely views. Excellent service and high-quality cooking are on offer in the Il Roseto restaurant. 目 ♥ ♥

THE RIVIERA DI LEVANTE

| **BONASSOLA:** *Villa Belvedere* | €€ | 22 | ● | ▨ | ● | ▨ |

Via Ammiraglio Serra 33. **Road Map** E4. ☎ *0187 813 622.* FAX *0187 813 709.*
@ hotelvillabelvedere@tin.it
The Villa Belvedere stands in an enchanting and panoramic position, and benefits from a climate that is mild all year round, thanks to the sea and the enclosing hills. Lovely garden and comfortable rooms.
● mid-Oct–Mar. ♥

| **CAMOGLI:** *La Camogliese* | €€ | 21 | ● | | ● | |

Via Garibaldi 55. **Road Map** D4. ☎ *0185 771 402.* FAX *0185 774 024.*
W www.lacamogliese.it
This gracious, family-run *pensione* by the sea provides attentive and courteous service. Rooms are simple but well cared for, and some have a small terrace. The restaurant overlooking the port is good. ♥ ♨ ♥

| **CAMOGLI:** *Cenobio dei Dogi* | €€€€ | 106 | ● | ▨ | ● | ▨ |

Via Cuneo 34. **Road Map** D4. ☎ *0185 72 41.* FAX *0185 772 796.*
W www.cenobio.it
A splendid pastel-pink building set between the hills and the sea, the Cenobio dei Dogi was the summer residence of the doges of Genoa. Spacious, very comfortable and extremely tasteful rooms offer wonderful views over the Golfo del Paradiso. Lovely grounds and a beautiful 17th-century chapel now open to visitors. 目 ♥ ♨ ♥ ♥

| **CHIAVARI:** *Santa Maria* | €€ | 36 | ● | ▨ | ● | ▨ |

Viale Tito Groppo 29. **Road Map** E4. ☎ *0185 363 321.* FAX *0185 323 508.*
W www.santamaria-hotel.com
Facing the Golfo del Tigullio, a short distance from the old heart of Chiavari, the Santa Maria has very comfortable rooms with modern furnishings. The hotel is set in pretty gardens and there is a panoramic terrace and solarium. 目 ♣ ♿

FIASCHERINO/TELLARO: *Il Nido* €€€ 36
Via Fiascherino 75. **Road Map** F5. (0187 967 286. FAX 0187 964 617.
W www.hotelnido.com
A real "nest" *(nido)* facing the sea of Fiascherino, with lovely light rooms
with panoramic balconies. Own beach. ● *mid-Nov–mid-Feb.*

LA SPEZIA: *Corallo* €€ 33
Via F Crispi 32. **Road Map** F4. (0187 731 366. FAX 0187 754 490.
W www.hotelcorallospezia.com
An unpretentious, reliable hotel lying in a quiet position a short
distance from the seafront (from where you can go on boat trips to
the resorts on the Golfo dei Poeti). The Corallo's excellent position
also makes it a good base from which to reach the city's important
sights.

LA SPEZIA: *Firenze e Continentale* €€ 67
Via Paleocapa 7. **Road Map** F4. (0187 713 210. FAX 0187 714 930.
W www.hotelfirenzecontinentale.it
Close to the railway station, this is a good hotel with spacious and
well-furnished rooms. The room where the breakfast buffet is served is
very pleasant and offers good views. ● *21 Dec–7 Jan.*

LAVAGNA: *Fieschi* €€€ 13
Via Rezza 12. **Road Map** E4. (0185 304 400. FAX 0185 313 809.
W www.hotelvillafieschi.it
This hotel occupies a lovely patrician 19th-century villa standing in
extensive grounds. Pleasant and pristine rooms in antique style are
equipped with minibars and satellite TV. ● *end Oct–Feb.*

LERICI: *Byron* €€ 30
Via Biaggini 19. **Road Map** F5. (0187 967 104. FAX 0187 967 409.
W www.byronhotel.com
Situated on the seafront at Lerici, in a splendid position not far from the
town centre, the Byron was built in the 1960s. Rooms are not particularly
fancy or spacious but some have balconies.

LERICI: *Florida* €€€ 37
Lungomare Biaggini 35. **Road Map** F5. (0187 967 332. FAX 0187 967 344.
W www.hotelflorida.it
This attractive hotel stands on the seafront road leading from Lerici to San
Terenzo. Light, airy and well-kept rooms have balconies with sea views.
Generous buffet breakfast. ● *20 Dec–Feb.*

LEVANTO: *Nazionale* € 38
Via Jacopo da Levanto 20. **Road Map** E4. (0187 808 102. FAX 0187 800 901.
W www.nazionale.it
This is one of the oldest hotels in the village. It has pretty, spacious and
comfortable rooms, a lovely garden with a swing, and a restaurant
serving elegant food. ● *Nov–Mar.*

LEVANTO: *Stella Maris* €€€€ 15
Via Marconi 4. **Road Map** E4. (0187 808 258. FAX 0187 807 351.
W www.hotelstellamaris.it
This delightful hotel close to the sea occupies an 18th-century palazzo,
though most of the interior decoration dates from the late 19th century.
The atmosphere is relaxing and the rooms, furnished with the occasional
antique, pretty. The restaurant offers good regional cooking. Also rooms in
a modern annexe. Half-board only. ● *Nov.*

MANAROLA: *Ca' d'Andrean* € 10
Via Discovolo 101. **Road Map** F4. (0187 920 040. FAX 0187 920 452.
W www.cadandrean.it
This small, family-run hotel is in a quiet position high up in the stunning
village of Manarola, in the Cinque Terre. Rooms are spacious and light,
some with a terrace. There's a pretty interior garden where you can have
breakfast and also a bar. ● *mid-Nov–mid-Dec.*

MONEGLIA: *B&B A Casa di Roby* €€€ 3
Strada San Lorenzo 7A. **Road Map** E4. (e FAX 0185 496 42.
W www.acasadiroby.it
Set among olive groves, this luxury bed & breakfast occupies an old
frantoio (olive presshouse) in a lovely position on the hill dominating
Moneglia. All three rooms offer views over the bay.
● *weekdays (excluding public holidays) during the winter.*

For key to symbols see back flap

Price categories are for a standard double room for one night including tax, service charges and breakfast:
€ under 85 euros
€€ 85–125 euros
€€€ 125–175 euros
€€€€ 175–225 euros
€€€€€ over 225 euros

CREDIT CARDS
Hotels which accept the main credit cards.

GARDEN OR TERRACE
Hotel in a park or garden or with a terrace with panoramic views.

PARKING
Garage or parking facilities for guests, either within the hotel or nearby.

RESTAURANT
Hotel with a particularly good restaurant which is also open to non-residents.

	ROOMS	CREDIT CARDS	GARDEN OR TERRACE	PARKING	RESTAURANT
MONTEROSSO AL MARE: *Meublé Agavi* €€	10				
Via Fegina 30. **Road Map** E4. 0187 817 171. FAX 0187 818 264. @ hotel.agavi@libero.it Situated on the Fegina seafront in the largest of the Cinque Terre towns, Le Agavi occupies the first floor of a palazzo (complete with a tower) and has been a hotel since the 1930s. Rooms are well-kept and some have lovely views over the sea.					
MONTEROSSO AL MARE: *Porto Roca* €€€€€	43	●	▨		▨
Via Corone 1. **Road Map** E4. 0187 817 502. FAX 0187 817 692. w www.portoroca.it In an enchanting spot, on a cliff with terraces offering fantastic sea views. The decor is elegant and Mediterranean in style, with some antiques. Pretty rooms and a panoramic terrace-restaurant. ● *Nov–Feb.* 目					
PORTOFINO: *Piccolo Hotel (Domina)* €€€€€	22	●	▨	●	▨
Via Duca degli Abruzzi 31. **Road Map** D4. 0185 269 015. FAX 0185 269 621. w www.dominapiccolo.it This old Ligurian villa by the sea has the discreet fascination of a small hotel in an exclusive location. The rooms and bathrooms have been furnished carefully and tastefully. Private access to the beach. ● *Nov–Feb.* 目					
PORTOFINO: *Splendido (Orient Express)* €€€€€	66	●	▨	●	▨
Viale Baratta 16. **Road Map** D4. 0185 269 551. FAX 0185 267 806. w www.hotelsplendido.com One of the most exclusive hotels in the world, the Splendido is proud of its long-standing ability to attract celebrities, from Groucho Marx to Madonna. Perched, half-hidden, in the greenery of the headland, the hotel has fantastic views. Many of the luxurious rooms have their own panoramic terrace. The restaurant, of course, is superb. ● *Oct–Apr.* 目					
PORTOVENERE: *Il Genio* €€	7	●	▨	●	
Piazza Basteri 8. **Road Map** F5. 0187 790 611. FAX 0187 790 611. The Genio, housed in part of the old town walls, has clean rooms and a small, flower-filled terrace overlooking the sea. Courteous service. ● *mid-Jan–mid-Feb.* 目					
PORTOVENERE: *Royal Sporting* €€€€	60	●	▨	●	▨
Via dell'Olivo 345. **Road Map** F5. 0187 790 326. FAX 0187 777 707. w www.royalsporting.com A top-quality, modern hotel with spacious, light rooms and a pool on a panoramic terrace. Pleasant garden. ● *Nov–mid-Mar.* 目					
RAPALLO: *Rosa Bianca* €€€	18	●		●	
Lungomare V. Veneto 42. **Road Map** E4. 0185 503 90. FAX 0185 650 35. w www.hotelrosabianca.it A small, tastefully furnished hotel in a good position by the sea. Rooms are simple but comfortable. Service is attentive and personal. 目					
RAPALLO: *Excelsior Palace* €€€€€	131	●	▨	●	▨
Via San Michele di Pagana 8. **Road Map** E4. 0185 230 666. FAX 0185 230 214. w www.excelsiorpalace.thi.it This is one of the most fascinating of the Italian Riviera's traditional hotels, with a string of illustrious and royal guests to its name, from Rita Hayworth to the Duke of Windsor and Wallis Simpson. The public areas are sumptuous, the rooms luxurious. The private bathing area is in a lovely position set into the cliffs. 目					
SAN FRUTTUOSO: *Da Giovanni* €€	7	●	▨		▨
Via San Fruttuoso 10. **Road Map** D4. 0185 770 047. FAX 0185 770 47. This small inn with simple rooms stands in a pretty position close to the famous abbey and the sea. The small restaurant offers a good menu of fish-based dishes. Half-board only. No en-suite rooms. ● *Nov–Apr.*					

SANTA MARGHERITA LIGURE: *Argentina* €€€ 12
Via Paraggi a Monte 56. **Road Map** E4. 📞 *0185 286 708.* 🅵🅰🆇 *0185 284 894.*
This small, graceful hotel is surrounded by Mediterranean maquis. Rooms
are simple and charming and some have sea views. ● *Nov–Feb.* 🏃 🛏

SANTA MARGHERITA LIGURE: *Grand Hotel Miramare* €€€€€ 81
Lungomare Milite Ignoto 30. **Road Map** E4. 📞 *0185 287 013.*
🅵🅰🆇 *0185 284 651.* Ⓦ www.grandhotelmiramare.it
A historic, early 1900s hotel on the seafront and with lovely gardens.
Lawrence Olivier and Vivien Leigh spent their honeymoon here. Barbecues
are held by the pool in summer. Many rooms have balconies. 🗐 🏊 🛏

SANTA MARGHERITA LIGURE: *Imperiale* €€€€€ 89
Via Pagana 19. **Road Map** E4. 📞 *0185 288 991.* 🅵🅰🆇 *0185 284 223.*
Ⓦ www.hotelimperiale.com
The symbol of Santa Margherita, the Imperiale (in what was once a private
villa) dominates the bay from its splendid position. The public areas and
the restaurant are sumptuous, with lavish use made of gilt and marble.
The attractive rooms have spectacular views. Pleasant gardens lead down
to the private beach. ● *Nov–Mar.* 🗐 🍴 🏊

SESTRI LEVANTE: *Grand Hotel dei Castelli* €€€€ 30
Via Penisola 26. **Road Map** E4. 📞 *0185 485 780.* 🅵🅰🆇 *0185 447 67.*
Ⓦ www.hoteldeicastelli.com
A trio of Art Nouveau castles built from often ancient salvaged materials.
Superbly located on a hill overlooking Sestri's Baia delle Favole. Luxuriant
park, private beach and pool, romantic sunsets. One lift takes you down to
the town, another to the sea. Excellent restaurant. 🗐 🍴 🏊 🎾 🏃 🛏

SESTRI LEVANTE: *Grand Hotel Villa Balbi* €€€€€ 99
Viale Rimembranza 1. **Road Map** E4.
📞 *0185 429 41.* 🅵🅰🆇 *0185 482 459.* Ⓦ www.villabalbi.it
This historic hotel, housed in a 17th-century villa on the Baia delle Favole,
has some exquisite features, including frescoed ceilings and Baroque
friezes. Antiques abound, the rooms and gardens are lovely, and the
service is discreet and efficient. ● *mid-Oct–end Dec.* 🗐 🏊 🏃

THE RIVIERA DI PONENTE

ALASSIO: *Beau Rivage* €€ 20
Via Roma 82. **Road Map** B4. 📞 *0182 640 585.* 🅵🅰🆇 *0182 640 585.*
Ⓦ www.hotelbeaurivage.it
Occupying a late 19th-century villa facing the sea, the Beau Rivage is an
attractive hotel with very pleasant public areas and guest rooms with the
occasional antique and panoramic balcony. Half-board only.

ALASSIO: *Grand Hotel Diana* €€€€ 54
Via Garibaldi 110. **Road Map** B4. 📞 *0182 642 701.* 🅵🅰🆇 *0182 640 304.*
Ⓦ www.hoteldianaalassio.it
With all the facilities that a Grand Hotel should offer: garden and terrace by
the sea, its own beach, indoor swimming pool with jacuzzi, gym, sauna, as
well as spacious guest rooms (some with a sea view) and two good
restaurants. 🗐 🍴 🏊 🏃 🛏

ALBENGA: *Marisa* €€ 31
Via Pisa 28. **Road Map** B4. 📞 *0182 502 41.* 🅵🅰🆇 *0182 555 122.*
The most distinctive of Albenga's hotels, with its scattering of antiques,
strange sculptures and bizarre modern paintings. Large roooms. 🗐

ALBISSOLA MARINA: *Garden* €€ 34
Viale Faraggiana 6. **Road Map** C3. 📞 *019 485 253.* 🅵🅰🆇 *019 485 255.*
Ⓦ www.hotelgardenalbissola.com
By the sea, but not far from the mountains and from some lovely walks,
this quiet hotel is entirely air-conditioned and soundproofed. Run by the
same family over five generations, the hotel is relaxed and welcoming, and
has pleasant, light rooms, each with a terrace. 🗐 🍴 🏊 🛏 ♿

APRICALE: *Locanda dei Carugi* €€ 6
Via Roma 12. **Road Map** A4. 📞 *0184 209 010.* 🅵🅰🆇 *0184 209 942.*
Ⓦ www.locandadeicarugi.it
The romantic heart of one of the most beautiful medieval towns in Liguria
is the location for this delightful inn, whose rooms provide lovely views
over the valley and over the town square. The comfortable and tastefully
furnished rooms are all different. 🗐 🛏

For key to symbols see back flap

		ROOMS	CREDIT CARDS	GARDEN OR TERRACE	PARKING	RESTAURANT

Price categories are for a standard double room for one night including tax, service charges and breakfast:
€ under 85 euros
€€ 85–125 euros
€€€ 125–175 euros
€€€€ 175–225 euros
€€€€€ over 225 euros

CREDIT CARDS
Hotels which accept the main credit cards.

GARDEN OR TERRACE
Hotel in a park or garden or with a terrace with panoramic views.

PARKING
Garage or parking facilities for guests, either within the hotel or nearby.

RESTAURANT
Hotel with a particularly good restaurant which is also open to non-residents.

	ROOMS	CREDIT CARDS	GARDEN OR TERRACE	PARKING	RESTAURANT
BORDIGHERA: *Villa Elisa* €€€	35	●	■	●	■

Via Romana 70. **Road Map** A5. **(** *0184 261 313.* **FAX** *0184 261 942.*
w www.villaelisa.com
A pleasant building surrounded by a flower-filled garden above the town. Rooms are very pleasant and facilities are good. There is a restaurant with a verandah in the garden. If you have children to keep entertained, this is a good place to come. 🖩 ♨ 👫 🏠

	ROOMS	CREDIT CARDS	GARDEN OR TERRACE	PARKING	RESTAURANT
BORDIGHERA: *Grand Hotel del Mare* €€€€€	107	●	■		■

Via Portico della Punta 34. **Road Map** A5. **(** *0184 262 201.* **FAX** *0184 262 394.*
w www.grandhoteldelmare.it
A modern, white hotel overlooking the sea and surrounded by lovely gardens filled with tropical plants. Offers luxury and comfort. Spacious rooms have balconies with sea views. There is also a beauty salon. Private beach. ● *mid-Oct–26 Dec.* 🖩 🍽 ♨ 🅿 🏠 ♿

	ROOMS	CREDIT CARDS	GARDEN OR TERRACE	PARKING	RESTAURANT
BORGIO VEREZZI: *Villa Delle Rose* €€	44	●	■	●	■

Via Nazario Sauro 1. **Road Map** C4. **(** *019 610 461.* **FAX** *019 610 461.*
w www.villarose.it
A modern and very comfortable hotel located just a stone's throw from the sea. It has a spacious garden, a piano bar and a restaurant with a terrace overlooking the Mediterranean. ● *mid-Nov–end Dec.* 🏠

	ROOMS	CREDIT CARDS	GARDEN OR TERRACE	PARKING	RESTAURANT
CERVO: *Miracervo* €	13	●	■	●	■

Via Aurelia 53. **Road Map** B5. **(** *0183 400 263.* **FAX** *0183 400 263.*
This is a comfortable, modern hotel right by the sea. All the rooms have private facilities and a terrace. From the verandah there are views towards the old town. The cuisine is typically Ligurian, with specials based on fish. The owner, Signora Maria, is hands-on. ● *Nov.* 🏠

	ROOMS	CREDIT CARDS	GARDEN OR TERRACE	PARKING	RESTAURANT
FINALE LIGURE: *Punta Est* €€€€	40	●	■	●	■

Via Aurelia 1. **Road Map** C4. **(** *019 600 611.* **FAX** *019 600 611.*
w www.puntaest.com
An exclusive hotel in the Mediterranean maquis, set on a headland overlooking the sea right at the end of the town. Guest rooms are in both the 19th-century villa and a more modern building close by.
● *mid-Oct–Apr.* 🖩 ♨ 👫 🏠

	ROOMS	CREDIT CARDS	GARDEN OR TERRACE	PARKING	RESTAURANT
IMPERIA: *Croce di Malta* €€	39	●		●	■

Via Scarincio 148. **Road Map** B5. **(** *0183 667 020.* **FAX** *0183 636 87.*
w www.hotelcrocedimalta.com
This hotel is right in the heart of Imperia's "Borgo Marina", the old part of town once inhabited mainly by fishermen. The comfortable rooms have balconies offering views either of the sea or over the marina. Facilities in the rooms include satellite and pay-TV, minibar and an Internet connection. 🖩 🏠

	ROOMS	CREDIT CARDS	GARDEN OR TERRACE	PARKING	RESTAURANT
IMPERIA: *Hotel Kristina* €€	34	●	■		■

Spianata Borgo Peri 8. **Road Map** B5. **(** *0183 293 564.* **FAX** *0183 293 565.*
w www.hotelkristina.com
During the summer season, when you book a room it is possible to also reserve a place on the beach in front of the hotel. Most of the rooms have terraces, from where it is possible to admire the whole of the bay of Imperia. 🏠 ♿

	ROOMS	CREDIT CARDS	GARDEN OR TERRACE	PARKING	RESTAURANT
LOANO: *Villa Beatrice* €	30	●	■	●	■

Via Sant'Erasmo 6. **Road Map** B4. **(** and **FAX** *019 668 244.*
@ hvbeatrice@tin.it
This quiet hotel in a 19th-century villa has rooms facing either on to the garden or the marina. Facilities include a swimming pool for children, a private beach, heated jacuzzi tubs and minigolf.
● *Oct.* 🍽 ♨ 👫 🏠

LOANO: *Grand Hotel Garden Lido* €€ 77
Lungomare Nazario Sauro 9. **Road Map** B4. (019 669 666.
FAX 019 668 552. W www.gardenlido.com
Facing the harbour, this hotel is more inviting than it looks, with spacious,
modern and well-equipped rooms and a large terrace. The pretty garden
has two swimming pools, and there is also a piano bar.

NOLI: *Miramare* €€ 28
Corso Italia 2. **Road Map** C4. (019 748 926. FAX 019 748 927.
W www.hotelmiramarenoli.it
Occupying an old fortification, the Miramare still has some of the original
features, most noticeably the thick walls. There is a small but pretty garden
and a smattering of antiques. The rooms offer lovely views. ● Oct.

PIETRA LIGURE: *Grand Hotel Royal* €€ 105
Via G. Bado 129. **Road Map** B4. (019 616 192. FAX 019 616 195.
W www.royalgrandhotel.it
Set in a delightful position between palms and gardens on the seafront
walk, the Grand Hotel Royal is a very pleasant seaside hotel. Most of the
rooms have sea views, but only some have air-conditioning.
● Oct–mid-Dec.

SAN REMO: *Paradiso* €€ 41
Via Roccasterone 12. **Road Map** A5. (0184 571 211. FAX 0184 578 176.
W www.paradisohotel.it
Situated in a quiet, leafy area away from the seafront, the Paradiso has a
lovely garden that you can enjoy from the verandah restaurant. The
rooms are comfortable.

SAN REMO: *Royal* €€€€€ 137
Corso dell'Imperatrice 80. **Road Map** A5. (0184 53 91.
FAX 0184 661 445. W www.royalhotelsanremo.com
For more than a century this traditional hotel has been offering among the
best facilities on the Riviera dei Fiori. The rooms vary in their size and
comfort but are mostly splendid and have sea views. In the enchanting
garden, full of tropical plants, there is a sea-water swimming pool, one of
the loveliest in Europe. ● Oct–mid-Dec.

SAVONA: *Riviera Suisse* € 80
Via Paleocapa 24. **Road Map** C4. (019 850 853. FAX 019 853 435.
W www.rivierasuissehotel.it
This hotel overlooks Savona's main street in the heart of the old city. It
occupies a fine 19th-century palazzo with an elegant arcade. Run by the
same family since the 1930s, the hotel offers a personal service. The
restaurant serves Ligurian and Piemontese dishes. ● Oct–19 Dec.

SPOTORNO: *Delle Palme* €€ 32
Via Aurelia 39. **Road Map** C4. (and FAX 019 745 161 or 019 745 180.
W www.hoteldellepalme.it
Part of the elegant seafront, this hotel faces the public gardens.
The rooms have all the usual facilities. The restaurant is known
for its regional cooking, particularly its fish dishes. ● Nov.

VARAZZE: *El Chico (Best Western)* €€€ 38
Strada Romana 63. **Road Map** C3. (019 931 388. FAX 019 432 423.
W www.bestwestern.it
This modern hotel built in the Mediterranean style stands in a large
park just above Varazze. Rooms are light and many have good views.
Relaxed atmosphere and good games room.
● end Nov–Jan.

VENTIMIGLIA: *Kaly* € 26
Lungomare Trento e Trieste 67. **Road Map** A5. (0184 295 218. FAX 0184 295 118.
W www.francescatohotels.com
A modern, comfortable hotel in the residential district by the sea, just
a few metres from the beach. There is a bar and garden.

VENTIMIGLIA: *Sole Mare* €€ 28
Passeggiata Marconi 22. **Road Map** A5. (0184 351 854. FAX 0184 230 988.
W www.hotelsolemare.it
Situated on the seafront walk a short distance from the centre, this hotel is
ideal for anyone in search of peace and quiet. All the rooms are spacious,
with balconies overlooking the sea.

For key to symbols see back flap

WHERE TO EAT

**Sign for a shop selling
Ligurian specialities**

MEAT does feature on menus in the region of Liguria, but anyone that doesn't eat fish is likely to feel that they are missing out: Ligurian cooking revolves around seafood, particularly on the coast. This is a land of strong flavours and long-standing traditions, where many cooks follow recipes that have not changed for many generations: a fact celebrated in many of the region's restaurants and trattorias. Liguria has some excellent upmarket restaurants, but more pleasure can often be derived from discovering a family-run trattoria by chance while strolling around the historic district of a resort or one of the hilltowns of the interior. A good opportunity to try the local specialities is during the many gastronomic festivals that take place in every season. *Agriturismo*, or farm holidays, also give visitors the chance to taste real home cooking.

OPENING HOURS AND PRICES

RESTAURANTS AND trattorias in Liguria operate similar opening hours to those in other northern regions of Italy. Lunch is usually served from midday to 2:30–3pm, while dinner is served from 7pm until late in the evening, the latest hours being kept in the big resorts with an active nightlife. Closing days depend both on the season and on the type of establishment; in general, restaurants and trattorias stay open most of the year, particularly in the towns along the coast.

Prices can obviously vary. In many restaurants the bill can easily exceed 50 euros a head, excluding wine, particularly if the meal includes fresh fish; in a more everyday trattoria, on the other hand, the bill is likly to come to around 20–25 euros.

In terms of tipping, it is usual to leave around 5 per cent of the total bill in a trattoria, and 10 per cent in a restaurant.

LOCAL PRODUCE

LIGURIAN cooking is inspired by an ancient tradition born out of the superb fruits of the land and the sea.

The fact that meat and cheese are of relatively small significance in Liguria leaves fish and vegetables to rule the roost. The variety of seafood on local menus is huge: bream *(orata)*, red mullet *(triglia)* and sea bass *(branzino)* are all popular, alongside staple shellfish such as prawns and mussels. Many restaurants offer fish soups and stews, a choice of grilled or roasted fish, or a mix of

Summer tables at a Ligurian restaurant, placed in the characteristic *carruggi*

fried fish. Fancier fish dishes include *cappon magro*, a salad of fish, greens and hard-boiled eggs in a garlicky sauce. Dried cod *(stoccafisso)* is also popular.

That the Ligurian diet is considered to be so healthy is due in part to the fact that fruit and vegetables (grown in abundance on the plain of Albenga) are central to the local diet. Any menu will show that chefs make good use of the local produce. As well as being combined with fish or meat, vegetables are also the focus of many dishes. Stuffed *(ripieni* or *farciti)* vegetables are very popular.

The olives that are the source of the region's rightly sought-after olive oil are also used in cooking. Olives known as *taggiasca*, meaning from the area around Taggia, are particularly renowned.

Basil, thyme, rosemary and marjoram, all grown in the mountain valleys, are the classic Ligurian herbs.

Fresh fish, abundant in the seas along the Riviera

Supreme among these is basil *(basilico)*, the basis for the region's world-famous pesto. This is served with the region's fantastic array of local pastas, with intriguing names such as *fidelini*, *fazzoletti* and *stracci*. The best-known pastas are *trofie* (twists from Genoa) and *trenette* (flat cousins of spaghetti). The most popular stuffed pastas are *pansôti (see p186)* and ravioli.

Relaxing at one of Liguria's many seaside bars

LIGURIAN TRATTORIAS

TYPICAL LIGURIAN trattorias may provide more modest decor and simpler menus than the average restaurant, but they often cook excellent meals. Unfortunately, tourist development along the coast has brought with it a proliferation of fast food joints and pizza parlours, which means that it can be hard to find a good trattoria along the coast. Your best chance of finding one is in the hinterland. Wherever you are, to find the best and most authentic trattorias just ask the local residents.

Vegetable tart and *focaccia*, typical produce

An alternative, if you want to eat genuine local food, is to visit an *agriturismo* farm, one that offers rooms and home-cooked meals to visitors *(see p174)*.

A traditional trattoria offering authentic Ligurian cuisine

BARS AND CAFÉS

A TYPICAL DAY in Liguria starts with a visit to a café or bar for breakfast. It's a daily ritual to sit at a table or counter, inside or out, reading the newspaper or just watching the world go by. Furthermore, drinking coffee in a bar or café can often provide good opportunities to get to know some of the local people. The best cafés offer cakes and pastries, as well as often delicious home-made ice creams. Note that in Liguria's most historic cafés and those in the fashionable resorts, prices can be high.

See pages 202–203 for details of some of the region's grandest cafés.

FOOD FESTIVALS

IN COMMON WITH the rest of Italy, food and village festivals in Liguria provide great opportunities for trying the local food. Among the region's main food festivals, highlights include: the Sagra delle Focaccette (focaccia festival) at Recco, at the end of April; the Festa dell'Olio (olive oil) in Baiardo, near San Remo, and the Festa del Basilico (basil) in Diano Marina, both in May; and

the famous Sagra del Pesce (fish) in Camogli, in mid-May. During the Festa del Limone (lemon festival), which is held in Monterosso, one of the towns on the famous Cinque Terre, at the end of May, the heaviest lemon wins a prize.

On the last Sunday in June, the Sagra dell'Acciuga (anchovy festival) takes place in Lavagna, while from 4–8 July Sestri Levante hosts the Sagra del Totano (squid). At Riva Trigoso, the popular Sagra del Bagnun (a local dish made with anchovies) is held on 15 July; on the same day, in Diano Borganzo, everyone turns out for the Sagra delle Trenette al Pesto (*trenette* are a traditional Ligurian pasta). Lastly, at Badalucco, in mid-September, around 500 kg (1,100 lb) of stockfish (dried cod) is cooked and distributed annually at the Sagra del Stoccafisso.

DISABLED ACCESS

RESTAURANTS IN LIGURIA are improving facilities for the disabled. Even so, in old-fashioned restaurants the disabled may still have difficulty moving around.

SMOKING

IT IS NOT EASY to find cafés and restaurants with separate smoking and non-smoking areas, though new legislation banning smoking in public places is due to come into force in 2005. Meanwhile, restaurant owners are usually willing to be accommodating.

What to Eat and Drink

Walnut sauce

D ESPITE THE REGION'S small size, Ligurian food is varied and tasty. It is often made from genuinely local produce which, thanks to the sun, the fertile land and the sea, is of high quality. Extra virgin olive oil, wine, vegetables and plenty of fish, either fresh, dried or preserved in oil: these are just some of the delights of Ligurian cuisine. Some of the region's most traditional foods are known worldwide, such as pesto sauce and *focaccia alla genovese* (a cross between pizza base and bread).

Torta pasqualina (Easter pie) *is made with puff pastry and has a filling of artichokes, spinach, courgettes (zucchini) and eggs.*

ANTIPASTI
Focaccia and savoury tarts are among the specialities served as *antipasti* (appetizers). A selection of sausages and salami is also served, as well as fish and seafood.

Mussels (cozze)   **Prawns (gamberi)**

Clams (vongole)   **Octopus (pulpo)**

Seafood *can feature in any course along the coast. Mussels, prawns and octopus are all local favourites, but expect to be offered a wide range.*

Fugassa *is a cheese* focaccia *for which the town of Recco, east of Genoa, is famous. It is also known as* focaccia al formaggio di Recco.

Fainà (farinata) *is a type of* focaccia *made from chickpea (garbanzo) flour and baked in a wood-fired oven. It is eaten warm.*

FIRST COURSES
As well as soups, made with fish or cereals and vegetables, first courses include fresh pasta, such as *trofie, trenette* or *pansôti* (stuffed pasta triangles), served with pesto or walnut sauce *(salsa di noci).*

Pansôti with walnut sauce *is pasta stuffed with vegetables or herbs and topped with a sauce of walnuts, herbs and ricotta cheese.*

Trenette al pesto, *a Genoese speciality, consists of noodles with a sauce of basil, pine nuts, garlic, Parmesan and oil.*

Mesciua, *literally "a mix", is a soup of white beans, spelt and chickpeas (garbanzos); it is typical of La Spezia.*

Ciuppin, *from Sestri Levante, is a puréed soup made from fish and shellfish, tomatoes, herbs, wine and garlic.*

Minestrone alla genovese (Genoese-style) *is a thick soup made with vegetables, aromatic herbs and a little pesto.*

Main Courses

Meat courses might include rabbit *alla ligure* (usually meaning with wine and herbs) and *la cima*, typical of the Genoa area, while fish may come in salads, stews or fried. Both meat and fish are usually served with locally grown vegetables: Albenga artichokes are highly sought after.

Focaccia

Fish, *fried or stewed, flavoured with aromatic herbs, is a constant feature of Ligurian cuisine.*

Bagnun, *a tomato-based stew of anchovies, started life as a fishermen's breakfast.*

La cima *is rolled veal stuffed with a filling made of meat, eggs, cheese and vegetables.*

Cakes

Liguria offers a wide range of special cakes and biscuits made from old recipes.

Cheeses

The best areas for the production of cheese are the mountains of the interior. San Stè cheese, from Santo Stefano d'Aveto, is a lovely cheese made from full-cream cow's milk. Local sheep cheeses are also good.

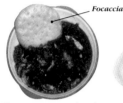

Caciotta di Brugnato

San Stè

Pandolce, *from Genoa, contains orange flower water, muscatel raisins and candied fruits.*

Baci (kisses), *made from nuts, eggs and cocoa, are filled with chocolate cream.*

Olive Oil

Ligurian extra virgin olive oil, made by cold-pressing the best quality olives, is light and fragrant and has a high reputation within Italy. Olives have been cultivated on the terraced slopes of Liguria for many centuries. Ancient granite millstones are still used in some of the old oil presses.

Canestrelli, *classically pale, fragrant and crumbly, make a fine morning snack.*

Amaretti *from Sassello are made with almonds, sugar and egg white.*

Olive oil

Olive oil

Pesto Genovese, *a blend of basil, salt, garlic, Parmesan (or pecorino). olive oil and pine nuts is best when freshly prepared, but is also sold in jars.*

Wine

The steep slopes of Liguria do not make it a natural vine-growing region, but the region produces some good wines, including eight DOC wines. Of these, the wines of the Cinque Terre (including a sweet wine called Schiacchetrà) and Rossese di Dolceacqua have a national reputation. Other good whites include Vermentino (from Lunigiana or around Imperia) and Pigato, a lightly fragrant white wine at its best from Albenga. Also look out for Lumassina di Finale Ligure and Bianco di Coronata (from Genoa), both white. Reds include Ormeasco, a rich wine with scents of cherry and blackberry.

Sciacchetrà *from the Cinque Terre is a renowned sweet white wine with an intensely flowery, fruity scent.*

Vermentino *is a dry but fruity white wine, good with fish and soups.*

Rossese, *a red wine often called simply Dolceacqua, goes well with strong cheese.*

Choosing a Restaurant

THESE RESTAURANTS have been selected for their good food and location. They are listed by region and then by price band. Use the colour-coded thumb tabs, which indicate the areas covered on each page, to guide you to the relevant section. The map references refer to the Genoa street finder on pages 94–9 or the road map at the back of the book.

	CREDIT CARDS	PARKING	OUTSIDE TABLES	TRADITIONAL COOKING	FISH COOKERY

GENOA

IL CENTRO STORICO: *Cantina di Colombo*　€
Via di Porta Soprana 57r. **Map** 2 F4. **(** *010 247 59 59.*
Low prices are charged in this pleasantly rustic trattoria, located just a short distance from the house where Christopher Columbus is said to have been born. The emphasis is on regional cuisine, with meat and vegetables dominating the menu. Good wines. ● *Sun; Aug, 25 Dec–mid Jan.* ▯

IL CENTRO STORICO: *Cantine Squarciafico*　€
Piazza Invrea 3r. **Map** 5 C3. **(** *010 247 08 23.*
Columns and vaulted ceilings are a feature in this restaurant, which offers a varied menu at lunchtime and in the evening. You may choose to have just a simple, one-course meal or a full menu, based on meat, fish and vegetables. Home-made pasta also available. ● *Aug.* ▯

IL CENTRO STORICO: *Da Rina*　€€€
Mura delle Grazie 3r. **Map** 2 F5. **(** *010 246 64 75.*
A restaurant in the old Genoese tradition, run by the same family that opened it in the 1940s. Simple but flavoursome dishes. Fish is prepared in various ways – poached, grilled, or cooked *alla genovese* (with anchovies, mushrooms and other vegetables). Lobster is also on offer. First courses are less impressive than the antipasti and main courses. ● *Mon; Aug.* ▯

IL CENTRO STORICO: *Vegia Zena*　€€€
Vico Serriglio 15r. **Map** 5 B2. **(** *010 251 33 32.*
Both an old Genoese trattoria and a classic restaurant, the Vegia Zena, close to the Aquarium, offers traditional Ligurian dishes, all prepared with the freshest ingredients and with the focus on fish. The fish antipasto is delicious; other specialities include *stoccafisso accomodato* (dried cod with potatoes and olives), *tortelli di pesce* (fish-stuffed pasta) and pasta with pesto. Good desserts. ● *Mon, Sun D; Aug, last week Dec.* ▯ ▯

IL CENTRO STORICO: *Zefferino*　€€€€
Via XX Settembre 20. **Map** 6 D–E4. **(** *010 591 990.*
This historic, centrally located restaurant (in the same family since the 1930s) was a favourite of Frank Sinatra, who had their pesto shipped to him in Las Vegas. It serves typical dishes such as *polpo alla ligure* (octopus with potatoes and herbs) and scampi with basil. Fantastic choice of desserts, such as lemon sorbet from Nervi, and attentive service. ▯ ▯

IL CENTRO STORICO: *Da Toto*　€€€€
Ponte F Morosini Sud 19/20. **Map** 5 A2. **(** *010 251 75 81.*
The restaurant is located in one of the most appealing places in the city, in the port. Appropriately, the cooking focuses firmly on fish. Antipasti include stuffed squid and fried Tigullio whitebait; among the first courses a highlight is the *pasta e fagioli ai frutti di mare* (pasta and beans with seafood). ● *Sun; Aug.* ▯ ▯

LE STRADE NUOVE: *Europa*　€
Galleria G Mazzini 53r. **Map** 6 D3. **(** *010 581 259.*
This pizzeria and *tavola calda* in the old aristocratic quarter of Genoa has a long and established tradition. It is busy day and night thanks to its proximity to the Teatro Carlo Felice. Good food is served promptly, from a menu that includes fish and roast meat. ● *Sun; Aug.* ▯

LE STRADE NUOVE: *Le Rune*　€€€
Vico Domoculta 14r. **Map** 6 D3. **(** *010 594 951.*
This welcoming, discreet restaurant is housed in an old palazzo in the heart of the old city. Traditional fish dishes and a range of olive oils (from Liguria and elsewhere) are features, along with a good selection of wines and cheeses. Excellent and varied desserts. Children's menu available.
● *Sat L.* ▯ ▯

		Price categories are for a complete meal with drinks (including wine):			
€ under 30 euros					
€€ 30–40 euros					
€€€ 40–50 euros					
€€€€ 50–60 euros					
€€€€€ over 60 euros					

CREDIT CARDS
Major credit cards are accepted.

PARKING
Parking or garage with attendant.

OUTSIDE TABLES
Restaurant offering the chance to eat outside, on a terrace, in a garden or piazza.

TRADITIONAL COOKING
Authentic regional dishes available.

FISH COOKERY
Restaurant offering fresh local fish and seafood.

	CREDIT CARDS	PARKING	OUTSIDE TABLES	TRADITIONAL COOKING	FISH COOKERY
LE STRADE NUOVE: *Pallavicini Celliere* €€€ Salita Pallavicini 25r. **Map** 6 D3. (010 252 882. An informal restaurant offering traditional Ligurian and Tuscan dishes as well as some more unusual dishes, including ostrich goulash. Large selection of excellent cheeses. Home-made desserts. ● Sun; Aug.	▦			●	▦
LE STRADE NUOVE: *Saint Cyr* €€€ Piazza Marsala 4. **Map** 3 A1. (010 886 897. Sophisticated cooking that brings together Ligurian, Piemontese and French traditions, served in classically elegant surroundings. The antipasti are particularly good, and the service delightful. Good range of both Italian and foreign wines available. ● Sat, Sun; Aug, end Dec.	▦	●		●	▦
FURTHER AFIELD (CENTRAL GENOA): *Enoteca Sola* €€ Via C Barabino 120r. **Map** 3 C4. (010 594 513. A simple but most congenial restaurant located east of the city centre, close to the Fiera Internazionale. On offer are purely Ligurian dishes. A Genoese flan or one of the other antipasti may be followed by minestrone made with carnaroli (risotto) rice, and then by a meat or fish course. Home-made desserts include an excellent peach tart. Efficient service. ● Sun; Aug.	▦			●	▦
FURTHER AFIELD (CENTRAL GENOA): *Gran Gotto* €€€€ Viale Brigata Bisagno 69r. **Map** 3 C4. (010 564 344. A good restaurant of long-established fame, east of the city centre. Its small but elegant dining room has the feel of an old *osteria*, albeit a modernized one. Recherché and delicious dishes are largely fish-based. Good service. Famous olive oil cellar. ● Sat L, Sun; Aug, New Year.	▦	●		●	▦
FURTHER AFIELD (CENTRAL GENOA): *La Bitta nella Pergola* €€€€€ Via Giuseppe Casaregis 52. **Map** 4 D4. (010 588 543. East of the city centre. Refined dishes are nicely presented in this restaurant where elegance and tradition are comfortably juxtaposed. The cooking combines Genoese and Neapolitan influences. Wonderful desserts, all home-made. ● Mon, Sun D; Jan, Aug.	▦				▦
FURTHER AFIELD (CENTRAL GENOA): *Le Perlage* €€€€€ Corso G Marconi 10r. **Map** 3 C5. (010 588 551. This dark, wood-panelled restaurant faces the Fiera Internazionale, in the heart of the commercial area. Light, fish-based dishes with inventive, original touches are served, in line with modern gastronomic trends. Highlights include octopus *alla greca* (Greek-style), sea bream pie and *gnocchetti* with octopus. Vast choice of cheeses. ● Sun; Aug.	▦				▦
FURTHER AFIELD (OUTER GENOA): *Bruxaboschi* €€ Via F Mignone 8, San Desiderio. **Road Map** D 3. (010 345 03 02. A restaurant just north of the city with a menu based around meat and vegetables, including mushrooms, truffles and game (in season), with just a few fish dishes. Wide choice of spirits available. Gluten-free dishes and a children's menu available. ● Mon, Sun D; Aug, 25 Dec–6 Jan.	▦	●	▦	●	▦
FURTHER AFIELD (OUTER GENOA): *Edilio* €€€ Corso A De Stefanis 104r. **Road Map** D3. (010 811 260. One of the most famous and high-class restaurants in Genoa, near the city's football stadium in the Marassi district. Elegant surroundings and attentive service. Diners can try fish and meat dishes prepared in the traditional way but with an original twist. Stuffed anchovies are among the Edilio's specialities. Excellent home-made desserts. ● Mon, Sun D; Aug.	▦			●	▦

<table>
<tr><td colspan="2">

Price categories are for a complete meal with drinks (including wine):
€ under 30 euros
€€ 30–40 euros
€€€ 40–50 euros
€€€€ 50–60 euros
€€€€€ over 60 euros

</td><td colspan="5">

CREDIT CARDS
Major credit cards are accepted.
PARKING
Parking or garage with attendant.
OUTSIDE TABLES
Restaurant offering the chance to eat outside, on a terrace, in a garden or piazza.
TRADITIONAL COOKING
Authentic Ligurian dishes available.
FISH COOKERY
Restaurant offering fresh local fish and seafood.

</td></tr>
</table>

	CREDIT CARDS	PARKING	OUTSIDE TABLES	TRADITIONAL COOKING	FISH COOKERY

FURTHER AFIELD (OUTER GENOA): *Toe Drue* €€€
Via C Corsi 44/r, Sestri Ponente. **Road Map** D3. 010 650 01 00.
A fashionable restaurant with the romantic look of an old *osteria*. The name of the restaurant (meaning "hard table") derives from the rustic tables which came, supposedly, from a monastery in Lombardy. The emphasis is on Ligurian cooking, but the family's roots in Trieste also influence the menu. In season, truffles, mushrooms and game feature, and there is a good choice of cheeses. Courteous service. *Sat L, Sun; 5–20 Aug.*

CREDIT CARDS			TRADITIONAL COOKING	FISH COOKERY

FURTHER AFIELD (OUTER GENOA): *Baldin* €€€€
Piazza Enrico Tazzoli 20r, Sestri Ponente. **Road Map** D3. 010 653 14 00.
A traditional restaurant, well-kept and spacious, located just west of the city. Serves mainly fish and, in season, mushrooms and truffles. Good selection of cheeses. Desserts are home-made. Pleasant service.
Mon, Sun; 1st week Jan, Aug.

FURTHER AFIELD (OUTER GENOA): *La Pineta* €€€€
Via Gualco 82, Struppa. 010 802 772.
Set in a pine wood just outside Genoa, this restaurant offers traditional dishes as well as more unusual fare. In addition to vegetable-filled tarts, *focaccia* with sage, ravioli and pansôti, the menu features plenty of game (for which La Pineta is famous), donkey ribs, meats from North America and horse (cooked *alla francese*, or French-style). *Mon, Sun D; Aug.*

FURTHER AFIELD (OUTER GENOA): *Antica Osteria del Bai* €€€€€
Via Quarto 12, Quarto dei Mille. **Road Map** D3. 010 387 478.
Located east of the city and open since the mid-19th century (Garibaldi ate here in 1869 before leaving for Sicily to fight for Italian unification). Good traditional Ligurian cooking rules: excellent fish and traditional Ligurian pastas, including *pansôti*. Diners sit in a wood-panelled room reminiscent of an old fishing inn, overlooking the sea. Service is prompt and courteous. *Mon; 10–20 Jan, 1–20 Aug.*

THE RIVIERA DI LEVANTE

AMEGLIA: *Locanda delle Tamerici* €€€€€
Via Litoranea 106, Fiumaretta di Ameglia. **Road Map** F5. 0187 642 62.
An intimate but relaxed restaurant (with rooms) east of Ameglia. Creative regional cooking that works wonders with the local vegetables and seafood: prawn flan on chick pea (garbanzo) sauce and scented with sea urchins; squid stuffed with vegetables and scampi; saffron *tagliatelle* with *finferli* (mushrooms) and mussels; *fidelini* (pasta) with seafood and crispy mullet scented with ginger and lemon; and sea bass wrapped in aubergine (eggplant). *Mon, Tue; 24 Dec–7 Jan.*

AMEGLIA: *Paracucchi* €€€€€
Viale XXV Aprile 60. **Road Map** F5. 0187 643 91-643 92.
A stylish and elegant restaurant in the Locanda dell'Angelo hotel. Among the often fascinating dishes, which make the most of the local produce, are: gazpacho of tomatoes and lemons with steamed prawns; escalope of foie gras with apricot compote; *farro* (spelt wheat) risotto with prawns and basil cream; medallions of lobster with *taggiasca* olives; and oven-roasted suckling pig with potatoes and peaches.
Mon, Tue L, Sun D; 20 days in Jan.

BOGLIASCO: *Il Tipico* €€€
Via Poggio Favaro 20, San Bernardo. **Road Map** D4. 010 347 07 54.
A superb, classic restaurant, just outside Bogliasco. Sample typically Ligurian dishes with a modern touch, such as *pansôti alle noci* (stuffed pasta with walnut sauce), *fettuccine verdi* with prawns and basil, and seafood risotto. Fish is simply and beautifully cooked, such as fish brochettes; roasted fish *alla ligure* with potatoes; and sea bass with baby vegetables. *Mon; 1st 2 weeks Jan, 10–20 Aug.*

CAMOGLI: *Nonna Nina*   €€€
Via F Molfino 126, San Rocco. **Road Map** D4. ☎ *0185 773 835.*
This informal, family-run restaurant is just south of Camogli. It occupies a
typical late 19th-century Ligurian country house. The dishes, essentially
based on old Ligurian recipes, include: fritters or soup of tiny anchovies
(gianchetti); stuffed anchovies; *taglierini* (thin noodles) with marjoram;
stewed dried cod; and rabbit *alla ligure* (with olives and white wine). A
house speciality is *trofie* (pasta) with nettles, pesto and quail.
● *Mon–Fri L, Wed; 15 days Jan, 15 days Nov.*

CAMOGLI: *Rosa*   €€€
Largo F Casabona 11. **Road Map** D4. ☎ *0185 773 411.*
A restaurant with a romantic setting in an Art Nouveau villa overlooking
the sea. The menu features a lot of fish: *tonnetto* (tuna) in sweet and sour
sauce; stuffed mussels; *taglierini* with red mullet; prawn risotto; clam soup;
moscardini affogati ("drowned" octopus); and bream with thyme. There is
also a choice of simply grilled or fried fish, as well *pansôti in salsa di noci*
(stuffed pasta in walnut sauce). ● *Tue; 7 Jan–6 Feb, 22 Nov–6 Dec.* 🍴 🧒

CASTELNUOVO DI MAGRA: *Da Armanda*   €€
Piazza Garibaldi 6. **Road Map** F5. ☎ *0187 674 410.*
A family-run, rustic restaurant serving traditional regional cooking,
including some excellent pastas. Choose from: vegetable flan; stuffed
lettuce; *tortelloni* with *salsa di noci* (walnut sauce); *tortelli* stuffed with
aubergines; *taglierini* with courgette (zucchini) flowers; saddle of rabbit
with olives or leg of lamb with thyme. ● *Wed; 24 Dec–6 Jan, mid–end Jun.* 🍴

CHIAVARI: *Da Felice*   €€
Via Luigi Risso 71. **Road Map** E4. ☎ *0185 308 016.*
A rustic restaurant serving Ligurian specialities such as *cappon magro*
(a salad of cooked fish), smoked fish, fish fritters, *buridda* (fish stew) with
cuttlefish, and some good pasta dishes, including *picagge* (pasta) with basil
and mushroom sauce. Small but good wine list. ● *Mon L.* 🍴 ♿

CHIAVARI: *Lord Nelson*   €€€€
Corso Valparaiso 27. **Road Map** E4. ☎ *0185 302 595.*
The Lord Nelson, furnished with seafaring motifs, calls itself a pub but
doesn't feel like one: this is, instead, the poshest restaurant in Chiavari.
International and Ligurian dishes fill the menu, including some beautiful
fish dishes: lobster in puff pastry with chick pea (garbanzo) cream;
carpaccio of seared tuna; *tagliolini* of pumpkin with shaved mullet roe;
ravioli of sea bass with a sauce of red mullet; and gurnard stew. Save room
for the excellent desserts, such as the fruits of the forest gratin.
Rooms also available. ● *Wed (except in Jul & Aug); Nov.* 🍴

LA SPEZIA: *Gabbiani*   €
Molo Italia. **Road Map** F4. ☎ *0187 779 177.*
A floating restaurant with lovely sea views. Ligurian fish cookery plus grills
in summer. Try the *antipasti di mare*, risotto with curled octopus, stuffed
mussels, or the delicious *spaghetti allo scoglio* (with seafood). ● *Mon.*

LA SPEZIA: *Il Sogno di Angelo*   €€€€
Via del Popolo 39. **Road Map** F4. ☎ *0187 514 041.*
In downtown La Spezia. Realizing his father Angelo's dream *(sogno)* to
open a restaurant, chef Davide has created an elegant, stylish and charming
atmosphere in which to eat his delicious food. Ligurian ingredients and
international cuisine are combined in dishes such as crab ravioli in saffron
broth and pheasant with black truffle. Home-baked bread and fantastic
desserts, such as walnut *semifreddo* and *crema cotta* (crème brûlée) with
mint coulis. ● *Sun; 1 week Jan, 2 weeks Aug.* 🍴

LAVAGNA: *Rajeu*   €€
Via Milite Ignoto 25. **Road Map** E4. ☎ *0185 390 145.*
A welcoming and friendly place, on the eastern side of Lavagna, decorated
like a sailors' inn. Specials include seafood salad; spaghetti with seafood;
ravioli stuffed with fish; local grilled or fried fish; and *buridda* (a traditional
Ligurian fish stew). ● *Mon; 1 week end Feb, Nov.* 🍴

LERICI: *La Barcaccia*   €€€
Piazza Garibaldi 8. **Road Map** F5. ☎ *0187 967 721.*
A classic restaurant, with a garden and a creative Ligurian menu. Try the
prawn salad with chestnut honey; the fish-stuffed *raviolini* with seafood; or
the pan-fried gurnard with onion *fonduta*.
● *Mon–Fri L, Thu (not Aug); Feb, Nov.* 🍴

....

Price categories are for a complete meal with drinks (including wine): € under 30 euros €€ 30–40 euros €€€ 40–50 euros €€€€ 50–60 euros €€€€€ over 60 euros	**CREDIT CARDS** Major credit cards are accepted. **PARKING** Parking or garage with attendant. **OUTSIDE TABLES** Restaurant offering the chance to eat outside, on a terrace, in a garden or piazza. **TRADITIONAL COOKING** Authentic Ligurian dishes available. **FISH COOKERY** Restaurant offering fresh local fish and seafood.

	CREDIT CARDS	PARKING	OUTSIDE TABLES	TRADITIONAL COOKING	FISH COOKERY
LERICI: *Il Frantoio* €€€ Via Cavour 21. **Road Map** F5. (0187 964 174. An elegant restaurant with a lively open kitchen. Choose from sophisticated dishes such as carpaccio of bream with spring leaves and extra virgin olive oil, potato *gnocchetti* with lobster sauce, and *trenette* with pesto and baby prawns. ● Mon (not Jul, Aug); Feb.	▦			●	▦
LERICI: *Vecchia Lerici* €€€ Piazza Mottino 10. **Road Map** F5. (0187 967 597. An intimate restaurant with a maritime theme and a terrace for use in the summer. The food is inspired by the Ligurian culinary tradition, and you can choose from dishes such as: tartare of bream and salmon; *tagliolini* with baby squid, tomato and rocket (arugula); velouté of porcini mushrooms, asparagus and baby prawns; and bream with local olives. ● Wed, Thu L (winter); Nov.	▦		▦	●	▦
LERICI: *Due Corone* €€€€ Via Vespucci 14. **Road Map** F5. (0187 967 417. An elegant restaurant by the port, where Ligurian-style fish and seafood dishes are, not surprisingly, the speciality. They do a wonderful mixed grill and great assorted antipasti, or fancier dishes such as ravioli stuffed with fish, steamed scampi tails on melted pecorino cheese, fillet of bream in a potato crust, and fillet of veal with balsamic vinegar. ● Tue; 7 Jan–8 Feb.	▦		▦	●	▦
MONEGLIA: *Ruota* €€€€ Lemeglio. **Road Map** E4. (0185 495 65. A rustic place in a tiny village just east of Moneglia. Its menu of Ligurian dishes includes successful creations such as hake salad with mayonnaise, scampi risotto, bream baked in salt, steamed local scampi, and cuttlefish with porcini mushrooms. ● Wed; Nov.	▦	●	▦	●	▦
PORTOFINO: *El Portico* €€ Via Roma 21. **Road Map** D4. (0185 269 239. A wonderfully unpretentious, family-run trattoria and pizzeria, where you can eat just as well – if less grandly – as at its more prestigious neighbours. Fresh fish, pasta and pizzas reign here, followed by some fine home-made desserts. Booking recommended. ● Tue; Jan, Feb.			▦	●	▦
PORTOFINO: *Da Puny* €€€€€ Piazza Martiri dell'Olivetta 5. **Road Map** D4. (0185 269 037. This is a good (and well-located) place to push the boat out. The pasta dishes are reliably excellent, and many of the seafood dishes memorable: try marinated swordfish with green beans and tomato, tuna sausage, pilaff with curled octopus, sea bass baked in salt, or fish cooked with bay leaves, black olives and potatoes. ● Thu; 15 Dec–15 Feb.			▦	●	▦
PORTOFINO: *Da U Batti* €€€€€ Vico Nuovo 17. **Road Map** D4. (0185 269 379. A congenial trattoria with a small dining room and a verandah. As well as tasty *pansôti con salsa di noci* and *trenette al pesto*, you can choose from some good seafood dishes. Scampi alla Batti is a signature dish, or try the poached sea bass with mayonnaise and rocket (arugula), rice with lobster, or simple grilled fish with the house sauce. ● Mon; 15 Nov–20 Jan.	▦		▦	●	▦
PORTOVENERE: *La Chiglia* €€€ Via dell'Olivo 317. **Road Map** F5. (0187 792 179. This popular trattoria offers lovely views towards the island of Palmaria, as well as creative versions of Ligurian favourites. Worth singling out are the *antipasti di mare* (an appetizer of mixed seafood), the mixed fried fish and the *tagliolini* with prawns and rocket (arugula). The grilled local fish is also a simple but reliable option. ● Wed; Nov.	▦			●	▦

RAPALLO: *U Giancu* €€€
Via San Massimo 78. **Road Map** E4. 0185 260 505.
This eccentric family restaurant just outside Rapallo has walls plastered
with cartoons and an owner famous for his hat collection. There is a lovely
garden with a playground for children. The menu caters well for both
children and adults, and includes *everything from pasta* with mushroom
sauce and grilled lamb cutlets to fried flowers of elder, borage, sage and
pumpkin, and porcini mushrooms *al cartoccio* (in paper). ● *Wed.*

RAPALLO: *Elite* €€€€
Via Milite Ignoto 19. **Road Map** E4. 0185 505 51.
Welcoming surroundings and a menu featuring a combination of Ligurian
and international dishes. The *linguine alla Nettuno* (a seafood pasta dish)
and the salmon risotto are both tasty, and there are also simple but good
dishes incorporating beef fillet, prawns and lobster. ● *Wed; Nov.*

RIOMAGGIORE: *Cappun Magru* €€€
Via Volastra 19, Groppo di Manarola. **Road Map** F5. 0187 920 563.
Intimate surroundings in a typical vinegrower's house in the Cinque Terre.
The menu always has *cappon magro* (fish salad) and other simple fish
dishes. The chick pea (garbanzo) and seafood timbale is good, and meat-
lovers can try the duck or sirloin steak. ● *Mon, Tue; 10 Dec–10 Feb.*

SANTA MARGHERITA LIGURE: *Da Nello* €€
Via Gramsci 105. **Road Map** E4. 0185 286 505.
A fish restaurant offering specials such as anchovies with lemon and *penne*
with scampi. The simplest fish dishes – such as the mixed fried fish – are
always a good choice. ● *Mon; Nov.*

SANTA MARGHERITA LIGURE: *Trattoria dei Pescatori* €€€
Via Bottaro 43. **Road Map** E4. 0185 286 747.
An unusual restaurant created in the 19th century from fishing net
workshops. Specialities from the Gulf of Tigullio form the basis of the
menu, including seafood salads and *ciuppin* (thick fish soup). Genoese
minestrone and *pansôti alla salsa di noci* are also on offer. ● *Tue; Feb.*

SANTA MARGHERITA LIGURE: *Oca Bianca* €€€
Via XXV Aprile 21. **Road Map** E4. 0185 288 411.
A friendly restaurant in the heart of the resort serving, unusually, no fish.
Creative cooking using mostly Ligurian ingredients, such as risotto with
duck breast, hare's liver terrine, pork cooked in beer, and excellent steaks.
Vegetarians and children are also well catered for. ● *Mon.*

SANTA MARGHERITA LIGURE: *Cesarina* €€€€
Via Mameli 2/c. **Road Map** E4. 0185 286 059.
A modern and elegant restaurant. *Triglia* (red mullet) is often on the menu,
either marinated or in a sauce to be served with pasta. The *trenette al pesto*
is always good; also worth trying are the cuttlefish stew and mixed fried
fish. ● *Tue; 10 Dec–31 Jan.*

SARZANA: *Napoleone* €€€
Via Buonaparte 16. **Road Map** F5. 0187 627 974.
This intimate, even romantic restaurant produces sophisticated dishes,
often featuring vegetables from their own garden. For once, fish does not
dominate, and dishes show a Tuscan influence. The *ravioli di lardo di
Colonnata* (ravioli stuffed with local bacon), the timbale of carrots with
black truffle, and the *tracci* (pasta) with rabbit sauce are all excellent.
Stuffed vegetables are also a house speciality. ● *Wed.*

SESTRI LEVANTE: *Polpo Mario* €€€
Via XXV Aprile 163. **Road Map** E4. 0185 480 203.
This smart family restaurant is popular with media types. The fish-based
menu (the restaurant has its own fishing boat) includes octopus pâté,
prawn and sea asparagus fritters, *tortino di leccia* (fish pie) and its famous
misto all'antica – cuttlefish, prawns, octopus, potatoes, sea asparagus, pine
nuts and olives, served au gratin. ● *Mon.*

SESTRI LEVANTE: *Fiammenghilla Fieschi* €€€€
Via Pestella 6, località Trigoso. **Road Map** E4. 0185 481 041.
Part of a 17th-century Ligurian villa just east of the town. Fish and Ligurian
dishes are the main focus: purée of beans with grilled prawns and olive oil;
buckwheat *lasagnette*, wild asparagus and Santa Margherita prawns; fillets
of skate in light batter with limoncello liqueur; and artichoke tart with red
mullet fillets and sauce. ● *Mon, Tue–Fri L; 15 days Oct–Nov, 15 days Jan–Feb.*

	CREDIT CARDS	PARKING	OUTSIDE TABLES	TRADITIONAL COOKING	FISH COOKERY

Price categories are for a complete meal with drinks (including wine):
€ under 30 euros
€€ 30–40 euros
€€€ 40–50 euros
€€€€ 50–60 euros
€€€€€ over 60 euros

CREDIT CARDS Major credit cards are accepted.
PARKING Parking or garage with attendant.
OUTSIDE TABLES Restaurant offering the chance to eat outside, on a terrace, in a garden or piazza.
TRADITIONAL COOKING Authentic Ligurian dishes available.
FISH COOKERY Restaurant offering fresh local fish and seafood.

TELLARO: *Miranda* €€€€€
Via Fiascherino 92. **Road Map** F5. ☎ 0187 968 130.
A rustic restaurant (with rooms) serving delicious food. Successful dishes include the prawn tart, angler fish steaks with tuna sauce, risotto with scampi and asparagus, bream in a fricassee of beans, and sea bass in asparagus cream. ● Mon; mid-Dec–mid-Jan.
Credit Cards, Outside Tables, Fish Cookery

THE RIVIERA DI PONENTE

ALASSIO: *La Palma* €€€€€
Via Cavour 5. **Road Map** B4. ☎ 0182 640 314.
This upmarket restaurant occupies rooms in an 18th-century palazzo in the old town. The main *menu degustazione* is based on Ligurian-Provençal dishes, featuring a range of surprising combinations: scallops with duck foie gras on a compote of potatoes, apples and a coffee sauce; squid stuffed with snails served on a purée of courgettes (zucchini) and black truffle; smoked mackerel with cuttlefish eggs and prawn ice cream; duck breast with wild black cherries and chocolate; and plums stuffed with foie gras in a vanilla sauce with pepper ice cream. ● Tue; 5 Nov–5 Dec.
Credit Cards, Traditional Cooking, Fish Cookery

ALBENGA: *Italia* €€
Viale Martiri della Libertà 8. **Road Map** B4. ☎ 0182 504 05.
A welcoming restaurant with tables outside in summer. The classically regional dishes include prawn and artichoke puffs, seafood antipasto au gratin and risotto with prawns and fresh vegetables, as well as mixed grilled fish. Meat dishes include ravioli with meat juices and porcini mushrooms and *filetto bordolese* (steak with mushrooms and red wine). ● Mon (except in summer); mid-Oct–mid-Nov.
Credit Cards, Outside Tables, Traditional Cooking, Fish Cookery

ALBENGA: *Il Pernambucco* €€€€
Viale Italia 35. **Road Map** B4. ☎ 0182 534 58.
A classic and elegant restaurant in an upmarket sport complex. It serves a good choice of fish-based dishes, such as pan-fried squid with artichokes, *pappardelle* with lobster, *tagliolini* with basil and crab, and black Venere rice with fish sauce. And there's always steak with green peppercorns for those in need of a break from fish. ● Wed in winter; Oct.
Credit Cards, Parking, Outside Tables, Traditional Cooking, Fish Cookery

ALBISOLA SUPERIORE: *Au Fundegu* €€€€
Via Spotorno 87. **Road Map** C3. ☎ 019 480 341.
A smart and romantic restaurant offering refined Ligurian fare. The menu includes dishes such as pan-fried shellfish with Ligurian herbs and fresh tomato, fillets of red mullet *(triglia)* scented with basil; *gnocchetti* of bream with prawns; oven-baked bream with olives and potatoes *alla ligure*; and *spaghettone napoletano* with squid and *trombetta* (large) courgettes (zucchini). ● Mon–Fri L, Wed; Jan, Sep.
Credit Cards, Parking, Outside Tables, Traditional Cooking, Fish Cookery

ALBISSOLA MARINA: *Ai Cacciatori da Mario* €€
Corso Bigliati 70. **Road Map** C3. ☎ 019 481 640.
A welcoming family restaurant, decorated with Albissola ceramics galore and with a terrace offering sea views where you can eat in the summer. Classic fish dishes, such as stuffed anchovies, seafood salad and thick fish soup *(ciuppin)*, dominate the menu, but there are also some excellent home-made pastas, including ravioli, *pennette* with squid and *linguine* with scampi. ● Wed; 15–30 Sep.
Credit Cards, Parking, Outside Tables, Traditional Cooking, Fish Cookery

ALTARE: *Quintilio* €€€
Via Gramsci 23. **Road Map** C3. ☎ 019 580 00.
A pleasant, family-run restaurant (with rooms) offering a mix of Ligurian and Piemontese cuisine. There are tasty vegetable dishes to choose from, including *tortino* (tart) of mushrooms, stuffed peppers, cannelloni stuffed with mushrooms, and Piemontese *fritto misto* (fried vegetables). *Cappon magro* (seafood salad) is also available. ● Mon, Tue–Sat L, Sun D; Jul.
Credit Cards, Parking, Traditional Cooking, Fish Cookery

ANDORA: *Casa del Priore* €€€€
Via Castello 34, Castello di Andora. **Road Map** B4. 0182 873 30.
A romantic restaurant in an old manor house. The food is Ligurian but with
the odd outside influence: the *ciuppin* (fish soup) is good, or try the
octopus terrine, black ravioli with sea bass, or the poached local fish.
Mon, Tue–Sun L; Jan.

ARMA DI TAGGIA: *La Conchiglia* €€€
Via Lungomare 33. **Road Map** A5. 0184 431 69.
A smart place in an old pink fisherman's home on the waterfront, with a
deservedly good reputation. Traditional Ligurian cooking is embellished by
creative thinking. Seafood predominates. Typical dishes include: raw fish
and shellfish on fennel and capers; *lasagnette* of aubergines (eggplant) and
swordfish with tomato and basil; and crispy cannelloni of potatoes and
mushrooms with prawns. Wed (not Jul & Aug); 15 days Jun, 15 days Nov.

BAIARDO: *Jolanda* €
Via Roma 47. **Road Map** A4. 0184 673 017.
Located right in the centre of Baiardo, Jolanda is as historical as it is
traditional. The menu offers dishes typical of the interior, including stuffed
vegetables, home-made ravioli and game in season, everything seasoned
with the fragrant local oil. Wild boar *(cinghiale)* is a speciality.
Mon (except in summer); Nov.

BERGEGGI: *Claudio* €€€€€
Via XXV Aprile 37. **Road Map** C4. 019 859 750.
A smart but charming restaurant in the hotel of the same name, with a
garden overlooking the sea. The seafood is beautifully prepared, with some
interesting variations on the Ligurian theme. The fried fish is simple but
delicious, or try the fish "mosaic" with Mediterranean lemons or the
tagliolini with borage and shellfish. Mon, Tue–Fri L; Jan.

BORDIGHERA: *La Reserve* €€€
Via Arziglia 20, Capo Sant'Ampelio. **Road Map** A5. 0184 261 322.
A great restaurant in a superb spot with a terrace overlooking the sea.
Using the freshest of ingredients, La Reserve produces some exquisite
dishes, such as the *tris di carpacci* (three different types of carpaccio),
sea bass ravioli, potato gnocchi in *salsa corallo*, and sea bass with
samphire. Mon, Wed; mid-Dec–mid-Jan.

BORDIGHERA: *Da Carletto* €€€€€
Via Vittorio Emanuele 339. **Road Map** A5. 0184 261 725.
At this attractive and sophisticated restaurant the menu shows a mix of
Ligurian and Provençal influences. Dishes are mainly fish-based: spaghetti
with lobster; *lasagnette* with prawns and artichokes; *gnocchetti* with a red
mullet sauce; John Dory with butter, rosemary, braised Tropea onions and
pan-fried duck's liver; and sea bass flambéed with Calvados and grated
apple. Wed; 15–29 Jun, 15 Nov–20 Dec.

BORDIGHERA: *La Via Romana* €€€€€
Via Romana 57. **Road Map** A5. 0184 266 681.
In the elegant Art Nouveau-style dining room you can enjoy cooking
inspired by Ligurian and Provençal traditions, with the occasional taste of
Sicily thrown in. Refined dishes include raw fish with lime and Szechuan
pepper and perfume of green radish; fillets of mullet pan-fried with ginger
and spices; *pansôti* stuffed with prawn and courgette (zucchini); *tagliolini*
with spicy prawns; and breast of guinea fowl with Pigato wine and thyme.
Wed, Thu L; 3 weeks in Oct, Christmas, New Year.

BORGIO VEREZZI: *DOC* €€€€
Via Vittorio Veneto 1. **Road Map** C4. 019 611 477.
A romantic restaurant in a 1930s villa. The cooking is fish-based but
incorporates beautifully prepared vegetables. Examples include: *fantasia di
mare* (assorted fish) with basil; gnocchi and beetroot with mullet roe;
tartare of shellfish with radicchio; and artichoke soufflé with velouté of
sun-dried tomatoes. Mon (not Jun–Aug).

CERVO: *San Giorgio* €€€
Via A. Volta 19 (Cervo Alta). **Road Map** B5. 0183 400 175.
A restaurant where Ligurian dishes are cooked with flair and imagination.
There are delicious squid or octopus stews and various seafood pasta
dishes, including *bavette* with small scampi and *trofiette* with squid. The
raw fish with grilled vegetables is also recommended.
Mon D, Tue L (winter only); 10–31 Jan, Nov.

	CREDIT CARDS	PARKING	OUTSIDE TABLES	TRADITIONAL COOKING	FISH COOKERY
Price categories are for a complete meal with drinks (including wine): € under 30 euros €€ 30–40 euros €€€ 40–50 euros €€€€ 50–60 euros €€€€€ over 60 euros	**CREDIT CARDS** Major credit cards are accepted. **PARKING** Parking or garage with attendant. **OUTSIDE TABLES** Restaurant offering the chance to eat outside, on a terrace, in a garden or piazza. **TRADITIONAL COOKING** Authentic Ligurian dishes available. **FISH COOKERY** Restaurant offering fresh local fish and seafood.				

DOLCEACQUA: *Gastone* €€

Piazza Garibaldi 2. **Road Map** A5. ☎ *0184 206 577.*

A rustic restaurant with an outside terrace. Being located inland, meat and vegetables predominate: smoked duck breast with avocado and endive; *tortino* (tart) of porcini mushrooms; ravioli stuffed with wild herbs and served with butter and sage; and lamb cutlets grilled with rosemary. ● *Mon D, Tue; 15 days Oct.* 🍷 ♿

FINALE LIGURE: *Lampara* €€€€

Vico Tubino 4, Finale Marina. **Road Map** C4. ☎ *019 692 430.*

This restaurant serves classic Ligurian food enlivened by some modern twists. There is a good choice of antipasti and some tasty pasta dishes: *spaghetti alle vongole* (with clams); *trofiette* with scampi and cannellini with salmon. The grilled and roasted fish is another good choice. ● *Wed; Nov.* 🍷

FINALE LIGURE: *Torchi* €€€€€

Via dell'Annunziata 12, Finalborgo. **Road Map** C4. ☎ *019 690 531.*

A smart restaurant run by a Sicilian-Neapolitan family in a 16th-century olive presshouse. Specials include rolled sea bass with thyme cream; stuffed lettuce; homemade spaghetti with shellfish sauce; risotto with cuttlefish and seafood; and warm carpaccio of shellfish. There is the odd meat dish, too. ● *Mon (winter only), Tue (not Aug); 10 Jan–10 Feb.* 🍴 🍷

IMPERIA: *Lanterna Blu da Tonino* €€€€€

Via Scarincio 32, Porto Maurizio. **Road Map** B5. ☎ *0183 638 59.*

This restaurant is furnished with antiques and overlooks the harbour. The Mediterranean menu serves exclusively fish. The hot seafood antipasti is delicious, while other dishes worth trying include the *linguettine* with lobster, *tagliolini* with cuttlefish ink, gurnard with tomatoes, olives and capers, and the turbot with "flavours of the Mediterranean". ● *Wed L (in summer); Jun, Oct–Nov, Christmas.* 🍷

LAIGUEGLIA: *Baia del Sole* €€€

Piazza Cavour 8. **Road Map** B4. ☎ *0182 480 026.*

An attractive and hospitable restaurant, serving traditional Ligurian dishes with an imaginative touch. *Taggiasca* olives are a common feature. Recommended dishes include the angler fish with olives, tomatoes and local *trombetta* courgettes (zucchini); seared fresh tuna with ginger; tartare of steamed octopus with celery, toasted pine nuts and basil sauce; fresh *stracci* (pasta) with pesto and green beans; potato gnocchi with octopus; asparagus *raviolini*; bream or sea bass with potatoes and olives; and turbot served with olives and capers. ● *Mon, Tue, Wed–Sun L; early Jan–Mar, mid-Oct–Dec.* 🍷

NOLI: *Lilliput* €€€

Via Zuglieno 49, Voze. **Road Map** C4. ☎ *019 748 009.*

A short distance inland from the coast, this restaurant is set in a pretty position with lovely views over gardens; diners can eat outside in summer. The Italian and Ligurian dishes use fish, meat and vegetables in equal measure. They do some good standard dishes, including minestrone, as well as less predictable dishes such as gnocchi with rosemary and fillets of bream with olives and potatoes. Leave room for the *semifreddo* ice with zabaglione and orange sauce. ● *Mon, Tue–Fri L; 10 Jan–10 Feb, 4–30 Nov.* 🍷

NOLI: *Scaletta* €€€

Via Verdi 16. **Road Map** C4. ☎ *019 748 754.*

A recommended restaurant with an outdoor dining area in summer. The imaginative cooking is mainly fish-based. In addition to well-produced staples such as grilled or oven-baked fish, the menu also offers interesting dishes such as carpaccio of salmon, stuffed anchovies, black *tagliatelle* with a gurnard sauce, fish-stuffed ravioli and *trofie* (pasta) with small prawns and courgettes (zucchini). ● *Tue; Oct–Nov.*

SAN REMO: *Bagatto* €€€
Via Matteotti 145. **Road Map** A5. 📞 *0184 531 925.*
A relaxed, appealing restaurant in a 16th-century palazzo. Expect
good-quality Ligurian cooking, with dishes such as mussels and clam soup;
panissetta (chick pea/garbanzo pancake) with artichokes scented with
marjoram; *pennette* with San Remo prawns and rocket (arugula) pesto;
purée of chick peas (garbanzos) and bay leaves with steamed baby squid;
and cuttlefish stew with spinach, pine nuts and thyme. There are also meat
(including lamb) dishes on the menu. ⬤ *Sun; Jul.* 🍷

SAN REMO: *Il Sommergibile* €€€
Piazza Bresca 12. **Road Map** A5. 📞 *0184 501 944.*
An elegant place created with great attention to detail. The acquaria
surrounding the dining room are designed to create the impression that
you are dining inside a submersible. The menu revolves around beautifully
fresh fish and shellfish. Try the house terrine and the grilled San Remo
gamberoni (extra large prawns). ⬤ *Thu (except in summer); Nov.* 🍷

SAN REMO: *Paolo e Barbara* €€€€€
Via Roma 47. **Road Map** A5. 📞 *0184 531 653.*
A small, smart restaurant rated among the best in Liguria. Paolo, the chef,
puts his own spin on the local traditions. His *gamberoni* (San Remo
prawns flambéed in whisky) are a signature dish. Other memorable
creations include *scabeccio* (escabeche) of red mullet and tartare of tuna
with basil. ⬤ *Wed, Thu; 2 weeks Jul, 3 weeks Dec.* 🍷 ♿

SAVONA: *Arco Antico* €€€€€
Piazza Lavagnola 26. **Road Map** C4. 📞 *019 820 938.*
An intimate, romantic restaurant. Dishes include crispy cannelloni of sea
bass and basil with sea bass roe; red mullet with goose foie gras and
balsamic vinegar; steamed squid with potato terrine and stuffed courgette
(zucchini) flowers. ⬤ *Mon–Sat L, Sun; 2 weeks Jan, 1 week Sep.* ♿

SAVONA: *A Spurcacciun-a* €€€€€
Via Nizza 89/r. **Road Map** C4. 📞 *019 264 065.*
A Savona institution perfect for an elegant evening out. The flavours of
Liguria and the Mediterranean influence the menu. As well as some
standard fare, such as *ciuppin* and *trofie al pesto*, there are some more
unusual dishes, including a warm salad of steamed white prawns in
gazpacho salsa and *mandilli neri* (black pasta squares) with prawns and
trombetta courgettes (zucchini). ⬤ *Wed; 22 Dec–22 Jan.* 🍷

SPOTORNO: *Pinna Rossa* €€
Vico Albini 10. **Road Map** C4. 📞 *019 745 161.*
An intimate, welcoming restaurant with stylish decor. It serves solidly
fishy food: *tortino* (tart) of octopus and potatoes with olive pesto;
lasagnette sautéed with squid and mussels; and dried cod *buridda* (stew).
⬤ *Mon; Nov.* 🍷 🧒

VARAZZE: *Antico Genovese* €€€€
Corso Colombo 70. **Road Map** C3. 📞 *019 964 82.*
Ligurian and Mediterranean cooking, with seafood predominating. The
most inspired creations include the crudités of local fish, warm fish salad in
a beetroot vinaigrette, *trenette al pesto genovese* with peas and potatoes,
and the *fettucce di farro* (spelt pasta) sautéed with baby squid. A few meat
dishes, too, such as breast of duck glazed with balsamic vinegar. Excellent
cheese trolley. ⬤ *Mon L, Sun; mid–end Jun, end Sep.* 🍷 🧒

VARIGOTTI: *Muraglia-Conchiglia d'Oro* €€€
Via Aurelia 133. **Road Map** C4. 📞 *019 698 015.*
A lovely restaurant with panoramic views and simple, authentic cooking
inspired by the nearby sea: raw fish, *fazzoletti* (traditional Ligurian pasta)
with scampi, salted prawns, scampi with apples and ginger, and mixed
grilled fish. Rooms available. ⬤ *Wed (Oct–May Tue also); 15 Jan–15 Feb.* 🍷

VENTIMIGLIA: *Balzi Rossi* €€€€€
Piazza De Gasperi, Grimaldi. **Road Map** A5. 📞 *0184 381 32.*
With a lovely terrace overlooking the sea right by the French border, this is
a friendly and hugely successful restaurant. There are some inspired dishes
to choose from, including: scallops in their shells, a gratin of artichokes and
fried leeks, buckwheat *lasagnette* with pesto, potatoes and green beans,
tagliolini with San Remo prawns and artichokes, and roasted duck breast
with braised fennel and dried tomatoes. The rabbit terrine is a speciality of
the house. ⬤ *Mon, Tue L, Sun L (Aug only); Mar, Nov–Dec.* 🍷 🍷 ♿

For key to symbols see back flap

SHOPPING

SHOPPING is an enjoyable experience in Liguria, as it is in the whole of Italy. If it's choice or designer clothes you're after, Genoa and San Remo are the places to go, though the big resorts have lots of boutiques, too. In terms of crafts, Liguria is a good place for buying ceramics, an ancient craft associated with Albisola and Savona. You can also find good-quality glass (Altare), lace (Rapallo and Portofino), macramé and woodcarving (Chiavari).

Characteristic sign

As in other regions of Italy, you can find some great markets. Most towns have a market every week, while larger places such as Genoa, Ventimiglia and Rapallo, have one every day. Most visitors may not consider taking any of Liguria's famous fresh flowers home, but San Remo's flower market, the largest in Europe, is well worth a visit.

Wherever you go there are shops selling local olive oil and wine, as well as Liguria's other gastronomic delights.

Throwing a pot, a tradition with a long history in Liguria

CERAMICS

THIS IS ONE OF the oldest handicrafts practised in Liguria. Evidence of ceramic production dates back to at least the 15th century. The twin-city of Albisola, the main ceramics centre in Liguria, has been a town of potters since the Renaissance. Here you can find all sorts of objects made from the local clay and typically coloured blue and white, from decorative tiles to old pharmacy jars.

In nearby Savona, pots are also traditionally painted blue and white, though you can find more modern designs and other colours, as well as figures from nativity scenes (*presepi*).

You can buy ceramics either in specialist shops and art galleries or, sometimes, from the potters' own workshops.

ANTIQUES

BEFORE YOU START shopping for antiques (or modern art, in fact), you should be aware that if you want to take any such object out of the country you will need to apply to the Italian Department of Exports for an export licence (for which you will have to pay). Any reputable antiques dealer will be able to give you the details.

Antique shops proliferate in Liguria, above all in the large towns, and some are of an excellent standard. Items for sale range from objets d'art to books and prints, furniture, statues, jewellery and antique posters. Model ships and other seafaring memorabilia, such as shipboard furniture, instruments and even figureheads, are particularly sought-after.

Several important antiques fairs are held in the region, including "Antiqua" and "Tuttantico" in Genoa, and the annual fair held in August in Sarzana. There is also a monthly antiques market in Genoa's Palazzo Ducale.

Wherever you shop, always ask for evidence of the authenticity of your purchase.

PLANTS AND FLOWERS

THANKS TO ITS mild climate, Liguria is one of Italy's foremost regions in the field of horticulture: nurseries and glasshouses housing everything from camellias, to citrus trees under one roof seem to dominate the landscape in some areas, and flower shops abound. Bonsai trees (including even miniature olive trees) are popular buys, as are cacti and orchids. All kinds of tropical plants are available, too.

Plants and flowers, the pride of Liguria

OLIVE OIL

A NATURAL PRODUCT that is of great importance to the region's economy is the olive, and also the oil made from it. No one knows who first planted olives along this coast

Shop selling locally made handicrafts

Dried beans sold by the sackful in a Ligurian market

but, in the Middle Ages, the monasteries played an important role in developing the art of olive-pressing.

Olives are cultivated all along the coast, but the best grow along the Riviera di Ponente, none more so than the small black olives of Taggia, which yield a golden olive oil with green tints and an almondy, lightly fruity aroma. In the area between Taggia and Albenga you can buy olive oil direct from the producers: look for signs saying *frantoio* (meaning presshouse).

Most Ligurian olive oil carries the quality mark of Denominazione d'Origine Protetta (DOP), which guarantees the provenance of the olives and the cold-pressing methods used in the manufacture.

Note that the price of a good-quality olive oil (ideally extra virgin) bought from a presshouse is higher than everyday oil from a supermarket or grocer's shop, but will definitely be worth taking home.

WINE

LIGURIA is not a major wine producer but still has some respected wines, both whites and reds *(see p187)*. It is fun to buy wine direct from the producers.

Olio Carli, a fine olive oil from Imperia

Sometimes you have to pay to taste the wine, which may be accompanied by cheese and salami, and you usually need to book ahead.

GASTRONOMY

THE MAIN PROBLEM with buying food in Liguria is that it's hard to know where to start, and stop. Much of what you see is best eaten on the spot. This applies to the wonderful snacks that the Ligurians love so much. Baked or fried snacks come in all shapes and sizes: from the famous *focaccia (see p186)* to *cuculli* (fritters) and *torta sardenaira*, a sort of pizza topped with tomatoes and anchovies (popular in San Remo). Bakeries and *pasticcerie* (pastry shops) sell all manner of wonderful cakes and biscuits, too.

In terms of foods to take home, you'd do better to concentrate on the local cured meats and preserved vegetables, such as sundried tomatoes, local artichoke paste and dried porcini mushrooms. Anchovies in olive oil are another good buy.

DIRECTORY

ANTIQUES

Antiqua & Tuttantico
Genoa
Fiera Internazionale
☎ 010 539 11.
ⓦ www.fiera.ge.it

CERAMICS

Bottega d'Arte
Albisola Superiore
Via San Giorgio 15.
☎ 019 488 604.

Ceramiche Fenice
Albisola Superiore
Corso Ferrari 1.
☎ 019 481 668.

Studio d'Arte Esedra
Dolceacqua
Via Castello 11.
☎ 0184 200 969.

GLASS AND LACE

Soffieria Bormioli (glass)
Altare
Via Paleologo 16
☎ 019 58 254.

E. Gandolfi (lace)
Rapallo
Piazza Cavour 1
☎ 0185 50 234.

PLANTS

Stern & Dellerba (cacti & succulents)
San Remo
Via Privata delle Rose 7.
☎ 0184 661 290.

Vivai Olcese (plants)
Genova
Via Borghero 6.
☎ 010 380 290.

LOCAL PRODUCE

Antico Frantoio Sommariva (oil)
Albenga
Via Mameli 7.
☎ 0182 559 222.

Bottega del Formaggio (cheese & salami)
Chiavari
Via Martiri della Liberazione 208.
☎ 0185 314 225.

Bruciamonti (deli)
Genoa
Via Roma 81.

Bottega della Strega (deli)
Triora
Corso Italia 48.
☎ 0184 94 278.

Cascina dei Peri (wine)
Castelnuovo Magra
Via Montefranco 71.
☎ 0187 674 085.

Enoteca Sciacchetrà (wine)
Vernazza
Via Roma 50.
☎ 0187 821 112.

Panificio Canale (bakery)
Portofino
Via Roma 30.
☎ 0185 269 248.

A'Pestun'à (bakery)
Genoa
Via Boccadasse 9.
☎ 010 377 75 75.

Revello Dolce e Salato (bakery)
Camogli
Via Garibaldi 183.

OUTDOOR ACTIVITIES

MORE THAN 300 KM (186 miles) of coastline provide a wonderful playground for anyone who loves sports associated with the sea, from windsurfing and diving to sailing (Liguria has more than 60 sailing clubs). Swimming is popular too, of course, though many beaches are pebbly. There is plenty to do away from the coast, too. In the hills of the interior there are numerous trails that are used by hikers, horse riders and

Exploring the countryside on horseback

mountain bikers, though the terrain makes any of these activities a relatively energetic option. The region's parks and nature reserves all have hiking trails, while the peaks of the Ligurian Alps and of the Apennines provide some scope for skiing and other winter sports. For those who take a more leisurely approach, there is always golf: there are courses in San Remo, Rapallo, Lerici, Garlenda (near Albenga) and Arenzano (near Genoa).

The breezy coastline, a boon for windsurfers

INFORMATION

FOR THOSE intending to do some serious sport, the best source of information is CONI, the Ligurian sports committee. The Club Alpino Italiano (CAI) is a good source for anyone venturing into the mountains, whether it's to hike, ski or rock-climb.

SAILING

LIGURIA has a most beautiful coastline and is a great place to go sailing. From La Spezia to Ventimiglia, the coast has countless beaches and inlets, some accessible only by boat. While it is not difficult to navigate along this coast, it is important not to underestimate the dangers of a changing sea, even in the summer. The to-and-fro

of sea bathers can be problematic in high season.

If you do not have a boat, there are many brokerage agencies which have plenty of yachts and motor-driven boats for hire.

A good source of general information are the Pagine Azzurre (published annually in English), which includes official charts and plans of every harbour.

CANOEING

CANOES ARE A COMMON sight along the coast. Inland, there are some opportunities for downhill canoeing during the winter and the spring thaw, when water is abundant in the local rivers.

WINDSURFING

WAVES AND year-round winds combine to make certain stretches of the Riviera di Ponente popular with windsurfers, though not everyone finds the relatively sheltered conditions exciting.

Arma di Taggia, around Porto Maurizio, Capo Mimosa (near Andora) and Levanto are among the best places to windsurf. You can hire boards in most of the big resorts along the coast, however.

DIVING

A FEW AREAS ALONG the coast of Liguria provide some great opportunities for diving. The most popular spots

include the headland of Portofino, Ventimiglia, Alassio and the Cinque Terre marine park (with diving centres in Riomaggiore and Monterosso). The latter, created only in 1997, has some rare white and black corals, and is also home to many of the species of dolphin and whale that inhabit the Ligurian Sea. Note that diving numbers are strictly controlled here, so it is worth booking ahead.

There are around 60 dive centres in Liguria: their addresses are given on the regional tourist board websites *(see Directory)*.

ROCK CLIMBING

STONY CLIFFS facing the sea enable rock climbers to enjoy the sport all year round. The most popular sites are

Exploring the fascinating sea beds along the coast

Players on one of Liguria's three 18-hole golf courses

found in the area of Le Manie near Finale Ligure *(see p144)*, and nearby at Capo di Noli. Cliffs explored and opened up only recently are at Muzzerone, near Portovenere, and Castelbianco (Albenga).

MOUNTAIN BIKING

THE AREA AROUND Finale Ligure is one of the most popular areas for mountain biking, with paths penetrating the Mediteranean maquis. Capo di Noli is an excellent place for exploring, for cyclists of all abilities.

HIKING

THE LONGEST signposted route in the region is the Alta Via dei Monti Liguri, which travels the full length of the Ligurian hinterland, from outside Ventimiglia to

north of La Spezia. At 440 km (275 miles), it is Italy's longest continuous walk. The terrain is not difficult and the route never isolated, passing through many villages.

The Cinque Terre is another walker's paradise and has several trails. Most famous of these is the Sentiero Azzurro (Blue Path), a relatively easy route which gets very busy in summer, when it can be hard to find a room for the night without booking ahead. A quieter option is the Sentiero Crinale, which runs along the clifftop. There are also spectacular but steep trails leading to the sanctuaries scattered around this area.

Another good area to walk in is in the French part of the Val Roja, north of Ventimiglia: particularly in the Vallée des Merveilles and on the slopes of Monte Bego.

HORSE RIDING

HORSE RIDING is popular in Liguria, and there are plenty of stables offering treks lasting a day or more. You can do some great day treks in the Cinque Terre. *Agriturismo* farms may also offer trekking opportunities.

SKIING

THE ALPS AND the Apennines provide some opportunities for skiing, though most resorts are small. Monte Saccarello (near Móneri di Triora) and Colizzano (north of Toirano) are both good for downhill skiing. Cross-country skiing is possible from Santo Stefano Aveto, in the Apennines.

A varied and challenging landscape for mountain bikers

DIRECTORY

INFORMATION

CONI
W www.coni.it

Club Alpino Italiano (CAI)
W www.cai.it

SAILING

Italian Sailing Federation (FIV)
Genoa
C 010 565 723

Italian Yacht Club (YCI)
W www.yachtclubitalia.it

Pagine Azzurre
W www.pagineazzurre.com.

Weather and shipping reports
W www.eurometeo.com

DIVING

Coopsus 5 Terre
Riomaggiore
C 0187 807 055

Punta Mesco
Levanto
W www.divingcenter.net

San Fruttuoso Diving Center
Santa Margherita Ligure
C 0185 280 862.

ROCK CLIMBING

Information
W www.thecrag.com

Rock Store
Finalborgo
C 019 690 208.

BIKE HIRE

Blu Bike
Finale Ligure
C 019 680 639.

HIKING

Information
W www.parks.it

Alta Via
W www.altaviadeimonti liguri.it

HORSE RIDING

Centro Turismo Equestre 5 Terre
Campiglia
C 0187 758 114.

Monte Beigua Riding
Alpicella (Varazze)
C 010 553 1878.

SKIING

Information
W www.liguriasci.it
W www.fisiliguria.org

GOLF

Information
W www.federgolf.it/circoli.asp

ENTERTAINMENT

Night club sign in Albenga

A LITTLE BIT OF everything summarizes the variety of entertainment available in Liguria. There are cinemas and theatres (the Teatro Carlo Felice in Genoa is one of Italy's most famous historic theatres), casinos, discos, nightclubs, wine bars and all sorts of venues hosting live music. The vast majority of such entertainment is, inevitably, focused along the coast, and the choice is greatest during the summer. Be warned that clubs and bars in the resorts tend to be very

expensive. For a cheaper night out, simply find the best bar on the seafront and watch the world go by.

Attending one of the region's numerous festivals can sometimes provide the highlight of a trip to Liguria. In addition to the many regattas and food festivals, there are various events focused around music, both modern and classical. The Festival della Canzone Italiana, held in San Remo in February *(see p28)*, is one of the most important dates in the Italian pop music calendar.

The casino in San Remo, one of Liguria's best-known nightspots

THEATRES

EVERY TOWN OF any size in Liguria has its own theatre, and some of the cities have several. Classical concerts, operas and ballet tend to be held in their own dedicated theatre, though San Remo's famous **Casino** hosts a whole range of entertainment, from touring ballet concerts to live music.

The main theatrical and classical music seasons tend to run in the winter, but Liguria is not a cultural desert during the summer. Outdoor performances are particularly common at this time of year. In Genoa, for example, films are shown in various parks around the city, and the ballet festival in the parks in nearby Nervi is hugely popular. The summer theatre season held in the pretty town square at Borgio Verezzi is also another permanent fixture.

DISCOS AND CLUBS

THERE IS A TREND nowadays for discos and clubs to offer far more than just a chance to dance and have a drink. Some of Liguria's major dance venues have been turned into multi-functional venues where, in addition to dance floors and bars, there are restaurants, shops, five-a-side football pitches and perhaps even a private beach. Such a description would fit **Estoril Moonlight**, one of the top clubs in Genoa.

San Remo has some of the best nightlife along the coast, and Santa Margherita is buzzing, too (it's just a short drive for revellers from Genoa): here, the **Carillon** is a gorgeous but trendy restaurant-

cum-disco, which can be very hard to get into unless you book a table.

BARS AND CAFES

ITALIANS SPEND half their lives in bars and cafés, and Ligurians are no exception. The beauty of these places is that many are open in the evening, sometimes even late into the night in the resorts, and serve snacks as well as coffee and alcohol.

Typical of the riviera are the fabulous historic cafés, in business since the region's heyday in the 19th century. These usually have wonderful decor and a great atmosphere. **Caffè Klainguti** is a fine example in Genoa. Founded in 1828, it was beloved of the composer Giuseppe Verdi and serves delicious coffee and pastries. In Santa Margherita Ligure, the Art Nouveau decor is one of the big attractions of the **Caffè Colombo**. In Chiavari, **Defilla** is well worth seeking out. The latter, with mirrors, paintings and stucco galore, becomes a piano bar at night. In San Remo, try the **Caffè Royal**, and in Alassio the **Giacomel**, which serves fantastic ice cream.

Increasingly, Italians are in the habit of meeting up with friends at a wine bar, whether it's before dinner or after the theatre. Wine

The Teatro Chiabrera at Savona

bars offer a good choice of wines, as well light snacks. In Genoa, one name that emerges above the rest is **I Tre Merli**, attractively located in the Palazzina Millo in the Porto Antico. Also in Genoa are **Monumento**, with a bar and terrace overlooking the sea at Quarto, and **La Lepre**, a popular place in which to chill out and enjoy a drink or two; both these open late.

Other famous names are **Winterose** in Portofino, a celebrity haunt, and **La Mandragola**, housed in an old mill in Santa Margherita.

LIVE MUSIC

THERE ARE all sorts of venues to which to go to hear live music, from the roof garden of San Remo's casino (in the summer) to the so-called disco-pubs, where you can have a drink, listen to some music, and maybe even have a dance, too.

In Genoa, **DLF**, in an old converted cinema west of the Lanterna, has live music in

THE GENOA DERBY

Local football fans love to attend matches played by the two city teams, Genova and Sampdoria, a lively meeting known as the "Derby della Lanterna". Genova, set up by a group of Englishmen in 1893, is the oldest football team in Italy, while Sampdoria was formed in 1946. Historically, Genova was the best team, but now it languishes in Serie B in the national league, while Sampdoria is in Serie A.

Sampdoria emblem

Genova emblem

addition to some of the hottest international DJs. For something rather different, try the **Louisiana Jazz Club**, a relaxed venue with a bar and both local and international musicians. In summer, there is usually a programme of jazz concerts all along the coast.

Sabot in Santa Margherita Ligure stages all manner of live bands that attract a predominantly young crowd. It also holds popular live music evenings outside during the summer. In Savona, the best bands appear at **Ju Bamboo**, a

club decked out in tropical fashion, complete with palms.

WATER PARKS

AIMED OF COURSE AT children, but also great fun for adults is the water park of **Le Caravelle** in Ceriale, a small resort just north of Albenga. This, the only aquapark in Liguria, has swimming pools with artificial waves, water slides, chutes, waterfalls, whirlpools and all sorts of seriously wet entertainment, as well as animated figures and shows.

DIRECTORY

THEATRES

Casino
San Remo
Corso Inglesi 18.
(0184 595 252/257.
W www.casinosanremo.it

Teatro Carlo Felice
Genoa
Passo Eugenio Montale 4.
(010 538 11.
W www.carlofelice.it

Teatro Comunale Chiabrera
Savona
Piazza Armando Diaz 2.
(019 838 69 95.

DISCOS & CLUBS

Carillon
Santa Margherita Ligure
Via Paraggi a Mare 10.
(0185 286 721.

Chez Vous
Lavagna
Piazza Milano 14.
(0185 324 738.

Estoril Moonlight
Genoa
Corso Italia 7/D.
(010 362 37 54.

La Capannina
Alassio
Regione Serre.
(0182 642 250.

Piscine dei Castelli
Sestri Levante
Piazza Marinai d'Italia 3.
(0185 480 001.

BARS & CAFES

Caffè Colombo
Santa Margherita Ligure
Via Pescino 13.
(0185 293 106.

Caffè Klainguti
Genoa
Piazza Soziglia 98r.
(010 247 45 52.

Caffè Royal
San Remo
Corso Imperatrice 80.
(0184 53 91.

Defilla
Chiavari
Piazza Matteotti.
(0185 309 829.

Giacomel
Alassio
Via Mazzini 65.

I Tre Merli
Genoa
Porto Antico, Pal. Millo.
(010 246 44 16.

La Lepre
Genoa
Piazza della Lepre 5r.
(010 251 7693.

Monumento
Genoa
Via V Maggio 28.
(010 386 239.

Winterose
Portofino
Calata Marconi 42.
(0185 269 500.

La Mandragola
Santa Margherita Ligure
Via dei Mulini 1.
(0185 284 900.

LIVE MUSIC

DLF
Genoa
Via Degola 9.
(010 593 650.

Ju Bamboo
Savona
Via Famagosta 2.
(019 800 624.

Louisiana Jazz Club
Genoa
Via San Sebastiano 36r.
(010 585 241.

Raggio di Luna
Albenga
Piazza Rossi 1.
(0182 540 216.

Sabot
Santa Margherita Ligure
Piazza Martiri della Libertà 32.
(0185 280 747.

WATER PARKS

Le Caravelle
Ceriale
Via Sant'Eugenio.
(0182 931 755.

PRACTICAL INFORMATION 206-209
TRAVEL INFORMATION 210-211

PRACTICAL INFORMATION

O N THE WHOLE, you will find that Liguria has a good standard of services and infrastructure. It is easy to travel around, particularly along the coast; the people are friendly; and, in a region that has such a long and well-established tourist season, there are good sources of information, whether you go to a local tourist office or surf the Internet – many of the tourist-oriented websites have text in English as well as Italian.

Liguria regional logo

Healthcare in its all its usual forms is available throughout the region, though the best facilities are inevitably found along the coast, where you are also much more likely to find English-speaking medical staff.

In general, Ligurian museums are modern and well laid-out. Many are also accessible to people with disabilities, who are well catered for in Liguria, with good sources of information as well as other services.

The crowded beach at Camogli in the summer

WHEN TO VISIT

O F ALL THE ITALIAN regions, Liguria is the one with the most temperate climate. Even in winter, its climate is generally warmer than in much of Italy, with the exception of Sicily. As a result, there is only a relatively short period when tourists don't visit. Furthermore, such are the cultural attractions of the region, that there is plenty to do even when the climate isn't hot enough for long stints by the seaside.

But while Liguria is virtually a year-round attraction, there is still an identifiable high season, which extends from May to the end of September. Tourists from Britain, France, Germany and Holland, as well as Italy, pour into the region during this period,

Sign for a local tourist office

when the entire coast can become extremely crowded.

Visitors more interested in cultural pursuits should consider visiting in March and April or September and October, when the weather is cooler and the hotels quieter.

TOURIST INFORMATION

T HERE ARE FOUR Ligurian provinces – Genoa, Imperia, La Spezia and Savona – but five tourist boards or Aziende di Promozione Turistica (APT): Riviera dei Fiori for Imperia; Riviera delle Palme for Savona; Genoa for the city and its environs; Tigullio, with responsibility for the rest of the province of Genoa; and lastly Cinque Terre e Golfo dei Poeti, which covers the La Spezia area.

In every good-sized town you will find a tourist office (or, in the smaller towns, a "Pro loco" office), which will have information about the local sights as well as the hotels and restaurants. Local tourist offices usually open from 8am–12:30pm and 3–7pm Monday to Friday, with some larger offices opening for longer during the summer. Some offices open on Saturday mornings.

The tourist information kiosks found at major transport terminals are generally fairly basic.

COMMUNICATIONS

P OST OFFICES are found in all Ligurian towns and there is often more than one branch. They are usually open in the morning only, from 8:30am to

Sailing along the coast, a very popular sport in Liguria

◁ **The unmistakably picturesque seafront of Portofino**

1:30pm (noon on Saturdays and the last day of the month), although in the large towns there are usually post offices that stay open until 5pm. You can also buy stamps (for postcards and normal letters) from any tobacconist shop, called a *tabaccaio*. Public telephones are not as commmon as they once were, owing to the growth in use of mobile phones. Those that remain are almost all operated by phone card, which you can buy from tobacconists, certain kiosks and in post offices.

Sign for an Internet café

There are plenty of Internet cafés along the coast for surfing the Internet or sending e-mails, and more are opening up all the time.

HOSPITALS AND PHARMACIES

PHARMACIES OBSERVE the hours of 9am–1pm and 4–8pm, closing on Saturday afternoons and all day Sunday. These hours may be extended in the larger tourist resorts on the coast, where some pharmacies stay open continuously until 8pm and sometimes later. Every city in Liguria has a hospital. EU citizens with form EIII are entitled to emergency medical assistance free of charge, but you may have to pay for other treatments. It is therefore vital that you take out proper travel insurance.

LIGURIA ON THE INTERNET

ALTHOUGH websites can vary considerably in terms of the information provided – in particular whether this is precise and up-to-date – the range of information available on the Internet about Liguria is of a much better standard than that provided in most other Italian regions.

All the five regional tourist offices, as well as each local tourist (APT) office has its own specific website, which can provide information about local events, among other things. Many museums and other attractions have their own websites, too.

For a greater overview, particularly if you haven't decided where in Liguria you wish to go, you should visit the Ligurian regional website (*see Directory*), which is a hugely useful resource and includes links to many other local websites.

Entrance to a pharmacy in the old centre of Albenga

DIRECTORY

APT

APT Cinque Terre e Golfo dei Poeti
(0187 770 900.

APT Genova
(010 246 26 33.

APT Riviera delle Palme
(0182 647 11.

APT Riviera dei Fiori
(0184 590 59.

APT Tigullio
(0185 292 91.

LOCAL TOURIST OFFICES

Alassio
(0182 647 027.

Albenga
(0182 558 444.

Albisola Superiore
(019 400 20 08.

Andora
(0182 681 004.

Arma di Taggia
(0184 437 33.

Bordighera
(0184 262 322.

Borgio Verezzi
(019 610 412.

Camogli
(0185 771 066.

Castelnuovo Magra
(0187 693 304.

Chiavari
(0185 325 198.

Dolceacqua
(0184 206 666.

Finale Ligure
(019 681 019.

Imperia
(0183 660 140.

La Spezia
(0187 770 900.

Lavagna
(0185 395 070.

Lerici
(0187 967 346.

Levanto
(0187 808 125.

Loano
(019 676 007.

Moneglia
(0185 490 576.

Pietra Ligure
(019 629 003.

Portofino
(0185 269 024.

Portovenere
(0187 790 691.

Rapallo
(0185 230 346.

Sarzana
(0187 620 419.

Santa Margherita Ligure
(0185 287 485.

Sestri Levante
(0185 457 011.

San Remo
(0184 590 59.

Spotorno
(019 741 50 08.

Varazze
(019 935 043.

INTERNET

Liguria Region
w www.regione.liguria.it
w www.turismo. liguriainrete.it

APT
Cinque Terre e Golfo dei Poeti
w www.aptcinqueterre. sp.it
Genoa
w www.apt.genova.it
Riviera delle Palme
w www.inforiviera.it
Riviera dei Fiori
w www.rivieradeifiori. org
Tigullio
w www.apttigullio. liguria.it

General
w www. liguriadascoprire.it

Other Useful Information

IN COMMON WITH THE OTHER regions of Italy, Liguria does not present any particular problems as far as crime is concerned, even in the most popular tourist resorts. You should, however, always observe the usual rules of common sense when travelling around. Every town possesses, besides a traffic police station, a police *(carabinieri)* station, which is open 24 hours a day and to which visitors should turn in an emergency. All towns have banks with cash machines where visitors can withdraw euros.

A team of *carabinieri* in their distinctive uniform

LAW AND ORDER

IN ITALY the forces of law and order are organized into two divisions: the *carabinieri* and the *polizia*. The former are responsible for public order, with communal, provincial or regional jurisdiction, and are commonly seen on patrol in the streets. The duties of the *polizia* are more wide-ranging, being generally more concerned with criminal investigations. At local level, you also find the municipal police, including the traffic police *(vigili urbani)*, who can deal with minor or emergency situations that do not involve traffic.

In the event of a theft, you should report the crime at the nearest police station in order to validate any insurance claim.

Municipal Policeman

FIREFIGHTERS

IN LIGURIA, forest fires, often encouraged by the constant wind that blows throughout the year, are suprisingly frequent. Therefore, if you are exploring the countryside it is essential to observe all the standard countryside code practices, especially with regard to not lighting a fire outside designated areas and making sure that cigarettes are completely extinguished.

The region is well equipped with fire stations, even in rural areas, and fire engines respond rapidly to alarm calls. Firefighters also attend other kinds of emergency.

PERSONAL SAFETY

USE COMMON SENSE when it comes to personal safety. Do not carry large sums of cash with you when you are out, and leave any valuables, at your hotel, in a safe if possible. You may wish to keep a separate photocopy of personal documents, so that you can request duplicates in the event of theft. Of course, you should never leave home without taking out full insurance cover.

Places where you are most likely to encounter pickpockets include railway stations and ferry terminals, or any crowded place, such as a bus, market or a street festival. If you are travelling by car, make sure that you always leave the vehicle locked, and don't leave any items in full view.

Genoa is a large bustling port city with, inevitably, some districts that it is best to steer clear of. (On arrival at your hotel, it is a good idea to ask the reception staff about areas that are best avoided.) In the countryside, however, and in the resorts, you need have few concerns about your personal safety, though it pays to be alert if you are out late at night.

If you wish to hire a taxi, make sure that you choose an official one. Your hotel should be able to recommend a reputable taxi firm. Make sure that the meter is switched on or that the fee is agreed in advance.

DISABLED VISITORS

LIGURIA PROVIDES relatively good information for people with disabilities. Genoa has a helpful service called Terre di Mare (www.terredimare), which is designed specifically for tourists. The national hotel site (www.italiapertutti) is also a useful resource.

It is always wise to phone a hotel or attraction in advance to check their facilities.

A firefighting plane in action during a summer fire in the hinterland

Entrance to one of the larger banks in Liguria

BANKS AND EXCHANGE

Currency can be changed in various ways. You will find bureaux de change in the larger airports and towns, and it is also possible to change money in hotels and travel agencies. As a general rule, however, the banks offer the best exchange rates. Banks in Italy normally open from 8:30am to 1:30pm, and from 3pm to 4pm, Monday to Friday; note that the banks often close early the day before a public holiday. Opening hours of bureaux de change are more variable.

Every town in Liguria has cashpoint/ATM machines (known as *bancomat*), where it is possible to withdraw money using a debit or credit card. These can normally be used 24 hours a day.

Despite these options, you are still advised to arrive in Liguria with at least a few euros for immediate use, particularly if you are due to arrive late in the day or at a weekend. Remember that for all kinds of transaction you will need to show some form of identification.

Credit cards are widely accepted for purchases and

can also be used to withdraw cash (though the latter transaction is not normally good value for money). VISA, American Express, MasterCard and Diners Club are the most commonly used cards.

THE EURO

Since January 2002 the euro has been the sole official currency in all participating states of the European Union. This means that euro notes and coins are valid throughout the so-called "eurozone", including Italy.

DIRECTORY

General emergencies
📞 113
Carabinieri (police)
📞 112
Fire Service
📞 115
Breakdown service
📞 116
Ambulance
📞 118
Coastguard
📞 15 30

Banknotes and Coins

Banknotes come in seven denominations. The 5-euro note is grey, the 10-euro is pink, the 20 is blue, the 50 orange, the 100 green, the 200 yellow and the 500 purple. There are eight different coins. The 1- and 2-euro coins are silver and gold; those worth 50, 20 and 10 cents are gold, while those worth 5, 2 and 1 cent are bronze.

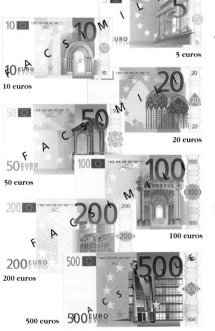

5 euros
10 euros
20 euros
50 euros
100 euros
200 euros
500 euros

2 euros   1 euro

50 cents   20 cents   10 cents

5 cents   2 cents   1 cents

TRAVEL INFORMATION

L IGURIA IS A narrow and relatively small region, so moving from place to place is usually easy. This is particularly

Typical coach, used by tourists to reach the coastal resorts of Liguria

true of the coast, which has good train and bus services as well as a decent road network (though traffic can be a problem in high season). While there are buses to the main inland towns, you need a car to explore inland areas properly. A car can be a hindrance on the coast in summer, however, when parking is virtually impossible in some places, including the Cinque Terre, to which you are advised to travel by

foot, train or boat. In terms of reaching Liguria, Genoa has one of Italy's major airports. There are also long-distance train and coach services, with good links from France and from other parts of Italy. There are various ferry services, too, though most of these operate from within Italy. Of more use to visitors are the ferries which ply between the main Ligurian resorts in summer. For those with a private yacht, there are plenty of marinas; most of these can offer good facilities and moorings for all sizes of craft.

ARRIVING BY AIR

T HE MAIN AIRPORT in Liguria is the Cristoforo Colombo at Genova-Sestri, west of the city. Ryanair and BA flights arrive here direct from the United Kingdom. Alternative entry points are Nice (with Easyjet, British Midland and BA), an easy train ride from the Riviera di Ponente, and Pisa (with Ryanair and BA), just 50 km (30 miles) from La Spezia. The closest airports receiving flights from North America are Milan and Rome.

Regular buses link Cristoforo Colombo airport with the ferry terminal and Principe and Brignole train stations in Genoa, running from 5:30am to 11:45pm.

There is also a small airport at Villanova d'Albenga, on the Riviera di Ponente, but at present this receives only domestic flights.

A stretch of the motorway linking Liguria's main towns

TRAVELLING BY CAR

S INCE DRIVING TO Liguria from the UK (either via the Swiss Alps or the French riviera) takes the best part of 24 hours, you would do better to fly and hire a car on arrival. The main rental companies have desks in the airport, but car hire in Italy can be expensive; you'll often

get a better rate if you arrange the car before leaving home.

A motorway *(autostrada)* – the A10 and its continuation the A12 – provides fast access along the Ligurian coast, though this route can get busy in holiday season and at weekends. Heading inland, motorways link the coast with Parma, Milan and Turin. The other principal route is state road no. 1 (SS1), the so-called Via Aurelia, first laid by the Romans. It runs the length of the coast, sometimes offering glimpses of the sea. Inland roads tend to be narrow and winding but are in good condition and pass through often stunning scenery.

If you plan to drive, note that parking in the resorts can be difficult (and stressful) in high season, and also that petrol stations are scarce in the hinterland once you head

Genoa's port and airport, both busy traffic hubs

away from the main towns, with few opening on Sundays or in the evening.

TRAVELLING BY TRAIN

IT IS MUCH SIMPLER to reach Liguria by train than it used to be, though it is a more expensive option than flying. From the UK, you can take the Eurostar to Paris, and then the TGV right down to Nice (a journery of around 12 hours), from where the coastal line runs east into Liguria.

Both fast and slow trains serve the towns along the Ligurian coast. In general, trains from the north or west arrive at Genoa's Stazione Principe, while those from the south and east arrive at Stazione Brignole. Both stations have good bus connections.

The historic Genoa–Casella line, which runs inland to the Apennines, is a rare example of a narrow-gauge railway *(see p88)*.

TRAVELLING BY COACH

EUROLINES RUNS coaches to Liguria from elsewhere in Europe, but travelling by train or air doesn't cost much more.

Within Liguria, coach travel (often more expensive than train travel) is most useful for journeys into the mountains: in many inland areas coaches are the only sole of transport. Coach services from Genoa (run by different companies) leave from Piazza Acquaverde and Piazza della Vittoria, close to Stazione Principe and Stazione Brignole respectively.

CITY TRANSPORT

BUSES IN GENOA, run by the Azienda Mobilità e Trasporti (AMT), are easy to use since they charge a flat rate for trips within the city limits and nearby suburbs. Tourist tickets valid for 24 or 48 hours are also available. Tickets, sold by newspaper kiosks and tobacconists, must be bought in advance and validated in the machine once on board.

Logo of Riviera Trasporti

Genoa also has a nascent metro, and two funiculars, which link Piazza del Portello and Largo della Zecca with Genoa's upper districts. From Piazza del Portello you can also take the lift up to the belvedere at Castelletto.

FERRIES AND MARINAS

IT IS POSSIBLE to travel to Liguria by sea, though most services are from within Italy. Genoa's splendid Stazione Marittima is the main hub for ferries, with connections to Cagliari and other ports in Sardinia, and Palermo in Sicily. Overseas links are with Corsica, Tunis and Barcelona. Ferries from Corsica also arrive at Vado, near Savona. Several companies operate these services, including Tirrenia and Grimaldi.

In summer, local ferry services run along the Ligurian coast, primarily in the Golfo del Tigullio, the Golfo dei Poeti and along the coast of the Cinque Terre.

For those with their own boat, there are more than 60 landing points and marinas along the coast, including the famous tiny harbour at Portofino. The marinas are generally well-equipped and can accommodate a total of around 16,000 boats.

The newly built railway station at San Remo

General Index

Page numbers in **bold type** refer to main entries

A

Abbeys
San Fruttuoso 21, 37, 111
San Venerio (Isola del Tino) 121
Sant'Andrea di Borzone 114
Adelasia 152
Airports 210
Agriturismo 174–5
Alassio 20, 24, 29, 43, 132, 151, **152**
Caffè Roma 152
Hotels 181
Muretto 29, 132, 152
Restaurants 194
Albenga 20, 24, 30, 36, 41, 102, 132, 146, **148–51**, 187
Baptistry 149, 150, **151**
Hotels 181
Loggia dei Quattro Canti 148
Piana di Albenga 148
Piazza dei Leoni 149
Porta Molino 149
Porta Torlaro 148
Restaurants 194
Torracco 148
Torre and Casa Lengueglia Doria 148
Via Bernardo Ricci 148
Albini Franco 53, 57, 72
Albisola Superiore 36, **135**, 150
Restaurants 194
Albissola Marina **135**, 198
Hotels 181
Lungomare degli Artisti 135
Restaurants 194
Aleramo 152
Alessi, Galeazzo 52, 53, 56, 60, 67, 88
Alta Via dei Monti 18, 201
Altare 133, 140
Restaurants 194
Ameglia 33, **126**
Restaurants 190
Andersen, Hans Christian 27, 116
Andora **152–3**
Restaurants 195
Ansaldo, Giovanni Andrea 76, 116
Antiques shops 198, 199
Antonello da Messina 23, 64
Ecce Homo 23, 64
Apennines 13, 24, 17, 19, 105, 140, 200
Apricale 160
Hotels 181

APT tourist offices 175, 206, 207
Architecture 24–5
Arenzano 19, 134
Ariosto, Ludovico 26
Arma di Taggia 20, 35, 158, 200
Restaurants 195
Art 22–3
Assereto, Gioacchino 23, 71, 75, 76
Augustines 57, 86

B

Bacezza 114
Baiardo 161
Restaurants 195
Baiardo, Giovanni Battista 59
Balbi family 46, 67, 77, 83
Balestrino 28
Balilla 42
Balzi Rossi 20, 33, 35, 82, 132, 168, **169**
Banco di San Giorgio 38, 58, 59
Banknotes and coins 209
Banks 209
Barabino, Carlo 43, 55, 76, 87
Barabino, Nicolò 108
Barbarian invasions 36
Barbieri, Giovan Francesco see Guercino
Barnaba da Modena 58, 164
Madonna and Child 58
Barnabite monks 86
Barocci, Federico 53
Crucifix with Mary, John and St Sebastian 53
Baroque in Liguria 102, 144, 152, 153
Bars 185, 202–203
Basilian monks 86
Basilicas see Churches
Battles
of Chioggia 40
of Curzola 40, 58, 65
of Meloria 38–9, 40
of Lepanto 41, 79, 124
of Pola 40
Bed & breakfast 174–5
Beerbohm, Max 109
Bellini, Vincenzo 26
Bianca e Fernando 26
Benedictines 37, 114, 165
Benso, Giulio 76, 77
Annunciation 76
Assumption 76
Berengarius 36
Bergeggi 18, **140**
Restaurants 195
Bianco family 77
Bianco, Bartolomeo 77
Bicknell, Clarence 165

Birolli, Renato 23
Bishops of Albenga 145, 154
Bishops of Savona 141
Bocca di Magra **126–7**
Boccanegra, Simone 22, 38, 40, 54
Bocciardo, Domenico 154, 157
Death of St Joseph 157
Gloria di San Biagio 154
Tobias burying the Dead 157
Bogliasco 21, **108**
Restaurants 190
Boldini, Giovanni 23, 89
Portrait of the Contessa de Byland 23
Portrait of Miss Bell 89
Bonassola 21, **117**
Hotels 178
Bonone, Carlo 76
Beheading of John the Baptist 76
Bonvicini, Alessandro 74
Bordighera 20, 42, 43, 102, 160, **165**
Hotels 182
Restaurants 195
Bordone, Paris 23, 74
Borgio Verezzi 20, **144–5**, 202
Hotels 182
Restaurants 195
Borgo Rotondo 106
Borzonasca 114
Braccesco, Carlo 64, 117
Saints Augustine and Jerome 117
Saints Blaise and Pantaleo 117
Bramante 135
Brea, Francesco 158, 165
Brea, Ludovico 58, 86, 139, 141, 158, **159**, 165
Annunciation 86
Assumption and Saints 139, 158
Baptism of Christ 159
Christ on the Cross between the Madonna and St John the Evangelist 159
The Conversion of St Paul 58, 159
Coronation of the Virgin 159
Crucifixion 159
Enthroned Madonna and Child, Angels and Saints 141
Madonna del Rosario 159
Madonna and Saints 159
Paradise 58
St Peter 159
Brignole Sale family 71, 72, 73, 74, 75

Brignole Sale, Giovan Francesco
72, 74, 75
Brignole Sale De Ferrari,
Duchess of Galliera 71, 72, 82
Brilla, Antonio 136, 138, 139
Deposition 139
Madonna della Misericordia 138
Bronze Age 24, 33, 35, 125, 136
Bronzino 79
Andrea Doria as Neptune 79
Brugnato 29
Buses and coaches 211
Bussana 164
Bussana Vecchia 164
Byron, Lord 27, 88, 121

C
Cafés 185, 202
Cairo Montenotte 140
Calendar of events 28–31
Calizzano 201
Cambiaso, Giovanni 158
Cambiaso, Luca 22, 56, 65, 68,
71, 83, 89, 114, 117, 153, 158
Last Supper 117
Nativity 83
Pietà 56
San Francesco di Paola 153
Camogli 13, 21, 28, 29, 41, 106,
108, 115
Hotels 178
Restaurants 190–91
Camp sites 175
Campi 88
Campiglia **120**
Canaletto 124
Canavesio, Giovanni 165
Passion of Christ 165
Polyptych of St Michael 165
Canoeing 200
Canova, Antonio 50, 57
Penitent Madonna 50, 57
Cantone, Bernardino 59, 70, 71
Cantoni, Gaetano 156
Cantoni, Simone 54
Canzio, Michele 84
Capo Mortola 170
Caravaggio 71, 124
Ecce Homo 71
Carbone, Giovanni Bernardo 75
Carcare 133
Carlone, Giovanni Andrea 75
Carlone, Giovanni Battista 54,
76, 116
Carlone, Taddeo 59, 71, 79
Fountain of Neptune 78, 79
Carracci, Agostino 74
Carracci, Annibale 74
Carracci, Ludovico 74
Annunciation 74

Carrega, Maurizio 157, 168
Carrega, Tommaso 157, 168
Life of St Peter 157
Cars 210
Casa Magni 27, 121
Casella train 89
Casella, Francesco 70
Cassini, Gian Domenico 160
Castel Vittorio 165
Castellari 24
Castello, Bernardo 65, 77
Castello, Giovan Battista
(il Bergamasco) 65, 71, 89
Castello, Valerio 55, 71, 77
Castelnuovo di Magra **127**
Restaurants 191
Castiglione, Giovan Battista
see Grechetto
Castles and fortresses
D'Albertis (Genoa) 83
di Ameglia 126
di Andora 152
dell'Annunziata (Ventimiglia)
168
di Apricale 160
d'Appio (Ventimiglia) 169
Begato (Genoa) 87
della Bocchetta (Altare) 140
di Bogliasco 108
Brown (Portofino) 111
di Cairo Montenotte 140
Castellaccio (Genoa) 87
di Castelnuovo di Magra 127
di Cervo 153
Diamante (Genoa) 87
Doria (Dolceacqua) 166, 167
Dragone (Camogli) 108
di Lerici 121
Mackenzie (Genoa) 87
Malaspina (Santo Stefano
d'Aveto) 115
di Millesimo 140
Monleone (Moneglia) 117
di Noli 141
del Priamàr (Savona)136, 139
di Pietra Ligure 145
di Portovenere 120
Puin (Genoa) 87
di Rapallo 109
di San Giorgio (La Spezia)
124–5
di San Terenzo 121
di Sant'Antonio (Albissola
Marina) 135
di Sarzanello 129
Sperone (Genoa) 87
di Spotorno 141
Tenaglia (Genoa) 87
di Torriglia 108
di Varese Ligure 116

Castles and fortresses (cont.)
di Varigotti 144
di Villafranca (Moneglia) 117
Castracani, Castruccio 129
Caves
Grotta del Caviglione 34
Grotta delle Arene Candide 35
Grotta delle Fate 35
Grotte dei Balzi Rossi *see*
Balzi Rossi
Grotte di Toirano 33, 35, **146–7**
Grotte di Valdemino 145
Cavour, Camillo 124
Celle Ligure 134
Ceramics 75, 135, 136, 198, 199
Ceresola, Andrea (Vannone)
54, 59
Ceriale 203
Ceriana 28, 30, 161
Cervo 102, 132, **153**
Hotels 182
Restaurants 195
Cevasco, Giovanni Battista 85,
87
Charles V, emperor 40, 78, 79
Chermayeff, Peter 62
Chiabrera, Gabriello 138
Chiavari 21, 33, 41, 106, **114**,
115
Hotels 178
Restaurants 191
Churches
dell'Annunziata (Altare) 140
dell'Assunta (Spotorno) 141
dell'Assunta (Triora) 158
dell'Assunta (Ventimiglia) 168
dei Cappuccini (Genoa) 86
dei Cappuccini (Santa
Margherita Ligure) 109
Cristo Risorto (Savona) 138–9
Duomo di Imperia 156
del Gesù (Genoa) 51, **54**, 77
Immacolata Concezione
(San Remo) 164
d'In Selàa (Tellaro) 126
Madonna della Punta
(Bonassola) 117
Madonna delle Grazie
(Bacezza) 22, 114
Madonnetta (Genoa) 86
della Natività (Bogliasco) 108
dei Neri (Ventimiglia) 168
Nostra Signora Assunta
(Savona) 139
Nostra Signora della Costa
(San Remo) 164
Nostra Signora del Boschetto
(Camogli) 109
Nostra Signora di Castello
(Savona) 139, 159

Churches (cont.)
Nostra Signora della
Concordia (Albissola Marina)
135
Nostra Signora delle Grazie
(Voltri), 82
Nostra Signora della Neve
(Albisola) 135
Nostra Signora dell'Orto
(Chiavari) 114
Oratorio d'In Selàa (Tellaro)
126
Oratorio del Cristo Risorto
(Savona) 138–9
Oratorio dell'Immacolata
Concezione (Sanremo) 164
Oratorio della Santissima
Annunziata (Spotorno) 141
Oratorio dei Neri
(Ventimiglia) 168
Oratorio di Nostra Signora
della Neve (Albisola) 135
Oratorio di San Bartolomeo
(Apricale) 160
Oratorio di San Leonardo
(Imperia) 157
Oratorio di San Salvatore
(Baiardo) 161
Oratorio di Santa Chiara
(Bogliasco) 108
Parrocchiale dell'Assunta
(Spotorno) 141
Parrocchiale della
Oregina (Genoa) 83, 86
Purificazione di Maria
(Apricale) 160
Russian Orthodox Church
(San Remo) 164
Sacro Cuore (Bussana
Vecchia) 164
San Bartolomeo (Apricale)
160
San Bartolomeo degli Armeni
(Genoa) 86
San Bernardo (Pigna) 165
San Biagio (Finale Ligure) 144
San Biagio (Imperia) 154
San Domenico (Varazze) 134
San Donato (Genoa) 57
San Francesco (Lerici) 121
San Francesco (Monterosso
al Mare) 118
San Francesco (Rapallo) 109
San Francesco (Ventimiglia)
168
San Francesco di Paola
(Genoa) 82
San Francesco di Paola
(La Spezia) 124
San Fruttuoso 21, 37, 111
San Giorgio (Dolceacqua) 166
San Giorgio (Tellaro) 126

Churches (cont.)
San Giovanni Battista
(Cervo) 102, 132, 153
San Giovanni Battista
(Chiavari) 114
San Giovanni Battista
(Finale Ligure) 144
San Giovanni Battista
(Imperia) 154
San Giovanni Battista
(Monterosso al Mare) 118
San Giovanni Battista
(Pieve di Teco) 153
San Giovanni di Pré (Genoa)
38, 78
San Leonardo (Imperia) 157
San Lorenzo (Cairo
Montenotte) 140
San Lorenzo (Genoa) 22, 24,
47, 49, 50, **52–3**
San Lorenzo (Portovenere) 120
San Lorenzo Vecchio
(Varigotti) 144
San Martino (Bergeggi) 140
San Matteo (Genoa) 38, 65
San Matteo (Laigueglia) 152
San Michele (Albenga) 102,
149, **150**
San Michele (Pigna) 165
San Michele (Ventimiglia) 169
San Nicola di Bari
(Pietra Ligure) 145
San Nicolò (Albisola) 135
San Nicolò (Andora) 153
San Nicolò (Baiardo) 161
San Nicolò (Perinaldo) 160
San Nicolò dell'Isola
(Sestri Levante) 116
San Paragorio (Noli) 132, 141
San Pietro (Borgio Verezzi) 145
San Pietro (Imperia) 157
San Pietro (Noli) 141
San Pietro (Portovenere)
103, 105, 120
San Pietro in Banchi
(Genoa) 59
San Pietro in Castello
(Genoa) 57
San Rocco (Vallecrosia) 160
San Salvatore (Baiardo) 161
San Salvatore dei Fieschi (San
Salvatore di Cogorno) 40, 115
San Siro (Genoa) 68, **76**
San Siro (San Remo) 164
San Siro di Struppa (Genoa) 88
San Tommaso (Dolcedo) 158
San Tommaso (Pigna) 165
San Venerio (Isola del Tino)
121
San Venerio (La Spezia) 125
Sant'Agostino (Borgio
Verezzi) 145

Churches (cont.)
Sant'Agostino (Genoa) 50
Sant'Ambrogio (Alassio) 152
Sant'Ambrogio (Varazze) 134
Sant'Ampelio (Bordighera)
165
Sant'Andrea (Levanto) 117
Sant'Andrea (Savona) 138
Sant'Andrea di Borzone 114
Sant'Antonio Abate
(Dolceacqua) 167
Sant'Eugenio (Altare) 140
Santa Caterina (Bonassola) 117
Santa Chiara (Bogliasco) 108
Santa Croce (Moneglia) 117
Santa Giulia di Centaura
(Lavagna) 115
Santa Maria (Luni) 127
Santa Maria Assunta (Camogli)
108
Santa Maria Assunta
(San Terenzo) 121
Santa Maria Assunta
(Sarzana) 22, 128
Santa Maria Assunta in
Carignano (Genoa) 56
Santa Maria di Nazareth
(Sestri Levante) 116
Santa Maria del Canneto
(Taggia) 158
Santa Maria del Prato
(Genoa) 38
Santa Maria dell'Assunta
(La Spezia) 125
Santa Maria della Ripa
(Pieve di Teco) 153
Santa Maria delle Grazie
(Portovenere) 120
Santa Maria delle Vigne
(Genoa) 50, **64**
Santa Maria di Castello
(Genoa) 50, **58**, 159
Santa Maria di Pia
(Finale Ligure) 144
Santa Maria in Fontibus
(Albenga) 149
Santa Maria Maddalena
(Bordighera) 165
Santa Maria Maddalena
(Castelnuovo di Magra) 127
Santi Filippo e Giacomo
(Castelnuovo di Magra) 127
Santi Giacomo e Filippo
(Andora) 153
Santi Giacomo e Filippo
(Taggia) 158
Santi Vincenzo e Anastasio
(Ameglia) 126
Santissima Annunziata
(Spotorno) 141
Santissima Annunziata
del Vastato (Genoa) 76

Churches (cont.)
  Santo Stefano (Borgio
  Verezzi) 145
  Santo Stefano (Genoa) 55
  Santo Stefano (Lavagna) 115
  Santo Stefano (Rapallo) 109
  San Barnaba (Genoa) 86
Chiodo, Domenico 124
Chiossone, Edoardo 70
Ciber, G 139
  Assumption 139
Cicagna 115
Cinque Terre 19, 21, 105, 106,
  118–9, 121, 127, 187, 200, 201
Clairmont, Claire 27
Classicism 89
Clavesana, Marchesi 153
Coast 16, 34, 20–21
Colla, Micheri 152
Colombiadi (Columbus
  celebrations) 25, 43, 57, 60
Columbus, Christopher 25, 41,
  50, 51, 56, 57, 71, 82
  House of 56–7
Cogoleto 19
Conca, Sebastiano 157
  Madonna with Child and
  Santa Caterina da Bologna
  157
Congress of Vienna 42
Constantius 151
Conte, Paolo 13
Convents and monasteries
  degli Agostiniani (Pieve di
  Teco) 153
  di Monte Carmelo (Loano)
  145
  di San Domenico (Taggia)
  158, 159
  di Santa Caterina (Finale
  Ligure) 144
  di Santa Chiara (Imperia) 157
Coppedé, Gino 87
Corniglia 119
Corradi, Pierantonio 72
Cortese, G 139
Cosini, Silvio 79
Cozzi, Geminiano 75
Cremona, Ippolito 64
Croce family 57
Crosa, Giuseppe 51
Crusades 37, 38, 39, 40
Cuisine 184–5, 186–7
Cuneo, Renata 137
  Ecce Homo 137
  Man Sleeping 137
  The Shell 137
  Summer 137

D

D'Albertis, Enrico Alberto 83
D'Andrade, Alfredo 57, 59, 83

Dante Alighieri 26, 146
Dapporto, Carlo 27
David, Claude 56
David, Gérard 71
David, Giovanni 39, 54
  Battle of Meloria 39
Davis, Sammy 202
De Amicis, Edmondo 27, 154
De André, Fabrizio 15, 26, 78
De' Bardi, Donato 22, 23, 136
  Crucifixion 22, 136, 137
De' Bianchi, Bianca 29
De Chirico, Giorgio 137
De Ferrari, Francesco 59
  Arms of Genoa with the
  symbols of Justice and
  Strength 59
De Ferrari, Giovanni Andrea
  71, 116, 141
De Ferrari Gregorio 55, 65, 72,
  75, 76, 77, 141, 154, 156, 157
  Allegory of Spring 72, 75
  Allegory of Summer 75
  Assumption of Mary 76
  Myth of Phaethon 75
  Our Lady of Sorrows and souls
  in Purgatory 157
  Predica di San Francesco
  St Clare drives out the
  Saracens 154
  Saverio 156
De Ferrari, Orazio 83, 114
  Washing of the Feet 83
De Nittis, Giuseppe 23
De Stefanis, Alessandro 83
Deiva Marina 20, 116
Del Carretto, Marchesi 140,
  141, 144, 153
Del Piombo, Sebastiano 23, 40,
  46
  Portrait of Andrea Doria 40
Della Porta, Gian Giacomo 59
Della Robbia family 144
Della Robbia, Andrea 125
  Coronation of the Virgin 125
Della Rovere, Francesco
  see Sixtus IV
Della Rovere, Francesco Maria
  135
Della Rovere, Giuliano
  see Julius II
Deserto di Varazze 134
Di Bartolo, Taddeo 23, 65, 158
  Christ on the rocky shores of
  Jordan 158
  Madonna 65
Di Credi, Lorenzo 164
Di Negro, Giancarlo 70
Dialects 27
Diano Marina 29
Dickens, Charles 27
Disabled Access 185, 208

Discos and Clubs 202
Diving 200
Doges 40, 42
Dolceacqua 14, 102, 132, 165,
  166–7, 187
  Restaurants 196
Dolcedo **158**
dolphins 16
Dominicans 58
Doria family 14, 38, 41, 50,
  65, 71, 83, 108, 110, 115, 145,
  153, 154, 166
Doria, Andrea 25, 38, 40, 41,
  46, 65, 67, 70, 78, **79**, 87, 154
Doria, Giacomo 55
Doria, Lamba 65
Doria, Martino 65
Doria, Oberto 39, 145
Dürer, Albrecht 23, 72, 74
  Portrait of a Young Man 72
Durazzo family 41, 74
Durazzo, Eugenio 77
Durazzo, Ippolito 70
Durazzo, Maria 71, 74

E

Emanuele Filiberto di Savoia 124
Embriaco, Guglielmo 39
Etruscans 33

F

FAI (Fondo Ambientale
  Italiano) 110
Falconet, Etienne 75
Farinata 15, 31, 186
Fattori, Giovanni 23
Fegina 118
Fei, Paolo Di Giovanni 23,
  124
  Annunciation 23
Ferrari, D 138
  Madonna del Buonconsiglio
  138
Ferret, Eugenio 164
Ferries 211
Festival della Canzone Italiana
  (San Remo) 26, 28, 102, 131,
  164, 202
Festival Internazionale
  della Danza (Nervi) 23, 89
Festivals **28–31**, 185
Fiascherino **126**
Fiasella, Domenico 54, 56, 76,
  116, 136, 151, 157
  Annunciation 151
  Deposition 116
  San Domenico Soriano
  and Madonna 157
Fieschi family 25, 38, 108, 114,
  115, 116, 124
Fieschi, Opizio 29

Finalborgo 132, 144
Finale Ligure 18, 35, 132, **144**, 187, 201
  Hotels 182
  Restaurants 196
Finale Marina 132, 144
Finale Pia 132, 144
Finale stone 71, 141
Fiumaretta di Ameglia
  Restaurants 191
Flower industry 29, 198, 199
Focaccia 15, 28, 186, 199
Focesi 152
Fontana, Carlo 77
Fontana, Lucio 135
Food and drink 184–5, 186–7
Football 203
Foppa, Vincenzo 23, 139
  Madonna and Saints 139
Foresta delle Lame 19, 115
Fortresses *see* Castles and Fortresses
Fossati, Ivano 26
Franciscans 83
Frederick I, Barbarossa 53, 56, 116

G

Gagini family 65, 154
Gagini, Domenico 53
Gagini, Elia 53
Gagini, Giovanni 165
Galletti, Guido 110
  Cristo degli Abissi 29, 110
Gallinara 18, **151**
Gardella, Ignazio 55
Gardens and Parks
  Giardini Ormond (Sanremo) 164
  Giardino Esotico Pallanca (Bordighera) 165
  Parco Casale (Rapallo) 109
  Parco Comunale di Villa Durazzo (Santa Margherita Ligure) 109
  Parco Durazzo Pallavicini (Pegli) 82, **83–4**, 87
  Parco Serra Gropallo (Nervi) 23
  Parco Urbano delle Mura (Genoa) 87
  Villa Hanbury (La Mortola) 132, 168, **170–71**
Garlenda 29, 201
Garibaldi, Giuseppe 42
Garibbe 160
Gassman, Vittorio 27
Gelasio, pope 53
Genoa 13, 15, 21, 22, 24, 25, 26, 28, 29, 30, 31, 33, 37, 38, 40, **45–89**, 102, 115, 121, 131, 136, 141, 174, 187, 198, 202, 203

Genoa (cont.)
  Albaro 81, **88**
  Albergo dei Poveri 76
  Aquarium 15, 25, 43, 46, 58, 60, 61, **62–3**
  Boccadasse 81, **89**
  Casa di Colombo 50, 51, **56–7**
  Casella train 89
  Centro Storico 48–65
  Cimitero di Staglieno 81, **87**
  Circonvallazione a Monte 81, 82, 86
  Città dei Bambini 61
  Football teams 203
  Fortresses 81, **87**
  Further Afield 80–9
  Hotels 176–78
  Houses of the Doria 49
  La Commenda 78
  Lanterna 25, 41, 49, **61**, 203
  Loggia dei Mercanti 59
  "Matitone" 57
  Nervi 81, **89**
  Pegli **82**
  Piazza Banchi 50, **59**
  Piazza De Ferrari 50, 51
  Piazza della Fontana Marose 68, **70**
  Piazza San Matteo 38, 49, 50, **65**
  Porta di Santa Fede 56
  Porta Soprana 51, **56**
  Porto Antico 31, 46, 58, **60–61**
  Porto Nuovo 25, 43
  Quartiere di Fassolo 83
  Quarto 43
  Restaurants 188–190
  Sottoripa 59
  Stazione Marittima 79
  Strade Nuove 25, 66–79
  Streetfinder 90–99
  Teatro Carlo Felice 26, 43, 49, 54, **55**, 84, 202
  Torre degli Embriaci 58
  Via Balbi 67, **77**
  Via di Sottoripa 50
  Via Garibaldi 47, 67, 69, **70**, 77
  Voltri 31, 81, **82**
  Walls 81, **87**
Gentile da Fabriano 74
Gentileschi, Orazio 76
  Annunciation 76
Ghibellines 39, 41
Ghirlandaio 82
Giambologna 77
Giambono, Michele 74
Giordano, Luca 77
Giovanni V Paleologo 86
Giuliano da Sangallo 138
Giulio Romano 55
  Martyrdom of St Stephen 55

Giustenice 145
Giustiniani, Luca 89
Golf 200, 201
Golfo dei Poeti 121
Golfo del Paradiso 108, 110
Golfo del Tigullio 21, 106, 109, 110, 114, 116
Golfo di La Spezia 19, 120, 126, 127
Golfo di Lerici 27, 121
Golfo di San Remo 20
Gothic architecture 24
Govi, Gilberto 27
Grasso, Giovanni Battista 87
Grechetto (Giovan Battista Castiglione) 55, 58, 64, 75, 77
  Agar and the Angel 75
  Flight of the Family of Abraham 75
  Virgin with the saints Catherine and Mary Magdalen and the effigies of St Dominic 58
Greeks 33
Grillo family 64
Grillo, Beppe 26, 27
Grimaldi 169
Grimaldi family 38, 58, 64, 71
Grimaldi, Nicolò 71
Gropallo, Gaetano 89
Grotte *see* Caves
Guardi, Francesco 124
Guelphs 39, 41
Guercino (Giovan Francesco Barbieri) 23, 56, 74
  Dying Cleopatra 23, 74
  God the Father with Angel 74
  Suicide of Catone Uticense 74
Guidobono, Bartolomeo 75, 136
Guttuso, Renato 23, 137

H

Hadrian V, pope (Ottobono Fieschi) 115
Haffner, Antonio 75
Haffner, Enrico 75
Hannibal 36, 136
Hanbury, Sir Thomas 169, 170, 171
Helg, Franca 57
Hemingway, Ernest 27, 152
Henry VII, emperor 22, 57, 64
Heruli 36
Heyerdahl, Thor 152
Hiking 201
Hills 17
  Colle della Madonna della Costa 117
  Colle di Cadibona 13, 36, 140
  Colle di San Benigno 61
  Colle di San Giacomo 117

Honorius, emperor 151
Horse riding 201
Hospitals 207
Hotels 174, 176–183
House of Columbus see Casa di Colombo

I

Imperia 29, 30, 102, 132, 153, **154–7**
  Hotels 182
  Oneglia 31, 154–5
  Piazza Dante 155
  Porto Maurizio 156–7, 200
  Restaurants 196
  Via Bonfante 154–5
Innocent IV, pope (Sinibaldo Fieschi) 115
Internet 207
Iron Age 125, 136
Islands
  Bergeggi 140–41
  Gallinara 18, **151**
  Palmaria **120–21**, 125
  Tinetto 120–21
  Tino 120–21

J, K

Jacopo da Varagine 134
  Legenda Aurea 134
Jesuits 51, 77, 86
Julius II, pope 135, 138
Julius III, pope 166
Justus von Ravensburg 58
  Annunciation 58
Knights of St John 38, 39

L

La Spezia 21, 23, 27, 28, 41, 102, 107, 121, **124–5**
  Hotels 179
  Naval base 124
  Restaurants 191
Lacroix, François 154
Lago degli Abeti 115
Lago del Brugneto 19, 108
Laigueglia 29, 152
  Restaurants 196
Landscape 16–19
Lauzi, Bruno 26
Lavagna 29, **115**
  Hotels 179
Lawrence DH 121
Lemeglio 117
Leoncino, Andrea 75
Lerici 21, 27, 43, **121**
  Hotels 179
  Restaurants 191–2
Levanto 21, 37, **117**, 120
  Hotels 179
Licini, Osvaldo 57

Ligurian tribes 33, 34–5, 36, 114, 136, 168
Ligurian cuisine 184–5, 186–7
Ligurian Romanesque 132, 141
Lippi, Filippino 71
Lippo di Benivieni 124
Literature 27
Livy 136
Loano 20, 30, 31, **145**
  Hotels 182–3
Lombards 36
Lomellini family 76
Lomi, Aurelio 56
Lorenzetti, Pietro 124
Lorenzo the Magnificent 129
Lotto, Lorenzo 23
Louis XIII 61
Louis XIV, king of France 42
Luni 24, 103, 106, 121, 125, **127**, 128

M

Madame De Staël 70
Maestro, Guglielmo 22
  Christ on the Cross 22
Maestri Comacini 164
Magellan 138
Magnasco Alessandro 71, 88, 89, 116
  Trattenimento in un Giardino di Albaro 71, 88
Malaspina family 108
Mameli, Goffredo 43
Manarola 119
  Hotels 179
Mannerism 89
Manzù, Giacomo 137
Maps
  Albenga Street-by-Street 148–9
  Exploring the Riviera di Levante 106–7
  Exploring the Riviera di Ponente 132–3
  Genoa: around Piazza Matteotti 50–51
  Genoa: around Via Garibaldi 68–9
  Genoa at a Glance 46–7
  Genoa: Centro Storico 49
  Genoa: Further Afield 81
  Genoa: Le Strade Nuove 67
  Italian Riviera Coastline 20–21
  Italian Riviera at a Glance 102–3
  La Spezia Town Centre 125
  Oneglia Town Centre 155
  Parks and nature reserves 18–9
  Porto Maurizio Town Centre 157
  Sarzana 128–9

Maps (cont.)
  Savona Town Centre 137
  Tour of the Armea and Crosia Valleys 160–61
Maragliano, Anton Maria **23**, 58, 83, 86, 108, 114, 135, 139, 141, 144, 153, 154, 156, 164
  Annunciation 139
  Crucifixion 153
  Immaculate Conception 58
  Pietà 86
  Virgin Mary 83
Maratta, Carlo 56, 74
  Martyrdom of St Blaise 56
  Rest on the Flight to Egypt 74
Marcenaro, Caterina 53, 72
Marconi, Guglielmo 116
Margaret of Brabant 57, 64
Maria Alexandrovna, czarina 164
Marieschi, Michele 124
Marinaldi, Francesco Maria 154
Martinengo, Filippo 139
  Addolorata 139
  Deposition 139
Martini, Arturo 89
Martin of Tours, saint 151
Marvaldi, Giovanni Battista 153
Mazone Giovanni 136
  Christ on the Cross between the Marys and St John the Baptist 136
Mazzini, Giuseppe 42, 43, 87, 136
  Tomb 87
Meloria, Battle of 38–9, 40
Mengs, Anton Raphael 55
Michelangelo 135
Middle Ages 22, 24, 59, 65, 88, 102, 121, 127, 136, 138, 140, 144, 148, 157, 158, 164, 166
Millesimo 133, 140
Minnelli, Liza 202
Miró, Joan 23, 137
Molini di Triora 30
Moneglia 116–7
  Hotels 179
  Restaurants 192
Monet, Claude 14, 165, 166
Montaldo, Leonardo, doge of Genoa 86
Montale, Eugenio 27, 105, 118, 121
Montaretto 117
Montemarcello **126**
Monterosso al Mare 118
  Fegina 118
  Hotels 180
Montesquieu 27
Morandi, Giorgio 23, 137
Mountains 17
  Monte Aiona 115
  Monte Antola 108

Mountains (cont.)
Monte Bego 34, 35, 201
Monte Beigua 18, 134
Monte di Portofino 21, 89, 110
Monte Granarolo 79
Monte Maggiorasca 114
Monte Peralto 87
Monte Sant'Elena 140
Monte Ursino 141
Montorsoli Giovanni Angelo
65, 79
Fontana del Tritone 79
Moore, Henry 23, 137
Museums and galleries
Accademia Ligustica di Belle
Arti (Genoa) 54, **55**, 70
Biblioteca Museo Clarence
Bicknell (Bordighera) 165
Civico Museo Archeologico
(Chiavari) 114
Civico Museo del Finale
(Finale Ligure) 144
Civico Museo Ingauno
(Albenga) 150
Civico Museo Naturalistico
(Loano) 145
Civico Museo Storico-
Archeologico (Savona)
136
Galata Museo del Mare 78
Galleria d'Arte Moderna
(Nervi) 23, 89
Galleria di Palazzo Bianco
(Genoa) 71, 159
Galleria di Palazzo Doria
Pamphilj (Genoa) 79
Galleria di Palazzo Rosso
(Genoa) 23, 73, 74–5
Galleria Nazionale della
Liguria (Genoa) 64
Galleria Nazionale di Palazzo
Reale (Genoa) 77
Galleria Nazionale di Palazzo
Spinola (Genoa) 23, 64
Galleria Rizzi (Sestri Levante)
116
Museo Amedeo Lia (La
Spezia) 23, 124
Museo Archeologico
Nazionale (Luni) 127
Museo Archeologico Gerolamo
Rossi (Ventimiglia) 168, 169
Museo Civico (San Remo) 164
Museo Civico Archeologico
Ubaldo Formentini
(La Spezia) 125
Museo Civico di Archeologia
Ligure (Pegli) 82, 134
Museo Civico di Storia
Naturale G Doria (Genoa) 55
Museo Civico Navale
(Pegli) 82

Museums and galleries (cont.)
Museo d'Arte Contemporanea
(Genoa) 57
Museo del Merletto (Rapallo)
109
Museo del Tesoro (Genoa) 53
Museo del Tesoro (Savona)
22, 139, 159
Museo del Vetro e dell'Arte
Vetraria (Altare) 140
Museo dell'Olivo (Imperia)
155
Museo della Canzone e della
Riproduzione Sonora
(Garibbe) 160
Museo della Ceramica Manlio
Trucco (Albisola) 135
Museo della Cultura
Materiale (Levanto) 117
Museo di Arte Orientale
E Chiossone (Genoa) 70
Museo di Sant'Agostino
(Genoa) 22, 57
Museo di Santa Maria
del Castello (Genoa) 58
Museo Diocesano d'Arte Sacra
(Albenga) 151
Museo Etnografico (Genoa) 83
Museo Etnografico del
Ponente Ligure (Cervo) 153
Museo Etnografico e della
Stregoneria (Triora) 158
Museo Giannettino Luxoro
(Nervi) 89
Museo Marinaro Gio Bono
Ferrari (Camogli) 108, 109
Museo Navale Internazionale
del Ponente Ligure (Imperia)
156
Museo Navale Romano
(Albenga) 150
Museo Nazionale dell'Antartide
Felice Ippolito (Genoa) 60
Museo Preistorico dei Balzi
Rossi (Ponte San Ludovico) 169
Museo Renata Cuneo
(Savona) 137
Museo Sandro Pertini
(Savona) 23, 137
Museo Tecnico Navale della
Marina Militare (La Spezia) 124
Pinacoteca Civica (Imperia) 156
Pinacoteca Civica (Savona)
23, 136, 159
Raccolta Frugone (Nervi) 89
Music 26, 203

N

Napoleon Bonaparte 42, 124,
140, 166
National parks *see* Parks and
nature reserves

Nativity scenes 86
Neanderthal man 33, 35
Nicola 127
Nicolò da Voltri 57
Madonna and Child 57
Nietzsche, Friedrich 27
Noli 18, 29, 37, 132, 140,
141
Hotels 183
Restaurants 196
Novaro, Antonio 145

O

Olive oil 28, 31, 186, 199
Olives 28, 31, 198
Oliverio, Frate 58
Oratories *see* Churches
Orengo, Marchesi 170, 171
Otto of Savoy (prince) 23, 82
Otto I of Saxony 152

P

Paganini, Niccolò 26, 43, 71
Paggi, Giovan Battista 76
Palazzi 25
Amati (Castelnuovo di Magra)
127
Balbi Senarega (Genoa) 77
Belimbau-Negrotto Cambiaso
(Genoa) 76
Bianco (Genoa) 68, 88
Borea d'Olmo (San Remo) 164
Cambiaso (Genoa) 70
Carrega Cataldi (Genoa)
69, 70
Comunale (Imperia) 155
Comunale (Loano) 145
Comunale (Noli) 141
Costaguta Rocca (Chiavari)
114
degli Anziani (Savona) 137
degli Ufficiali (Savona) 136
dei Conti Fieschi (San
Salvatore di Cogorno) 115
dei Conti Leale Franchelli
(Pietra Ligure) 145
dei Pavoni (Savona) 136
del Comandante (Loano) 145
del Commissario (Savona)
136
del Comune (Perinaldo) 160
del Podestà (Ameglia) 126
della Borsa (Genoa) 54
della Commenda (Genoa)
38, 78
della Loggia (Savona) 23, 136,
137
della Rovere (Savona) 138
della Sibilla (Savona) 136
dell'Università (Genoa) 77
di Andrea Doria (Genoa) 65

Palazzi (cont.)
di Domenicaccio Doria (Genoa) 65
di Lamba Doria (Genoa) 65
di Negro (Genoa) 59
Doria (Dolceacqua) 167
Doria Pamphilj, or del Principe (Genoa) 46, 67, **78**
Doria Tursi (Genoa) 25, 68, **69**, 70, 71
Ducale (Genoa) 25, 39, 47, 49, 50, **54**
Durazzo Pallavicini (Genoa) 77
Durazzo Pallavicini (Sestri Levante) 116
Franzone (Lavagna) 115
Giacomo Doria (Genoa) 69
Interlano Pallavicini (Genoa) 70
Lercari Parodi (Genoa) 70, 71
Martinengo (Savona) 138
Morchio (Cervo) 153
Pagliari (Imperia) 157
Peloso Cepolla (Albenga) 150
Podestà (Genoa) 69, 71
Pubblico (Ventimiglia) 168
Reale (Genoa) 46, **77**
Rosso (Genoa) 68, 71, **72–5**
San Bernardo (Savona) 137
San Giorgio (Genoa) 38, 49, 50, **58–9**
Spinola (Genoa) 22, 49, 50, **64**
Spinola "dei Marmi" (Genoa) 70
Vannoni (Levanto) 117
Vecchio del Comune (Albenga) 150
Vescovile (Albenga) 151
Viale (Cervo) 153
Paleolithic 144, 169
Pallavicini, Ignazio Alessandro 84
Pallavicini Durazzo, Clelia 84
Palma il Vecchio 74
Madonna and Child, St John the Baptist and Mary Magdalen 74
Palmaria, isola 120–21, 125
Paraggi 111
Parasio (Imperia) 157
Parks and Nature Reserves 18–9, 105
Parco Culturale Golfo dei Poeti 121
Parco Culturale Riviera delle Palme 151
Parco del Finalese 18, **144**
Parco dell'Antola 19
Parco della Val d'Aveto 201
Parco Naturale del Monte Beigua 18, 131, **134–5**
Parco di Portofino 19, 102

Parks and Nature Reserves (cont.)
Parco Naturale Regionale dell'Aveto 115
Parco Naturale Regionale di Montemarcello-Magra 19, 116, **126**
Parco Nazionale delle Cinque Terre 19, 102, 118
Parco Regionale del Monte Antola 108
Riserva Naturale delle Agoraie 115
Parodi, Domenico 58, 75, 77, 86, 165
Assumption 58
Pietà 86
Parodi, Filippo 77, 138
Madonna della Misericordia 138
Parodi, Francesco 139
Pecorile 134
Peluzzi, Eso 136
Pentema 108
People 14
Perin del Vaga 46, 55, 79
Giants struck by Jove 79
Polyptych of St Erasmus 55
Stories of the Kings of Rome and *Military Triumphs* 79
Perinaldo 160
Pertini, Sandro 23
Pharmacies 207
Piaggio, Giuseppe 51
Piaggio Teramo 114
Piano, Renzo 25, 43, 49, 60, 61, 62
Aquarium (Genoa) 62
Bigo (Genoa) 25, 60
Sfera (Genoa) 61
Piazza, Albertino 139
Enthroned Madonna with Child and saints Peter and Paul 139
Pietra Ligure 29, 31, **145**, 146
Hotels 183
Pieve di Teco 102, **153**, 187
Pieve Ligure 21, 31
Pigna 102, **165**
Pino 88
Piola, Domenico 23, 59, 75, 76, 77, 115, 141, 151
Allegory of Autumn 75
Allegory of Winter 75
Crucifixion 115
Madonna, Queen of Genoa and St George 59
Last Supper 151
Piola, Paolo Geronimo 75
Piovene, Guido 14
Viaggio in Italia 14
Pirates 37, 41
Pisanello 23, 74

Pisano Giovanni 57, 64
Justice 64
Margaret of Brabant monument 22, 57, 64
Poggio, Marcantonio 153
Pogli d'Ortovero 29
Pogliaghi, Lodovico 58
Polo, Marco 58
Pontormo (Iacopo Carucci) 23, 124
Self Portrait 124
Ponzello, Domenico 71
Ponzello, Giovanni 71
Poor Clares 138
Portofino 13, 19, 21, 36, 41, 43, 103, 105, 106, 109, **110–3**, 114, 115, 202, 203
Hotels 180
Restaurants 192
Portovenere 16, 19, 21, 29, 103, 106, **120**, 121, 201
Hotels 180
Restaurants 192
Post offices 206–7
Practical Information 206–9
Prehistory 33–5, 144
Presepi *see* Nativity scenes
Preti Mattia 74
Clorinda saving Olindo and Sofronia from the stake 74
Resurrection of Lazarus 74
Procaccini, Giulio Cesare 55, 74
Provost, Jan 22
Przewalskii horse 34
Public holidays 31
Puget, Pierre 56, 76
St Sebastian and Beato Alessandro Sauli 56

Q

Quarries, slate (Lavagna) 115

R

Restaurants 191
Raphael 23, 79, 135
Rapallo 21, 105, 106, **109**, 201
Hotels 180
Restaurants 193
Ratti, Giovanni Agostino 136, 138, 141
Immaculate Conception 138
Realdo 158
Recco 21, 28, 30
Reni, Guido 23, 54, 64, 74, 151
Martyrdom of St Catherine 151
St Sebastian 23, 74
Reinhart, Fabio 55
Renaissance 22–3, 25
Republic of Genoa 38, 40–41, 82, 117, 128, 136, 140, 145, 156
Republic of Savona 139

Resasco, Giovanni Battista 87
Riccomanno, Leonardo 128
Riomaggiore 119
   Restaurants 193
Restaurants 188–197
Risorgimento 42–3
Rivers
   Arroscia 153
   Aveto 105
   Bisagno 87
   Bormida 140
   Carrea 134
   Centa 20, 150
   Crovana 116
   Entella 21, 114, 115
   Ghiararo 117
   Impero 156
   Magra 19, 21, 36, 105, 126,
    127, 128
   Merula 152
   Nervia 20, 166, 167
   Prino 158
   Roia 20, 168
   Sturla 114
   Trebbia 36
   Vara 36, 105, 116, 126
Riviera dei Fiori 131, 154, 170
Riviera delle Palme 131, 132, 152
Riviera di Levante 104–129
Riviera di Ponente 130–171
Robert of Anjou 40
Rock climbing 201
Romans 33, 36
Romano, Luzio 79
Rosa, Salvator 164
Rosai, Ottone 23
Rossese 166, 187
Rossi, Aldo 49, 55
Rubens, Pieter Paul 22, 23, 51,
   54, 64, 67, 68, 71, 77
   Circumcision 54
   Equestrian portrait of Gio
   Carlo Doria 22, 23, 64
   St Ignatius Exorcising the
   Devil 54, 77
   Venus and Mars 68
Ruffini, Giovanni 27
Rustichello 58

S

Sacchi, Pier Francesco 88
   Polyptych of San Siro 88
Sampdoria football team 203
San Fruttuoso 29, 105, 106, **110**
   Hotels 180
San Remo 15, 28, 34, 40, 41, 43,
   102, 131, 160, **164**, 198,
   201, 202
   Casino 102, 164
   Hotels 183
   Restaurants 197
San Salvatore di Cogorno 115

San Terenzo 121
Sanctuaries *see* Churches
Sansovino Andrea 53
   John the Baptist 53
   Madonna 53
Santa Margherita Ligure 21, 43,
   105, **109**, 202, 203
   Hotels 181
   Restaurants 193
Sant'Olcese 88
Santo Stefano d'Aveto 114–5, 201
Sardorella 88
Sarzana 106, 127, **128–9**
   Restaurants 193
Sassello 29, 201
Sassetta 124
Sassu Aligi 23, 135, 137
Savoy, House of 43, 46, 77, 140,
   154
Savona 28, 36, 37, 40, 41, 102,
   131, 132, **136–9**, 150
   Bastions 136
   Cittadella 136
   Hotels 183
   Piazza d'Armi 136
   Piazza Salineri 138
   Restaurants 197
   Torre degli Aliberti 138
   Torre del Brandale 137
   Torre di Leon Pancaldo 138
   Torre Ghibellina 138
   Via Paleocapa 136, 138
Scarampi family 140
Schiacchetrá 118, 119, 187
Schiaffino, Bernardo 108
   Virgin Mary 108
Schiaffino, Francesco 77
Scorza, Sinibaldo 75
Seborga 165
Security 208
Self-catering apartments 175
Semino, Francesco 108
Sestri Levante 36, 105, 106, 114,
   115, **116**, 187
   Hotels 181
   Restaurants 193
Shelley, Percy Bysshe 27, 121
Shopping 198–9
Simone da Pavia 134
   Blessed Jacopo and other
   saints 134
Sinatra, Frank 202
Sironi, Mario 137
Sixtus IV, pope 134, 139
Slate 115
Solenghi, Tullio 27
Sorri, Pietro 59
   Madonna and child and
   saints John the Baptist and
   George 59
Spinola family 38, 64, 83, 138
Sport 200–201

Spotorno **141**
   Hotels 183
   Restaurants 197
Strozzi, Bernardo 23, 55, 71, 73,
   74, 77
   Carità 74
   The Cook 23, 73, 75
   Incredulity of St Thomas 75
   Madonna with Child and
   San Giovannino 75

T

Taggia 29, 31, 158, 199
Tavarone, Lazzaro 53, 54, 58,
   64, 78
   Exploits and Personalities in
   the Grimaldi family 64
   Glory of Mary 65
   Martyrdom of the Saint 53
   San Lorenzo and the Church
   treasury 53
Tavella, Carlo Antonio 75
Tellaro 21, 31, 106, **126**
   Restaurants 194
Tenco, Premio 26
Theatine fathers 68, 76
Theatre 26–7, 202
Tinetto, isola 120–21
Tino, isola 120–21
Tintoretto 74
Titian 23, 124
   Portrait of a Gentleman 124
Torrazza 88
Torriglia 108
Tourism 14–15
Tourist offices 206, 207
Tours
   Armea and Crosia valleys
  160–61
Trains 211
Tramonti 120
Trensasco 88
Triora 14, 131, 132, **158**
Tuccio d'Andria 139
   Madonna and Saints 139

U

UNESCO 118
University of Genoa 77, 88, 170

V

Vado 36
Valeriani Giuseppe 54
Vallecrosia Alta 160
Valleys
   Val d'Aveto 19, 115
   Val Bisagno 88
   Val Crosia 160
   Val di Magra 121
   Val di Vara 14, 29, 116
   Val Nervia 34, 165, 168, 187

Valleys (cont.)
  Val Polcevera 88
  Val Trebbia 19
  Val Varatella 146, 147
  Valle Argentina 158
  Valle Armea 160, 161
  Valle Arroscia 187
  Valle Bormida 140
  Valle del Po 37
  Valle del Polcevera 87
  Valle di Fontanabuona 115
  Valle Roia 168
  Valle Scrivia 19, 88
  Vallée des Merveilles 34, 35,
    201
Van Cleve, Joos 22, 57, 64
  Adoration of the Magi 57
Van Dyck, Anthony 23, 64, 68,
  71, 72, 75, 77
  *Equestrian Portrait of Anton
  Geronima Brignole Sale and
  her daughter Aurelia* 75
  Giulio Brignole Sale 72, 75
  *Paolina Adorno Brignole
  Sale* 75
Vanni, Turino 87
  Madonna and Saints 87
Varazze 30, **134**
  Hotels 183
  Restaurants 197
Varese Ligure 106, 116
Varigotti 144
  Restaurants 197
Varni, Santo 87
  Faith 87

Ventimiglia 20, 29, 37, 40, 102,
  131, 132, **168–9**, 170, 200
  Hotels 183
  Restaurants 197
Vernazza 118
Veronese, Bonifacio 74
  Adoration of the Magi 74
Veronese, Paolo 23, 71, 74
  Judith and Holofernes 23, 74
Vezzano Ligure 30
Via Aurelia 43, 107, 133,
  152, 168, 210
Via Julia Augusta 144, 151
Viano, Giacomo 71
Villaggio, Paolo 27
Villanova d'Albenga 151
Villas
  Brignole Sale (Voltri) 82
  Croce (Genoa) 57
  Di Negro (Genoa) 68, 70
  Doria Centurione (Pegli) 82
  Durazzo Pallavicini
    (Pegli) 81, 82
  Faraggiana (Albissola Marina)
    135
  Gavotti (Albisola) 135
  Giustiniani Cambiaso
    (Albaro) 88
  Grimaldi Fassio (Nervi) 23, 89
  Gropallo (Nervi) 89
  Hanbury (Capo Mortola)
    132, 168, **170–71**
  Magni (Lerici) 27
  Marigola (San Terenzo) 121
  Nobel (San Remo) 164

Villas (cont.)
  Saluzzo Bombrini (Albaro) 88
  Saluzzo Mongiardino (Albaro)
    88
  Serra (Nervi) 89
  Tigullio (Rapallo) 109
Visigoths 36
Vittorio Emanuele I 71
Vouet, Simon 54

W
Walks
  Alta Via dei Monti Liguri
    201
  Strada dei Santuari 119
  Via dell'Amore 119
  see also Hiking
Water parks 203
Wedgwood, Josiah 75
Whales 16
Wildlife 17
Windsurfing 200
Wine 30, 118, 119, 160, 187,
  198
  Cinque Terre 198
  Rossese 160, 187, 198
  Schiacchetrá 118, 119, 187
  Vermentino 187, 198
Wine bars 202–3
witchcraft 14, 158
World War II 13, 43, 72, 79

Z
Zoagli 21, 109
Zurbarán, Francisco de 71

Acknowledgments

DORLING KINDERSLEY would like to thank the following people and institutions whose contributions and assistance have made the preparation of this book possible.

SPECIAL THANKS
Agenzia Regionale per la Promozione Turistica "In Liguria"; APT Cinque Terre e Golfo dei Poeti; APT di Genova; APT Riviera Ligure delle Palme; APT Riviera dei Fiori; APT Tigullio; Banca Carige, Genoa; Emma Brown; Giardini Botanici Hanbury, Ventimiglia; Grotte di Toirano, Toirano; Soprintendenza per i Beni Archeologici della Liguria, Genoa; the restaurant *Il Sommergibile* in San Remo.

PHOTOGRAPHY PERMISSIONS
Thanks are due to those bodies and societies who authorized the reproduction of images, in particular: Accademia Ligustica di Belle Arti, Genoa; Acquario di Genova; Banca Carige (coin collection and photographic archive, Genoa); Galleria di Palazzo Rosso (photographic archive of Genoa town council); Genoa Cricket and Football Club, Genoa; Museo Amedeo Lia, La Spezia; Museo Archeologico dei Balzi Rossi, Ventimiglia; Regione Liguria; Palazzo Ducale, Genoa; Società Editrice Buonaparte, Sarzana; UC Sampdoria, Genoa.

While every effort has been made to contact the copyright holders, we apologize for any omissions and will be happy to include them in future editions of the guide.

PICTURE CREDITS
Top part: t = top; tl = top left; tcl = top centre left; tc = top centre; tcr = top centre right; tr = top right.
Centre part: ctl = centre top left; ct = centre top; ctr = centre top right; cl = centre left; c = centre; cr = centre right; cbl = centre bottom left; cb = centre below; cbr = centre bottom right.
Lower part: b = bottom; bl = bottom left; bcl = bottom centre left; bc = bottom centre; bcr = bottom centre right; br = bottom right.

COMMISSIONED PHOTOGRAPHS
LUCIO ROSSI, POLIS, Milan: 1, 2–3, 8–9, 14bc, 15bl, 16tr, 16ctl, 16ctr, 16cbr, 16br, 17ctl, 17cbl, 18tr, 18br, 19tl, 20, 21bl, 21br, 22ctr, 23tl, 23bl, 24, 26br, 28cbr, 28bl, 29ctr, 30bl, 31br, 32, 33c, 35cl, 36tl, 43cr, 46cl, 46bl, 47, 48, 49, 50tr, 50ctl, 50cbr, 51, 52–3, 54, 55tr, 55br, 56, 57tr, 58tr, 58c, 59, 60, 61tr, 64, 66, 67, 68tr, 69, 70cr, 71c, 71bl, 76, 78tl, 78cr, 79c, 79b, 80, 82, 83t, 84–5, 86, 87tr, 88t, 88cl, 89b, 102–3, 104, 106cl, 107, 108tl, 109, 111tl, 112–3, 114, 115t, 115bl, 116, 117br, 120, 121t, 121c, 122–3, 124tl, 124ctl, 125, 126tl, 126br, 127br, 128–9

(except 128bl), 130–31, 132–3, 134tr, 134bl, 135tr, 135bl, 136cl, 136br, 137c, 138, 139t, 140–41, 144–5, 146–7, 148–9 (except 149br), 150–51, 152–3 , 154–5, 156–7, 158, 159tc, 159bl, 159bc, 159br, 160–61, 162–3, 164–5, 166–7 (except 167br), 168, 169tl, 170tl, 170tr, 170cl, 171, 173 (section), 174bl, 175, 184bl, 185tr, 186tl, 186tr, 186ct, 186ctr, 186cbr, 187tl, 187ct, 187ctr, 187cbc, 187cbr, 187cbl, 187bc, 187br, 198, 199tl, 202tr, 202bc, 206cb, 207, 209tl, 210, 211b.

PHOTO CREDITS
ALAMY IMAGES: Robert Harding World Imagery 172–3,; Natalie Tepper 61c. FABRIZIO ARDITO, Rome: 14tl, 15t, 100–1, 105, 108br, 142–3, 169c, 208br. ARCHIVIO ELECTA, Milan: 37cr, 38cr, 42tl.

EUGENIO BERSANI, POLIS, Milan: 13, 19bl, 117t, 118, 119t.

CORBIS: Archivo Iconografico 39cr; Owen Franken 35br; John Heseltine 167br; Gianni Dagli Orti 34bl; Royalty-free 204–5; Gustavo Tomisch 35tr..

IL DAGHERROTIPO: Giorgio Oddi 149bl; Marcio Melodia 200t; Salvatore Barba 44–5. DK IMAGES: 186cr; John Heseltine 208c; Clive Streeter 186bca, 186bra, 187tr.

MARY EVANS PICTURE LIBRARY: 41t.

FARABOLAFOTO, Milan: 9 (section), 12, 14cr, 15cr, 17tl, 17tr, 17bl, 17br, 21tr, 26tr, 26ctl, 26cbr, 27, 28ctl, 34tr, 42c, 43t, 43bc, 43br, 45 (section), 61bc, 65tr, 65cl, 101 (section), 106br, 110cl, 111cbr, 127tl, 174cr, 184t, 184cr, 185c, 200cl, 205, 206ctl.

MARKA, Milan: Danilo Donadoni 128bl.

PETER NOBLE: 208tr.

LINO PASTORELLI, Sanremo: 30ctl. ANDREA PISTOLESI: 68cl.

FRANCINE RECULEZ: 168cla. DANIELE ROBOTTI, Alessandria: 77tl, 88bl, 119cr, 119br. ROGER-VIOLLET, ARCHIVI ALINARI, Firenze: 37tc. GHIGO ROLI, Modena: 17ctr, 17cbr, 18ctl, 19ctr, 170bl.

PHOTO SCALA, Florence: Museo Navale di Pegli 38bl. MARCO STOPPATO, Milan: 81.

Jacket: FARABOLAFOTO (steps and flowers), LUCIO ROSSI, POLIS (Tellaro, flowers, Fortezza di Sarzanello, pestle, church of San Pietro).

All the other photos are from ARCHIVIO FABIO RATTI, ARCHIVIO MONDADORI, ARCHIVIO ARNOLDO MONDADORI EDITORE, Milan.

Phrase Book

IN EMERGENCY

Help!	Aiuto!	eye-**yoo**-toh
Stop!	Fermate!	fair-**mah**-teh
Call a doctor.	Chiama un medico	kee-**ah**-mah oon **meh**-dee-koh
Call an ambulance.	Chiama un' ambulanza	kee-**ah**-mah oon am-boo-**lan**-tsa
Call the police.	Chiama la polizia	kee-**ah**-mah lah pol-ee-**tsee**-ah
Call the fire brigade.	Chiama i pompieri	kee-**ah**-mah ee pom-pee-**air**-ee
Where is the telephone?	Dov'è il telefono?	dov-**eh** eel teh-**leh**-foh-noh?
The nearest hospital?	L'ospedale più vicino?	loss-peh-**dah**-leh pee-**oo** vee-**chee**-noh?

COMMUNICATION ESSENTIALS

Yes/No	Sì/No	see/ noh
Please	Per favore	pair fah-**vor**-eh
Thank you	Grazie	**grah**-tsee-eh
Excuse me	Mi scusi	mee **skoo**-zee
Hello	Buon giorno	bwon **jor**-noh
Goodbye	Arrivederci	ah-ree-veh-**dair**-chee
Good evening	Buona sera	**bwon**-ah **sair**-ah
morning	la mattina	lah mah-**tee**-nah
afternoon	il pomeriggio	eel poh-meh-**ree**-joh
evening	la sera	lah **sair**-ah
yesterday	ieri	ee-**air**-ee
today	oggi	**oh**-jee
tomorrow	domani	doh-**mah**-nee
here	qui	kwee
there	là	lah
What?	Quale?	**kwah**-leh?
When?	Quando?	**kwan**-doh?
Why?	Perché?	pair-**keh**?
Where?	Dove?	**doh**-veh?

USEFUL PHRASES

How are you?	Come sta?	**koh**-meh stah?
Very well, thank you.	Molto bene, grazie.	**moll**-toh **beh**-neh **grah**-tsee-eh
Pleased to meet you.	Piacere di conoscerla.	pee-ah-**chair**-eh dee coh-**noh**-shair-lah
See you later.	A più tardi.	ah pee-oo **tar**-dee
That's fine.	Va bene.	va **beh**-neh
Where is/are ...?	Dov'è/Dove sono ...?	dov-**eh**/doveh **soh**-noh?
How long does it take to get to ...?	Quanto tempo ci vuole per andare a ...?	**kwan**-toh **tem**-poh chee voo-**oh**-leh pair an-**dar**-eh ah ...?
How do I get to ...?	Come faccio per arrivare a ...?	koh-meh **fah**-choh pair arri-**var**-eh ah..?
Do you speak English?	Parla inglese?	**par**-lah een-**gleh**-zeh?
I don't understand.	Non capisco.	non ka-**pee**-skoh
Could you speak more slowly, please?	Può parlare più lentamente, per favore?	pwoh par-**lah**-reh pee-oo len-ta-**men**-teh pair fah-**vor**-eh?
I'm sorry.	Mi dispiace.	mee dee-spee-**ah**-cheh

USEFUL WORDS

big	grande	**gran**-deh
small	piccolo	**pee**-koh-loh
hot	caldo	**kal**-doh
cold	freddo	**fred**-doh
good	buono	**bwoh**-noh
bad	cattivo	kat-**tee**-voh
enough	basta	**bas**-tah
well	bene	**beh**-neh
open	aperto	ah-**pair**-toh
closed	chiuso	kee-**oo**-zoh
left	a sinistra	ah see-**nee**-strah
right	a destra	ah **dess**-trah
straight on	sempre dritto	**sem**-preh **dree**-toh
near	vicino	vee-**chee**-noh
far	lontano	lon-**tah**-noh
up	su	soo
down	giù	joo
early	presto	**press**-toh
late	tardi	**tar**-dee
entrance	entrata	en-**trah**-tah
exit	uscita	oo-**shee**-ta
toilet	il gabinetto	eel gah-bee-**net**-toh
free, unoccupied	libero	**lee**-bair-oh
free, no charge	gratuito	grah-**too**-ee-toh

MAKING A TELEPHONE CALL

I'd like to place a long-distance call.	Vorrei fare una interurbana.	vor-**ray far**-eh oona in-tair-oor-**bah**-nah
I'd like to make a reverse-charge call.	Vorrei fare una telefonata a carico del destinatario.	vor-**ray far**-eh oona teh-leh-fon-**ah**-tah ah **kar**-ee-koh dell dess-tee-nah-**tar**-ree-oh
I'll try again later.	Ritelefono più tardi.	ree-teh-**leh**-foh-noh pee-oo **tar**-dee
Can I leave a message?	Posso lasciare un messaggio?	**poss**-oh lash-**ah**-reh oon mess-**sah**-joh?
Hold on.	Un attimo, per favore	oon **ah**-tee-moh, pair fah-**vor**-eh
Could you speak up a little please?	Può parlare più forte, per favore?	pwoh par-**lah**-reh pee-**oo** for-teh, pair fah-**vor**-eh?
local call	telefonata locale	te-leh-fon-**ah**-tah loh-cah-leh

SHOPPING

How much does this cost?	Quant'è, per favore?	kwan-**teh** pair fah-**vor**-eh?
I would like ...	Vorrei ...	vor-**ray**
Do you have ...?	Avete ...?	ah-**veh**-teh.. ?
I'm just looking.	Sto soltanto guardando.	stoh sol-**tan**-toh gwar-**dan**-doh
Do you take credit cards?	Accettate carte di credito?	ah-chet-**tah**-teh **kar**-teh dee **creh**-dee-toh?
What time do you open/close?	A che ora apre/ chiude?	ah keh **or**-ah **ah**-preh/kee-**oo**-deh?
this one	questo	**kweh**-stoh
that one	quello	**kwell**-oh
expensive	caro	**kar**-oh
cheap	a buon prezzo	ah bwon **pret**-soh
size, clothes	la taglia	lah **tah**-lee-ah
size, shoes	il numero	eel **noo**-mair-oh
white	bianco	bee-**ang**-koh
black	nero	**neh**-roh
red	rosso	**ross**-oh
yellow	giallo	**jal**-loh
green	verde	**vair**-deh
blue	blu	bloo

TYPES OF SHOP

antique dealer	l'antiquario	lan-tee-**kwah**-ree-oh
bakery	il forno /il panificio	eel **forn**-oh /eel pan-ee-**fee**-choh
bank	la banca	lah **bang**-kah
bookshop	la libreria	lah lee-breh-**ree**-ah
butcher	la macelleria	lah mah-chell-eh-**ree**-ah
cake shop	la pasticceria	lah pas-tee-chair-**ee**-ah
chemist	la farmacia	lah far-mah-**chee**-ah
delicatessen	la salumeria	lah sah-loo-meh-**ree**-ah
department store	il grande magazzino	eel **gran**-deh mag-gad-**zee**-noh
fishmonger	il pescivendolo	eel pesh-ee-**ven**-doh-loh
florist	il fioraio	eel fee-or-**eye**-oh
greengrocer	il fruttivendolo	eel froo-tee-**ven**-doh-loh
grocery	alimentari	ah-lee-men-**tah**-ree
hairdresser	il parrucchiere	eel par-oo-kee-**air**-eh
ice cream parlour	la gelateria	lah jel-lah-tair-**ee**-ah
market	il mercato	eel mair-**kah**-toh
newsstand	l'edicola	leh-**dee**-koh-lah
post office	l'ufficio postale	loo-**fee**-choh pos-**tah**-leh
shoe shop	il negozio di scarpe	eel neh-**goh**-tsioh dee **skar**-peh
supermarket	il supermercato	eel su-pair-mair-**kah**-toh
tobacconist	il tabaccaio	eel tah-bak-**eye**-oh
travel agency	l'agenzia di viaggi	lah-jen-**tsee**-ah dee vee-**ad**-jee

SIGHTSEEING

art gallery	la pinacoteca	lah peena-koh-**teh**-kah
bus stop	la fermata dell'autobus	lah fair-**mah**-tah dell **ow**-toh-booss
church	la chiesa	lah kee-**eh**-zah
	la basilica	lah bah-**seel**-i-kah
closed for holidays	chiuso per le ferie	kee-**oo**-zoh pair leh **fair**-ee-eh
garden	il giardino	eel jar-**dee**-no
library	la biblioteca	lah beeb-lee-oh-**teh**-kah
museum	il museo	eel moo-**zeh**-oh
railway station	la stazione	lah stah-tsee-**oh**-neh
tourist information	l'ufficio di turismo	loo-**fee**-choh dee too-**ree**-smoh

STAYING IN A HOTEL

Do you have any vacant rooms?	Avete camere libere?	ah-**veh**-teh **kah**-mair-eh **lee**-bair-eh?
double room	una camera doppia	oona **kah**-mair-ah **doh**-pee-ah
with double bed	con letto matrimoniale	kon **let**-toh mah-tree-moh-nee-**ah**-leh
twin room	una camera con due letti	oona **kah**-mair-ah kon **doo**-eh **let**-tee
single room	una camera singola	oona **kah**-mair-ah **sing**-goh-lah
room with a bath, shower	una camera con bagno, con doccia	oona **kah**-mair-ah kon **ban**-yoh, kon **dot**-chah
porter	il facchino	eel fah-**kee**-noh
key	la chiave	lah kee-**ah**-veh
I have a reservation.	Ho fatto una prenotazione.	oh **fat**-toh oona preh-noh-tah-tsee-**oh**-neh

EATING OUT

Have you got a table for ...?	Avete una tavola per ... ?	ah-**veh**-teh oona **tah**-voh-lah pair ...?
I'd like to reserve a table.	Vorrei riservare una tavola.	vor-**ray** ree-sair-**vah**-reh oona **tah**-voh-lah
breakfast	colazione	koh-lah-tsee-**oh**-neh
lunch	pranzo	**pran**-tsoh
dinner	cena	**cheh**-nah
The bill, please.	Il conto, per favore.	eel **kon**-toh pair fah-**vor**-eh
I am a vegetarian.	Sono vegetariano/a.	**soh**-noh veh-jeh-tar-ee-**ah**-noh/nah
waitress	cameriera	kah-mair-ee-**air**-ah
waiter	cameriere	kah-mair-ee-**air**-eh
fixed price menu	il menù a prezzo fisso	eel meh-**noo** ah **pret**-soh **fee**-soh
dish of the day	piatto del giorno	pee-**ah**-toh dell **jor**-noh
starter	antipasto	an-tee-**pass**-toh
first course	il primo	eel **pree**-moh
main course	il secondo	eel seh-**kon**-doh
vegetables	il contorno	eel kon-**tor**-noh
dessert	il dolce	eel **doll**-cheh
cover charge	il coperto	eel koh-**pair**-toh
wine list	la lista dei vini	lah **lee**-stah day **vee**-nee
rare	al sangue	al **sang**-gweh
medium	al puntino	al poon-**tee**-noh
well done	ben cotto	ben **kot**-toh
glass	il bicchiere	eel bee-kee-**air**-eh
bottle	la bottiglia	lah bot-**teel**-yah
knife	il coltello	eel kol-**tell**-oh
fork	la forchetta	lah for-**ket**-tah
spoon	il cucchiaio	eel koo-kee-**eye**-oh

MENU DECODER

l'acqua minerale gassata/naturale	**lah**-kwah mee-nair-**ah**-leh gah-**zah**-tah/ nah-too-**rah**-leh	mineral water fizzy/still
agnello	ah-**niell**-oh	lamb
aceto	ah-**cheh**-toh	vinegar
aglio	**al**-ee-oh	garlic
al forno	al **for**-noh	baked
alla griglia	ah-lah **greel**-yah	grilled
l'aragosta	lah-rah-**goss**-tah	lobster
arrosto	ar-**ross**-toh	roast
la birra	lah **beer**-rah	beer
la bistecca	lah bee-**stek**-kah	steak
il brodo	eel **broh**-doh	broth
il burro	eel **boor**-oh	butter
il caffè	eel kah-**feh**	coffee
i calamari	ee kah-lah-**mah**-ree	squid
i carciofi	ee kar-**choff**-ee	artichokes
la carne	la **kar**-neh	meat
carne di maiale	**kar**-neh dee mah-**yah**-leh	pork
la cipolla	la chip-**oh**-lah	onion
i contorni	ee kon-**tor**-nee	vegetables
i fagioli	ee fah-**joh**-lee	beans
il fegato	eel **fay**-gah-toh	liver
il finocchio	eel fee-**nok**-ee-oh	fennel
il formaggio	eel for-**mad**-joh	cheese
le fragole	leh **frah**-goh-leh	strawberries
il fritto misto	eel free-toh **mees**-toh	mixed fried dish
la frutta	la **froot**-tah	fruit
frutti di mare	**froo**-tee dee **mah**-reh	seafood
i funghi	ee **foon**-ghee	mushrooms
i gamberi	ee **gam**-bair-ee	prawns
il gelato	eel jel-**lah**-toh	ice cream
l'insalata	leen-sah-lah-tah	salad

il latte	eel **laht**-teh	milk
lesso	**less**-oh	boiled
il manzo	eel **man**-tsoh	beef
la melanzana	lah meh-lan-**tsah**-nah	aubergine
la minestra	lah mee-**ness**-trah	soup
l'olio	loh-lee-oh	oil
il pane	eel **pah**-neh	bread
le patate	leh pah-**tah**-teh	potatoes
le patatine fritte	leh pah-tah-**teen**-eh **free**-teh	chips
il pepe	eel **peh**-peh	pepper
la pesca	lah **pess**-kah	peach
il pesce	eel **pesh**-eh	fish
il pollo	eel **poll**-oh	chicken
il pomodoro	eel poh-moh-**dor**-oh	tomato
il prosciutto cotto/crudo	eel pro-**shoo**-toh **kot**-toh/**kroo**-doh	ham cooked/cured
il riso	eel **ree**-zoh	rice
il sale	eel **sah**-leh	salt
la salsiccia	lah sal-**see**-chah	sausage
le seppie	leh **sep**-pee-eh	cuttlefish
secco	**sek**-koh	dry
la sogliola	lah **soll**-yoh-lah	sole
i spinaci	ee spee-**nah**-chee	spinach
succo d'arancia/ di limone	**soo**-koh dah-**ran**-chah/ dee lee-**moh**-neh	orange/lemon juice
il tè	eel **teh**	tea
la tisana	lah tee-**zah**-nah	herbal tea
il tonno	eel **ton**-noh	tuna
la torta	lah **tor**-tah	cake/tart
l'uovo	loo-**oh**-voh	egg
vino bianco	**vee**-noh bee-**ang**-koh	white wine
vino rosso	**vee**-noh **ross**-oh	red wine
il vitello	eel vee-**tell**-oh	veal
le vongole	leh von-goh-leh	clams
lo zucchero	loh **zoo**-kair-oh	sugar
gli zucchini	lyee dzu-**kee**-nee	courgettes
la zuppa	lah **tsoo**-pah	soup

NUMBERS

1	uno	**oo**-noh
2	due	**doo**-eh
3	tre	treh
4	quattro	**kwat**-roh
5	cinque	**ching**-kweh
6	sei	**say**-ee
7	sette	**set**-teh
8	otto	**ot**-toh
9	nove	**noh**-veh
10	dieci	dee-**eh**-chee
11	undici	**oon**-dee-chee
12	dodici	**doh**-dee-chee
13	tredici	**tray**-dee-chee
14	quattordici	kwat-**tor**-dee-chee
15	quindici	**kwin**-dee-chee
16	sedici	**say**-dee-chee
17	diciassette	dee-chah-**set**-teh
18	diciotto	dee-**chot**-toh
19	diciannove	dee-chah-**noh**-veh
20	venti	**ven**-tee
30	trenta	**tren**-tah
40	quaranta	kwah-**ran**-tah
50	cinquanta	ching-**kwan**-tah
60	sessanta	sess-**an**-tah
70	settanta	set-**tan**-tah
80	ottanta	ot-**tan**-tah
90	novanta	noh-**van**-tah
100	cento	**chen**-toh
1,000	mille	**mee**-leh
2,000	duemila	**doo**-eh **mee**-lah
5,000	cinquemila	**ching**-kweh **mee**-lah
1,000,000	un milione	oon meel-**yoh**-neh

TIME

one minute	un minuto	oon mee-**noo**-toh
one hour	un'ora	oon **or**-ah
half an hour	mezz'ora	medz-**or**-ah
a day	un giorno	oon **jor**-noh
a week	una settimana	oona set-tee-**mah**-nah
Monday	lunedì	loo-neh-**dee**
Tuesday	martedì	mar-teh-**dee**
Wednesday	mercoledì	mair-koh-leh-**dee**
Thursday	giovedì	joh-veh-**dee**
F. day	venerdì	ven-air-**dee**
Saturday	sabato	**sah**-bah-toh
Sunday	domenica	doh-**meh**-nee-kah

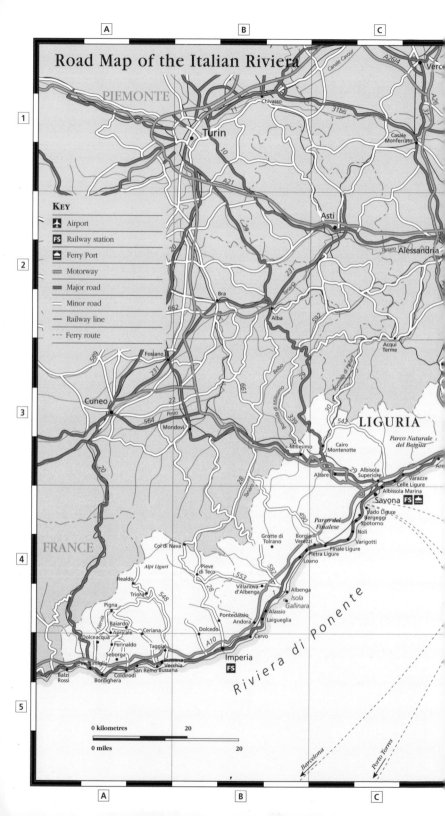

Road Map of the Italian Riviera

KEY

✈	Airport
FS	Railway station
⚓	Ferry Port
▬	Motorway
▬	Major road
─	Minor road
─	Railway line
┄	Ferry route

PIEMONTE

Chivasso

Turin

Casale Monferrato

Asti

Alessandria

Tanaro

Acqui Terme

Bra

Alba

Fossano

LIGURIA

Parco Naturale del Beigua

Cuneo

Mondovì

Millesimo

Cairo Montenotte

Altare

Albisola Superiore

Varazze

Celle Ligure

Albissola Marina

Savona FS ⚓

Vado Ligure

Bergeggi

Spotorno

Noli

Varigotti

FRANCE

Col di Nava

Alpi Liguri

Pieve di Teco

Grotte di Tolrano

Borgio Verezzi

Parco del Finalese

Finale Ligure

Pietra Ligure

Loano

Realdo

Triora

Villanova d'Albenga

Albenga

Isola Gallinara

Pigna

Baiardo

Apricale

Ceriana

Dolceacqua

Perinaldo

Seborga

Taggia

Pontedassio

Andora

Alassio

Laigueglia

Cervo

Dolcedo

Imperia FS

Ventimiglia

San Remo

Bussana

Bordighera

Coldirodi

Balzi Rossi

Bordighera

Riviera di Ponente

Barcelona

Porto Torres

0 kilometres 20

0 miles 20